A Short History
of Opera

VOLUME TWO

SCENE FROM MONTEMEZZI'S "L'AMORE DEI TRE RE"

A Short History
of Opera

by DONALD JAY GROUT

PROFESSOR OF MUSIC, CORNELL UNIVERSITY

VOLUME TWO

COLUMBIA UNIVERSITY PRESS · NEW YORK

1947

Part 5

From Romanticism to Modernism

LIST OF ABBREVIATIONS

AfMf	*Archiv für Musikforschung*
AfMw	*Archiv für Musikwissenschaft*
AMZ	*Allgemeine musikalische Zeitung*
art.	article
B&H	Breitkopf & Härtel
C.E.	Collected Edition (*Gesamtausgabe*)
C.F.	*Chefs d'œuvre de l'opéra français*
DdT	*Denkmäler deutscher Tonkunst*
DTB	*Denkmäler der Tonkunst in Bayern*
DTOe	*Denkmäler der Tonkunst in Oesterreich*
ed.	edition, editor, edited by
HAM	*Historical Anthology of Music*, Vol. II (Davison and Apel)
JMP	*Jahrbuch der Musikbibliothek Peters*
K	Köchel, *Chronologisch-thematisches Verzeichnis sämtlicher Tonwerke Wolfgang Amade Mozarts*, 3d ed., rev. Einstein
MA	*Musical Antiquary*
MfMg	*Monatshefte für Musikgeschichte*
M&L	*Music & Letters*
MM	*Mercure musical*
MMus	*Modern Music*
MQ	*Musical Quarterly*
MTNA	*Proceedings of the Music Teachers National Association*
mus.	music (by)
OHM	*Oxford History of Music*
perf.	performed, performance
PIMG	Publikationen der internationalen Musikgesellschaft
PMA	*Proceedings of the Musical Association* (London)
RassM	*La rasssegna musicale*
RdM	*Revue de musicologie*
RHCM	*Revue d'histoire et de critique musicales* (with No. 10 of Vol. II, 1902, became SIM *Revue musicale*)
RM	*Revue musicale* (Paris, 1920–)
RMl	*Rivista musicale italiana*
SB	Schering, *Geschichte der Musik in Beispielen*
SIM	*Société internationale de musique*
SIMG	*Sammelbände der internationalen Musikgesellschaft*
SzMw	*Studien zur Musikwissehschaft* (Beihefte der DTOe)
VfMw	*Vierteljahrsschrift für Musikwissenschaft*
ZfMw	*Zeitschrift für Musikwissenschaft*
ZIMG	*Zeitschrift der internationalen Musikgesellschaft*

24

French Opera from
1870 to 1914[1]

THE STATE OF MUSICAL TASTE IN PARIS (that is to say, in France) from 1840 to 1870 is sufficiently illustrated by three facts: the adoration of Meyerbeer, the neglect of Berlioz, and the craze for Offenbach. The disaster of the Franco-Prussian War was a salutary shock to both public and musicians. In 1871 the Société Nationale de Musique was founded, with the device *Ars gallica*. The rise of the modern French school dates from this event. Undiscriminating acceptance of incongruous musical styles on the one hand, and a frivolous addiction to the trivialities of operetta on the other, were succeeded by a conscious and strenuous effort to restore in modern terms the great musical individuality which had belonged to France in the sixteenth, seventeenth, and eighteenth centuries. The range of creative activity was widened. Whereas before 1870 composers had centered nearly all their efforts on opera, now choral, symphonic, and chamber music began to be important; higher standards of musical education were introduced, and a more cultivated and exacting public gradually came into being. This renewal of national musical life made the opera more vital, original, and adventurous. And although the highest rewards of popular success still went to those composers who were able and willing to bend their talents to the public fancy, nevertheless the best work found hearing and appreciation; there were no scandals like those of the Second Empire, when *Tannhäuser* was hissed off the stage and *Les Troyens* was closed after only twenty-one performances. It is worthy of remark that almost every important new operatic work in Paris after 1870

[1] *Almanach des spectacles*, Paris 1874–1913; *Cinquante Ans de musique française*, ed. Rohozinski; Bruneau, *La Musique française*; Rolland, *Musiciens d'aujourd'hui*; Seré, *Musiciens français d'aujourd'hui* (contains excellent bibliographical lists); Hill, *Modern French Music*; Coeuroy, *La Musique française moderne*; Jullien, *Musiciens d'aujourd'hui*, 2 vols. (1892–1894); Tiersot, *Un Demi-siècle de musique française* [1870–1917]; Aubry, *La Musique française d'aujourd'hui*.

was produced not at the Opéra but at the more enterprising and progressive Opéra-comique. The old distinction between the forms of opera and opéra comique had practically disappeared by the end of the nineteenth century, for the latter had by then largely abandoned the traditional spoken dialogue; so the repertoire of the two theatres contrasted simply as large-scale, established, conventional works in the one, and new, often experimental works in the other— alternating, of course, with the light, operetta-like pieces, which continued to flourish. Composers of large serious operas which should have been produced at the Paris Opéra frequently had recourse to the Théâtre de la Monnaie at Brussels for the first performances. Monte Carlo was also the scene of some notable premières. How little the term "opéra comique" in this period had to do with "comic" opera will be realized by recalling that Bizet's *Carmen,* Delibes' *Lakmé,* Lalo's *Roi d'Ys,* Massenet's *Manon,* Bruneau's *Attacque du moulin,* D'Indy's *Fervaal,* Charpentier's *Louise,* and Debussy's *Pelléas et Mélisande* were all staged, originally or eventually, at the Théâtre de l'Opéra-comique in Paris.

One of the first new operas of distinction to be produced in Paris after 1870 was Bizet's *Carmen* (1875).[2] The success of this work at Paris did not begin until some eight years after its composer's death, but it stands today as the most popular and vital French opera of the later nineteenth century. Its Spanish subject was a reflection of the exotic trend in French music which had begun a generation earlier with David; but more important than this feature was the realism with which scenes and characters were depicted, a realism which the librettists had somewhat toned down from Mérimée's original story (especially with respect to Carmen herself), but which still was strong enough to scandalize Paris in the seventies. The tragic ending of this opéra comique was also a novelty. As to the music, Bizet had formed his style from many sources. Probably the least important feature is the mild Spanish local color evident in such numbers as the Habañera, the Toreador Song, and the seguidilla "Près des ramparts de Seville" (Act I). Many of the choruses and ensembles are in characteristic operetta style. Fundamental, however, is the clear, firm, concise, and exact musical expression of every situation

---

[2] The most recent biography of Georges Bizet (1838–1875) is by Martin Cooper (1939); see also special Bizet number of RdM (November, 1938).

in terms of which only a French composer would be capable: the typical Gallic union of economy of material, perfect grasp of means, and an electric vitality and rhythmic verve, together with a completely objective, cool, yet passionate sensualism. This opera contains some spoken dialogue and is otherwise divided into the conventional arias, ensembles, and other numbers. So far as Bizet was concerned, Wagner's music dramas and theories might never have existed. The occasional repetition of certain motifs is of no more significance in *Carmen* than in Verdi's *Rigoletto* a quarter of a century earlier. The whole structure and aesthetic of Carmen was such that Nietzsche, after he had become disgusted with Wagner, might point to it as the ideal opera according to the principles of a properly "Mediterraneanized" European art.[3] It is hard to imagine what was in the minds of those contemporary critics who found the music untuneful, lacking in definite outlines, and overpowered by a too rich orchestration—charges, in a word, of Wagnerianism, such as had been leveled earlier at Gounod. But "Wagnerian" was a convenient word at this time for damning anything a critic disliked or could not understand. The styles of Gounod and Bizet do, indeed, have much in common, but the affinity is much more apparent in Bizet's earlier operas *Les Pêcheurs de perles* ("The Pearl Fishers," 1863) and *Djamileh* (1872). Both these works are still occasionally given in France and Italy, but they have less musical individuality and interest than *Carmen;* in fact, the only other work of Bizet's which compares with this opera is his incidental music to Daudet's play *L'Arlésienne* (1872).

The slight exotic flavor of *Carmen* and *Les Pêcheurs de perles* is found again in *Lakmé* (1883), the best opera of Léo Delibes,[4] with a Hindu locale and a tragic plot faintly reminiscent of Meyerbeer's *Africaine* and more than faintly foreshadowing Puccini's *Butterfly*. Delibes' music is elegant, graceful, and well orchestrated but lacks the intense quality of Bizet's. In *Lakmé* the oriental perfume is blended with an otherwise conventional idiom. Delibes' amusing and tuneful opéra comique *Le Roi l'a dit* ("The King Said So," 1873)

---

[3] "Der Fall Wagner," ¶3; "Jenseits von Gut und Böse," Pt. VIII *passim*.

[4] Delibes (1836–1891) wrote a dozen operettas before making a hit with his opéra comique *Le Roi l'a dit* in 1873. He was at his best as a composer of ballets: *La Source* (1866), *Coppélia* (1870) and *Sylvia* (1876). He became professor of composition at the Conservatoire in 1881. See biography by H. de Curzon.

is still remembered; a more serious work, *Jean de Nivelle* (1880),
was almost equally successful at first but has not remained in the
repertoire.

A more substantial figure than Delibes in French nineteenth-
century opera was Ernest Reyer.[5] Reyer belongs with those composers
whose music often compels more respect for its intentions than admiration for its actual sound. He had "genius without talent," [6] that
is, lofty and ideal conceptions without the technique for realizing
them fully in an attractive musical form. This incapacity may have
been due in part to his defective early training, but it was also partly
a matter of temperament; as a critic he was a despiser of mere pret-
tiness, a rebel against the superficial, snap judgments of the Paris
public,[7] and an early defender of Berlioz and Wagner. Reyer was
influenced by the fashionable orientalism in his choice of subjects,
as seen in his symphonic ode *Sélam* (1850) and a ballet-pantomime
Sacountala (1858). His first important operatic work, *La Statue* (1861),
is also an oriental story. A similar background is found in his
last opera, *Salammbô* (1890), taken with few alterations from Flau-
bert's novel and treated in an austere oratorio-like style, yet with a
grandeur of line recalling the spirit of Berlioz's *Troyens;* the plot
in general and the closing scene in particular are reminiscent of
Verdi's *Aïda*. The most successful of Reyer's operas was *Sigurd* (composed in the 1870's, first performed 1884); the subject is almost
identical with that of Wagner's *Siegfried* (Act III) and *Götterdämmerung*, with a touch of *Tannhäuser* in the shape of a seductive ballet, with a wordless chorus of elves, in Act II. But the resemblance
to Wagner is only skin-deep, even in the libretto: Sigurd talks in the
accents of Quinault's Renaud rather than like the great blond lad
of the *Ring;* and the rest of the personages likewise somehow seem
more Gallic than Teutonic. In the music there is no sign whatever
of Wagner; we find the old separate numbers of grand opera, a
distinctly periodic melody, and very little chromaticism. There is
some recurrence of motifs, but this is not a distinctly Wagnerian

---

[5] Reyer (1823–1909) was mostly self-taught in music, the principal influence on his style
being that of Berlioz. He wrote little except dramatic music but was active as journalist
and critic. See his *Notes de musique* and *Quarante Ans de musique;* also biography by
De Curzon and the same author's *Légende de Sigurd.*

[6] Alfred Bruneau, quoted in Combarieu, *Histoire* III, 389.

[7] See Lavignac, *Encyclopédie,* Pt. I, Vol. III, pp. 1727–28.

trait. The musical style is serious and even has a certain nobility; [8]
its model, clearly enough, is *Les Troyens.*

Parisian journalists had been crying "Wolf! wolf!" for years before any serious reflection of Wagner's ideas or musical style became
apparent in French music. The bitterness of the Franco-Prussian
War, aggravated by Wagner's silly gibes in his playlet *Eine Kapitula-
tion,* delayed his acceptance still longer. Yet by the early eighties
apparently all was forgiven, and Wagner became the rage in Paris
for some ten or twelve years. "From 1885 Wagner's work acted directly or indirectly on the whole of artistic thought, even on religious
and intellectual thought of the most distinguished people of Paris.
. . . Writers not only discussed musical subjects, but judged painting, literature, and philosophy, from a Wagnerian point of view.
. . . The whole universe was seen and judged by the thought of
Bayreuth." [9] A remarkable evidence of this enthusiasm was the
flourishing periodical *La Revue Wagneriénne* (1885–1888), contribu-
tors to which included Verlaine, Mallarmé, Huysmans, and practically every other important writer in Paris (Baudelaire had been
converted already in 1861). One effect of all this was to introduce the
subject of music to many people who would otherwise not have taken
an interest in it; another was to stimulate symphonic composition.
In opera, the risks involved in the magic garden of Wagnerism were
so patent that the composers for the most part withstood temptation,
though not always without effort. It is sometimes difficult to decide
what is to be called imitation of Wagner and what is simply acceptance of new ideas, such as the abolition of formal separate arias and
recitatives. Taken altogether, however, the direct influence of Wagner on French opera, in both literary and musical treatment, is seen
most strongly in works by three composers: Chabrier, D'Indy, and
Chausson. [10]

Chabrier [11] seems at first an unlikely person to be an apostle of
Wagner, for the pieces by which he is best known (the orchestral

[8] See example in OHM VII, 339–42.　　　[9] Rolland, *Musicians of Today,* p. 253.
[10] Cf. D'Indy, *Richard Wagner et son influence sur l'art musical français.*
[11] Alexis Emanuel Chabrier (1841–1894) was one of the most important composers in
the development of the modern French school, as well as a pianist of exceptional ability.
He was trained for the law; during fifteen years of service in the Ministry of the In-
terior he cultivated music as an amateur and kept abreast of contemporary movements
in painting and literature. See Hill, *Modern French Music,* chap. IV, and the separate
studies by Martineau and Servières.

rhapsody *España,* the *Bourrée Fantasque*) show him as a composer of typical Gallic vivacity, wit, and rhythmic exuberance. It is these qualities which are uppermost in his first important comic opera *L'Etoile* ("The Star," 1877), [12] and in his best-known stage work, *Le Roi malgré lui* ("The King in Spite of Himself," 1887), harmonically one of the most original opéras comiques of this period. But in 1879 Chabrier heard a performance of *Tristan und Isolde* at Munich which made a strong impression on him, reinforced by his experience shortly afterwards in directing rehearsals of *Lohengrin* and *Tristan* for performances at Paris. His opera *Gwendoline* (first performed at Brussels in 1886) is obviously influenced by Wagnerian elements: in the libretto there are echoes of *Der fliegende Holländer,* of the Valhalla mythology, and above all of *Tristan,* even to a love duet in the second act and a love-death at the end of the third. The form is a compromise between continuous drama and the older number opera. The music shows more than a trace of Wagner in its systematic use of leitmotifs, chromatics, chords of the seventh and ninth, and the characteristic appoggiaturas and suspensions. However, this must not be taken to mean that it is a mere copy of Wagner's idiom. Chabrier had a very individual harmonic style, one which was extremely advanced for his time; and as a second facet of his musical personality he had a genuine and sometimes profound gift of serious expressiveness. The most interesting portions of *Gwendoline* are the Spinning Song in Act I (incorporating an air from Moore's *Irish Melodies*), the love duet (strongly reminiscent of *Tristan*), and the orchestral prelude to Act II, the style of which has been well described as one of the links between Wagner and Debussy.[13] The skillful voice writing and the highly colorful and poetic orchestration of this opera should also be noted. But the uneven quality of the music as a whole, together with the rather dull and awkwardly proportioned libretto, have worked against its success. In his unfinished opera *Briseïs* (Act I performed 1899) Chabrier demonstrated even more daring harmonies than in *Gwendoline.*

Somewhat similar in subject matter to *Gwendoline,* and likewise tinctured with Wagnerian conceptions, is César Franck's opera

12 This work was produced in America as *The Merry Monarch* and elsewhere under various titles. See Loewenberg, *Annals,* p. 551.
13 Abraham, *A Hundred Years of Music,* p. 238.

Hulda (first performed in 1894).[14] But the most thorough, and at the same time the most individual, adaptation of Wagner's methods to French opera was brought about by Franck's pupil Vincent d'Indy in his *Fervaal* (1897) and *L'Etranger* ("The Stranger," 1903).[15] Like Wagner, D'Indy wrote his own librettos. The background of *Fervaal* is vaguely mythological, and the action in both operas is treated as symbolic of broad moral issues—the conflict between pagan religion and sacrificial love in *Fervaal,* and the expiation of unlawful love through death in *L'Etranger.* But whereas Wagner's symbolism is nearly always in practice subordinated to the aim of theatrical effect, with D'Indy there is evident a purpose to make art a vehicle for essentially religious teachings and to use every possible artistic means consistently for this end. The almost medieval combination of this austere ideal with a catholic breadth of resource, welded into unity by superb technical skill, is the clue to D'Indy's style.[16] It explains how he was able to take over many features of Wagner's music dramas without sacrificing his own individuality: pseudo mythology, symbolism, continuity of the music, harmonic sophistication, the symphonic orchestral texture with cyclical recurrence of motifs, free arioso treatment of the voice line, Wagnerian instrumental sonorities, even (in the love music of the first and third acts of *Fervaal*) actual reminiscences of *Tristan.* Indebtedness to Wagner is much less apparent in *L'Etranger* than in the earlier opera. The profound suggestiveness of the musical landscape in the introduction to Act II of *Fervaal* and the uniquely somber, mysterious poetry of the following scene are especially noteworthy. The third scene of Act II of *L'Etranger* is remarkable for imaginative and pictorial power (Example 110). As in his dramatic choral works, *Le Chant de la cloche* ("The Song of the Bell," 1879–1883) and *La Légende de St. Christophe* (composed 1908–1915), in the operas too D'Indy has effective

14 This opera was composed 1882–1885. The plot is similar to that of Lalo's *Roi d'Ys.* On Franck (1822–1890) see the biography by D'Indy and other works listed in Lynn's *Bio-bibliography.* Franck's other operas, less dramatic on the whole than his oratorios and of little importance in his total work, are: *Le Valet de ferme,* opéra comique, composed 1851–1852; and an unfinished lyric opera *Ghiselle,* performed in 1896 with the orchestration completed by Franck's pupils.
15 The most recent study of D'Indy (1851–1931) is by De Fraguier (1933). There are the following special studies: Bréville, *Fervaal;* Calvocoressi, *L'Etranger;* Destranges, *Le Chant de la cloche; idem, Fervaal; idem, L'Etranger.* See also D'Indy's own *Wagner et son influence sur l'art musical français.*
16 Rolland, chapter on D'Indy in *Musiciens d'aujourd'hui.*

L'ÉTRANGER, Act II, sc. 3

Ex. 110.

D'Indy

choral treatments of Gregorian melodies, notably the "Pange lingua" in the transcendently beautiful closing scene of *Fervaal*.[17] That neither of these operas has become popular may be owing in part to the unusual character of their librettos but more to the music, which lacks the simple, salient, easily perceived qualities apparently necessary for success on the stage. One cannot help feeling that, for the theatre, the music has many of the defects of Wagner without the latter's constant, compelling emotional power. Yet *Fervaal* in particular deserves respect as one of the outstanding French operas of the later nineteenth century in the noble tradition of Berlioz's *Troyens*. If musicians alone could dictate the repertoire of opera houses, *Fervaal* would be more often performed.

The influence of Wagner is still noticeable in Chausson's *Roi Arthus* (1903), a curious and not very successful combination of old grand-opera formal elements with the new Wagnerian idiom, including the inevitable Tristanesque love duet in Act I. Neither

[17] Cf. also the quotation of the intonation of the "Credo" in Act II, sc. 1 of the same opera; and in Bruneau's *Messidor* (also 1897) the plainsong passage from the litany in the finale.

libretto nor music offers any passages of real distinction.[18] The composer himself regarded *Le Roi Arthus* as only an experiment. This is perhaps the final word for all the attempts by French composers to assimilate Wagner's methods in the nineteenth century, since no consistent or historically important school grew from them. Along with these experiments the natural line of French lyric opera in descent from Gounod continued to flourish. We now turn our attention to the composers of this distinctively national group.

The first is Camille Saint-Saëns,[19] whose *Princesse jaune* ("The Yellow Princess," 1872) set the fashion for Japanese subjects in comic opera. Saint-Saëns' most famous dramatic work is the biblical *Samson et Dalila* (1877), half opera and half oratorio, like Liszt's *Legende von der heiligen Elisabeth* or D'Indy's *St. Christophe*. Saint-Saëns was not by nature a dramatic composer, but his technical facility and knowledge of many different musical styles enabled him to construct smooth and competent, though not exciting, works in the dramatic field. Of his sixteen stage works the most successful (next to *Samson et Dalila*) were *Henri VIII* (1883), *Ascanio* (1890), and the opéra comique *Phryné* (1893). Another composer of conservative national tendency was Edouard Lalo [20] with *Le Roi d'Ys* (1888), based on a Breton legend. The music of this opera is original in style, of remarkable rhythmic vitality, varied in color, and admirably adapted to the stage—qualities which have assured its survival to the present day. Three other French composers of the late nineteenth century should be mentioned in passing, though their work is less important than that of Saint-Saëns or Lalo: Emile Paladilhe (*Patriel*, 1886), Benjamin Godard (*La Vivandière*, 1895), and Isidore De Lara (*Messaline*, 1899).[21]

---

18 Ernest Chausson (1855–1899) was a pupil of Massenet and César Franck. *Le Roi Arthus* was his only opera ever to be performed. (It was not performed at Karlsruhe in 1900, as most books of reference say. See Loewenberg, *Annals*, p. 654.)

19 The most recent book on Saint-Saëns (1835–1921) is by Langlois (1934); cf. also his own writings, especially *Portraits et souvenirs*. See bibliography in Baker's *Dictionary* (4th ed., 1940) p. 946, and add: Du Tillet, "A propos du *Drame lyrique*," *Revue politique et littéraire* (July 3, 1897) pp. 27–30.

20 Lalo (1823–1892) had established his reputation as a symphonist before completing his only successful opera; the latter had been sketched as early as 1878. See Servières, *Edouard Lalo*.

21 Paladilhe (1844–1926) was a pupil of Halévy and winner of the Prix de Rome in 1860; Godard (1849–1895) was a composer of facile and pleasing melodic gifts, of which the well known "Berceuse" from his opera *Jocelyn* (1888) furnishes a good example. De Lara (1858–1935) was born in London and lived there chiefly, but most of his operas

The most representative and successful French opera composer of the late nineteenth and early twentieth centuries was Jules Massenet.[22] Massenet was an exceptionally productive worker, whose music is marked by characteristic French traits that we have already had occasion to notice in earlier composers such as Monsigny, Auber, Thomas (Massenet's teacher), and Gounod. First among these is the dominance of melody. Massenet's melody is of a highly personal quality: lyrical, tender, penetrating, sweetly sensuous, rounded in contours, exact but never violent in interpreting the text, sentimental, often melancholy, sometimes a little vulgar, and always charming. This melody determines the whole texture; the harmonic background is sketched with delicacy and a fine sense of instrumental color. Every detail of the score shows smooth craftsmanship and unhesitating choice of means. There is no commitment to particular theories of opera, Wagnerian or otherwise, but within the limits of his own style Massenet never hesitated to make use of any new device which had proved effective or popular, so that his works are not free of eclecticism and mirror in their own way most of the successive operatic tendencies of his lifetime. The subjects and their treatment also show the composer's sensitiveness to popular taste. Thus *Le Roi de Lahore* (1877) is an oriental story, *Le Cid* (1885) is in the manner of grand opera, *Esclarmonde* (1889) is Wagnerian, *La Navarraise* (1894) shows the influence of Italian *verismo,* and *Cendrillon* (1899) recalls Humperdinck's *Hänsel und Gretel;* but *Le Jongleur de Notre Dame* (1902) is a miracle play for which there could have been no public demand, but which the composer treated with special affection and thereby produced one of his best and most enduring operas. The suspicion is sometimes aroused that Massenet's choice of subjects, as well as his use of certain fashionable musical devices, was due to a desire to give his audiences what he knew they wanted rather than to any impulsion of his own. But there is no sacrifice of musical individuality in all this; and in the case of a composer whose instincts were so completely of the theatre, who always succeeded in achieving so neatly and spontaneously just the effect he intended, it seems a little ungracious to insist too strongly on an issue of artistic

were to French texts and were performed in France; his style was based on that of Massenet.

22 The principal biography of Massenet (1842–1912) is by L. Schneider. See also the study by Bruneau (1934) and the composer's own *Mes Souvenirs.*

sincerity. Massenet excelled in the musical depiction of passionate love, and most of his best works are notable for their heroines—unforgettable ladies all, of doubtful virtue perhaps, but indubitably alive and vivid. To this gallery belong Salomé in *Hérodiade* (1881), the heroines of *Manon* (1884), *Thaïs* (1894), *Sapho* (1897), and Charlotte in *Werther* (1892). With these works should also be mentioned *Thérèse* (1907), one of the last operas of Massenet to obtain general success.

Massenet traveled the main highway of French tradition in opera and his natural gifts so corresponded to the tastes of his day that success seemed to come almost without effort. Nor was his style without influence, direct or indirect, on later French composers. But he was the last to produce operas so easily. Changing musical idioms and new literary movements had their effect on the next generation, giving its work a less assured, more experimental character. Only two French serious operas so far in the twentieth century have even begun to equal the popularity of Massenet's: Charpentier's *Louise* (1900) and Debussy's *Pelléas et Mélisande* (1902). Each represents a characteristic operatic school of the period: the former that of naturalism, the latter that of symbolism.

The word "naturalism" and the related word "realism," however useful they may be in the study of literature or the graphic arts, are exceedingly vague when applied to music. Unless they refer to the obvious and unimportant practice of imitating everyday sounds by voices or instruments in a musical composition (as, for example, the bleating of sheep in Strauss's *Don Quixote*), it is difficult to see what meaning they can have that is related directly to music itself. What some writers call "realistic" or "naturalistic" music is simply, in effect, a certain kind of program music; the realism is deduced not from the music but from an extramusical fact (such as a title) about the composition in question. When we speak of realistic or naturalistic opera, therefore, we have reference primarily to the libretto; we mean that the opera presents persons, scenes, events, and conversations which are recognizably similar to the common daily experience of its audience, and that these things are treated seriously, as becomes matters of real moment, not with persiflage or fantasy as in an operetta. It goes without saying that such tendencies in opera grew out of earlier tendencies in literature. Thus Bizet's *Car-*

men, the first important realistic opera in France and one of the principal sources of the Italian verismo, was based on Mérimée's story. The chief disciples of realism in later nineteenth-century French literature were Guy de Maupassant (1850–1893) and Emile Zola (1840–1902). The latter found a musical interpreter in Alfred Bruneau,[23] the librettos of whose most important operas were either adapted from Zola's books or written especially for the composer by Zola himself; to the former class belong *Le Rêve* ("The Dream," 1891) and *L'Attacque du moulin* ("The Attack on the Mill," 1893), to the latter *Messidor* (1897), *L'Ouragan* ("The Hurricane," 1901), and *L'Enfant roi* ("The Child King," 1905). These works were concerned with current social and economic problems, presented in compact, tense dramatic situations, with symbolical additions. Another realistic detail was the prose form of the text instead of the customary verse. Unfortunately, this did not always inspire the composer to achieve a plastic musical rhythm; the regular accentuation indicated by the bar lines often becomes monotonous. The melodic line is declamatory rather than lyrical. The music is austere; it is especially apt in the creation of moods through reiterated motifs, but with all its evident sincerity and undoubted dramatic power, the important quality of sheer sensuous charm is often lacking. Bruneau is significant as a forerunner of some modern experiments in harmony [24] and as an independent, healthy force in the growth of modern French opera, counterbalancing to some extent the romanticism of D'Indy and the frank hedonism of Massenet.

A fuller measure of success in the field of operatic naturalism was granted to another pupil of Massenet, Gustave Charpentier.[25] *Louise,* a "musical novel," is his only important work, a strange but effective combination of several distinct elements. In scene, characters, and plot it is realistic; Charpentier, writing his own libretto, has almost gone out of his way to introduce such homely details as a bourgeois family supper, the reading of a newspaper, and a scene in a dressmak-

[23] Bruneau (1857–1934) was a pupil of Massenet and winner of the Prix de Rome in 1881. He was active not only as a composer of operas (thirteen) and ballets but also as a critic and writer (cf. the works listed in bibliography). See Boschot, *La Vie et les œuvres d'Alfred Bruneau.*

[24] An example from *L'Attaque du moulin* is found in OHM VII, 337–38.

[25] Charpentier (b. 1860) won the Prix de Rome in 1887. His only other opera is *Julien* (1913), a sequel to *Louise* but comparatively unsuccessful. See Delmas, *Gustave Charpentier et le lyrisme français;* Himonet, *Louise.*

ing shop; many of the minor personages are obviously taken "from life," and sing in a marked Parisian dialect. The crude melodrama of the closing scene recalls the mood of the Italian verismo composers. There is also, as in Bruneau, some touching on social questions: the issue of free love, the obligations of children to their parents, the miseries of poverty. But along with realism there is symbolism, especially in the weird figure of the Noctambulist, personification of "the pleasure of Paris." Paris itself is, as Bruneau remarked,[26] the real hero of this opera. Behind the whole action is the presence of the great city, seductive, mysterious, and fatal, enveloping persons and events in an atmosphere of poetry like that of the forest in Weber's *Freischütz*. Its hymn is the ensemble of street cries, running like a refrain through the first scene of Act II and echoing elsewhere throughout the opera. To realism and symbolism is added yet a third factor: sentiment. The dialogue between Louise and her father in Act I is of a convincing tenderness, while the love music of Act III, with the often-heard "Depuis le jour," is not only a great scene of passion but also one of the few of its kind in late nineteenth-century French opera which is never reminiscent of *Tristan und Isolde*—or hardly ever. It was the achievement of Charpentier to take all this realism, symbolism, and sentiment, holding together only with difficulty in the libretto itself, and mold it into one powerful whole by means of music. The score reminds one in many ways of Massenet: there is the same spontaneity and abundance of ideas, the same simple and economical texture, obtaining the maximum effect with the smallest apparent effort. The harmonic idiom is more advanced than Massenet's but not so daring or experimental as Bruneau's. The orchestral music is continuous, serving as background for spoken as well as sung passages,[27] and organized by means of a set of leitmotifs. A number of standard operatic devices are cleverly adapted to the libretto: Julien's serenade with accompaniment of a guitar, the ensemble of working girls in Act II (where the tattoo of the sewing machine replaces the whirr of the old romantic spinning wheel), and the grand ballet-like scene where Louise is crowned as the Muse of Montmartre in Act III. On the whole, it will be seen that when

---

26 *Musiciens d'aujourd'hui*, p. 154.
27 Both orchestrally accompanied spoken dialogue and the use of Parisian street cries are found in Massenet's *Manon;* there are street cries also in Puccini's *Bohême* (1896).

this opera is cited as an example of naturalism, the word needs to be taken with important qualifications. In any case it is not the naturalism which has caused it to survive, for this was but a passing fashion. *Louise* remains in the repertoire for the same reasons as other successful operas: because it has tuneful and moving music, wedded to a libretto which permits the music to operate as an effective partner in the creation of an interesting drama.

Beyond question, the most important French opera of the early twentieth century was Debussy's *Pelléas et Mélisande,* first performed at the Opéra-comique on April 30, 1902, "one of the three or four red-letter days in the history of our lyric stage" as Romain Rolland said.[28] The first sketches for this work are dated 1893, and Debussy revised it continually up to the time of performance. It is customary, and in the main correct, to regard *Pelléas et Mélisande* as a monument to French operatic reaction from Wagner. It is at the same time a focal point of French dramatic music, gathering up many essential national traits and giving them exceptionally clear and perfect expression, though colored by the individual genius of Debussy. The personal qualities of the music are so evident that they tend to usurp attention, and it is therefore well to emphasize that *Pelléas* is not only characteristic of Debussy but also of France.

There are four things which have marked French opera from the beginning of its history. The first is the belief that an opera is fundamentally a drama in words, to which music has been added; from this doctrine comes the insistence on clear and realistic declamation of the text. Both the contemporary admiration for Lully's recitative and Rousseau's later objections to it as "mannered" came from the same interest in the text as basic to the drama and hence to the opera. In no other country has so much attention been given to this issue. The flourishing of the opéra comique with its spoken dialogue was a constant witness that the French were willing to do without music rather than let it interfere with the understanding of the words. *Pelléas et Mélisande* conforms to this ideal. It is one of the rare in-

---

[28] *Musiciens d'aujourd'hui,* essay on Debussy. The standard books on Debussy (1862–1918) in English are those of Vallas (first publ. in French, 1932), Lockspeiser (1936), Thompson (1937), and Dumesnil (1940). See also the volume of Debussy's essays published under the title *Monsieur Croche, anti-dilettante.* There are special studies of *Pelléas et Mélisande* by Gilman, Jardillier, and M. Emmanuel. Debussy's only other stage work was the miracle drama *Le Martyre de Saint-Sebastien* (1911), based on D'Annunzio's play.

stances where a long play, not expressly made for music, has been turned into an opera with practically no rearranging.[29] In most places the music is no more than an iridescent veil covering the text; the orchestral background is shadowy, evanescent, almost a suggestion of sound rather than sound itself; and the voice part, with its independence of the bar line, narrow range, small intervals, and frequent chanting on one tone, adheres as closely as possible to the melody of French speech. Only in a few places, as in Mélisande's song at the beginning of Act III or in the love duet (Act IV, scene 4), does the melody become really lyric. How typical this narrow melodic line is of French music may be realized by comparing the contours of French folk-song melodies with those of German, English, or Italian folk songs, the instrumental themes of Saint-Saëns or César Franck with those of a German like Richard Strauss, or French nineteenth-century recitative in general with the wide-sweeping arioso of Verdi or Wagner. The use of the Wagnerian type of melody with French words, such as we find in the operas of Chabrier and D'Indy (and, to a lesser extent, in Bruneau and Charpentier) was soon felt to be unnatural. In the return to a more natural declamation and in the damping of orchestral sonorities, therefore, Debussy was in accord not only with the traditional French practice but with an even more ancient ideal, that of the early Florentine founders of opera, Peri, Caccini, and Gagliano.

The second historical feature of French opera is its tendency to center the musical interest not in the continuous orchestra or in the solo aria but in the divertissements, that is, interludes in the action where music might be enjoyed without the attention being divided by the necessity of following the drama at the same time. In early French opera and through the nineteenth century the common form of divertissement was the ballet with choruses. There are no ballets in *Pelléas,* and only one quite unimportant chorus, but the function of the divertissement is fulfilled by the orchestral preludes and the interludes which are played for changes of scene. Here, and here only, music has the foreground and the full symphonic resources are employed. But the interludes are not independent of the action;

29 The following scenes in the play are omitted in the opera: Act I, sc. 1; Act II, sc. 4; Act III, sc. 1; and Act V, sc. 1. There are very many other small omissions ranging from a single phrase to a dozen lines, and numerous alterations in wording. Some words have been added: see especially Act III, sc. 1 of the opera.

rather, they resume in wordless and concentrated form what has just passed and, by gradual transition, prepare for what is to come. Thus Debussy combines the Lullian form of opera with the new nineteenth-century practice of treating every detail as a means toward the central dramatic purpose.

Still another constant feature of French opera has been the deliberate choice of measured, objective, well-proportioned, and rational dramatic actions. The French have not been misled, except momentarily, either by the desire to be forceful at any cost or by the attractions of the world of metaphysical speculation. Not that French opera is as direct and uninhibited in its approach as the Italian; but the French prefer to suggest a hidden meaning by subtle juxtaposition of facts, trusting to stimulate the imagination rather than overwhelm it with exhaustive details, as Wagner tends to do. Now the quintessence of this subtle, indirect, and suggestive method in literature is found in the movement known as symbolism, of which Maeterlinck's five-act drama *Pelléas et Mélisande* is an outstanding example. The story is purposely vague and seems slight indeed when reduced to a bare summary. But the whole effect is in the manner, not the matter. As Edmund Gosse has said: "Maeterlinck is exclusively occupied in revealing, or indicating, the mystery which lies, only just out of sight, beneath the surface of ordinary life. In order to produce this effect of the mysterious he aims at an extreme simplicity of diction, and a symbolism so realistic as to be almost bare. He allows life itself to astonish us by its strangeness, by its inexplicable elements. Many of his plays are really highly pathetic records of unseen emotion; they are occupied with the spiritual adventures of souls, and the ordinary facts of time and space have no influence upon the movements of the characters. We know not who these orphan princesses, these blind persons, these pale Arthurian knights, these aged guardians of desolate castles, may be; we are not informed whence they come, nor whither they go; there is nothing concrete or circumstantial about them. Their life is intense and consistent, but it is wholly of a spiritual character; they are mysterious with the mystery of the movements of a soul." [30]

The mysterious, spiritual character of the drama is perfectly sup-

[30] "Maeterlinck," in *Encyclopædia Britannica* (11th ed.) XVII, 299a. Quoted by permission.

plemented by the music. The latter does everything by understate-
ment, by whispered suggestion. The full orchestra is hardly ever
heard outside the interludes. Instrumental doubling is avoided; solo
timbres and small combinations are the rule. Strings are often muted
and divided. There are only four fortissimos in the whole score.
Debussy's almost excessive "genius for good taste" [31] is apparent if
we contrast the wild greeting of the lovers in the second act of *Tristan*
with the meeting of Pelléas and Mélisande in Act IV (Example 111),

PELLÉAS ET MÉLISANDE, Act IV, sc.4

or the simple and touching scene of Mélisande's death in Act V with
Isolde's Liebestod.

However, soft music is not of necessity better than loud music; restraint is of no artistic value unless we are made aware that there is
something to be restrained. And here we come to the fourth and last
quality characteristic of French opera, which Debussy carries to the
ultimate degree, namely a capacity for the appreciation of the most
refined and complex sensory stimuli. In the quality of its acceptances
as well as of its refusals, French opera has always tended to be aristocratic. The style of musical impressionism which *Pelléas et Mélisande* exemplifies is essentially one of aristocratic sensualism, treating
sounds as of primary value for themselves irrespective of accepted
grammatical forms, and creating moods by reiterated minute impacts

[31] Rolland, *Musiciens d'aujourd'hui,* essay on Debussy.

of motifs, harmonies, and timbres. These elements in *Pelléas* sounded so completely unprecedented in themselves, and so completely detached from the familiar system of musical progressions, that audiences were at first bewildered; but they soon learned to associate the musical moods with those of the poetry and discovered a marvelous correspondence between the two. For as Maeterlinck's drama moved in a realm outside ordinary time and space, so Debussy's music moved in a realm outside the then known tonal system; lacking any strong formal associations within the field of music itself, his harmonies were irresistibly attracted to the similarly free images of the poet. Never was a happier marriage of music and verse. The technical methods of Debussy are familiar to all students of music and will be only briefly indicated here.[32] Modal, whole-tone, or pentatonic melodies and harmonies suggest the far-off, dreamlike character of the play. The free enchainment of seventh and ninth chords, often in organum-like parallel movement, and the blurring of tonality by complex harmonic relationships are also typical. There are definite leitmotifs which recur and are transformed and harmonically varied, but they are not treated in the continuous symphonic manner of Wagner. D'Indy has well expressed their function by the term "pivot themes." [33]

The influence of Wagner on Debussy is to be felt chiefly in a negative fashion, that is, by the care Debussy took to avoid writing like Wagner. In those days it was not easy. Debussy complained of his first draft of the duet in Act IV that "the ghost of old Klingsor, alias R. Wagner, keeps peeping out." [34] But the final score cannot be said to owe anything to Wagner beyond the orchestral continuity, the use of leitmotifs, and the exclusion of all merely ornamental details; in technique, idiom, feeling, and declamation it is Debussy's own. Whatever he had learned from *Tristan* or from Mussorgsky's *Boris Godunov*, from Massenet, Grieg, or from oriental music had been completely assimilated. So peculiarly was the musical style fitted to Maeterlinck's drama that it is no wonder Debussy was never able to find another suitable libretto. *Pelléas et Mélisande*, like *Fidelio*, remains an isolated masterpiece of its composer in the field of opera.

[32] See further M. Emmanuel, *Pelléas et Mélisande*, pp. 97–114 *et passim*.
[33] *Richard Wagner et son influence sur l'art musical français*, p. 81.
[34] Letter to Chausson, quoted in Abraham, *A Hundred Years of Music*, p. 278.

The next notable French opera of the twentieth century was Dukas' [35] *Ariane et Barbe-Bleue* ("Ariadne and Bluebeard," 1907); like *Pelléas,* it is the composer's only opera, and its libretto is likewise a symbolist drama by Maeterlinck. The influence of Debussy is apparent in the declamation and in some details of the harmony, but the recitative is less supple and poetic than Debussy's. The orchestration is very sonorous, using the brasses with brilliant effect, and the musical style on the whole is anything but impressionistic. Dukas was a composer of great technical attainment whose strong point was the development of ideas in large symphonic forms. Unfortunately, his themes are too often undistinguished in themselves, and their development marked less by inspiration than by system and perseverance; for example, the constant practice of repeating the exposition of a theme immediately in a new key (compare the exposition in the first movement of César Franck's symphony) becomes almost a mannerism. Dukas' harmony is very subtle, but here again one sometimes feels the absence of any compelling musical or dramatic reason for some of his complicated chord progressions. Another defect is the excessive reliance on the augmented triad in association with the whole-tone scale, a device which has lost the attraction of novelty since 1907. So much must be stated by way of negative criticism of *Ariane et Barbe-Bleue.* On the other hand, its many excellences must be emphasized. The work is less an opera than a huge symphony with the addition of choruses (essential to the drama, not mere embellishments) and solo voices. Cyclical recurrence and transformation of themes are used to create an architectural structure of grand and satisfying proportions. The great coda which forms the end of Act III is particularly impressive, summing up with Beethovenian finality all the principal themes of the opera and rounding off the whole with the theme which was first heard in the opening measures of the prelude to Act I. Among the many fine details of the score is the song of the "five daughters of Orlamonde," a striking folk-songlike melody and a source from which many of the leitmotifs of the opera are derived (Example 112). Altogether, *Ariane et Barbe-Bleue* is the most important French lyric drama of the early twentieth

[35] Paul Dukas (1865–1935) is best known for his orchestral scherzo *L'Apprenti sorcier.* His pianoforte Sonata in E-flat minor is an important work. See study by Samazeuilh and special Dukas issue of RM (May–June, 1936).

century next to *Pelléas et Mélisande*—important, that is, if measured in terms of artistic qualities rather than popular following. It is none the less significant musically for lacking those traits which made the success of Massenet and Charpentier.

ARIANE ET BARBE-BLEUE, Act I

Ex.112.   Dukas

There are four more operas of this period which merit special mention, each being in its own way a distinctive contribution. Déodat de Sévérac's *Coeur du moulin* ("The Heart of the Mill,"

1909),[36] a simple and poignant love story in a pastoral setting, has a musical score in which the influence of Debussy is modified by an original gift for direct, spontaneous expression and a charming regional flavor of southern France, evident especially in the choruses. Although its individual features were acclaimed by critics, *Le Coeur du moulin* has not had any popular success. Ravel's *Heure espagnole* ("The Spanish Hour," 1911),[37] on the contrary, has been widely performed. It is a one-act opera buffa in French, a tour de force of rhythm and orchestration, varied and witty in declamation, with a libretto in which the art of the *double-entendre* is carried to a height worthy of Favart. The vocal lines are suggestive of Richard Strauss, while under them the orchestra carries on a suite of Spanish dances ending with a mock-grand "scena and habañera." The scene being laid in a clockmaker's shop gives occasion for many charming and clever sound effects, among which the cuckoo motif is, of course, prominent. The strength of this opera is in just those qualities which Dukas' *Ariane* lacks, namely piquant details and a sense of lightness, gaiety, and improvisation. *Le Pays* ("The Country," 1912), by Guy Ropartz,[38] is a dramatic, solid, and well-proportioned score, with symphonic treatment of the orchestra, original in inspiration, evidencing the sound classical training its composer received from César Franck. One can detect a modified Wagnerianism (via D'Indy) in the melody and harmony, as well as the then fashionable obsession with the sound of the augmented fifth chord. Fauré's *Pénélope* (1913) [39] is a beautiful example of the composer's exquisite harmonic style, which lends to the classical subject matter an appropriate atmosphere of repose and remoteness, evoking the feeling of the antique world as no more common idiom could. From the viewpoint of theatrical

36 De Sévérac (1873–1921) was a pupil of D'Indy. Besides *Le Coeur du moulin* he composed two other operas (not produced), incidental music to plays, symphonic poems, and pianoforte pieces. The most recent study is by Selva (1930).
37 On Maurice Ravel (1875–1937) see Manuel, *Maurice Ravel et son œuvre dramatique;* special numbers of RM (April, 1925; December, 1938). Ravel's opera ballet *L'Enfant et les sortilèges* ("The Child and the Sorceries"), first performed in 1925, is simpler in style than *L'Heure espagnole,* with the orchestra subordinated to the voice parts, and some traces of jazz idiom.
38 J. Guy Ropartz (b. 1864) was director of the conservatories at Nancy (1894–1919) and Strasbourg (1919–29). His chief musical works are orchestral (four symphonies, two suites).
39 On Gabriel Urbain Fauré (1845–1924) see biographies by Bruneau (1925), Koechlin (1927), and Servières (1930); special number of RM (October 1922). Fauré's opera *Prométhée* was performed in 1900.

effectiveness, however, *Pénélope* is perhaps too refined; the slow tempo of the action (in Acts I and II especially) emphasizes the statuesque quality which is both the greatest musical beauty and the most serious dramatic weakness of this opera.

The dominant tendency of late nineteenth- and early twentieth-century French opera was idealistic; the noble, if somewhat vague, striving of *Fervaal* and *L'Etranger,* the mood of meditation on destiny in *Pelléas* and *Ariane,* the naïve religious faith of *Le Jongleur de Notre Dame,* the moral earnestness of *Le Coeur du moulin* and *Le Pays,* the serene, contemplative beauty of *Pénélope*—all show this. Even the so-called "naturalistic" operas of Bruneau and Charpentier used realism largely as a means of calling forth idealistic sentiment. Thus motivated, composers sought to bring into the theatre the most subtle and comprehensive resources of a highly developed musical art, aspiring toward universality of expression, freely using any and all means to which they found themselves attracted. Viewed from a later age, it seems an art of leisure and luxury, such as is possible only in a time of prosperity and peace. But leisure gave time for the unfolding of ideals, while luxury provided the material means for their realization on a scale which we have not seen since and probably shall not in this generation.

Among the minor composers of serious opera in this period were Gabriel Pierné (*La Fille de Tabarin,* 1901), Alexandre Georges (*Charlotte Corday,* 1901), Xavier Leroux (*La Reine Fiamette,* 1903, influenced by Puccini and Massenet; *Le Chemineau,* 1907), Henri Février (*Monna Vanna,* 1909), and Jean Noguès, whose *Quo Vadis* (1909) is a mild blend of Massenet and Fauré.[40] Distinguished especially for works in a lighter vein were the French-Venezuelan composer Reynaldo Hahn (1875–1946; *La Carmélite,* 1902), and Camille Erlanger (1863–1919; *Le Juif polonais,* 1900; *Aphrodite,* 1906). More individual in style was Raoul Laparra (1876–1943) with his operas on Spanish subjects; the most popular were *La Habanera* (1908) and *L'Illustre Fregona* (1931). Ernest Bloch's (b. 1880) opera *Macbeth,* composed in 1903, was given at the Opéra-comique in 1910. The music is strongly influenced by Debussy, with declamatory vocal lines, much parallelism in the orchestral texture, and a monotonously constant use of the augmented 5-7 chord, which seems to have fascinated opera composers of this period as much as the diminished seventh had fascinated their predecessors a hundred years earlier. *Macbeth* was severely criticized on account

[40] Pierné's dates are 1863–1937; Georges, 1850–1938; Leroux, 1863–1919; Février, b. 1875; Noguès, 1876–1932.

of its modernistic harmonies and rhythms [41] and soon dropped out of the repertory; in spite of much favorable comment, it has not yet been revived. Silvio Lazzari (1857–1944) with *La Lépreuse* (1912) and Louis Aubert (b. 1877) with *La Forêt bleue* (Geneva, 1913) had no great success, but Henri Rabaud's (b. 1873) oriental opéra comique *Mârouf, savetier de Caire* ("Marouf, Cobbler of Cairo," 1914), witty, modern in harmony, and brilliantly scored, has become a favorite both in Paris and abroad. It is undoubtedly one of the finest modern comic operas, a worthy descendant of the long French line of works in this style and on similar subjects. Another oriental opera was Gabriel Dupont's (1878–1914) *Antar*, finished in 1914 but not performed until 1921.[42] The Belgian Albert Dupuis (b. 1877; *La Passion*, Monte Carlo, 1916) in his operas reverted to the style of Massenet.

It must be remembered that throughout the period we have been considering the semidramatic form of the ballet occupied much of the attention of French composers. Lalo's *Namouna* (1882) never received the recognition it merited, but in the early twentieth century the performances of such works as Florent Schmitt's mimodrama *La Tragédie de Salomé* (1907), Ravel's *Daphnis et Chloé* (1912), and Stravinsky's *Firebird, Petrouchka,* and *The Ceremonial of Spring* (1910, 1911, and 1913 respectively) were very important musical events.

Fashions in opera might come and go, but the operetta and kindred forms went their way unperturbed. The line of French light opera, established in the nineteenth century by Auber, Adam, and Offenbach, was continued after 1870 by Alexandre Charles Lecocq (*La Fille de Madame Angot,* 1872), Robert Planquette (whose sentimental, fantastically successful *Cloches de Corneville* came out in 1877), Edmond Audran (*La Mascotte,* 1880), and Louis Varney (*Les Mousquetaires au couvent,* 1880).[43] Somewhat later began the long and popular series of operettas by André Messager (1853–1929), distinguished conductor and facile composer in a straightforward, attractively melodious vein (*La Basoche,* 1890; *Les P'tites Michu,* 1897; *Monsieur Beaucaire,* 1919). At the beginning of the twentieth century appeared the operettas of Claude Terrasse (1867–1923; *Le Sire de Vargy,* 1903; *Monsieur de la Palisse,* 1904).

[41] See Slonimsky, *Music Since 1900,* p. 106; Cohen, "Ernest Bloch's *Macbeth*," M&L XIX (1938) 143–48; Hall, "The Macbeth of Bloch," MMus XV, No. 4 (May–June, 1938) 209–15.

[42] See Dumesnil, "Gabriel Dupont," MQ XXX (1944) 441–47.

[43] On Lecocq (1832–1918) see Schneider, *Les Maîtres de l'opérette;* Planquette (1848–1903), Audran (1840–1901), and Varney (1844–1908) have not yet been subjects of separate studies.

Italian Opera after Verdi

AS ITALIANS IN THE EIGHTEENTH CENTURY would have nothing to do with Gluck, so in the nineteenth they cared little for Wagner. It was not until the eighties that even *Lohengrin* began to be accepted. With the exception of Boïto there were no important out-and-out Wagner disciples in Italy. There was considerable talk about Wagner and considerable skepticism as to the future of Italian opera, but the only result of any consequence was to call forth a vigorous national reaction of which the greatest monument is Verdi's *Otello*. Italian opera was too secure in its tradition and methods, too deeply rooted in popular life, to be susceptible to radical experiments, especially experiments resulting from aesthetic theories of a sort in which Italians were temperamentally uninterested. A mild influence of German romanticism, but hardly more, may be found in a few composers of the late nineteenth century. Alfredo Catalani with *Loreley* (1890, a revision of his *Elda*, 1880) and *La Wally* (1892) is the most distinguished of this group. His melodies are refined and musical, nearly always free of exaggerated pathos, supported by interesting and original harmony in a varied texture and with excellent balance of interest between voice and orchestra. Along with some curious traces of "Tristan chromaticism" there are experiments in modern devices (parallelism, augmented triads) which anticipate many of the characteristics of Puccini. The robust and vital rhythms are notable, especially in the choruses and dances of *La Wally*. Unfortunately, Catalani appeared just at a time when the Italian public was being seduced by Mascagni and Leoncavallo, so that his reserved and aristocratic music was drowned by the bellow of realism. With Antonio Smareglia (*Nozze istriane,* "Istrian Wedding," 1895), the influence of Wagner is apparent in the harmonic idiom and relative importance of the orchestra, but he lacked the popular touch in the lyrical parts, and his operas were not favorably received in his own country. Alberto Franchetti has been called "the Meyerbeer of Italy" because of his fondness for massive scenic effects (*Asrael,* 1888; *Cristo-*

foro Colombo, 1892; *Germania,* 1902), but the music is, on the whole, undistinguished. None of these composers[1] was attracted by the verismo movement of the 1890's, which was the popular trend in Italy at that time.

The most explosive reaction against Wagner, and the typical Italian adaptation of late nineteenth-century literary and dramatic movements, was launched with the performance of Mascagni's *Cavalleria rusticana* ("Rustic Chivalry," 1890) and Leoncavallo's *Pagliacci* ("The Clowns," 1892).[2] These two one-act operas are the classics of the school of verismo, or realism. The Italian verismo resembles the French naturalism in the use of scenes and characters from common life; but the naturalists use these materials as a means for the development of more general ideas and feelings, idealizing both scene and music, whereas the goal of the verists is simply to present a vivid, melodramatic plot, to arouse sensation by violent contrasts, to paint a cross section of life without concerning themselves with any general significance the action might have. Verismo is to naturalism what the "shocker" is to the realistic novel. The music corresponds to this conception. It aims simply and directly at the expression of intense passion through melodic or declamatory phrases of the solo voices, to which the orchestra contributes sensational harmonies. Choral or instrumental interludes serve only to establish a mood which is to be rent asunder in the next scene. Everything is so arranged that the moments of excitement follow one another in swift climatic succession. Now it cannot be denied that there was plenty of precedent

[1] Catalani (1854–1893) studied at Paris and Milan and was successor to Ponchielli as professor of composition at the Milan conservatory. See Klein, "Alfredo Catalani," MQ XXIII (1937) 287–94.

Smareglia (1854–1929) studied at Vienna and Milan; he became professor of composition at the Tortini Conservatory, Trieste, in 1921. See studies by Nacamuli, M. Smareglia, and A. Smareglia.

Franchetti (b. 1860) studied at Dresden and Munich. The most recent of his nine operas is *Glauco* (Naples, 1922).

[2] Pietro Mascagni (1863–1945) became famous overnight with *Cavalleria rusticana,* which remained his one big success, though *L'amico Fritz* (1891) and the romantic operas *Guglielmo Ratcliff* (1895) and *Iris* (1898) have been widely performed. His last operas were *Il piccolo Marat* (1921), *Nerone* (1935), and *I bianchi ed i neri* (1940). See studies by De Donno and biography by Pompei (1912).

Ruggiero Leoncavallo (1858–1919) is another one-opera composer. A projected early trilogy, *Crepusculum,* was left uncompleted after the failure of the first part. *La Bohème* (1897) suffered by comparison with Puccini's more popular work of the same title, but *Zaza* (1900) was fairly successful. Neither of these is of the verismo type.

On the aesthetic of verismo in general, see Rinaldi, *Musica e verismo.*

in Donizetti and the earlier works of Verdi for melodramatic situations in opera. But by comparison the action of the veristic operas takes place as in an atmosphere from which the nitrogen has been withdrawn, so that everything burns with a fierce, unnatural flame, and moreover quickly burns out. The one-act form is due not so much to concentration as to rapid exhaustion of the material. Much the same is true of the verismo movement as a whole, historically considered. It flared like a meteor across the operatic sky of the 1890's, but by the end of the century it was practically dead, for it had no possibilities of growth. Neither Mascagni nor Leoncavallo, nor any of their imitators in that style, were able to repeat the sensational success of *Cavalleria rusticana* and *Pagliacci*.

The chief figure in Italian opera of the late nineteenth and early twentieth centuries was Giacomo Puccini,[3] who resembles Massenet in his position of mediator between two eras, as well as in many features of his musical style. Puccini's rise to fame began with his third opera, *Manon Lescaut* (1893), which is less effective dramatically than Massenet's opera on the same subject (1884) but rather superior in musical interest—this despite occasional reminiscences of *Tristan,*[4] which few composers in the nineties seemed able to escape. Puccini's world-wide reputation rests chiefly on his next three works: *La Bohême* (1896), *Tosca* (1900), and *Madama Butterfly* (1904). *La Bohême* is a sentimental opera with dramatic touches of realism, on a libretto adapted from Henri Murger's *Scènes de la vie de Bohême* ("Scenes of Bohemian Life");[5] *Tosca,* taken from Victorien Sardou's drama of the same name (1887), is "a prolonged orgy of lust and crime"[6] made endurable by the beauty of the music; and *Madama Butterfly* is a tale of love and heartbreak in a Japanese setting. (In 1904 it was customary to regard the Japanese as a lovable, somewhat fragile, and altogether quaint set of people.) The musical characteristic of Puccini which stands out in all these operas is the intense, concentrated, melting quality of expressiveness in the vocal melodic

[3] Puccini (1858–1924) studied under Ponchielli at Milan and made his debut as an opera composer with *Le Villi* in 1884. By the early years of the twentieth century he had become the most successful and popular Italian composer since Verdi. See biographies by Fraccaroli and Specht; Puccini's letters, ed. by Adami; Gatti, "The Works of Giacomo Puccini," MQ XIV (1928) 16–34.

[4] E.g., the love duet in Act II, from the words "è fascino d'amor."

[5] Dramatized successfully as *La Vie de Bohême* in 1849.

[6] R. A. Streatfeild, in *Grove's Dictionary* (4th ed.) IV, 282.

line. It is like Massenet without Massenet's urbanity. It is naked emotion crying out, and persuading the listener's feeling by its very earnestness. For illustrations the reader need only recall the aria "Che gelida manina" and the ensuing duet in the first scene of *La Bohême*, the closing scene of the same work, or the familiar arias "Vissi d'arte" in *Tosca* and "Un bel di" in *Butterfly*. The history of this type of melody is instructive. It will be remembered that in Verdi we encountered from time to time a melodic phrase of peculiar poignancy which seemed to gather up the whole feeling of a scene in a pure and concentrated moment of expression, such as the "Amami, Alfredo" in *La traviata* (Ex. 103), the recitative "E tu, come sei pallida" of *Otello* (Ex. 104), or the kiss motif from the same work. For later composers, lacking the sweep and balance of construction found in Verdi at his best but perceiving that the high points of effectiveness in his operas were marked by phrases of this sort, naturally became ambitious to write operas which should consist entirely (or as nearly so as possible) of such melodic high points, just as the verismo composers had tried to write operas consisting entirely of melodramatic shocks. Both tendencies are evidence of satiety of sensation. These melodic phrases in Verdi are of the sort sometimes described as "pregnant"; their effect depends on the prevalence of a less heated manner of expression elsewhere in the opera, so that they stand out by contrast. But in Puccini we have, as an apparent ideal if not always an actuality, what may be called a kind of perpetual pregnancy in the melody, whether this is sung or entrusted to the orchestra as a background for vocal recitative. The musical utterance is kept at high tension, almost without repose, as though it were to be feared that if the audiences were not continually excited they would go to sleep. This tendency toward compression of language, this nervous stretto of musical style, is characteristic of the *fin de siècle* period. We shall find it once more, in the realm of harmonic procedure, when we come to the operas of Richard Strauss.

The sort of melody we have been describing runs through all of Puccini's works. In the early operas it is organized in more or less balanced periods, but later it becomes a freer line, often skillfully embodying a series of leitmotifs. The leitmotifs of Puccini are admirably dramatic in conception and effectively used either for recalling earlier moments in the opera or, by reiteration, to establish a mood, but they do not serve as generating themes for musical development.

Puccini's music was enriched by the composer's constant interest in the new harmonic developments of his time; he was always eager to put current discoveries to use in opera. One example of striking harmonic treatment is the series of three major triads (B-flat, A-flat, E-natural) which opens *Tosca* and is associated throughout the opera with the villainous Scarpia. The harmonic tension of the augmented fourth outlined by the first and third chords of this progression is by itself sufficient for Puccini's purpose; he has created his atmosphere with three strokes, and the chord series has no further use but to be repeated intact whenever the dramatic situation requires it. There is no use in making comparisons between Puccini's procedure and that, for example, of D'Indy in *Istar* or Sibelius in the Fourth Symphony, both of which works are largely developed out of the same augmented-fourth interval; but no contrast could show more starkly the difference between good opera music on the one hand and good symphonic music on the other. One common trait of Puccini's, found in all his operas from the early *Edgar* (1889) down to his last works, is the "side-slipping" [7] of chords (Example 113); doubtless this de-

MADAMA BUTTERFLY, Act II

Ex.113.   Puccini

vice was learned from Verdi (compare the passage "Oh! come è dolce" in the duet at the end of Act I of *Otello*) or Catalani, but it is based on a practice common in much exotic and primitive music and going back in European music history to medieval organum and faux-bourdon. Its usual purpose in Puccini is to break a melodic line into a number of parallel strands, like breaking up a beam of white light by

[7] Abraham, *A Hundred Years of Music*, p. 222.

a prism into parallel bands of color. In a sense it is a complementary effect to that of intensifying a melody by duplication at the unison and octaves—an effect dear to all Italian composers of the nineteenth century and one to which Puccini also frequently resorted. Parallel duplication of the melodic line at the fifth is used to good purpose in the introduction to scene 3 of *La Bohême* to suggest the bleakness of a cold winter dawn; at the third and fifth, in the introduction to the second scene of the same opera, for depicting the lively, crowded street scene (a passage which may or may not have been in the back of Stravinsky's mind when he wrote the music for the first scene of *Petrouchka*); and parallelism of the same sort, extended sometimes to chords of the seventh and ninth (compare Debussy), is found at many places in the later operas.

The most original places in Puccini, however, are not dependent on any single device; take for example the opening scene of Act III of *Tosca*, with its broad unison melody in the horns, the delicate descending parallel triads over a double pedal in the bass, the Lydian melody of the shepherd boy, and the faint background of bells, with the veiled, intruding threat of the three Scarpia chords from time to time—an inimitably beautiful and suggestive passage, technically perhaps owing something to both Verdi and Debussy, but nevertheless thoroughly individual.

An important source of color effects in Puccini's music is the use of exotic materials. Exoticism in Puccini was more than a mere borrowing of certain details but rather extended into the very fabric of his melody, harmony, rhythm, and instrumentation.[8] It is naturally most in evidence in the works on oriental subjects, *Madama Butterfly* and *Turandot* (1926). *Turandot,* based on a comedy of the eighteenth-century Carlo Gozzi, was completed after Puccini's death by Franco Alfano; it is "so far the last world success in the history of opera." [9] It shows side by side the most advanced harmonic experimentation (compare the bitonality at the opening of Acts I and II), the utmost development of Puccinian expressive lyric melody, and the most brilliant orchestration of any of his operas.

Puccini did not escape the influence of verismo, but the realism

[8] See the excellent study (with musical examples) by Carner, "The Exotic Element in Puccini," MQ XXII (1936) 45–67.
[9] Loewenberg, *Annals,* p. 727.

in his operas is always tempered by, or blended with, romantic and exotic elements. In *La Bohême,* common scenes and characters are invested with a romantic halo; the repulsive melodrama of *Tosca* is glorified by the music; and the few realistic details in *Madama Butterfly* are unimportant. A less convincing attempt to blend realism and romance is found in *La fanciulla del West* ("The Girl of the Golden West"), taken from a play by David Belasco and first performed at the Metropolitan Opera House in 1910. Though enthusiastically received by the first American audiences, *La fanciulla* did not attain as wide or enduring popularity as the preceding works. The next opera, *La rondine* ("The Swallow," 1917), was even less successful. A return was made, however, with the *trittico,* or triptych, of one-act operas performed at the Metropolitan in December 1918: *Il tabarro* ("The Clock"), a veristic melodrama; *Suor Angelica* ("Sister Angelica"), a miracle play; and *Gianni Schicchi,* the most popular of the three, a delightful comedy in the spirit of eighteenth-century opera buffa. Puccini's comic skill, evidenced also in some parts of *La Bohême* and *Turandot,* is here seen at its most spontaneous, incorporating smoothly all the characteristic harmonic devices of his later period. Only the occasional intrusion of sentimental melodies in the old vein breaks the unity of effect.

Puccini was not one of the great composers, but within his own limits (of which he was perfectly aware) he worked honorably and with mastery of his technique. Bill Nye remarked of Wagner's music that it "is better than it sounds"; Puccini's music, on the contrary, often sounds better than it is, owing to the perfect adjustment of means to ends. He had the prime requisite for an opera composer, an instinct for the theatre; to that he added the Italian gift of knowing how to write effectively for singers, an unusually keen ear for new harmonic and instrumental colors, a receptive mind to musical progress, and a poetic imagination excelling in the evocation of dreamlike, fantastic moods. Even *Turandot,* for all its modernistic dissonance, is essentially a romantic work, an escape into the exotic in both the dramatic and the musical sense.

A younger contemporary of Puccini was Umberto Giordano,[10] whose *Andrea Chénier* (1896) is like a rescue opera of the French Revolution period, but without the rescue; both plot and music show

[10] Giordano (b. 1867) studied at the Naples Conservatory. See Galli, *Umberto Giordano.*

the influence of verismo in the exaggerated emphasis on effect at all
costs (Example 114). Apart from its undoubted dramatic qualities,
the score offers little of interest; the harmonies are heavy and old-
fashioned, and there are few notable lyric passages in the voice parts.
Some local color is provided by the use of revolutionary songs ("Ça

ANDREA CHÉNIER, sc. 2

Ex.114.   Giordano

ira," "La Carmagnole," "La Marseillaise"). *Fedora* (1898) and
Siberia (1903) are in the same style, with Russian instead of French
background. In *Madame Sans-Gêne* (New York, 1915) the composer's
skill at producing effective theatre music is brilliantly applied in a
vivacious and tuneful comedy drama. Of Giordano's later operas,
La cena delle beffe ("The Feast of Jests," 1924), a lurid four-act melodrama, has been the most successful. None of these are of much significance musically; they are the work of a gifted but not profound

composer, operating within the framework of traditional Italian opera and skillfully adapting it to the current fashion of orchestral continuity. A similar, but less conspicuous, position must be assigned to Francesco Cilèa;[11] his *Adriana Lecouvreur* (1902) is an involved drama of the age of Louis XV, with expertly contrived music of a lyrical-tragic sort obviously influenced by Puccini, unadventurous harmonically or rhythmically, but good theatre and grateful for the singers.

One of the most popular composers of the early twentieth century was the German-Italian Ermanno Wolf-Ferrari,[12] who has specialized in comedy operas on librettos either adapted from the eighteenth-century Goldoni or of a similar type: *Le donne curiose* ("The Curious Ladies," 1903); *Il segreto di Susanna* ("The Secret of Suzanne," 1909), his most famous work; and *Sly* (1927), a comic opera distantly reminiscent of Verdi's *Falstaff*, and likewise on a Shakespearean subject (prologue to *The Taming of the Shrew*). His only tragic opera, an experiment with some of the methods of verismo, is *I gioielli della Madonna* ("The Jewels of the Madonna," 1911), a work strongly suggestive of Donizetti with modern trimmings in harmony and rhythm. The Serenade in Act II, perhaps the best-known number in the opera, is a good illustration of the vivacity and rather superficial harmonic cleverness of the style. One of the last composers of the verismo school, whose work is full of the old traditional Italian opera devices, was Mascagni's pupil Riccardo Zandonai (1883–1944); his most important opera is *Francesca da Rimini* (1914), based on D'Annunzio's tragedy of the same name—a smoothly contrived score with a pleasant tincture of late romantic harmony.

The decline of verismo and the effort to combine some of its features with a neoromantic or exotic type of opera, which we find in Puccini, Giordano, and others, is one symptom of a new spirit rising in Italian musical life in the early years of the twentieth century. By comparison with the previous period, this was a time of internationalism and even a certain amount of eclecticism. After Wagner, came

---

11 Cilèa (b. 1866) likewise studied at Naples. He is one of the first Italian opera composers of this period to have busied himself with music in other forms (orchestral and chamber works). See *Bollettino bibliografico musicale* VII (June, 1932) 5–16.
12 Wolf-Ferrari (b. at Venice, 1876, of a German father and an Italian mother) studied under Rheinberger at Munich, and all but the first of his operas up to 1914 were first performed in Germany. See De Rensis, *Ermanno Wolf-Ferrari, la sua vita d'artista;* Grisson, *Ermanno Wolf-Ferrari.*

Strauss, Debussy, and Stravinsky in turn to make their impress on Italian composers. Interest was aroused in symphonic and chamber music (Martucci, Sgambati); an important renewal of church music was led by Don Lorenzo Perosi and Enrico Bossi. Evidence of this broadened outlook is found in the neoromantic operas of Italo Montemezzi,[13] especially *L'amore dei tre re* ("The Love of the Three Kings," 1913) and *La nave* ("The Ship," 1918), where the influence of both Wagner and Debussy is blended with a native Italian lyricism to produce music sound in workmanship, rich in instrumental color, conservative in idiom though not merely imitative, and of enduring beauty. *L'amore dei tre re* is without doubt the greatest Italian tragic opera since Verdi's *Otello*. Its most notable quality is the refinement of the style; the chromaticism of the period is treated with intelligence and restraint, intensifying the expression of feeling by the very refusal to dwell on obvious tricks of theatrical effect. There are memorable moments of classic breadth, as at the end of the love duet in Act II (Example 115). The voice line is an admirable ad-

L'AMORE DEI TRE RE, Act II

Ex. 115.　　　　　　　　　　　　　　　　　　Montemezzi

[13] Montemezzi (b. 1875) studied at the Milan Conservatory. His first two operas were *Giovanni Gallurese* (1905) and *Hellera* (1909). His most recent opera, *La notte di Zoraima* (1931), has been widely performed in Italy.

SCENE FROM ZANDONAI'S "FRANCESCA DA RIMINI"

justment of vocal melody to a continuous symphonic texture; recurring motifs and a carefully worked out key scheme make a formal whole of satisfying proportions. Altogether this opera, with its night-shrouded castle, its lovers swooning in sensual ecstasy, and the tragic figure of the blind Archibaldo, with its music which seems from beginning to end one low cry of voluptuous pain, of delicately scented agony and hopeless fatalism, is an appropriate work with which to close our contemplation of the course of Italian opera at the end of the romantic period: the ripe and languid fruit of a dying age, the sunset of a long and glorious day.

26

German Opera after Wagner [1]

WAGNER AFFECTED THE COURSE OF LYRIC drama like a new planet hurled into a solar system. The center of the operatic universe shifted; all the old balances were disturbed; regroupings took place, accompanied by erratic movements. These consequences were least marked in Italy, more so in France, and most of all, naturally, in Germany. Yet even there they did not appear quickly. Most of Wagner's contemporary rivals [2] either ignored him or fondly hoped to patch selected details from his system onto the old structure of grand opera. Only Peter Cornelius, with his comic *Barbier von Bagdad* and epic *Cid* (1865), combined a full appreciation of Wagner's achievements with a discriminating independence. Max Bruch's *Loreley* (1863) was a romantic opera of the old nineteenth-century type.[3] Karl Goldmark's *Königin von Saba* ("The Queen of Sheba," 1875),[4] one of the most popular German works of the later nineteenth century, is an agreeable but old-fashioned grand opera in the heavy manner of Meyerbeer, complete with set numbers, ballets, pageantry, and some conventional strokes of oriental color. Goldmark had obviously accepted Wagner as far as *Tannhäuser*, but

---

1 General bibliography: Schiedermair, *Die deutsche Oper;* R. Louis, *Die deutsche Musik der Gegenwart* (1909); Istel, "German Opera Since Richard Wagner," MQ I (1915) 260–90; *idem, Die moderne Oper* (2d ed., 1923); Bitter, *Die deutsche komische Oper der Gegenwart* (1932); Korngold, *Deutsches Opernschaffen der Gegenwart* (1922); *Monographien moderner Musiker,* ed. Segnitz; Pisk, "Die Moderne: Deutsche: Die Oper," in Adler, *Handbuch* II, 1029–38; Moser, *Geschichte der deutschen Musik* III, 351–451, *passim;* Wellesz, "Opera in the Twentieth Century," in *Grove's Dictionary* (4th ed.), *Supplementary Volume,* pp. 477–88.

2 A list of these forgotten men will be found in Adler, *Handbuch* II, 883–87.

3 Bruch (1838–1920) is best known as a composer of secular oratorios and for his two violin concertos. He wrote two other operas. The libretto of *Die Loreley* was originally intended for Mendelssohn, who apparently composed only three numbers from it.

4 Goldmark (1830–1915) wrote five more operas after *Die Königin von Saba,* but only *Das Heimchen am Herd* ("The Cricket on the Hearth," 1896, after Dickens) was successful. See biographies by Keller and L. Koch, also the composer's own *Erinnerungen.*

he was evidently not acquainted with, or at any rate not at all influenced by, the later style of *Tristan* and the *Ring*.

The composers of comic and popular opera concerned themselves even less with Wagner's dramatic and musical reforms. Thus Hermann Goetz [5] seems to ignore the existence of *Die Meistersinger* in his *Der Widerspenstigen Zähmung* ("The Taming of the Shrew," 1874). This work, like Cornelius' *Barbier,* has never had the wide public success that the clever libretto and Mozartean humor of the music would seem to deserve. Greater popularity was achieved by two other comic operas of the same period: Ignaz Brüll's *Das goldene Kreuz* ("The Golden Cross," 1875),[6] a harmless and pleasant comic opera slightly reminiscent of Auber; and Nessler's *Trompeter von Säckingen* ("The Trumpeter of Säckingen," 1884),[7] an example of *Volksoper,* or "people's opera," with men's choruses, arias, and dances all in the simple, tuneful, sentimental style of nineteenth-century German popular music.

The direct influence of Wagner on German opera began to be felt in the 1880's. It was evidenced by the choice of Germanic, Greek, or Hindu myths as subject matter (often with symbolical overtones and a redemption motive), and in music by the cultivation of the leitmotif system, emphasis on the orchestra, and a harmonic and melodic idiom of an obviously Wagnerian type. (Heinrich Dorn [8] had composed a five-act *Niebelungen* opera in 1854, but neither the poem nor the music had any resemblance to Wagner's *Ring*.) The principal composers of the Wagnerian school in the late nineteenth century were Felix von Weingartner (*Sakuntala,* 1884; *Genesius,* 1892; *Orestes,* a trilogy, 1902), Heinrich Zöllner (*Faust,* 1887; *Der Überfall,* 1895; *Die versunkene Glocke,* "The Sunken Bell," a fairytale opera, 1899), and especially August Bungert, whose *Homerische Welt* ("The Homeric World"), consisting of two cycles of six operas in all, was the most ambitious musico-dramatic undertaking since the *Ring* but nevertheless failed to make its way with the public

[5] On Goetz (1840–1876) see biographies by Kreuzhage and Kruse.
[6] Brüll (1846–1907), a close friend of Brahms, studied and taught at Vienna. He composed ten stage works in all.
[7] Viktor Nessler (1841–1890), Alsatian composer and conductor, was active at Strasbourg and Leipzig.
[8] Dorn (1804–1892) composed fourteen stage works and many songs. See his autobiography, *Aus meinem Leben.*

because of appallingly uninteresting music.[9] These composers for the most part followed Wagner in writing their own librettos. Among other Wagnerian works of this period may be mentioned some early operas by composers who later developed a more personal style: Kienzl's *Urvasi* (1886), Schillings' *Ingwelde* (1894), R. Strauss's *Guntram* (1894), Pfitzner's *Arme Heinrich* (1896), and D'Albert's *Kain* (1900).

The inevitable consequence of all this imitation of Wagner was a reaction. Both public and composers, growing tired of more or less feeble repetitions of a style in which Wagner had already said the definitive, final word, were ready for something new, and a way out was discovered quite inadvertently. In 1885 Alexander Ritter [10] had produced a one-act opera *Der faule Hans* ("Lazy Hans"), of a type known in Germany as a *Märchenoper*, that is, a fairy-tale opera. Though this work had no immediate successors, it is of interest as the forerunner of a most important fairy-tale opera which came out in 1893: Humperdinck's *Hänsel und Gretel*.[11] Humperdinck first wrote this music for a play which his sister's children performed at home; made into a full opera, it caught the public fancy to such a degree as to start a whole new school in Germany. People turned with relief from the misty heights of mythology to the homely, familiar, enchanted world of the fairy tale, to subjects like those which their grandparents had enjoyed in the days of Marschner and Lortzing.

9 Weingartner (1863–1942) was known principally as a conductor but was also a prolific composer. His later operas include *Kain und Abel* (1914); *Dame Kobold* (1916); the veristic *Dorfschule* (1920); the comic *Meister Andrea* (1920), with spoken dialogue and separate numbers in early nineteenth-century style; and *Der Apostat* (1938). See his own writings, especially *Die Lehre von der Wiedergeburt des musikalischen Dramas* (1895) and *Lebenserinnerungen*.

Zöllner (b. 1854) was a choral conductor and teacher at Cologne, New York, and Leipzig. He composed ten operas. See essay in Vol. II of Segnitz's *Monographien moderner Musiker*.

Bungert (1845–1915) studied at Cologne and Paris. Besides the operas mentioned (the first cycle, two operas, was not completed) he wrote orchestral and choral works. See Chop, *August Bungert*.

10 Ritter (1833–1896) was a friend of von Bülow, and married Wagner's niece in 1854. In music he was a disciple of Liszt, his symphonic poems marking a stage between that master and R. Strauss; he is also of importance as a song composer. See von Hausegger, *Alexander Ritter*.

11 Engelbert Humperdinck (1854–1921) was a pupil of F. Hiller and Rheinberger, a friend of Wagner's, and teacher of many noted opera composers. His most important later works were *Königskinder* ("The Royal Children"), written first in 1898 as incidental music to a play and recast as an opera ten years later, and the comedy opera *Die Heirat wider Willen* ("The Reluctant Marriage," 1905). See biography by O. Besch.

The transition was made easier for intellectuals by the fact that Humperdinck kept up an appearance of loyalty to Wagner. The music of *Hänsel und Gretel* is, in fact, a peculiar mixture of German folk melody and Wagnerian polyphony. Perhaps the texture is too complicated for the subject matter, but if this be a fault, it is one easy to forgive in view of the many musical beauties and the heartfelt, simple emotion of the work. The music brings together many qualities rooted in the affections of Germans over generations: the delightful songs and dances of the children, the idyllic forest scenes, just enough of the supernatural (but with a comic touch), and the chorale-like feeling of the "Evening blessing" melody, which recurs in the finale to the words

> When past bearing is our grief,
> God himself will send relief.

Among the many fairy-tale operas which followed the successful appearance of *Hänsel und Gretel* were Thuille's *Lobetanz* (1898) and *Gugeline* (1901), Klose's *Ilsebill* (1903), Sommer's *Rübezahl* (1904), and two works by Humperdinck's pupil Leo Blech: *Alpenkönig und Menschenfeind* ("Alpine King and Man's Enemy," 1903; revised in 1917 under the title of *Rappelkopf*) and *Aschenbrödel* ("Cinderella," 1905).[12] Here in varying degrees the post-Wagnerian musical idiom was adapted to popular subjects. To this group of composers belongs also Richard Wagner's son Siegfried Wagner,[13] another Humperdinck pupil, whose *Bärenhäuter* (1899) was the first and best of a long series of fairy-tale operas to his own texts, attempt-

[12] Ludwig Thuille (1861–1907) was a pupil of Rheinberger and taught piano and theory at the Munich Conservatory. See biography by Munter.

Friedrich Klose (1862–1942) was Thuille's successor at Munich. A composer in the tradition of Liszt and Wagner, his principal works are choral and orchestral. See biography by Knappe.

Hans Sommer (1837–1922), originally a professor of physics, resigned in 1884 to devote himself to music. He is known as a song composer as well as for his operas. See essay by Stier in Segnitz's *Monographien* I.

Leo Blech (b. 1871) has had a long career as opera conductor in Germany. He composed seven stage works, the best of which was the comedy *Versiegelt* (1908; see below). See biography by W. Jacob.

[13] Siegfried Wagner (1869–1930) was active as conductor and supervisor of the Bayreuth festivals. He composed twelve operas. See his *Erinnerungen;* letters, ed. by Rebois; Glasenapp, *Siegfried Wagner und seine Kunst;* Du Moulin-Eckart, *Wahnfried;* other studies by Pretsch and Daube. (*Der Bärenhäuter* is untranslatable. The story on which it is based will be found under the title "Des Teufels russiger Bruder" in Grimm, *Kinder- und Haus-Märchen* [Berlin, 1815] II, 100–105.)

ing to combine legend, symbolism, and humor in a popular style. None of these composers equaled Humperdinck in either merit or public favor. A genuine school of people's opera appeared in Austria, stemming from Wilhelm Kienzl's *Evangelimann* (1895).[14] Kienzl, like Humperdinck, founded his appeal on the application of the Wagnerian technique to nonheroic subjects, but his texture is less complex than Humperdinck's, and some of his musical material has an equal or even greater folklike flavor (Example 116). *Der Evange-*

DER EVANGELIMANN, Act I

Ex.116.   Kienzl

O Zit-ter-bart, o Zit-ter-bart, o Franz Xa-ve-rius Zit-ter-bart! Du

triffst ja nicht den La-den mehr; die Ku-gel ist für dich zu schwer.

limann is, in fact, a kind of anthology of popular dance and song types, together with sentimental melodies in the style of Nessler, and amusing reminiscences of *Lohengrin, Tristan, Die Meistersinger,* and *Hänsel und Gretel*—all attached to a libretto of the most unashamedly melodramatic-romantic sort. Its popularity in Germany and Austria may be judged by the fact that *Der Evangelimann* had over 5,300 performances in the first forty years of its existence. Closely related to Kienzl's work is that of another Austrian, Julius Bittner,[15]

---

14 Kienzl (1857–1941) composed songs and chamber music as well as ten operas. His most successful work after *Der Evangelimann* was *Der Kuhreigen* (1911, on a French Revolution subject). He was also noted as an essayist and scholar. Two *Festschriften* (1917, 1937) have been dedicated to him. See his autobiography, *Meine Lebenswanderungen,* and essay by Morold in Segnitz's *Monographien* III (1909). (The personage of the "Evangelimann" has no English equivalent; he is a wandering mendicant who receives alms in return for reading and telling stories from the Scriptures.)

15 Bittner (1874–1939), a graduate in law and for many years a magistrate in Vienna, composed over seventeen stage works (the last in 1935), also orchestral and choral music. See Specht, *Julius Bittner.*

whose operas (to his own texts) are based on a folklike type of melody, alternating closed numbers with declamatory passages and combining sentiment with humor. *Die rote Gred* ("Red-headed Gred," 1907) and *Der Musikant* ("The Musician," 1910) show his characteristic style in purest form; *Der Bergsee* ("The Mountain Lake," 1911) has curious post-Wagnerian reminiscences. *Das höllisch Gold* ("The Infernal Gold," 1916), a humorous miracle play, was his most varied and most popular work. Likewise in the field of people's opera must be noted the Viennese Heuberger's *Barfüssele* (1905) and the Czech Karel Weis's *Polnische Jude* ("The Polish Jew," 1901),[16] both of which were very popular in their day. Finally, we may mention the Viennese operetta in the early twentieth century, represented by Franz Lehár (*Die lustige Witwe*, "The Merry Widow," 1905), Oskar Straus (*Ein Walzertraum*, "A Waltz Dream," 1907; *Der tapfere Soldat*, "The Chocolate Soldier," 1908), and Leo Fall (*Die Dollarprinzessin*, "The Dollar Princess," 1907).[17]

Meanwhile there developed in Germany a more sophisticated type of comic opera, less national in subject matter and going back for musical inspiration either to Cornelius' *Barbier* or Wagner's *Meistersinger*. The most celebrated example of this school, though seldom performed, is Hugo Wolf's *Corregidor* (1896),[18] a sincere and in many respects inspired attempt to create a gay, original German comic opera "without the gloomy, world-redeeming ghost of a Schopenhaurian philosopher in the background." [19] This laudable intention was frustrated by Wolf's long-standing admiration for Wagner's music: the orchestra of *Der Corregidor* is as heavily polyphonic as that

[16] Richard Heuberger (1850–1914) composed three operas, six operettas, two ballets, and numerous choral and orchestral works. See his collected essays, *Musikalische Skizzen* and *Im Foyer*.

Karel Weis (1862–1937) studied and worked chiefly at Prague. Of his many operas and operettas (some in Czech), only *Der polnische Jude* won wide acclaim.

[17] Lehár (b. 1870) was born in Hungary but has lived mostly in Vienna. See biographies by Decsey and Czech.

Straus (b. 1870) studied under Bruch, conducted at many German theatres, and has written much music for Hollywood films. See R. Bizet, *Une Heure . . . avec Oskar Straus*.

Fall (1873–1925) is musically the most interesting of these three composers.

[18] On Wolf (1860–1903) see biographies by Decsey and Newman; also Hellmer, *Der Corregidor*. This, Wolf's only completed opera, was based on a story *El sombrero de tres picos* by P. A. de Alarcón; the same subject was used by Manuel de Falla for a ballet (1919) and by Zandonai for his opera *La farsa amorosa* (1933).

[19] Letter of Wolf to Grohe, 1890. See Istel, "German Opera Since Wagner," MQ I (1915) 278–79.

of *Die Meistersinger,* and the music is full of leitmotifs—a style completely unsuited to Wolf's libretto. Moreover Wolf, like Schubert and Schumann, was not at home in the theatre: his invention seems to have been paralyzed by the requirements of the stage; the music goes from one song to the next like a Liederspiel; neither persons nor situations are adequately characterized. This composer, "who could be so dramatic in the lied, here in the drama remained above all a lyricist." [20] *Der Corregidor,* though not lacking in finely wrought details,[21] was a failure as an opera. Another Spanish subject, from Lope de Vega, was treated by Anton Urspruch in his comic opera *Das Unmöglichste von allem* ("The Most Impossible of All," 1897), with light parlando dialogue and intricate contrapuntal ensembles derived from the style of Mozart. A more spirited and dramatic composer in this field was von Reznicek,[22] whose *Donna Diana* (1894; another Spanish subject) gave promise of a future which was not realized in his next few operas; but with *Ritter Blaubart* ("Knight Bluebeard," 1920), "an eclectic score embodying elements of Italian cantilena style and the technique of French impressionism," [23] he renewed his reputation.

One of the best German comic operas of the later nineteenth century was D'Albert's *Abreise* ("The Departure," 1898), a fine example of swift-moving dialogue with a tuneful, spontaneous, and deftly orchestrated score, somewhat reminiscent of Cornelius. More in the *Meistersinger* idiom were Blech's comic operas *Das war ich* ("That was I," 1902) and the more ambitious *Versiegelt* ("Sealed," 1908); but these, like Wolf's *Corregidor,* suffered from the music being, as a rule, too heavy and polyphonic for the simple librettos. Two other similar comic operas of this period were Schillings' *Pfeifertag* ("The Parliament of Pipers," 1899), and R. Strauss's *Feuersnot* ("The Fire Famine," 1901), the latter an extraordinary combination of humor, eroticism, and autobiography, with music which shows the composer

20 Moser, *Geschichte der deutschen Musik* III, 397.

21 For instance: the duet "In solchen Abendfeierstunden," Act II; Frasquita's "In dem Schatten meiner Locken" (Act I), a charming song taken from Wolf's earlier *Spanisches Liederbuch;* Lukas's monologue (Act III, sc. 3), the most nearly dramatic music in the opera.

22 Urspruch (1850–1907) was a pupil of Raff and Liszt. The Austrian Emil Nikolaus Freiherr von Reznicek (1860–1945), an esteemed conductor, wrote eleven operas, nine major symphonic works, a violin concerto, and smaller pieces. See studies by Chop and Specht.

23 Slonimsky, *Music Since 1900,* p. 209.

in transition from his early Wagnerian style to that of *Salome* and *Elektra.*

Altogether, German comic opera in the late nineteenth- and early twentieth-century period, apart from folk opera, is disappointing. No unified authoritative tradition was evolved, and individual works of talent remained isolated experiments which their composers seemed unable to repeat. The only exceptions, other than Strauss's *Rosenkavalier,* were the comic operas of Wolf-Ferrari, but he was half Italian by birth and more than half Italian by temperament.

One of the most esteemed German opera composers of this period is Hans Pfitzner,[24] a confessed romantic and explicit antimodernist, in whom a musical language deriving fundamentally from Wagner is modified by a more diatonic melody, a certain asceticism of feeling, long dwellings on mystical, subjective moods, and frequently dissonant contrapuntal texture with long-breathed melodic lines (Example 117). Pfitzner's masterpiece, the "musical legend" *Palestrina* (1917), is a romanticized version of the well-known story of the composition of Palestrina's "Pope Marcellus" Mass,[25] motifs from which are incorporated in the score. It does not require any great penetration to perceive that Pfitzner (who in this one instance was his own librettist) has treated the legend with reference to his own position as defender of the ancient, good tradition of music against the modernists and Philistines. This implication, which is not unrelated to the dramatic idea of Wagner's *Meistersinger,* has doubtless been responsible in part for the success which *Palestrina* has had with a large public in Germany—a success which has found little or no echo elsewhere. A more advanced harmonic style and partial return to the form of separate numbers is seen in Pfitzner's most recent opera, *Das Herz* ("The Heart," 1931).

A composer of somewhat similar romantic tendencies, though on a more modest scale, was the Swiss Hans Huber (1852–1921), whose

[24] Pfitzner (b. 1869) has composed many songs and choral works as well as operas and has also written many essays on musical subjects (*Gesammelte Schriften,* 3 vols.). The most recent biographies and studies are by Abendroth, Valentin, and Müller-Blattau. See also Dent, "Hans Pfitzner," M&L IV (1923) 119–32; Riezler, *Hans Pfitzner und die deutsche Bühne;* Halusa, *Pfitzners musikdramatisches Schaffen;* studies of separate operas by R. Louis (*Die Rose vom Liebesgarten,* 1901), Hirtler, and Berrsche (*Der arme Heinrich*).
[25] This legend is due to Baini, a nineteenth-century historian. See summary of the historical evidence in *Grove's Dictionary,* art. "Palestrina," and cf. Jeppeson, "Marcellus-Probleme," *Acta Musicologica* XVI/XVII (1944/45) 11–38.

romantic operas had considerable popularity in his own country
(*Die schöne Bellinda,* 1916).

Although the principal musical influence on German opera composers in the early twentieth century was still that of Wagner, there

PALESTRINA, prelude

Ex.117.

Pfitzner

were some reflections of foreign trends. The methods of Italian
verismo and French naturalism are apparent in *Tiefland* ("The Low-
lands," 1903) by Eugen d'Albert,[26] a brutal, realistic drama with an

[26] D'Albert (1864–1932) was born at Glasgow, studied piano under Pauer and Liszt, and
as a virtuoso was famous for his Beethoven interpretations. In addition to twenty operas

extremely effective musical score in which Italian-style parlando recitative alternates with a Puccinian leitmotif technique and Wagnerian harmonies. This was D'Albert's most successful opera, though among his later works the extravagantly theatrical *Die toten Augen* ("The Dead Eyes," 1916), with its cleverly eclectic music, was widely performed. Another German veristic work was Max von Schillings' *Mona Lisa* (1915),[27] murder and melodrama against a Renaissance background, with a modern frame of prologue and epilogue, one of the most popular German operas of the present century. The music lies strongly under the influence of Puccini in melody and instrumentation, and apparently also of early Debussy in the harmony; the score shows a slight tendency toward closed numbers in place of the symphonic continuity of von Schillings' early Wagnerian operas, but the leitmotif still flourishes. Another opera of the German realist school was Waltershausen's *Oberst Chabert* ("Count Chabert," 1912),[28] written in a nonmelodic declamatory style with the dramatic situations underlined by rapidly fluctuating harmonies; the constant alternation of two triads at the interval of an augmented fourth has the effect of a leitmotif.

Impressionism made its mark in Germany with Franz Schreker,[29] whose first opera, *Der ferne Klang* ("The Distant Tone"), was composed 1903–1909, though not performed until 1912. The first notable feature of Schreker's music is the harmony, which basically is like that of Debussy (seventh and ninth chords as consonant units; free use, singly or in combination, of chromatic alteration, pedal points, and organum-like parallel progressions; treatment of sensuous effect as an end for itself). But it is the Debussy of *L'Après-midi,* the *Nocturnes,* and *La Mer* rather than of the subdued *Pelléas et Mélisande* who is Schreker's model. The texture is exceedingly full, often

---

he composed concertos, orchestral works, piano and chamber music, and songs. See study by Raupp; also Schmitz, "Eugen d'Albert als Opernkomponist," *Hochland* VI, No. 2 (1909) 464–71.

[27] Von Schillings (1868–1933) was assistant conductor at Bayreuth from 1892 and conducted at many other theatres. He composed four operas and a number of choral and orchestral works. See study by Raupp.

[28] Hermann Wolfgang von Waltershausen (b. 1882) composed five operas, but has been most influential in German musical life as a teacher and writer. Some of his writings are listed in the bibliography.

[29] Schreker (1878–1934) was also influential as a teacher (Křenek, Haba, and others). See studies by Bekker, Kapp, and R. S. Hoffmann, also numerous articles in *Anbruch* (especially Jahrg. II, VI, X).

with complicated decorative rhythmic motifs within the beat, or making use of several separated tone masses (as in the opening of Act II of *Der ferne Klang*). All this is, of course, supported by an orchestration of corresponding richness, in which harps, muted strings and horns, glissandi, tremolos, and similar effects are prominent. The feeling of tone impressions (*Klang*) in Schreker's operas is so strong as to lead naturally to a symbolism in which sounds become the embodiment of ideal, mystic forces. There are other signs of the late romantic period as well: occasional Straussian storm and stress in the harmony, reminiscences of Verdi in a melodic line, and traces of Puccini's declamation and orchestral treatment.

The whole, nevertheless, is not mere patchwork but an original and very effective theatrical style which made Schreker, during the war and postwar years, one of the most highly regarded opera composers in Germany. His librettos (written by himself) have been criticized for awkwardness of language and for their preoccupation with sex in exaggerated, pathological forms. *Die Gezeichneten* ("The Stigmatized Ones," 1918), a Renaissance subject, has this feature to an extreme degree. His chief work, *Der Schatzgräber* ("The Treasure Digger," 1920), shows a tendency toward more triadic harmony (with much parallelism) and a somewhat less complicated texture. The leitmotif system is much less prominent here, and in *Irrelohe* (1924) it was abandoned altogether. Meanwhile *Das Spielwerk und die Prinzessin* ("The Playthings and the Princess"), considerably revised in 1920 from its original 1913 form, experimented with pandiatonism and other modern harmonic devices. An even more advanced harmonic idiom is found in the postwar operas of Zemlinsky,[30] though his most important influence has been indirect, through his pupils Arnold Schönberg and E. W. Korngold.

A unique figure in music of the early twentieth century was Ferruccio Busoni,[31] of mixed German and Italian ancestry, one of the

---

[30] Alexander von Zemlinsky (1872–1942) had a distinguished career as conductor and teacher. See special number of *Der Auftakt* (Prague, 1921).

[31] The main biography of Busoni (1866–1924) is by Edward Dent. See also Bekker, *Klang und Eros;* Gatti, "The Stage Works of Ferruccio Busoni," MQ XX (1934) 267–77; "Nota bio-bibliografica su Ferruccio Busoni," RassM XIII (1940) 82–88; and Busoni's *Entwurf einer neuen Aesthetik der Tonkunst, Von der Einheit der Musik* (collected essays), and *Über die Möglichkeiten der Oper.* Busoni wrote all his own librettos. *Turandot* (1917), his only opera not mentioned in the text, was arranged from his earlier incidental music to Gozzi's play.

greatest pianists of his day, a scholar, philosopher, and international figure, reminding one of an artist of the Renaissance in his breadth and clarity of outlook. In his thoroughgoing rejection of Wagner and adherence to the operatic ideals of Mozart, Busoni was an important influence in the neoclassic movement. His first opera, *Die Brautwahl* ("The Bridal Choice," 1912), revives the old principle of set numbers, though the libretto and music still retain many romantic traits. The one-act *Arlecchino* (1917) is an ironical comedy making use of the old commedia dell' arte masks and including some spoken dialogue. Busoni's masterpiece, *Doktor Faust* (completed by Jarnach and posthumously produced in 1925), is, from both the literary and the musical viewpoint, the most significant treatment of this subject in the twentieth century. The highly mystical and symbolical libretto is joined to a score conceived in the same spirit, realized in large forms, worked out with uncompromising musical idealism and logic, but—by reason of these very qualities—lacking the emotional dramatic force which is necessary for wide popular appeal in opera. Professor Dent has said that "one cannot apply to *Doctor Faust* the ordinary standards of operatic criticism. It moves on a plane of spiritual experience far beyond that of even the greatest of musical works for the stage." [32] This may be true; indeed, the more carefully one studies the score the greater his respect for the composer. But, like many another high plane of "spiritual experience," it is sometimes dull for outsiders. The fact remains that the music is so condensed, so completely objective, unromantic, and contrapuntal, so complex and varied in its harmonic tendencies,[33] so remote from the familiar notions of tonality, in short, so remote from all common musical experience, as to prove a stumbling block for any listener who has not prepared himself by a long education in Busoni's peculiar style and aesthetic. Unless this idiom, or one similar to it, becomes an important part of our general musical background, *Doktor Faust* is all too likely to remain a book of wisdom written in a language few can understand and none translate.

[32] *Ferruccio Busoni*, p. 304.
[33] The music is not atonal, but tonality is nearly always blurred by one or more of the following devices: pandiatonic chords, parallelism, dissonances against pedal points or ostinato motives, linear dissonant counterpoint, modality and organum-like chords, cross relations, atonal melodies (often including octave transposition of single notes in the line), and polytonal chord combinations.

If we now summarize the course of German opera from the death of Wagner to the end of the First World War, we find that the period begins with imitations of the master in almost every detail; but soon there appear various branches, in which the basic Wagnerian musical idiom, the leitmotif technique, and the Gesamtkunstwerk aesthetic are still for the most part retained but applied to different subject matters: the fairy-tale (Humperdinck), realistic drama (D'Albert, von Schillings), or comedy (Wolf, Blech). A modification of the harmonic idiom comes with Schreker's impressionism, while Pfitzner continues in the romantic path. There is a more or less unconscious revolt against Wagner in the Volksoper and operetta, a revolt manifest in both subjects and musical style. As we approach the 1920's, we note that the gradual emancipation from Wagner is marked by one or more of the following signs: (1) thoroughgoing adoption of a neoclassical or other antiromantic idiom, (2) abandonment of the leitmotif system, and (3) return to the old principle of the number opera with set musical forms (Busoni, and the later works of von Schillings, Pfitzner, and Schreker). We now turn our attention to the composer in whose works this entire evolution is embodied, the most important representative of German opera in the early twentieth-century period, Richard Strauss.[34]

Strauss was already famous for his symphonic poems before he attracted world-wide notice with his third opera, *Salome* (1905), the libretto of which is a German translation of Oscar Wilde's drama (written originally in French). The peculiar blend of oriental sensuousness and decadent luxuriance of horror offered by this text has been perfectly caught in Strauss's music. The power of emotional expressiveness shown by Wagner in depicting the agonies of Amfortas is displayed to an equal degree by Strauss in the final scene of *Salome* in the musical treatment of a form of sexual perversion (necrophilism) not commonly found in opera. There is no need either to apologize for or to condemn the subject; in a work of art, morality is a matter of taste. The only relevant point is that Strauss deals with the scene successfully. It is but one instance of his amazing skill in musical characterization. Formally, *Salome* is in the Wag-

[34] The principal biography of Richard Strauss (b. 1864) is by R. Specht. There are biographies in English by Newman (1908) and Finck (1917). On the operas more particularly see E. Schmitz, *Richard Strauss als Musikdramatiker;* Hübner, *Richard Strauss und das Musikdrama;* and Gregor, *Richard Strauss.*

nerian style: the orchestra is dominant, the music is continuous (in one act), there is a system of leitmotifs, the texture is uniformly thick and polyphonic, the rhythms are nonperiodic, and the voice parts are mostly of an arioso character. Strauss's mastery of orchestral effect, the individuality and variety of his instrumental coloring, are as evident in the operas as in the symphonic poems. His harmony, which sounded so daring and dissonant at the turn of the century, is no longer novel, but just for this reason we can now better appreciate how appropriate it is for the dramatic purposes. Technically it may be regarded as a continuation of Wagner, with progressions generally conditioned by chromatic voice leading but less bound up with romantic expressiveness, more remote and sudden in its modulations, and much more dissonant. It is a type of harmony which assumes a familiarity with Wagner on the listener's part, and which as it were telescopes the characteristic Wagner progressions in a manner analogous to the treatment of a fugue subject in stretto. (We have already noticed a similar evolution from the Verdi melodic style in Puccini's operas.) The melodies in *Salome* are of two sorts: either declamatory, with many unusual intervals rising out of the harmonic progressions, or else long-sustained, impassioned outpourings, marked by a very wide range and wide leaps. Strauss has managed to combine the characteristics of the music drama with the striking dramatic quality of the Italian verismo and to introduce also some features of grand opera (for example, the Dance of the Seven Veils).

All the characteristics of *Salome* are pushed to an extreme in *Elektra* (1909, with libretto by von Hofmannsthal [35]). Here the central passion is Elektra's insane thirst for vengeance on the murderers of her father, and here again Strauss has matched the somber horrors of the libretto with music of fearful dissonance, lurid melodramatic power, and a harmonic idiom in which for long stretches polytonality is the normal state, becoming at times in effect completely atonal. Perhaps the most noticeable feature of the score is the contrast between this dissonant idiom and the occasional stretches of lush, late-romantic sentimentality, with cloying sevenths, ninths, chromatic alterations,

[35] Hugo von Hofmannsthal (1874–1929) also wrote for Strauss the librettos of *Der Rosenkavalier, Ariadne auf Naxos, Die Frau ohne Schatten* (1921) and *Die aegyptische Helena* (1928). See F. Strauss, *Richard Strauss Briefwechsel mit Hugo von Hofmannsthal;* Holländer, "Hugo von Hofmannsthal als Opernlibrettist," *Zeitschrift für Musik* XCVI (1929) 551–54; Krüger, *Hugo von Hofmannsthal und Richard Strauss.*

and suspensions. Whatever the composer's intentions may have been, these portions give the final dreadful touch of spiritual abnormality to the whole action; they are like something familiar suddenly seen in a ghastly, strange light.

Der Rosenkavalier ("The Cavalier of the Rose," 1911), Strauss's best and most successful opera, is a pleasant comedy of Viennese life in the time of Maria Theresa (*ca.* 1750). It is an ideal libretto, with humor, farce, sentiment, swiftly moving action, variety of scenes, and superb characterizations. The music is as varied as the drama. In some portions it is no less complex (though considerably less dissonant) than that of *Salome* and *Elektra*. The erotic quality of the love music in the first part of Act I is equal to Strauss's best in this familiar vein. For the most part, however, the style of *Der Rosenkavalier* is relatively simple and tuneful. The famous waltzes are anachronistic; the waltzes of Schubert, Lanner, and J. Strauss, which these imitate, were not, of course, a feature of eighteenth-century Vienna. But this is of little importance, and it is still less important that Strauss has seen fit to decorate the waltz themes with some of his own characteristic harmonic twists. The best musical characterizations are those of the Princess, a near-tragic figure, and Baron Ochs, the perfect type of comic boor. The music of Octavian and Sophie is music of situations and general sentiment rather than of personalities, but it is none the less fine on that account. The scene of the presentation of the silver rose and the following short duet (near the beginning of Act II) is one of the most beautiful passages in all opera. It is remarkable that here Strauss writes in an almost purely diatonic idiom, even emphasizing the triads by outlining them in the melodies; one of the composer's happiest inspirations, the theme of the silver rose (high, dissonant appoggiatura triads with celesta, flutes, harps, and three solo violins), tinkles against this background. The ensembles are virtuoso creations, particularly the scene of the levee in Act I: a dissolution and at the same time an apotheosis of the eighteenth-century opera buffa ensemble, bringing together all the elements of this form in seeming confusion and with complete realism. The introduction of a stylized Italian aria (compare the old interpolated number in opera) is accomplished in the spirit of sporting with the formal technique. The ensemble of Act II is less elaborate, but the first two-thirds of Act III is really one long ensemble of broad farcical nature, laid on musically with a rather heavy hand perhaps, but of an irresistible comic dash which can only be compared to the similar scenes in *Die Meistersinger* (end of Act II) and *Falstaff* (end of Act III). After all this hurly-burly follows one of those transformations of mood which are so characteristic of *Der Rosenkavalier*. The trio for three soprano voices (Sophie, Princess, Octavian) [36] is another superlative number, a luxurious and melting texture of long-spun, expressive, interweaving lines above a comparatively simple harmonic basis. The long decrescendo continues: the last song is a duet in G major, two strophes of a simple lyric melody in thirds and sixths, in the style of the old German Singspiel. The themes of the silver rose and the lovers' first meeting sound once more. The opera closes with a pantomime of the Princess's little negro pageboy, to the same music which was heard at his first appearance near the beginning of Act I.[37]

Der Rosenkavalier was hardly finished before Strauss and von Hofmannsthal were at work on their next collaborative effort, *Ariadne auf Naxos* (1912), designed as a pendant to a German version of Molière's *Bourgeois Gentilhomme*. This one-act piece, which von Hofmannsthal considered one of his "most characteristic productions," [38] is a profoundly poetic and sensitive treatment of the myth of Ariadne and Bacchus, in form and spirit suggesting the pastorales and ballets of Lully and Molière, which were likewise usually enclosed within a comedy; [39] like these models, it introduces comic-satirical elements through personages borrowed from the Italian commedia dell' arte. Strauss's music continues the trend toward diatonism and simplicity already evident in *Der Rosenkavalier;* harmonically, it starts from the point which the composer had reached in the silver-rose scene of the earlier opera and becomes progressively less and less chromatic. There is a trio in scene 3 for three sopranos,

[36] Octavian's part is a "trouser role"—a man's part sung by a woman; this practice, fairly frequent in nineteenth-century opera, is an interesting historical survival of the castrato hero roles of earlier days.

[37] The whole masterly finale of Act III was largely shaped by Strauss's suggestions. Von Hofmannsthal at one time feared it would be feeble in effect, but Strauss wrote "It is precisely at the end that the composer, when he has found the right idea, can get his best and loftiest effects—on a matter of this kind you may safely leave it to me to judge. . . . I will guarantee the end of the act . . . if you will be answerable for the other portions." (Letter, Sept. 7, 1910; in *Correspondence*, pp. 86–87.)

[38] Letter of Dec. 18, 1911 (*Correspondence*, p. 144).

[39] The analogy will be seen most clearly by comparison with the following works of Molière: *La Princesse d'Elide* (1664), *Psyché* (a *tragédie-ballet*, 1671), the pastorale in *La Comtesse d'Escarbagnas* (1671) and the pastoral *intermèdes* in *Georges Dandin* (1668) and *Le Malade imaginaire* (1673), music by M.-A. Charpentier.

similar to the trio in the last act of *Der Rosenkavalier* and likewise followed by a simple folklike song. A new element is the light, swift, parlando style of the comic scenes and of the prologue which was added in 1916 when *Ariadne* was taken out of its original setting in the Molière play. One role (Zerbinetta) is especially written for a high coloratura soprano. The leitmotif technique is used to a slight extent, but the orchestra (only thirty-six players) is subordinated to the voices, and there is a distinct tendency toward division into separate numbers.

Ariadne auf Naxos is the definitive stage of Strauss's conversion to a Mozartean style, an intimate opera in which the musical idiom is refined to classic purity in comparison with the earlier works. From this point on, Strauss became musically conservative. He had summed up in his own creative career the transition from Wagnerian music drama to the postwar, anti-Wagnerian opera. "I give you my word I have now definitely cast off the whole armour of Wagner forever more." [40] But the flame of inspiration no longer burned so brightly; most of his later operas had little more than a *succès d'estime,* even in Germany. Perhaps the best of them are the comedies *Intermezzo* (1924, text by the composer) and *Arabella* (1933). The former is notable for Strauss's conscious attempt to lighten the orchestral texture and make a precise distinction between recitative and cantilena styles in the singing in order to make the words clearer; perhaps by way of compensation, there are important symphonic interludes. *Arabella* combines an operetta-like libretto with attractive and melodious music which is more than once reminiscent of *Der Rosenkavalier.* *Die Frau ohne Schatten* ("The Woman without a Shadow," 1919) and *Die aegyptische Helena* ("The Egyptian Helen," 1928) are serious works, though less complex musically than *Salome* or *Elektra.* *Die schweigsame Frau* ("The Silent Woman," 1935, libretto by Stefan Zweig) [41] is in the manner of Italian opera buffa. There is not one of these works but has its moments of genius; any of them might have been hailed with applause in the composer's earlier days, but they had nothing new to say to the postwar generation. The same holds even more strongly for *Friedenstag, Daphne* (both 1938), and *Das Liebe der Danae* (1945).

[40] Letter to von Hofmannsthal, August, 1916; *Correspondence,* p. 291.
[41] See Mathis, "Stefan Zweig as Librettist," M&L XXV (1944) 163–76, 226–45.

27

National Opera in Russia
and Other Countries

THE SECOND HALF OF THE NINETEENTH century saw the rise of independent schools of composition in many countries which had previously been only tributary to the chief musical nations of Europe, or which, like Spain and England, had been for a long time in an inferior position. In the growth of musical nationalism opera played an important part. The use of characteristic national subjects, often from patriotic motives, stimulated composers to seek an equally characteristic national expression in their music. National operas, as a rule, were not exportable; only exceptionally (as in the case of some Russian operas) did these works make their way into foreign countries. Nevertheless, they are an important feature of the history of opera in the late nineteenth- and early twentieth-century period. It is the purpose of the present chapter to survey the development of these national schools.

RUSSIA.[1]—There was no native opera in Russia before the end of the eighteenth century. In the late medieval period there were religious mystery plays, and in the seventeenth-century biblical school dramas with incidental music. The first public theatre was opened at St. Petersburg in 1703, giving for the most part foreign plays brought in by way of Germany, with some use of incidental music. There are records of Italian opera at the court from 1735, but the

---

[1] Bibliography (chief works in English): Newmarch, *The Russian Opera;* Montagu-Nathan, *History of Russian Music;* Sabaneiv's *History of Russian Music* is available in German; his *Modern Russian Composers* (tr. Joffe) contains little that bears directly on opera but is nevertheless valuable. See also Mooser, *L'Opéra-comique français en Russie au XVIIIᵉ siècle.* Most important are the following recent books: Calvocoressi and Abraham, *Masters of Russian Music* (1936; contains bibliography of Russian periodicals and books); Abraham, *Studies in Russian Music* and *On Russian Music.*

Titles in this section are given only in English translation. Transliteration of names and titles usually follows that of Baker's *Biographical Dictionary of Musicians,* 4th ed. (1940). Works in Russian are not included in the bibliographies unless translations in English, French, German, or Italian exist.

heyday of Italian opera in Russia came under Catherine II ("The Great," reigned 1762–1796) when Galuppi, Paisiello, Cimarosa, Salieri, and others sojourned at St. Petersburg for varying lengths of time. Already in the eighteenth century a few native composers had begun to write operas on national subjects and occasionally introduced national melodies, but these were amateur affairs of no importance. The upsurge of national spirit under Alexander I (reigned 1801–1825), imbued in Russia as elsewhere with the spirit of Byron's romanticism, encouraged such productions. Curiously, one of the earliest composers of national Russian opera was a versatile Neapolitan, Catterino Cavos (1776–1840), who same to St. Petersburg near the end of the eighteenth century and remained for the rest of his life. He composed, to Russian, French, or Italian texts, over forty operas, including *Ivan Susanin* (1815; same subject as Glinka's *Life for the Czar*) and *The Firebird* (1822). Among the Russian composers of this period was A. N. Verstovsky,[2] some of whose operas (*Askold's Grave*, 1835; *Thunder*, 1857) held the stage in Russia almost to the end of the century.

Essentially in the same native dilettante tradition was Glinka's *Life for the Czar* (1836),[3] from which the Russian national school of opera is usually dated. It is on account of its story, which became a focal point for patriotic feeling, and on account of its immense popularity that *A Life for the Czar* holds this position. Its music is unexpectedly lacking in strongly national qualities; the material for the most part is as much French or Italian as Russian. The melody of the Bridal Chorus in Act III (Example 118) is as close as Glinka

A LIFE FOR THE CZAR, Act III

Ex.118.   Glinka

2 Alexiey Nikolaievitch Verstovsky (1799–1862) was inspector and later manager of the imperial theatres in Moscow, where all of his eight operas were first produced. See Findeisen, "Die Entwickelung der Tonkunst in Russland," SIMG II (1900–1901) 279–302.
3 On Michail Ivanovich Glinka (1804–1857) see biographies by Calvocoressi and Montagu-Nathan, also von Riesemann's *Monographien zur russischen Musik;* bibliography by Inch.

comes to the folk-song idiom in this opera,[4] though the choral theme of the epilogue so took hold of popular fancy as to become almost a second national anthem. There is compensation for the undistinguished quality of much of the music in the clear and varied orchestration, which was a model for all the later Russian nationalists, including Rimsky-Korsakov. Moreover, in the extensive use of leitmotifs Glinka was far in advance of any opera composer before Wagner. The Polish soldiers, for example, are characterized by themes in the national dance rhythms of polonaise and mazurka, which, first heard in the ball scene of Act II, recur in Act III at the entrance of the Poles, and the mazurka rhythm again at their appearance in Act IV. The quasi-folk-song theme of the opening chorus is used as a leitmotif of Russian heroism, sung by the hero Susanin in Act III as he defies the Polish conspirators; the opposing national motifs are again contrasted in the orchestral introduction to the epilogue. Susanin's last aria (Act IV) is to a large extent made up of previously heard themes, the recurrences here producing a purposeful dramatic effect. The theme of the final chorus, repeated again and again with cumulative power, has been subtly prepared by two or three statements earlier in the opera. This brilliant epilogue is not only the climax of patriotic emotion but also of the highly colored mass effect of sound and spectacle so beloved in Russian opera.

Although *A Life for the Czar* was more popular, the real musical foundations for the future were laid in Glinka's second and last opera, *Russlan and Ludmilla* (1842). The libretto, a fantastic and incoherent fairy tale, is adapted from a poem of Pushkin. In spite of some traces of Weber, the music is much more original than in Glinka's earlier opera, and the musical characterizations are more definite. The leitmotif system is abandoned; almost the only recurring motif is the descending whole-tone scale associated with the wicked magician Chernomor.[5] There are at least five distinct styles or procedures characteristic of all later Russian music which appear in *Russlan and Ludmilla:* (1) the heroic, broad, solemn, declamatory style, with modal suggestions and archaic effect (introduction and song of the Bard, Act I); (2) the Russian lyrical style, with expressive melodic lines of a folkish cast, delicately colored harmony featuring

---

[4] There are folk-song quotations in the opening of Susanin's aria, No. 3, and in the accompaniment to Susanin's last two solo passages at the end of Act IV.
[5] This is said to be the earliest in European music of the whole-tone scale.

the lowered sixth or raised fifth, and chromatically moving inner
voices (Fina's ballad and Russlan's first aria in Act II); (3) expression
of fantastic occurrences by means of unusual harmonies, such as
whole-tone passages or chord progressions pivoting about one note
(scene of Ludmilla's abduction, toward the end of Act I); (4) oriental
atmosphere, sometimes using genuine oriental themes (Persian
chorus at opening of Act III), sometimes manufactured melodies
(Ratmir's romance, Act V), but always characterized by fanciful ara-
besque figures in the accompaniment and a languorous harmony
and orchestration; (5) the vividly colored choruses and dances, with
glittering instrumentation and often daring harmonies (chorus in
honor of Lel, finale of Act I; Chernomor's march and following
dances, especially the *lezginka*, finale of Act IV)—models for such
scenes in Borodin's *Prince Igor*, Rimsky-Korsakov's *Sadko*, and even
Stravinsky's *Sacre du Printemps*.

Almost the only Russian opera of any importance for twenty years
after *Russlan and Ludmilla* was Dargomyzhsky's *Russalka* (1856),[6]
likewise on a text from Pushkin and somewhat similar in subject to
Glinka's work. Musically, however, it was inferior to *Russlan;* its
best feature was the realistic declamation of the recitative, which
Dargomyzhsky proceeded to develop to the highest degree in his
last opera, *The Stone Guest*. This work (a setting of Pushkin's Don
Juan drama) was completed after Dargomyzhsky's death by Cui,
orchestrated by Rimsky-Korsakov, and first performed in 1872. It
is no masterpiece and never had a popular success, but it was influential on later Russian opera because of the composer's attempt
to write the entire work (except for some songs near the beginning
of Act II) in a melodic recitative, a vocal line which should be in
every detail the equivalent of the words. The result, though accurate
in declamation and dramatic in some places, lacks sharp characterization or melodic interest, and there is no compensation for the
melodic poverty in the orchestral part, which is conceived as accompaniment rather than a continuous symphonic tissue. In his re-
pudiation of set musical forms and high respect for the words,
Dargomyzhsky may have been influenced to a slight degree by Wag-

[6] Alexander Sergievitch Dargomyzhsky (1813–1869) wrote four operas (one uncompleted) and numerous minor works, as well as several orchestral pieces which were very
popular in Russia. See works mentioned in general bibliography above; there are no
separate studies in English.

ner's theories, though there is no trace of Wagner in the musical substance itself. Harmonically there is some interest in Dargomyzhsky's use of whole-tone scale fragments as leitmotifs for the Statue (Example 119), and some passages constructed entirely on this scale.

Dargomyzhsky had arrived in his own way at certain features of the

THE STONE GUEST, Act II

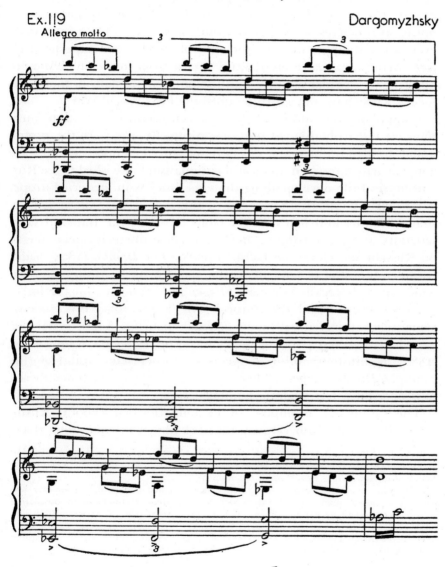

Ex.119   Dargomyzhsky

Wagnerian music drama. The most explicit and self-conscious disciple of Wagner in Russia was Serov,[7] whose first opera, *Judith* (1863),
shows the composer's admiration for all the methods of grand opera
of the Meyerbeer and early Wagner type. In his third and last opera,
The Power of Evil (completed by N. T. Soloviev and first produced
in 1871), Serov aimed "to embody the Wagnerian theories in a music
drama written in Russian, on a Russian subject," and to keep "more
closely than has yet been done [*sic*] to the forms of Russian popular
music, as preserved unchanged in our folksongs." [8] The result, however, was a disappointing hybrid, full of striking but superficial effects. Serov's operas received little regard from musicians but were
nevertheless popular enough with the public to remain in the repertory of Russian opera companies until the First World War.

From about the middle of the nineteenth century, Russian musicians were sharply divided into two groups. In one were the profes-
sional, foreign-trained, and officially supported composers who were
not primarily interested in musical nationalism but wished to see Russian musical life develop along the same lines as in western Europe,
particularly Germany. The head of this school was Anton Rubinstein,[9] founder and first director (1862–1867) of the Imperial Conservatory at St. Petersburg. Of Rubinstein's nineteen operas (eight
on Russian and eleven on German texts), *The Demon* (1875) had a
considerable success, both in Russia and abroad. It is on a libretto
which strongly recalls Wagner's *Fliegende Holländer,* but the forms
are conventional and the musical style is that of pre-Wagnerian
romanticism mingled with some oriental elements. A more vital and
varied, though less popular, opera was *The Merchant Kalashnikov*
(1880). Rubinstein's biblical operas, or rather stage oratorios (for
example, *Die Makkabäer,* "The Maccabees," 1875), are remembered
now only for a few separate numbers.

The leading opera composer of the nonnationalist school in Russia
in the late nineteenth century was Tchaikovsky,[10] in whom Slavic

[7] Alexander Nikolaievitch Serov (1820–1871) was a lecturer, teacher, and essayist as well
as a composer. See von Riesemann, *Monographien* I.

[8] Quoted in Newmarch, *The Russian Opera,* p. 157.

[9] Rubinstein (1829–1894) was a celebrated concert pianist and prolific composer (orchestral, chamber, piano, and vocal music). See his Memoirs (in German translation
by E. Kretschmann as *Erinnerungen*); Bowen, *Free Artist* (life of A. Rubinstein and
his brother Nikolai).

[10] On Peter Ilyitch Tchaikovsky (1840–1893) see his *Diaries* (English tr., 1945), biographies
by Newmarch and Evans, also Bowen and von Meck, *"Beloved Friend."*

temperament and German training were leavened by a distinct lyrical gift and a lively appreciation of Italian opera and French ballet. Reckoned by bulk, if not also by musical excellence, Tchaikovsky's achievement is as important in the field of opera as in that of the symphony. After two early works [11] in which he experimented with the then fashionable nationalism, he produced his masterpiece, *Eugen Onegin,* at Moscow in 1879. In both the libretto (after Pushkin) and the musical style this is an old-fashioned romantic opera, but the music is in Tchaikovsky's happiest vein, with lyrical, graceful melodies, expressive harmonies, transparent and imaginative orchestration—true and living in expression without any of the hysterical emotionalism of some of the later works (such as the Fifth and Sixth symphonies). The character of the heroine, Tatiana, is delineated with especial sympathy, and that of Onegin himself is scarcely less vivid. The ballet music (particularly the waltz in Act II) is tuneful and charming, as are also the choruses in Act I. Tchaikovsky's next three operas were in a more heavily dramatic style. *The Maid of Orleans* (1881, libretto after Schiller) was less successful than *Mazeppa* (1884, from a poem of Pushkin), which contains two of the composer's finest dramatic moments: the monologue of Kochubey and the extremely pathetic final scene. *The Enchantress* (1887) had such a disappointing reception that Tchaikovsky returned to his more characteristic lyrical medium for his last two operatic works: *The Queen of Spades* (1890), his most popular opera next to *Onegin,* and *Iolanthe* (1892). In *The Queen of Spades,* based on a melodramatic tale of Pushkin, Tchaikovsky attained a more nearly perfect balance than in any of his other operas between dramatic declamation, lyrical expressiveness, and divertissement music (see especially the ballets in Act II).

The struggle for Russian national music, begun by Glinka and Dargomyzhsky, was carried on after 1860 by a group of five composers: Balakirev, Cui, Mussorgsky, Borodin, and Rimsky-Korsakov. All were amateurs; only Rimsky-Korsakov—and he only at a comparatively late stage of his career—ever had a thorough conventional technical training in composition. Balakirev wrote no operas. Cui [12]

11 *The Guardsman* (1874) and *Vakula the Smith* (1876); the latter is known in a later version as *The Little Slippers* and also as *Oxana's Caprice*. There were two still earlier operas which Tchaikovsky destroyed.
12 Cesar Antonovitch Cui (1835–1918) was a military engineer by profession. He studied

wrote ten, but most of them are not Russian in subject, none are Russian in musical style, and, with the possible exception of *William Ratcliffe* (1869) they are unimportant from any point of view. The Russian national opera in its highest development, therefore, is the work of the remaining three composers of the "mighty five."

The lack of the usual technical musical education (which meant, at this time, a German conservatory training) had the advantage of turning the nationalist composers to the resources of their own country for dramatic and musical material, and to their own instincts and national traditions for the means of shaping this material into operatic form. These conditions were especially important for Mussorgsky,[13] the most individual genius of the group. In *Boris Godunov* (1874) Mussorgsky created one of the great masterpieces of nineteenth-century opera, a monument of much that is most typical in Russian musical drama and at the same time an absolutely personal, inimitable work. *Boris Godunov* was first composed in 1868–1869 and rewritten in 1871–1872. In 1896 Rimsky-Korsakov prepared a thoroughly revised version, with "corrections" of the harmony, improvements in the orchestration, a different order of scenes, and many cuts; the deleted portions were restored in a second revision (1908), and in this form the opera made its way into the repertory of all foreign opera houses. After the revolution of 1918 the composer's own score was revived for performances in Russia, and both his original and recast versions were published in 1928. In 1941 another revision, with new orchestration, was made by Shostakovitch.

The libretto of *Boris Godunov* was prepared by Mussorgsky himself; its sources were Pushkin's drama of the same title and N. M. Karamzin's *History of the Russian Empire*. The character of the half-mad emperor Boris (reigned 1598–1605), especially as sung and acted by the late Feodor Chaliapin, is one of the most vivid and moving in all opera. Yet an equally potent force in the action is the cruel, anonymous mass of the Russian people—a force visibly present in

---

music with the Polish composer Moniuszko and with Balakirev. In addition to operas he wrote many orchestral suites, chamber works, and short pianoforte pieces. He completed Mussorgsky's opera *The Fair at Sorochinsk* in 1917. His *Musique en Russie* (publ. 1880) is the source of many errors concerning the Russian national school.

[13] On Mussorgsky (1839–1881) see biographies by Calvocoressi, Montagu-Nathan, and von Riesemann; also Godet, *En Marge de Boris Godounof;* Abraham, "Moussorgsky's *Boris* and Pushkin's," M&L XXVI (1945) 31–38.

the mighty crowd scenes but also invisibly working like the relentless pressure of Fate at every step toward the catastrophe of the drama. With grim poetic vision Mussorgsky set this primeval force in the closing scene of the opera [14] over against the figure of the Idiot Boy, who, left alone at the last on a darkened stage, keens his lament: "Weep, ye people; soon the foe shall come, soon the gloom shall fall; woe to our land; weep, Russian folk, weep, hungry folk!" One senses in such scenes the influence of the democratic ideals prevalent in Russia during the sixties and seventies in the period after the liberation of the serfs under Alexander II, ideals so eloquently expounded in the writings of Tolstoy. In comparison to the elemental power of most of Mussorgsky's opera, the love episode (Act III) seems both dramatically and musically a pale diversion (as does most of the love interest in Russian opera generally). In form, *Boris Godunov* is a series of detached scenes rather than a coherently developed plot; it thus illustrates the Russian habit, in both musical and literary creation (compare Tolstoy's *War and Peace*), of complete absorption in the present moment, leaving the total impression to be achieved by the cumulative impact of many separate effects.

The most striking feature of Mussorgsky's music is the way in which, in the declamation, the melodic line always manages to convey the emotion of the text in the most direct, compressed, and forcible manner imaginable. Perhaps the best examples of this are the two most familiar scenes of the opera, the last part of Act II (including the "clock scene") and the farewell and death of Boris in Act IV.[15] Here Mussorgsky realized the supreme ideal of dramatic, semi-melodic recitative, which Glinka had foreshadowed in *Russlan and Ludmilla* and which Dargomyzhsky had sought in *The Stone Guest*. Much of the same gloomy power, though with less violence, is displayed in the monastery scene at the beginning of Act I. A more song-ful idiom, equally characteristic of the composer, is heard in the first part of the Inn scene (Act I, scene 2). Still more characteristic are the children's songs in the first part of Act II—examples of a psychological insight and musical style in which Mussorgsky is almost unique, and which he had demonstrated in his song cycle *The*

14 References are to Mussorgsky's 1874 version, piano-vocal score published by J. & W. Chester, Ltd., London, cop. 1926.
15 The music of the latter scene, like several other numbers in *Boris*, was adapted from an early opera of Mussorgsky's, *Salammbô* (composed 1863–1865).

Nursery (composed 1870–1872). It is to be noted that in all these songs—declamatory or lyrical—the melodic line is the guiding factor. It is a style of melody which, with its peculiar intervals (especially the falling fourth at cadences), monotonous reiteration of patterns, irregularity of phrase structure, and archaic, modal basis, has grown most intimately out of Russian folk-song. To this melodic line the harmony is generally a mere added support, but it is likewise of a strongly personal type,[16] blended of modal feeling, impressionistic (often childlike) fondness for the mere sound of certain combinations, an unconventional harmonic training, and (at least, so one suspects) the happy outcome of improvisation at the piano. While it remains relatively consonant, and far from any suspicion of atonality, nevertheless any effort to analyze a really typical passage of Mussorgsky according to the principles of textbook harmony will show how completely foreign his methods were to the conventional practice of the nineteenth century. Not unrelated to the naïveté of his harmonic effects is Mussorgsky's reveling in brilliant, crude, and massive effects of color. This trait is seen most clearly in the great crowd scene of the coronation, the orchestral introduction of which is also an example of the frequent Russian mannerism of alternating chords pivoting on one common tone (in this case A-flat^7 and D^7 on the common tone G-flat = F-sharp). The chorus itself in this scene is built on the same folk tune which Beethoven used in his second "Razumovsky" Quartet.

Of Mussorgsky's other operas the principal one is *Khovantchina* (1896, libretto by Strassov). This work is, if possible, even more intensely national in subject and musical style than *Boris Godunov* but less concentrated dramatically and less unified in total musical effect. Its finest numbers are the orchestral prelude, the aria of Shaklovity in Act III, and some of the choruses of the Old Believers, in which Mussorgsky has distilled the whole spirit of the ancient Russian church style (Example 120).

The cardinal aesthetic principle of Mussorgsky was the search for realistic expression at any cost: "truth before beauty." To this end, he avoided conventional formulae, evolving a style which is as restrained, economical, and as incapable of successful imitation as that of Debussy. By temperament, he was led to depict predominantly

16 Cf. Calvocoressi, "Moussorgsky's Musical Style," MQ XVIII (1932) 530–46.

that side of the Russian character which gives itself over to gloom and mysticism, to the emotions of violence, brutality, and madness which dominate *Boris Godunov.* A totally different, though no less normal,

KHOVANTCHINA, Act V

Ex.120   Mussorgsky

aspect of the national personality comes to life in Borodin's *Prince Igor* (1890).[17] The libretto is by the composer, after a plan by Stassov;

[17] Alexander Porfirievitch Borodin (1833–1887) was a professor of chemistry; his principal teacher in music was Balakirev. He wrote two operas, three symphonies, chamber music, and songs. See Habets, *Borodin and Liszt;* Abraham, *Borodin.*

the score, unfinished at Borodin's death, was completed by Glazounov and Rimsky-Korsakov and orchestrated by the latter. The story is taken from a medieval Russian epic (apparently genuine, though long suspected to be an eighteenth-century forgery), but the central plot is of little importance except to give occasion for the many episodic scenes which make up most of the opera. Some of these scenes are comic in style, others are love scenes, but an exceptionally large place is reserved for spectacle, dances, and choruses (for example, the well-known Polovtsian ballets in Act II). The musical ancestor of *Prince Igor* is Glinka's *Russlan and Ludmilla,* and its principal descendant is Rimsky-Korsakov's *Sadko.* The style of *Prince Igor* is predominantly lyric, with many of the arias in conventional Italian forms; there is some arioso writing, but little dramatic recitative in the manner of Dargomyzhsky. Indeed, the music is not dramatic at all in the sense in which *Boris Godunov* is dramatic; it does not so much embody a drama as present a series of musical tableaux to accompany and complete the stage pictures.[18] In technical details also it is less unconventional than Mussorgsky; the most original portions are the oriental scenes, for which Borodin evolved an idiom partly based on Central Asiatic themes but fundamentally an out-growth of his eighteen-year-long absorption in the subject and study of all available musical and historical material. His ancestry (he was the illegitimate son of a Caucasian prince) may also have given him a particular bent toward this style which, with its persistent rhythmic patterns, chromatic intervals, and melodic arabesques, dominates the second and third acts of the opera. *Prince Igor,* like *Boris Godunov,* makes some use of leitmotifs, but a more important source of unity is the derivation, unobtrusive but unmistakable, of many of the themes of Acts II and III from phrases in the melody of the first Polovtsian chorus.[19]

If *Boris Godunov* represents a darkly fanatical aspect of the Russian character and *Prince Igor* a cheerful, hearty one, then the picture is completed by Rimsky-Korsakov,[20] whose most characteristic operas

[18] Abraham, *Studies in Russian Music,* p. 128.   [19] *Ibid.,* pp. 132–41.
[20] Nikolai Andreyevitch Rimsky-Korsakov (1844–1908) served as an officer in the Russian Navy before devoting himself entirely to music. He studied counterpoint by himself after his appointment as professor of instrumentation and composition at the St. Petersburg Conservatory in 1871. See his memoirs, *My Musical Life,* one of the principal sources of our knowledge about the Russian nationalists. His *Principles of Orchestration* is a standard treatise. See also Gilse van der Pals, *N. A. Rimsky-Korssakow, Opernschaffen.*

reflect a fairy-tale world of fantasy, romance, and innocent humor. This individual musical and dramatic style of Rimsky-Korsakov was not arrived at without some experimentation, and even after it had been achieved, he still continued to experiment. His first two operas, *The Maid of Pskov* (1873) and *May Night* (1880), showed the influence of Dargomyzhsky and Glinka. *The Snow Maiden* (1882) was more spontaneous and original, based on a fairy legend with vaguely symbolic touches. *Mlada* (1892), in which some traces of Wagner may be seen, was adapted from a libretto which was to have been collectively composed by Cui, Mussorgsky, Rimsky-Korsakov, and Borodin twenty years before (this joint undertaking was never completed). *Christmas Eve* (1895) was, like *May Night,* taken from a story by N. V. Gogol (1809–1852). Both these works are village tales, with love stories and comic-supernatural additions; the subject of *Christmas Eve* is the same as that of Tchaikovsky's *Vakula the Smith.* In 1898 appeared Rimsky-Korsakov's masterpiece, *Sadko,* an "opera legend," a typical combination of the epic and fantastic in a libretto adapted jointly by the composer and V. I. Bielsky from an eleventh-century legend and drawing much of the musical material from Rimsky-Korsakov's early symphonic poem (1876) of the same title. Then followed several experimental works: *Mozart and Salieri, Boyarinya Vera Sheloga* (both 1898), and *The Czar's Bride* (1899), the last a real tragedy with arias and concerted numbers in the old Italian style, "the old operatic convention of the first half of the nineteenth century decked out with Wagnerian leit-motives and Dargomïzhskian 'melodic recitative' and mildly flavoured here and there with the Russian folk-idiom." [21] *Czar Saltan* (1900), another fairy tale, returned to distinctive national traits in both libretto and music. *Servilia* (1902) and *Pan Voyevode* (1904) were unsuccessful essays in more dramatic plots with Wagnerian influence in the music. *Kaschey the Immortal* (1902) was also Wagnerian in technique with declamatory lines and constant use of leitmotifs, as well as the redemption idea woven into the legendary story; the music represents Rimsky-Korsakov's extreme excursion in the direction of chromaticism and dissonance. The last two operas were, with *Sadko,* the most important: *The Legend of the Invisible City of Kitezh* (1907) and *The Golden Cockerel* (1909). *Kitezh* has been called "the Russian Parsi-

21 Abraham, *Studies in Russian Music,* p. 248.

fal" because of its mystical and symbolical story, based on two ancient legends. But beyond an evident aspiration to combine the best features of pagan pantheism and orthodox Christianity in the figure of the heroine Fevronya, the symbolism is vague and not of fundamental importance. *The Golden Cockerel,* from a humorous-fantastic tale of Pushkin, is more objective and ironic, even satirical, but equally unclear as to the detailed application of its moral.

Other than a gradual growth in complexity of idiom and an increasing skill in the fabrication of piquant harmonic and coloristic effects, there is little that can be called an evolution in Rimsky-Korsakov's musical style through these fifteen operas—nothing remotely comparable to the change in Wagner from *Die Feen* to *Parsifal.* Rimsky-Korsakov was a lyrical and pictorial composer, resembling Mendelssohn in exquisiteness of detail as well as in the absence of strongly emotional and dramatic qualities. The realism of Mussorgsky was not for him: art, he once said, was "essentially the most enchanting and intoxicating of lies" [22]—no doubt an extreme statement, but one which explains much in his own music. The dramatic force of the last act of *The Maid of Pskov* and the serious musical characterization of Fevronya in *Kitezh* are exceptional in his work; his original, personal contribution lies in another realm. "[He] must be granted the quite peculiar power of evoking a fantastic world entirely his own, half-real, half-supernatural, a world as limited, as distinctive and as delightful as the world of the Grimms' fairy-tales or as Alice's Wonderland. It is a world in which the commonplace and matter-of-fact are inextricably confused with the fantastic, naivete with sophistication, the romantic with the humorous, and beauty with absurdity. He was not its inventor, of course; he owed it in the first place to Pushkin and Gogol. But he gave it a queer touch of his own, linking it with Slavonic antiquity and hinting at pantheistic symbolism, which makes it peculiarly his. And musically, of course, he reigns in it undisputed. He invented the perfect music for such a fantastic world: music insubstantial when it was matched with unreal things, deliciously lyrical when it touched reality, in both cases coloured from the most superb palette musician has ever held." [23]

[22] Quoted in Calvocoressi and Abraham, *Masters of Russian Music,* p. 411.
[23] *Ibid.,* p. 422. Quoted by permission of the publisher.

DESIGN FOR RIMSKY-KORSAKOV'S "COQ D'OR"

For Rimsky-Korsakov an opera was primarily a musical rather than a dramatic-literary work; hence the importance of musical design, which frequently dominates both the poetry and the scenic plan (for example, the rondo form in the fourth tableau of *Sadko*). Along with this there is usually a definite association of certain keys with certain moods. In most of the operas there is a consistent use of leitmotifs. These are not, as in Wagner, the material out of which a symphonic fabric is developed but are rather melodic fragments (sometimes only a phrase from a large theme) or even inconspicuous harmonic progressions, woven into the opera in a kind of mosaic pattern; they are as often given to the voices as to the orchestra.[24] In the harmony, there are as a rule two distinct idioms in each opera: one chromatic, fanciful, cunningly contrived, for the imaginary scenes and characters (Example 121), and the other diatonic, solid,

LE COQ D'OR, introduction

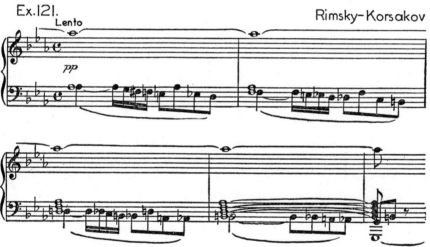

Ex.121.
Lento
Rimsky-Korsakov
pp

often modal, for the "real" world. The vocal parts, as usual in Russian opera, alternate between melodic recitative and closed aria-like forms. In his lyrical melodies, Rimsky-Korsakov owes much to the model of Glinka; his own melodies are elegant and graceful, though marked by certain persistently recurring formulae. An important factor in his style is the extensive use of folk tunes, and of original

[24] Cf. Rimsky-Korsakov, *My Musical Life,* p. 204.

tunes of the folk-song type; the source or inspiration for many of
these was his own collection of Russian folk songs, made in 1876.
Church melodies are also occasionally used, notably in *Kitezh*. The
oriental idiom, however, is much less extensive and less significant in
Rimsky-Korsakov's music than in that of either Balakirev or Borodin.
Like all Russian opera composers, he excelled in the depiction of
crowd scenes, especially in *The Maid of Pskov* (Act II), *Sadko*, *Kitezh*
(Act II and finale), and the humorous ensembles in *May Night,
Christmas Eve,* and *Sadko*. Above all, of course, he is distinguished
for his mastery of orchestral effects, a virtuosity in the treatment of
instrumental color such as few composers in history have equaled.

A number of minor Russian opera composers of the late nineteenth- and
early twentieth-century period can be only briefly mentioned. Eduard
Frantsovitch Napravnik (1839–1916), as conductor of the St. Petersburg
Opera from 1869, was influential in bringing out the works of the native
school; the most successful of his own operas was *Dubrovsky* (1895). A
pupil of Rimsky-Korsakov, but influenced in opera by Tchaikovsky, was
Anton Stepanovitch Arensky (1861–1906; *Raphael,* 1894). Also under the
influence of Tchaikovsky were the operatic works of Sergei Vassilievitch
Rachmaninov (1873–1943), Alexander Tikhonovitch Gretchaninov (b.
1864), and Michail Michaelovitch Ippolitov-Ivanov (1859–1935). Sergei
Ivanovitch Taneiev [25] produced an *Orestes* trilogy (1895) in severe contrapuntal style with admixtures of Rubinstein and Tchaikovsky. The impressionist movement was reflected in Russian opera in the works of
Vladimir Ivanovitch Rebikov (1866–1920).

The early works of Stravinsky [26] are in effect a continuation of
Rimsky-Korsakov's operatic style, but with preponderant or exclusive
emphasis on its pictorial aspects. Thus the ballet *The Firebird* (1910)
is based on a national legendary subject, uses national folksongs, and
in both orchestration and formal treatment is thoroughly Russian
in feeling. *Petrouchka* (1911) introduces an element of caricature,

---

[25] Taneiv (1850–1918) is an unusual personality in music. By early training a piano
virtuoso (pupil of N. Rubinstein), he became interested in the study of counterpoint
and brought out in 1909 a two-volume treatise on the subject, the result of nearly twenty
years' work. His later compositions were chiefly chamber music. He lived the life of an
ascetic, caring little for recognition or even publication of his work. See Sabaneiev,
Modern Russian Composers.

[26] On Igor Stravinsky (b. 1882) see his autobiography and his *Poétique musicale,* also
studies by Schloezer, Schaeffner, and Handschin; Blitzstein, "The Phenomenon of Stravinsky," MQ XXI (1935) 330–47: Armitage (ed.), *Stravinsky;* special Stravinsky issue of
RM (1939); Sternfeld, "Some Russian Folk Songs in Stravinsky's *Petrouchka,*" *Music Library Association Notes, Second Series* II, No. 2 (March, 1945) 95–107.

and *The Ceremonial of Spring* (1913) exaggerates the neoprimitive —departures from the pure nationalist tradition which are reflected in the novel, experimental features of the music of both works. In the opera *The Nightingale* (1914) the Russian elements begin to have the character of exotic material. So far as national qualities are concerned, the burlesque chamber opera *Renard* (composed 1916–1917) and the one-act opera buffa *Mavra* (1922) are wholly satirical in spirit, while in *The Story of the Soldier* (1918) and *The Wedding* (1923) the national subject matter as well as the musical idiom has become stylized. The neoclassic ballet *The Fairy Kiss* (1928), on themes from Tchaikovsky, may be regarded as the last faint echo of Russian nationalism in Stravinsky's work.

CENTRAL AND SOUTHEASTERN EUROPE.[27]—Although there were Polish operas as early as 1778 by Matthias Kamienski (1734–1821), the real founder of Polish national opera was Stanislaw Moniuszko,[28] a contemporary of Chopin and a song composer of undoubted lyric gifts. His *Halka* (1854) is still performed in Poland. Other works in a similar romantic vein, some of which are still revived, include *The Raftsman* (1858), *The Countess* (1860), and especially a comic work, *The Haunted Castle* (1865), next to *Halka* his most popular opera. Conditions in Poland were not favorable to native opera during the latter part of the nineteenth century, and therefore the promising work begun by Moniuszko did not come to full fruition.

The principal composers and works of this period were: Ludwik Grossman, 1835–1915 (*The Ghost of the Voyvod*, 1873); Adam Minhejmer, 1831–1904 (*Mazeppa*, composed before 1875 but not performed until 1900); Ladislas Zelenski, 1873–1921, a composer of chamber and orchestral music influenced by Brahms, and who in opera remained faithful to the pre-Wagnerian form and style (*Goplana*, 1896); Sigismund Noskowski, 1846–1909 (*Livia Quintilla*, 1898); Roman Statkowski, 1860–1925, whose two operas won prizes in international competitions, their style being in transition between the pre-Wagnerian and the music drama (*Philaenis*, 1904; *Marya*, 1906);[29] Ignace Jan Paderewski, 1860–1941 (*Manru*, 1901);

[27] Bibliography: Opieński, *La Musique polonaise;* Newmarch, *The Music of Czechoslovakia;* Nosek, *The Spirit of Bohemia;* Harászti, *La Musique hongroise;* Adorján, "L'Opérette hongroise," *Revue de Hongroie* VI (1910) 269–80; Dobronic, "A Study of Jugoslav Music," MQ XII (1926) 56–71.
[28] Moniuszko's dates are 1819–1872. See Jachimecki, "Moniuszko," MQ XIV (1928) 54–62.
[29] The text of *Marya* is from a poem by A. Malczewski; there are other operas on this subject by Melcer, Soltys, W. Gawronski, and H. Opienski (Loewenberg, *Annals*, p. 663).

Miecyslaw Soltys, 1863–1929 (*Panie Kochanku*, 1924); and Felician Szopski, b. 1865 (*Lilje*, 1917, in Wagnerian style).

A new generation whose music showed more progressive tendencies came to recognition in opera for the most part only after the restoration of Polish nationality in 1919.

This group included the pianist Henrik Melcer, 1869–1928 (*Marya*, 1904); the conductor Emil Mlynarski, 1870–1935 (*Summer Night*, composed 1915, performed 1923); the musicologist Henrik Opieński, 1870–1942 (*Marya*, 1924; *Jacob the Lutenist*, 1927); Taddeusz Joteyko, 1872–1932, the most successful of the group (*Sigmund August*, 1925); Felix Nowowiejski, 1877–ca. 1945, choral composer, conductor, winner of many prizes, whose *Baltic Legend* (1924) abounds in massive effects; and Adam Táddeusz Wieniawski, b. 1879, pupil of D'Indy and Fauré, a more subtle talent (*Megae*, 1912; *Wyzolony*, 1928).

The most productive and most naturally dramatic modern Polish opera composer is Ludomir Rózycki (b. 1883), whose works include *Boleslav the Bold* (1909), *Eros and Psyche* (1917, and winning the Polish state prize in 1931), the comic opera *Casanova* (1923), and the tragic *Beatrice Cenci* (1927). Karol Szymanowski (1883–1937),[30] by common consent the greatest Polish composer of the present century, was primarily interested in other than operatic forms. His *Hagith* (composed 1912) was influenced by Strauss's *Elektra*. *King Roger* (1926) is an outstanding modern opera. Its libretto, on a subject perhaps suggested by Schreker's *Der ferne Klang*, is exceptionally well constructed; the music is rich, sonorous, and original, deriving some of its material from Greek church modes (parallel-organum choruses in Act I) and oriental motifs (ballets in Act II).

The father of Bohemian music and opera was Bedřich Smetana,[31] whose first great success came with *The Bartered Bride* in 1866. This melodious comic opera, so permeated with the rhythms and spirit of national music, has become famous all over the world. Two other comic operas of Smetana, *The Kiss* (1876) and *The Secret* (1878),

---

[30] Jachimecki, "Szymanowski," *Slavonic . . . Review* XVII (July, 1938) 174–85.
[31] There were a few operas with Bohemian texts before Smetana, notably several by František Škroup (1801–1862) produced at Prague from 1826. Other early composers were František Skuherský (1830–1892), Karel Šebor (1845–1903; *The Hussite Bride*, 1868), Karel Bendl (1838–1897), and Vilém Blodek (1834–1874; especially noted for comic operas); one of the first Slovenian opera composers was Anton Foerster (1837–1909). For other names in this early period see Adler, *Handbuch* II, 925. On Smetana (1824–1884) the principal biography is that of Nejedlý, which has not been translated; there is a smaller work on Smetana by Nejedlý in English translation (London, 1924).

showed advances in technical skill and were almost as successful in the composer's own country as *The Bartered Bride*. Smetana's serious operas, especially *Dalibor* (1868) and *Libussa* (composed 1872, performed 1881), were attacked by patriotic critics because of their use of certain procedures associated with Wagner, such as leitmotifs and the declamatory character of the vocal parts. But the alleged Wagnerisms hardly ever penetrated to the substance of the music, which remained stoutly individual. The leader of the next generation of Bohemian composers, Antonin Dvořák,[32] was primarily a symphonic rather than a dramatic musician, though several of his nine operas were successful at Prague. *The Cunning Peasant* (1878) was inspired by Smetana's *Bartered Bride*. *The Devil and Kate* (1899) was Dvořák's most popular work in the comic style. In serious opera, he underwent the influence first of Meyerbeer and then of Wagner; the height of his achievement in this field was attained in a late work, *Rusalka* (1901), the libretto of which was well adapted to his lyrical powers. A third early figure in Bohemian music was Zdenko Fibich,[33] a prolific composer who, more internationally minded than either Smetana or Dvořák, came fully under the influence of romanticism and the Wagnerian music drama. He was noted especially for the classical trilogy *Hippodameia* (1890–91), set entirely as a melodrama —that is, orchestral music accompanying a spoken text—a form established by the eighteenth-century Bohemian composer Georg Benda. Fibich's best opera was *Šarka* (1897), based on a story from Czech mythology.

Other composers of this generation were Adalbert Hřimalý, 1842–1908 (*The Enchanted Prince*, 1872), Joseph Nešvera, 1842–1914 (*Woodland Air*, 1897), and Hanuš Trneček, 1858–1914.

An important Bohemian composer of the late nineteenth-century was Joseph Bohuslav Foerster,[34] whose most successful operas were *Eva* (1889) and *Jessika* (1905). Four pupils of Fibich also made their mark in Bohemian opera: Karel Kovařič, 1862–1920 (*On the Old*

[32] On Dvořák (1841–1904) see Hadow, *Studies in Modern Music, Second Series*, 10th ed. There are biographies in English by Paul Stefan (based on the monumental Czech biography by Otakar Šourek) and Karel Hoffmeister.
[33] Fibich (1850–1900) composed five overtures, three symphonies, five symphonic poems, some chamber music, songs, and piano pieces, in addition to his six operas and eight melodramas. See study by C. L. Richter.
[34] Foerster (b. 1859) is notable for choral works as well as for his seven operas. See biography by Nejedlý.

Bleaching Ground, 1901), Karel Weis (1862–1937), Antonín Horák (1875–1910), and Otakar Ostrčil, 1879–1935 (*The Bud,* 1911). An influential composer and teacher was Vitěslav Novák,[35] with four operas of which the most important was *The Imp of Zvikov* (1915). The Moravian Leoš Janáček [36] in his operas cultivated an intense style based on the rhythms of Czech speech, with a varied harmonic vocabulary influenced by Mussorgsky and the French impressionists, though modern in its primitive directness of expression and economy of resource (*Her Foster Daughter,* 1904, better known under the title *Jenufa; Káta Kabanová,* 1921; *The Sly Vixen,* 1924; *The Makropulos Case,* 1926).

Modern Czechoslovak composers of opera are: Otakar Zich, 1879–1934 (*The Sin,* 1922); Rudolf Karel, 1880–1945, a pupil of Dvořák (*Godmother Death,* 1933); Jaroslav Křička, b. 1882; Alois Haba, b. 1893 (*Die Mutter,* Munich 1931, the first quarter-tone opera); Marij Kogoj, b. 1895 (*Black Masks,* 1929); and Jaromir Weinberger, b. 1896, whose folk opera *Schwanda the Bagpiper* (1927) is one of the only two Czech operas which have become widely known outside their own country. Weinberger's *Outcasts of Poker Flat* (1932, from Bret Harte's story) shows American jazz influence. Bohuslav Martinu, b. 1890, better known for his symphonic and chamber music, is also the composer of six operas.

The founder of opera in Hungary was Ferenc Erkel (1810–1893), whose works have been performed more often than those of any other Hungarian composer (*Hunyady László,* 1844; *Bánk-Bán,* 1861). Others of the early nationalist group were András Bartay, 1798–1856 (*The Trick,* 1839, the first Hungarian comic opera); György Czászár, ca. 1820–? (*The Cumans,* 1848); Michael Brand, called Mosonyi, 1814–1870 (*Fair Ilonka,* 1861); and August von Adelburg, 1830–1873 (*Zrynyi,* 1868). Later nationalists included Jenö Hubay, 1858–1937 (*The Violin Maker of Cremona,* 1894), and Ede Poldini, b. 1869 (*The Vagabond and the Princess,* 1903). Wagnerian influence came with Ödön Mihalovich, 1842–1929 (*Toldi's Love,* 1893), and a pronounced flavor of late German romanticism is heard in the operas of Géza Zichy [37] and Erno Dohnányi, b. 1877 (*The Tower of the*

---

[35] On Novák (b. 1870) see Newmarch, "New Works on Czechoslovakia," *The Chesterian* XII (1931) 213–19.

[36] Janáček (1854–1928) was an enthusiastic student of folk songs and wrote two books on harmonic theory. See biography by D. Muller; also Holländer, "Leoš Janáček and His Operas," MQ XV (1929) 29–36.

[37] Zichy (1849–1924) has left an autobiography, *Aus meinem Leben.*

Voyvod, 1922). The leading modern Hungarian composer was Béla Bartók,[38] whose only opera, *Duke Bluebeard's Castle* (Budapest. 1918), is a masterpiece of orchestral color and somber dramatic power within the confines of a single act and using only two characters. Less individual but equally nationalistic in his music is Zoltán Kodály (b. 1882), with two Hungarian ballad operas: *Háry János* (1926) and *The Spinning Room of the Szekelys* (1932). Finally to be mentioned is Jenö Zádor, b. 1894 (*The Isle of the Dead*, 1928).

The principal opera composers of Rumania were: Liubicz Skibinski (*Verfel cu Dor*, 1879); Eduard Caudella, 1841–1923 (*Petru Rares*, 1900); Georg Kosmovici (*Marioara*, 1904); Theodor von Flondor, d. 1908 (*Mosul Ciokârlan*, 1901); Sabin Dragoi, b. 1894, a pupil of Dvořák and Janáček, with sophisticated modern use of Rumanian folksong in *Napasta* (1928); and Georges Enesco, b. 1881, with one opera, *Oedipe* (Paris, 1936).

Croatian opera is represented by Vatroslav Lisinski, 1819–1854 (*Ljubav i Zloba*, 1846); Ivan Zajc, 1832–1914 (*Nikola Šubič Zrinski*, 1876); Franjo Serafin Vilhar, 1852–1928 (*Smiljana*, 1892); Petar Konjović, b. 1882 (*Koštana*, 1931); Krešimir Baranović, b. 1894 (*Striženo-Košeno*, 1932); and Jacov Gotovac, b. 1895 (*Morana*, 1930).

In Serbia the only opera composer of importance is Alexander Savin, b. 1881 (*Ksenia*, 1919). Bulgarian opera has two composers: Georgi Athanassov, 1872–1931, a pupil of Mascagni (*Borislav*, 1911), and Pantcho Vladigerov, b. 1899, with the nationalist opera *Czar Kalojan* (1936). The only nationalist opera composer of Greece is Manuel Kalomiris, b. 1883 (*The Master*, 1915; *Mother's Ring*, 1917).

GERMANIC, SCANDINAVIAN, AND BALTIC COUNTRIES.—On the whole, opera found no very congenial ground in these countries, but there are sporadic examples, of which some of the most important will be mentioned.

Holland throughout the nineteenth century was under the musical domination of Germany.[39] Opera composers in this period included Richard Hol, 1825–1904 (*Floris V*, 1892); Cornelis van der Linden, 1842–1908 (*The Relief of Leyden*, 1893); Henry Brandts-Buys, 1850–1905 (*Albrecht Beiling*, 1891); Karl Dibbern, b. 1855 (*Odja*, 1901); Emile van Brucken-Fock, b. 1857 (*Seleneia*, 1895); Cornelis Dopper, 1870–1939 (*The Cross of Honor*, 1903); and Charles Grelinger, b. 1873, with the successful

---

[38] On Bartók (1881–1945) see biography by Harászti.
[39] Dresden, *Het Muziekleven in Nederland sinds 1880*; Sanders, *Moderne nederlandsche Componisten*. The earliest Dutch opera, *De triomferende Min* ("Love's Triumph"), by Carolus Hacquart (*ca.* 1649–*ca.* 1730), was published in 1680 but not performed until 1920, at Antwerp. (See Loewenberg, *Annals*, p. 36.)

opera *Op Hoop van Zegen* ("On Board the 'Hope of Blessing,' " 1907). Jan Brandts-Buys, 1868–1933, was more German than Dutch (*Die drei Schneider*, Dresden, 1916), but national traits appeared in the realistic-satiric operas of Hol's pupil Johan Wagenaar, b. 1862 (his *Doge van Venetie*, 1904, and *De Cid*, 1916, are serious operas). A modern Dutch opera is *Halewijn* (1933) by Willem Pijper (1894–1947).

Flemish opera composers of the nineteenth and twentieth centuries were: Joseph Mertens, 1834–1901 (*De zwarte Kapitein*, 1877); Jan Blockx (*De Herbergprinses*, 1896); [40] Paul Gilson, 1865–1942 (*Prinses Zonneschijn*, 1903); and Auguste de Boeck, 1865–1937 (*La Route d'Emeraude*, 1921).

Denmark, like Holland, has been to a large extent a musical province of Germany.[41] The earliest national opera composers were Johan Hartmann, 1805–1900 (*Liden Kirsten*, 1846); Henrik Rung, 1807–1871 (*Storm over Copenhagen*, 1845); Siegfried Saloman, 1816–1899 (*The Diamond Cross*, 1847); and Peter Arnold Heise, 1830–1879 (*King and Marshal*, 1878). Four operas by Peter Erasmus Lange-Müller (1850–1926) were produced at Copenhagen (*Spanske Studenter*, 1883). One of the most successful Danish comic operas was Carl August Nielsen's (1865–1931) *Maskarade* (1906). The most prolific recent Danish opera composer was August Enna, 1860–1939 (*The Witch*, 1892; *The Match Girl*, 1897).

The first Norwegian opera was *A Mountain Adventure* by Waldemar Thrane (1790–1828), which was published by 1824 but not performed on the stage until 1850 [42] Twenty years later came *The Knight and the Fluberg Sprite* by Martin Andreas Udbye (1820–1899), and in 1894 the first of Johannes Haarklou's (1847–1925) five operas, *Of Olden Days*. Ole Olsen (1850–1927) wrote four operas, of which *Leila* was performed at Christiana in 1908. Gerhard Schjelderup (1859–1933), though of Norwegian birth, composed most of his operas to German texts; the same is true of Sigwardt Aspestrand (b. 1856). Catherinus Elling (b. 1858) wrote one opera, *Kosakkerne* (1897).

Sweden from the seventeenth century had been in touch with the general development of opera in Europe.[43] Italian, French, and German subjects and musical styles, as might be expected, dominated Swedish opera houses in the late eighteenth and early nineteenth centuries. The earliest attempt at a Swedish historical subject was made by Carl Stenborg with *King Gustavus Adolphus's Hunting Party* (1779).[44] The first grand opera in Swedish was *Thetis och Pelée* (1773), by the Italian composer Francesco

---

[40] Solvay, *Notice sur Jan Blockx* [1851–1912].

[41] On the Danish branch of the eighteenth-century Singspiel see above, p. 267. The German composer Franz Gläser (1798–1861) wrote three operas to Danish texts.

[42] Loewenberg, *Annals*, p. 448. *See also* Kindem, *Den norske operas historie.*

[43] See Moberg, "Essais d'opéras en Suède," in *Mélanges de musicologie*, pp. 123–32; Engländer, *Joseph Martin Kraus.*

[44] This "comedy mingled with songs" was imitated from Collet's French opéra comique text, *La Partie de chasse de Henri IV*, part of which had been used by Weisse and J. A. Hiller for their popular Singspiel *Die Jagd* (1770).

Antonio Uttini (1723–1795). Swedish opera composers in the early and middle nineteenth century included J. N. Ahlström (1805–1857), Adolf Lindblad (1801–1878), Siegfried Saloman (1816–1899), and August Johan Södermann (1832–1876). Some German composers in this period also occasionally wrote operas to Swedish texts. A more definitely national type of Swedish opera, using native legends and folk melodies, appeared toward the end of the nineteenth century with the works of Ivar Hallström, 1826–1901 (*The Mountain King*, 1874). Nationalism was temporarily pushed aside, however, by the desire to emulate the Wagnerian music drama, as in the earlier operas of Anders Hallén, 1846–1925 (*Harald the Viking*, Leipzig, 1881), though more independent traits are evident in his *Valdemar's Treasure*, written for the opening of the new Stockholm Opera in 1899. A Wagner propagandist in Sweden was Richard Henneberg (1853–1925), who wrote a comic opera, *Drottningen's Pilgrimage*, in 1882. A combination of the Wagner style with national melodies is found in the operas of Vilhelm Stenhammar, 1871–1927 (*Tirfing*, 1898; *Das Fest auf Solhaug*, Stuttgart, 1899). A more definite step toward national opera, though still on a Wagnerian basis, was *Arnjlot* (1910), by Olof Wilhelm Peterson-Berger.[45] Natanaël Berg (b. 1879) and Kurt Atterberg (b. 1887) are distinguished chiefly in the field of the symphony, though both have produced operas. A contemporary opera composer is Ture Rangström, 1884–1947 (*Die Kronbraut*, Stuttgart 1919; in Swedish, at Stockholm, from 1922; based on Strindberg's drama).

In Finland there was no national opera before the twentieth century. *Kung Carls Jakt* by Fredrik Pacius (1809–1891), performed at Helsinki in 1852 and sometimes called the "first Finnish opera," was by a German-born composer and on a Swedish text.[46] The first opera composed to Finnish words was Oskar Merikanto's (1868–1924) *Pohjan Neiti* ("The Maid of Bothnia"), performed at Viipuri in 1908. Merikanto's subsequent works (*Elinan Surma*, "Elina's Death," 1910; *Regina von Emmeritz*, 1920) were somewhat influenced by Italian verismo methods. Other composers of this period were Erkki Gustaf Melartin, 1875–1937 (*Aino*, 1909), and Selim Palmgren, b. 1878 (*Daniel Hjort*, 1910; Swedish text). A more distinctly national style, with folk melodies and recitative rhythms adapted to the Finnish language, was exemplified by Armas Launis, b. 1884 (*Seitsemän Veljestä*, "Seven Brothers," 1913; *Kullervo*, 1917). Another Finnish folk-song scholar, Ilmari Krohn (b. 1867), produced an opera *Tuhotulva* ("The Deluge") at Helsinki in 1928. The most important modern Finnish operas are by Leevi Madetoja (b. 1887), a pupil of D'Indy: *Pohjalaisia* ("The East Bothnians," 1924) and *Juha* (1935).

A few national operas were produced in the smaller Baltic states after the First World War. In Latvia an opera company was organized at Riga

[45] Peterson-Berger (1867–1942) is the author of several books and a collection of essays published at Stockholm in 1923.
[46] See Loewenberg, *Annals*, p. 458.

in 1919. Native composers include Alfreds Kalnins, b. 1879 (*Banuta*, 1920; *Dzimtenes Atmoda*, "The Country's Awakening," 1933, a historical opera); Jazeps Medins, b. 1877 (*Vaidelote*, "The Virgin," 1927); Janis Medins, b. 1890 (*Uguns un Nakts*, "Fire and Night," 1921); and Janis Kalnins, b. 1904 (*Hamlets*, 1936). A Lithuanian opera house was opened at Kaunas toward the end of 1920, and the first Lithuanian opera, *Birute*, by Petrauskas Miskas, was performed in 1921. Another Lithuanian composer is Jurgio Karnavičius, b. 1885 (*Grazina*, 1933). Estonian operas have been composed by Arthur Lemba, b. 1885 (*Armastus ja Surm*, "Love and Death," Tallinn 1931; *Elga*, 1934).

SPAIN, PORTUGAL, AND LATIN AMERICA.[47]—With the disappearance of the old tonadilla in the first half of the nineteenth century, Spanish national opera went into an eclipse from which it did not emerge until about 1850. The first signs of reaction against the reign of Italian opera and French opéra comique in Spanish theatres appeared, strangely enough, in the works of a resident Italian composer, Basilio Basili, who in the late thirties and early forties brought out at Madrid a number of comic operas in Spanish. The first of these (1837) was labeled a *zarzuela-comedia,* thus reviving the ancient Spanish designation. Within a decade there was a flourishing school of the new zarzuela, a form derived essentially from the eighteenth-century tonadilla, using music of a light, popular, national style with admixture of some French and Italian elements. Many of the early librettos were from French sources—an instance of the influence which France has constantly exerted on the growth of national Spanish music. The leading composer of this first period of the revival was Francisco Asenjo Barbieri (1823–1894), who produced over seventy zarzuelas between 1850 and 1880, including the classic work of this type, *Pan y toros* ("Bread and Bulls," 1864). This and other zarzuelas of Barbieri [48] were long popular and have been influential on the development of national music in both Spain and South America. The principal contemporaries of Barbieri were Rafael José Maria Hernando (1822–1888), Joaquín Gaztambide (1882–1870), Cristóbal Oudrid y

[47] See Chase, *The Music of Spain,* for the most recent survey of this subject, with bibliographies. Further consult: Lavignac, *Encyclopédie,* Pt. I, Vol. IV, pp. 2290–2351, 2470–84; Salazar, *La música contemporánea en España;* music dictionaries of Saldoni and Pedrell and the "Espasa" encyclopedia; Trend, *A Picture of Modern Spain;* Peña y Goñi, *La ópera española.* Cf. also titles under early Spanish opera (above, pp. 270 ff.).

[48] E.g., *Tramoya* ("The Trick," 1850); *Jugar con fuego* ("Playing with Fire," 1851); *El barberillo de Lavapiés* ("The Little Barber of Lavapiés," 1874).

Segura (1829–1877), and Emilio Arrieta y Corera (1823–1894).[49]

Two distinct types of zarzuela developed at Madrid, corresponding to the two types of French opéra comique which evolved during the nineteenth century. On the one hand was the *genero chico*—comic, popular, informal, often quite ephemeral pieces in one act. These were produced in immense numbers throughout the century and indeed have continued up to the present day. The other type was the *zarzuela grande,* usually in three acts, which might be on a serious subject and even in some cases approach the scale and style of grand opera. Most composers of the later nineteenth century wrote zarzuelas of both kinds. Some of the most popular works of the genero chico were *La gran via* ("The Great Road," 1886) by Federico Chueca (1846–1908), in collaboration with Joaquín Valverde (1846–1910); *La viejecita* ("The Old Woman," 1897) by Manuel Fernández Caballero (1835–1906); *La bruja* ("The Witch," 1887) and *La revoltosa* ("The Revolutionary Girl," 1897) by Ruperto Chapí y Lorente (1851–1909); and above all *La verbena de la paloma* ("The Festival of Our Lady of the Dove," 1894) by Tomas Bretón y Hernández.[50]

Along with the rise of the popular zarzuela there was a growing desire for a national serious opera in Spain. Spanish composers of the earlier nineteenth century had rarely used Spanish texts or national subjects, and their music seldom had anything differentiating it from the contemporary Italian style.[51] A solitary early crusader for Spanish opera was Joaquín Espín y Guillén (1812–1881), one act of whose *Padilla, o el Asedio de Medina* ("Padilla, or the Siege of Medina") was performed at Madrid in 1845. Later in the century, however, the zarzuela composers interested themselves in the task of creating a more permanent and artistic form of national lyric drama than could be made of the genero chico pieces to which they chiefly owed their popular success. Barbieri had definite ideas on the

---

[49] Chief works: Hernando: *Colegiales y soldados* ("College Girls and Soldiers"), 1849; *El duende* ("The Ghost"), 1849. Gaztambide: *La mensanjera* ("The Errand Girl"), 1849. Oudrid: *Buenas noches, Don Simón* ("Good Night, Don Simon"), 1852. Arrieta: *El domino azul* ("The Blue Domino"), 1853; *Marina,* 1855.

[50] See biography of Bretón (1850–1923) by Salcedo.

[51] Composers of this period were: Ramón Carnicer, 1789–1855 (*Cristoforo Colombo,* 1831); Tomás Genovés y Lapetra, 1806–1861; Baltasar Saldoni, 1807–1889 (*Ipermestra,* 1838); Vicente Cuyas, 1814–1839 (*La Fattuchiera,* 1838); and Miguel Hilarión Eslava, 1807–1878 (*Il solitario del Monte Selvaggio,* 1841).

subject;[52] Arrieta, who had composed a number of Italian operas, expanded his two-act zarzuela *Marina* into a three-act Spanish opera with recitatives (1871). Chapí wrote several serious zarzuelas (*La tempestad* "The Storm," 1882; *Curro Vargas,* 1898) as well as operas (*Margarita la Tornera,* 1909), but his genius was for the comic rather than the serious. Bretón, who had also written Italian operas, composed an important Spanish opera, *La Dolores,* in 1895. Still another composer of this period was Emilio Serrano y Ruiz (1850–1939), with the operas *Irene de Otranto* in 1891 and *Gonzalo de Cordoba* (to his own text) in 1898.

The honorable title of "father of modern Spanish music" belongs to Felipe Pedrell,[53] distinguished scholar, composer, and teacher (or at least mentor) of most of the Spanish composers of the following generation. Pedrell combined a deep feeling for the qualities of Spanish folk-song and the great Spanish music of the past with a romantic-mystical temperament which led him frequently into paths where the general public could not follow. He was a greater idealist than composer, and his beneficent influence on Spanish music is out of all proportion to the very slight outward success of his own works. He was dubbed "the Spanish Wagner"; his most successful opera, *La Celestina* (1904), was called "the Spanish *Tristan.*" These expressions exaggerate the resemblance of his work to Wagner's. That there was some influence is, of course, unquestionable, but the examples of Glinka, Mussorgsky, and the other Russian opera composers were at least equally potent. As a matter of fact, if comparisons must be made, the composer whom Pedrell most closely resembles is D'Indy. The likeness is one of both temperament and musical style: each was irresistibly drawn into the orbit of Wagner; each, being an ardent nationalist and an artist of high ethical purpose, adapted the technique of the music drama for his own aims; and each succeeded in being individual in spite of this debt. D'Indy was a better technician than Pedrell and was more at home in the realm of purely

---

[52] Chase, *Music of Spain,* p. 141.
[53] Pedrell (1841–1922) composed seven operas, several symphonic poems, and choral works. He was editor of the *Hispaniae schola musica sacra* and the Complete Edition of Victoria. See Tebaldini, *Felipe Pedrell ed il dramma lirico spagnuolo;* Curzon, *Felipe Pedrell et Les Pyrénées;* Istel, "Felipe Pedrell," MQ XI (1925) 164–91; Gilbert Chase, "Felipe Pedrell" (unpublished essay); Pedrell's own *Jornadas de arte* (essays and critical writings); and catalogue of works by Reiff, AfMw III (1921) 86–97.

musical expression; Pedrell, on the other hand, drew his musical idiom from more varied sources.

The most important of Pedrell's ten operas is *Los Pirineos* ("The Pyrenees"), a trilogy in three acts with prologue, composed to a Catalan text of Victor Balaguer in 1890–1891 and first performed in Italian translation at Barcelona in 1902.[54] The poem offers a number of effective scenes, but on the whole its nature is more that of an epic than of a dramatic work. Pedrell's setting is unified by the use of leitmotifs. An idea of his style may be gained from Example 122, part of the Funeral March in the second act. The orchestra has a much less conspicuous position than in Wagner, and the voice parts are nearly always melodic. An important proportion of the score is

LOS PIRINEOS, Act II

Ex.122.   Pedrell

---

[54] *Los Pireneos* is itself the first opera of a larger trilogy, of which *La Celestina* is the second number; the third, *Raymond Lully,* was not completed.

given to set pieces, which appear in great variety. The composer's scholarly conscience is shown in his evident care to reproduce as authentically as possible the oriental idiom in the solos of the heroine, "Moon-Ray"; the scene of the Love Court in Act I offers modern adaptations of trouvère and troubadour art forms—*tenso, lai,* and *sirventes.* There are quotations from plainsong and from sixteenth-century Spanish church composers, and the excellent choral writing throughout the opera should be especially mentioned. The prologue in particular should make a very effective concert number for a choral society.

It is too much to claim that Pedrell is to be numbered among the greatest opera composers. His dramatic sense often failed him. Too many pages of *Los Pirineos* are thin in inspiration, repetitious, and lacking in rhythmic vitality and variety. But, out of a sincere artist's soul, enough moments of greatness have emerged to make this work an honor to its composer and country and to entitle it to at least an occasional performance, even if in a shortened version.

The national spirit which Pedrell did so much to inspire achieved world-wide recognition in the piano music of two of his pupils, Albéniz and Granados.[55] Both these composers essayed opera, but without important results. Albéniz, apparently under a mistaken notion of his own gifts, and also instigated by a wealthy English patron who fancied himself a dramatic author, devoted several years to writing operas in a heavy, pseudo-Wagnerian style but finally obtained a moderate success with a comic work, *Pepita Jiménez* (1896). Granados, like many of his contemporaries, was interested in trying to re-create the spirit of Madrid as typified in Goya, and the music of his principal opera, *Goyescas* (New York, 1916), was expanded from a series of piano pieces of the same title. The plot of this opera has a strong tinge of Italian verismo.

The mixture of romanticism and nationalism with a musical idiom related to that of Franck and D'Indy which was so characteristic of Pedrell is found likewise in the operas of Angel Barrios (b. 1862) and Conrado del Campo y Zabalata (b. 1879); their jointly composed *El Avapiés* [56] was performed at Madrid in 1919. Another Pedrell

[55] On Isaac Albéniz (1860–1909) see Klein, "Albéniz's Opera, *Pepita Jiménez*," *Musical Times* LIX (March, 1918) 116–17; Collet, *Albéniz et Granados;* Istel, "Isaac Albéniz," MQ XV (1929) 117–48. On Enrique Granados y Campina (1867–1916) see studies by Boladeres Ibern and Subirá.

[56] The title is the name of a quarter in Madrid.

disciple was Amadeo Vives (1871–1932), composer of many zarzuelas and other dramatic works, including the "lyric eclogue" *Maruxa* (1914) and the three-act comic opera *Doña Francisquita* (1923), which has been very successful in both Spain and South America. Joachín Turina (b. 1882) is significant chiefly for his orchestral and pianoforte compositions, though he has produced a few operas (*Margot*, 1914; *La adúltera penitente*, 1917; *Jardín de Oriente*, 1923). A more conservative composer was Vicente Arregui Garay (1871–1925), with his prize-winning opera *Yolanda* (performed 1923). Two of the best known modern Spanish operas are by Manuel de Falla.[57] *La vida breve* ("Life Is Short"; composed 1905, performed 1913) is less notable for its dramatic qualities than for its effective and authentic Andalusian musical background, and especially for the ballets in Act II. The marionette opera, *El retablo de Maese Pedro* ("Master Peter's Puppet Show," 1923), is an interesting dramatic experiment in a more modern idiom, using an orchestra of only twenty-five players. De Falla's ballets *El amor brujo* (1915) and *El sombrero de tres picos* (1919) should also be mentioned as important modern works for the theatre.

In addition to his influence on what may be called the main stream of modern Spanish opera, Pedrell is also the founder of the regional school of Catalonia. The leading figure in this school is Jaime Pahissa (b. 1880), with *La presó de Lleida* ("The Prison of Lérida," 1906; rewritten in 1928 as a three-act opera *La Princèsa Margarida*) and *Gala placidia* (1913). Other Catalan composers are Enric Morera (*Emporium*, 1906),[58] Juan Lamote de Grignon, b. 1872 (*Hesperia*, 1907), and Joan Manén, b. 1883 (*Acté*, 1903). Independent regional development is characteristic of Spanish music, but the only extensive regional opera outside Catalonia is found in the Basque country. The outstanding composer here was José María Usandizaga (1887–1915) with the nationalistic *Mendi-Mendyian* (1910) and the very successful Puccinian melodramatic opera *Las golondrinas* ("The Swallows," 1914). Another Basque composer is Jesús Guridi (b. 1886), whose national folk opera *Mirentxu* (1910) was followed in 1920 by a more ambitious work with some Wagnerian traits, *Amaya*, and a successful zarzuela *El Caserio* ("The Hamlet") in 1926.

The early history of dramatic music in Portugal [59] is similar to that of Spain, except that there was no distinct national form of as great

57 See biography of De Falla (1876–1946) by R. Manuel.
58 See biography of Morera (1865–1942) by Iglesias.
59 Bibliography: Luper, "The Music of Portugal," in Chase, *Music of Spain*, chap. XVIII; Vieira, *Diccionario biographico de musicos portuguezes*; Fonseca Benevides, *O real theatro de S. Carlos de Lisboa*; Lavignac, *Encyclopédie*, Pt. I, Vol. IV, pp. 2422–35, 2447–57.

importance as the tonadilla. The first opera in Portuguese was *La vida do grande D. Quixote de la Mancha* (1733) by Antonio José da Silva (1705–1739), an isolated attempt which led to nothing. Italian opera came to Portugal as early as 1682, but its flourishing period began only about 1720. Of the Portuguese composers who devoted themselves to writing in the Italian style, the chief was Marcos Antonio Portugal,[60] whose thirty-five operas were widely performed in Europe in the late eighteenth and early nineteenth centuries. He was also the composer of twenty-one comic operas to Portuguese texts. Italian and French opera continued to dominate the Portuguese stage throughout the nineteenth century; Miguel Pereira's (1843–1901) opera *Eurico* (1870), with Italian text arranged from a Portuguese novel, is typical of this tendency. Native composers only occasionally adopted their own language or musical idiom, except for comic pieces. In this genre, however, there were successful works by Antonio Luiz Miró, d. 1853 (*A marqueza*, 1848); Guilherme Cossoul, 1828–1880 (*A cisterna do diablo*, "The Devil's Cistern," 1850); Francisco Alves Rente, 1851–1891 (*Verde gaio*, "Light Yellow," 1876); and Domingo Cyriaco de Cardoso, 1846–1900 (*O burro do Senhor Alcaide*, "The Mayor's Donkey," 1891). An outstanding nationalist composer was Alfredo Keil, of whose serious Portuguese operas *Serrana* (1899) was most frequently performed. The principal contemporary composer of operas in Portugal is Ruy Coelho, b. 1891 (*Belkiss*, 1938).

Opera in Latin America [61] has been for the most part only an off-

---

60 M. A. Portugal (1762–1830), after producing some operas at Lisbon, rose to fame in Italy from 1793 to 1799. He was conductor at Lisbon from 1799 to 1810, then fled to Brazil, where he remained the rest of his life. See study by Carvalhaes.

61 Chase, *A Guide to Latin-American Music* (1945). Publications of the Pan American Union, Washington, D.C.: *Music in Latin America* (1942); *The Music of Argentina*, by Albert T. Luper (1944); *The Music of Brazil*, by Albert T. Luper (1944). Periodicals: *Handbook of Latin American Studies* (Cambridge, Mass., annually from 1935); *Boletín latino-americano de música*, 5 vols. (Montevideo, 1935–1941); *Rivista brasileira de música* (quarterly, from 1934); special number of RM, February–March, 1940 ("La Musique dans les pays latins"). See further: Slonimsky, *Music of Latin America*; Chase, *The Music of Spain*; idem, articles with bibliographies in *Harvard Dictionary of Music* (by countries); Alfredo Fiorda Kelley, *Cronología de las óperas . . . etc. cantados en Buenos Aires* [1825–1933]; Almeida, *História da música brasileira* (2d ed., 1942); Cernicchiaro, *Storia della musica nel Brasile*; Ayesterán, *Crónica de una temporada musical en el Montevideo de 1830*; Abascal Brunet, *Apuntes para la historia del teatro en Chile*; Saldívar, *Historia de la música en México*; Galindo, *Nociones de historia de la música mejicana*; Mayer-Serra, *Panorama de la música mexicana*; Alarcón, "La ópera en Mexico," *Boletín del instituto mexicano de musicología* I (1940) 5–9; Maria y Campos, *Una temporada de opera italiana en Oaxaca* [1874–1875]; Tolón, *Operas cubanas y sus autores.*

shoot of Italian and Spanish opera. In the colonial period the missionaries promoted plays with music, and at larger centers (for example, Lima) there were performances of the works of Calderón and other Spanish dramatists with music. A few tonadillas were imported in the eighteenth century. There is an eighteenth-century opera, *La Partenope,* composed by Manuel de Sumaya and performed at Mexico City in 1711. Regular performances of opera began in many Latin-American countries during the second quarter of the nineteenth century. Brazil had a national Opera from 1857; a famous Brazilian composer was Antonio Carlos Gomez, some of whose operas used native subjects, though all were in an Italian style of music modeled on Verdi.[62] The same Italianism is found in Henrique Eulalio Gurjão (1833–1885), whose best-known opera was *Idalia* (1881). Leopoldo Miguez (1850–1902) was influenced by Wagner in *Os Saldunes* (1901). Even the so-called "nationalist" composer Alberto Nepomuceno (1864–1920) did not develop an independent musical style in his operas.

In Argentina the Italian influence was even stronger, though national subjects were occasionally used, as in *La indigena* (1862) by Wenceslao Fumi (1823–1880) and in *Pampa* (1897) and *Yupansky* (1899) by Arturo Berutti (1862–1938). Justin Clérice (1863–1908) won recognition in Europe for his French comic operas and ballets.

In Mexico, Italian operas were composed by Melesio Morales, 1838–1908 (*Ildegonda,* 1865), and works in the German romantic style by Ricardo Castro, 1864–1907 (*Atzimba; La leyenda de Rudel*). A distinguished national one-act opera, using popular melodies, was *Guatimotzin* (1871) by Aniceto Ortega (1823–1875).

Most of the favorite Spanish zarzuelas were immediately brought to the new world and inspired similar works by local composers in all Latin American countries. Thus the Venezuelan José Angel Montero (1839–1881) produced fifteen zarzuelas as well as an opera, *Virginia* (1873). In Colombia, zarzuelas and similar pieces were composed by Juan Crisóstomo Osorio y Ricaurte (1863–1887) and Santos Cifuentes (1870–1932); in Mexico there was a popular comic opera, *Keofar* (1893) by Felipe Villanueva. Other Latin American opera

[62] Gomez (1836–1896) was educated at Rio de Janeiro and Milan. His most famous opera, *Il Guarny* (1870), is still given in Italy and Brazil. See studies by Seidl, Marchant, and Andrade; also Correa de Azvedo, "Carlos Gomez," *Boletin latino-americano de música* III (1937) 83–87; Castro, *Carlo Gomez.*

composers in this period were: in Colombia, Augusto Azzali (*Lhidiac*, 1893) and José María Ponce de León, 1846–1882 (*Ester; Florinda*); in Peru, Daniel Alomias Robles, 1871–1942 (*Illa-Cori*), and Theodoro Valcárcel, 1902–1942 (*Suray-Surita*, ballet opera); in Chile, Eleodoro Ortiz de Zarate, b. 1865 (*La fioraia di Lugano*, 1895; Italian text); and in Cuba, Eduardo Sánches de Fuentes y Peláez, b. 1876 (*Dolorosa*, 1910; *Kabelia*, 1942).[63]

The twentieth-century national musical renaissance in Latin America has not brought forth operas comparable in either numbers or importance to the music produced in other forms. In Argentina, where there is more native opera than anywhere else, the Italian influence is still predominant. This is especially the case with Ettore Panizza (b. 1875), the dean of living Argentine opera composers, whose works include *Il fidanzato del mare* ("The Bridegroom of the Sea," 1897), *Medio evo latino* (1900; three one-act operas, each placed in a different Latin country and a different medieval century), *Aurora* (1908, commissioned for the opening of the new Teatro Colón at Buenos Aires), and *Bisanzio* (composed about 1925). Alfredo Schiuma's (b. 1885) Italian opera *Tabaré* (1925), closely patterned after Verdi's *Forza del destino*, has been very successful; a highly praised recent work of Schiuma is *Las Virgenes del sol* (1939).[64] A more definitely national group is represented by Felipe Boero (b. 1885) with his folk opera *El matrero* ("The Rogue," 1929). Others in this group are Pascual de Rogatis, b. 1881 (*Hemac*, 1916; *La novia del hereje*, "The Heretic's Bride," 1935), Raul Espoile, b. 1889 (*La ciudad roja*, "The Red City," 1938), and Enrique Casella, b. 1891 (*La tapera*, "The Ruin").

In Brazil the new nationalism is evident in the works of Oscar Lorenzo Fernandez, b. 1897 (*Malazarte*, 1941), Francisco Mignone (b. 1897), and Comargo Guarnieri, b. 1907 (one-act comic opera *Pedro Malazarte*, 1942). Heitor Villa-Lobos (b. 1881), the leading present-day South American composer, wrote five operas early in his career, but only one (*Izaht*, composed 1912–1914) has been performed, and that only in a concert version (1940).

63 See Chase, "Some Notes on Afro-Cuban Music and Dancing," *Inter-American Monthly* (Washington, D.C.) I, No. 8 (December, 1942) 32–33.
64 Ferrari Nicolay, "En torno a *Las Vírgenes*," *Estudios* (Buenos Aires) Año 29 (1939) tomo 62, pp. 29–46.

A recent Mexican opera is *Tata Vasca* (1941), by Miguel Bernal Jimenez (b. 1910).[65]

THE BRITISH ISLES [66] AND THE UNITED STATES OF AMERICA.—"English Opera—the darkest page of our musical history," wrote Henry Davey.[67] His despairing estimate holds with all force for the nineteenth century, when serious opera in England was universally understood to mean Italian opera, that "exotic and irrational entertainment" which the British had been patronizing ever since the days of Dr. Johnson.[68] Almost the only English musical stage works to have any success at all in the nineteenth century were those of the light variety—Balfe, Wallace, Benedict, and (later) Sullivan. The Carl Rosa Opera Company, beginning in 1875, commissioned a few English works, including some from Arthur Goring Thomas, 1851–1892 (*Esmeralda*, 1883; *Nadeshda*, 1885) and the zealous Wagner apostle Frederick Corder (1852–1932). Sullivan's *Ivanhoe* made a great stir at its first production in 1891 but has long since disappeared from the stage. Other operas of a romantic cast were produced by Cowen, Mackenzie, and Stanford.[69] Mackenzie's most popular opera was *The Cricket on the Hearth* (composed about 1900, performed 1914). Stanford attempted to create an English *Meistersinger* in *The Canterbury Pilgrims* (1884), but is best known for his comic opera *Shamus O'Brien* (1896); his *Much Ado about Nothing* made a favorable impression at its first performance in 1901 and was revived in 1935. A later work, *The Critic* (1916), is said to be equally deserving. One of the best English opera composers in the early twentieth century was Dame Ethel Smyth (1858–1944), whose *Wreckers* (first given at Leipzig in 1906 in German as *Strandrecht*) is a very effective work;

---

[65] See Barros Sierra, "*Tata Vasco* y su partitura," *Romance* II (April, [1941]) 23.

[66] Streatfeild, *Musiciens anglais contemporains* (1913); Holbrooke, *Contemporary British Composers* (1925).

[67] *History of English Music*, 2d ed., p. 442.

[68] Cf. Mapleson, *Memoirs*, and Carlyle, "The Opera," in *Critical and Miscellaneous Essays* IV, 397–403.

[69] Sir Frederic Hymen Cowen (1852–1935) wrote four operas and two operettas, as well as many symphonies and oratorios, but is remembered chiefly for some of his shorter pieces. See his memoirs, *My Art and My Friends*.

Sir Alexander Campbell Mackenzie (1847–1935), noted conductor and educator, wrote four operas and an operetta, as well as many orchestral pieces.

Sir Charles Villiers Stanford (1852–1924) wrote seven operas and many orchestral works and edited several volumes of Irish folk songs. See studies by Fuller-Maitland (*The Music of Parry and Stanford*, chap. 9) and H. P. Greene.

a comic opera in the tradition of Sullivan, *The Boatswain's Mate* (1916), has been frequently performed in England.[70]

Frederick Delius [71] composed six operas, the best of which is *A Village Romeo and Juliet*, first performed (in German) at Berlin in 1907. This work, which from its story might almost have been entitled "A Village Tristan and Isolde," is full of lovely music in a late romantic style somewhat influenced by impressionism—rich textured, chromatic, with long expressive melodic lines for the solo voices and some fine choral scenes. The use of Celtic folk-song idiom, as in Vreli's song at the opening of scene 4, is also worthy of remark. The popular orchestral selection *"The Walk to Paradise Gardens"* (from the end of scene 5) may be taken as typical of the general style.

The revival of Celtic literature in the late nineteenth and early twentieth centuries led to a number of operas on Celtic legends. Most notable among these was Josef Holbrooke's mythological Welsh trilogy *The Cauldron of Anwen*,[72] broadly conceived along Wagnerian lines and written in a neo-romantic musical style strongly influenced by that of Wagner. Welsh subjects have also attracted Joseph Parry (1841–1903), Granville Bantock, 1868–1946 (*Caedmar*, 1892; *The Seal Woman*, 1924), and George Lloyd (b. 1913). Scottish stories or legends have been used by Hamish MacCunn, 1868–1916 (*Jeanie Deans*, 1894; *Diarmid*, 1897), and Irish by Robert O'Dwyer, b. 1860 (*Eithne*, 1910), and Geoffrey Palmer, b. 1882 (*Sruth na Maoile*, "The Sea of Moyle," 1923).

English operetta and light opera of this period were represented by Alfred Cellier (1844–1891); Edward Soloman (1853–1895); George H. Clutsam (b. 1866); Sidney Jones 1869–1946 (*The Geisha*, 1896); Edward German, 1862–1936 (*Merrie England*, 1902); Ivan Caryll, 1861–1921 (*The Duchess of Dantzic*, 1903); Edward Naylor, 1867–1934 (*The Angelus*, 1909); and Hubert Bath, 1883–1945 (*Bubbles*, 1923). Recent comic operas by English composers are Lord Berners's (b. 1883) *Carosse du Saint-Sacrement* (1923) and Arthur Benjamin's (b. 1893) *The Devil Take Her* (1931)—both witty one-act pieces in a fluent modern style.

In the present century many serious operas have been written for the English stage, though most have met with only indifference from the general public. Nearly all these works are distinguished by good

[70] See Capell, "Dame Ethel Smyth's Operas at Covent Garden," *Monthly Musical Record* LIII (1923) 197–98; also the composer's own writings, especially *Impressions That Remained* (1919).

[71] See biography of Delius (1862–1934) by Heseltine.

[72] See G. Lowe's biography of Holbrooke (b. 1878). The three operas of his trilogy were performed as follows: *The Children of Don*, 1912; *Dylan, Son of the Wave*, 1914; *Bronwen*, 1929.

literary quality and patent artistic sincerity in the musical settings, and the composers deserve recognition for having labored in the face of such discouraging conditions. John Edmund Barkworth's (1858–1929) *Romeo and Juliet* (1916) is the most important of his three operas. Alick Maclean's (1872–1936) *Quentin Durward,* published in 1894, was produced in 1920, and Robert Ernest Bryson's (1867–1942) *The Leper's Flute* in 1926. Philip Napier Miles [73] was active in organizing opera productions in England and wrote two operas (*Markheim,* 1924; *Westward Ho,* 1913). Effective in performance, though simple and conservative in musical style, are the operas of Nicholas Comyn Gatty (b. 1874): *Duke or Devil* (1909), the three-act romantic Shakespearean *Tempest* (1920), and the charming fairy opera *Prince Ferelon* (1919–1921). Eugène Goossens (b. 1893) has had considerable success with two operas in modern idiom, both to librettos by Arnold Bennett: *Judith* (1929) and *Don Juan de Mañera* (1937).

Other composers in this group are Sir Donald Francis Tovey, 1875–1940 (*The Bride of Dionysus,* 1929); Colin Macleod Campbell, b. 1890 (*Thais and Talmaae,* 1921); Lawrance Arthur Collingwood, b. 1887 (*Macbeth,* 1934); and the distinguished conductor Albert Coates, b. 1882 (*Samuel Pepys,* 1929; *Pickwick,* 1936.)

A recent movement has developed from interest in a type of opera adapted to limited conditions of performance and aiming to revive the chamber-opera spirit of Blow and Purcell. The leader of this revival was a disciple of Wagner's theories of the music drama, and one who in his own music followed a frankly romantic line during a period when romanticism was decidedly unfashionable. Rutland Boughton [74] dreamed of founding a British Bayreuth at Glastonbury, where festivals were organized in 1914 and for several years after the First World War. The project was finally abandoned, but its influence remained. Of Boughton's own nine operas, the most successful was *The Immortal Hour* (1914); many of his librettos were based on Arthurian legend. Equally national in subject, but of less heroic scope, were chamber operas by such composers as Charles Wood (1866–1926), Cyril Bradley Rootham (1875–1938), Martin Shaw

---

[73] On Napier Miles (1865–1935) see a study by Colles, M&L XVII (1936) 357–67.
[74] On Boughton (b. 1878) see his own books listed in bibliography, and Antcliffe, "The British School of Music-Drama," MQ IV (1918) 117–27.

(b. 1876), and Cecil Armstrong Gibbs (b. 1889). To these may be added from a younger generation the name of Benjamin Britten (b. 1913), whose *Paul Bunyan* was produced at Columbia University, New York, in 1941. Performances of his *Peter Grimes* at Tanglewood in 1946 have attracted much attention; his most recent opera is *The Rape of Lucretia* (1946).

The two most notable English composers of the early twentieth century, Gustav Holst and Ralph Vaughan Williams,[75] have made significant contributions to opera. Holst's *Savitri* (composed 1908, performed 1916) is a chamber opera of exquisite tenderness and simple emotion, in a musical style which suggests the Eastern setting of the story without attempt at literal imitation of Hindu melodies, and which contains some beautiful writing for women's chorus. Holst's principal opera, a one-act comedy *The Perfect Fool*, had very successful performances at Covent Garden in 1923; the music shows the composer fully emancipated from the neo-Wagnerian tendencies of his earlier dramatic works. *At the Boar's Head* (1925) is a Shakespearean intermezzo for *Henry IV*, a jolly work made up very largely of traditional English tunes, somewhat in the manner of ballad opera. The influence of these works is not to be reckoned so much by their outward success as by the fact that they represent the serious, original, and uncompromising efforts of a first-rank English composer in the restricted and thankless field of native opera. Much the same may be said of Vaughan Williams' dramatic works. *The Shepherds of the Delectable Mountains*, a pastoral episode after Bunyan, has been frequently revived in England since its first performance in 1922. *Hugh the Drover, or Love in the Stocks* (1924) is a ballad-type opera with continuous music, containing allusions to a number of traditional tunes without direct quotation, and as thoroughly English in spirit as any of Gilbert and Sullivan. *Sir John in Love* (1929), based on Shakespeare's *Merry Wives of Windsor*, is the composer's biggest work for the stage (four acts); the music is similar to that of *Hugh the Drover*, but more highly developed both formally and harmonically—a truly English *Falstaff* not unworthy of comparison with Verdi's Italian one. The Gilbert and Sullivan tradition

75 On Holst (1874–1934) see biography by his daughter, Imogen Holst; on Vaughan Williams (b. 1872) see Howes, *The Dramatic Works of Ralph Vaughan Williams*.

is carried on in *The Poisoned Kiss* (1936), a tuneful comic opera with spoken dialogue. *Riders to the Sea* (1937) is a restrained but moving setting of Synge's play, in neomodal style with much parallel chord progression and with a subdued intensity of feeling reminiscent of the composer's well-known song cycle, *On Wenlock Edge*.

The early history of opera in the United States of America [76] is similar to that in the other nations of the Western Hemisphere. It begins in colonial times with the importation of comic operas from Europe (in this case English ballad opera instead of the Spanish zarzuela); during the nineteenth century fashion favors alternately Italian opera, French grand opera, and German music drama. Tentative and unsuccessful efforts are made by native composers to imitate the musical style currently in vogue, sometimes applying it to "American" subjects, the Indians and the Puritan colonists being the two commonest sources of material for librettos. Prizes are offered and awarded; new operas by American composers are produced with great fanfare, given a few performances, then shelved and forgotten. There is no continuously subsidized theatre specifically for American opera, and in the absence of any assurance of adequate performance no first-rate composer will undertake to write one unless he is motivated by an irresistible inner urge or is an inveterate optimist. A few experimental works on a small scale are produced, but the American public at large shows little interest in them, preferring to hear *La Bohême* or *Die Walküre* in sumptuous settings and sung by expensive stars. In a word, American opera at the present time is in much the same state as English opera: an unrealized ideal. All the more honor, then, to those composers who have essayed this difficult field without much hope of reward or recognition. It must be added, unfortunately, that in many cases the honor is due for good intentions rather than actual results, though one should not too severely reproach American opera composers for shortcomings rising only out of their lack of experience and limited opportunity to hear their own works in performance.

[76] General bibliography: histories of American music by Ritter (to 1880), Elson, and Howard; *Dictionary of American Biography;* Howard, *Our Contemporary Composers:* Hipsher, *American Opera and Its Composers;* Graf, *The Opera and Its Future in America;* Mattfeld, *A Hundred Years of Grand Opera in New York;* Kolodin, *The Metropolitan Opera;* Gatti-Casazza, *Memories of the Opera;* Moore, *Forty Years of Opera in Chicago;* Carson, *St. Louis Goes to the Opera.*

It is possible that the first opera performance in the United States took place as early as 1703, but the earliest date which can yet be substantiated is 1735, when *Flora, or Hob in the Well,* a ballad opera, was presented at Charleston, South Carolina. *The Begger's Opera* and several similar works were played in New York in 1750–1751, and a like repertoire was heard in Annapolis and Upper Marlborough, Maryland, in 1752. In the same year ballad operas were given at Williamsburg, Virginia. Philadelphia followed two years later. All during the latter half of the eighteenth century there were seasons of opera, fairly regularly at New York and sporadically at other places; the total number in proportion to the population was actually greater than at any period since. Most of the works so presented were English comic operas (Shield, Storace, Dibdin, and others), but there were also a few French opéras comiques (Grétry, Monsigny, Philidor), usually in translation and with the music more or less extensively altered and adapted by English and American arrangers, besides many pantomimes and ballets. French opera, both grand and comic, flourished at New Orleans from 1791 until the Civil War and even afterwards. The first season of regular Italian opera in New York was in 1825. From that time on, the uneven career of foreign opera in the United States becomes too complicated to follow here even in outline, the more since our chief concern is not with "opera in America" but "American opera."

The known American operas of the eighteenth century have been thoroughly studied by Oscar G. T. Sonneck.[77] Many of these were of the type of *The Beggar's Opera,* with characters and dialects appropriate to the American locale. Toward the end of the century there were imitations and adaptations of popular plays, such as *The Archers* (1796), with music by the English-born composer Benjamin Carr (1769?–1831), which plainly was inspired by Schiller's *Tell;* in 1797 there was a melodrama, *Ariadne Abandoned,* probably imitated from Benda. Still other "operas" were on patriotic themes, with battle scenes and allegorical tableaux. None of these pieces had continuous music; most, in fact, were merely plays with incidental songs. The composers (or arrangers) included Francis Hopkinson (*The*

---

[77] "Early American Operas," SIMG VI (1904–1905) 428–95; also in his *Miscellaneous Studies,* pp. 16–92. See also Sonneck's *Bibliography of Early Secular American Music* (new ed., 1945); *Early Concert Life in America; Early Opera in America;* and further, Wegelin, *Micah Hawkins; idem, Early American Plays;* Seilhamer, *History of the American Theatre.*

Temple of Minerva, 1781),[78] James Hewitt (*Tammany,* 1794),[79] and Victor Pelissier (*Edwin and Angelina,* 1796).[80]

So little is known about the history of American music in the first half of the nineteenth century that it is impossible to make any definitive statement about American opera in this period. So far as present information goes there were no operatic works by American composers, except for the plays-with-incidental-music type, until 1845. In that year was produced at Philadelphia "the first publicly performed grand opera written by a native American," *Leonora,* by William Henry Fry [81]—a work of considerable competence and musical interest, modeled on the styles of Donizetti and Meyerbeer. Fry's next opera, *Notre-Dame de Paris,* was given at Philadelphia in 1864. Another American composer of this period was George Frederick Bristow,[82] whose *Rip Van Winkle* (New York, 1855) is arranged from Irving's tale with added love scenes and other episodes. There is some spoken dialogue; the music, unfortunately, is completely conventional and undistinguished, a lame imitation of the fashionable European light-opera style.

Of the many German-descended or German-trained American composers in the later nineteenth century, the most important in the field of opera was Walter Damrosch,[83] whose first success with *The Scarlet Letter* (1896) was hardly equaled by his two later works, *Cyrano* (1913) and *The Man without a Country* (1937). Damrosch's music is pleasantly put together, technically well fashioned, but does not depart from the style of late nineteenth-century German romanticism. A rather more original score, though one still strongly suggestive of Wagner, is John Knowles Paine's *Azara* (published 1901; performed only in concert version, 1907).[84]

---

78 On Hopkinson (1737–1791) see study by Sonneck.

79 Hewitt (1770–1827) was born in England and came to New York in 1792. He wrote music (almost none preserved) for at least seven operas. See Howard, "The Hewitt Family in American Music," MQ XVII (1931) 25–39.

80 The dates of Pelissier's birth and death are not known. He was undoubtedly a native of France, coming to America in 1792 or earlier.

81 Fry (1813–1864) was one of the earliest active propagandists for American music. He composed four program symphonies and several choral works in addition to his two operas. See Upton, *The Musical Works of William Henry Fry.*

82 Bristow (1825–1898) wrote several large choral and symphonic works, two quartets, and many smaller pieces.

83 Damrosch was born in Germany in 1862 but has lived most of his life in the United States. See his autobiography, *My Musical Life.*

84 Paine (1839–1906), the first professor of music in an American university (Harvard, 1875), composed many choral, symphonic, and chamber works.

Two earlier opera composers of German birth were Eduard Sobolewski, 1808–1872 (*Mohega*, Milwaukee, 1859) and Johann Heinrich Bonawitz, 1839–1917 (*Ostrolenka*, Philadelphia, 1874). With this group may also be listed the Americans Frederick Grant Gleason, 1848–1903 (*Otho Visconti*, Chicago, 1907) and Louis Adolphe Coerne, 1870–1922, of whose three operas only *Zenobia* was ever performed (Bremen, 1905). To the same generation as Coerne belong Arthur Finley Nevin, 1871–1943 (*Poia*, Berlin, 1910; *The Daughter of the Forest*, Chicago, 1918), Joseph Carl Breil, 1870–1926 (*The Legend*, New York, 1919), and John Adam Hugo, b. 1873 (*The Temple Dancer*, New York, 1919).

The German influence was still preponderant in American music in the early part of the twentieth century, but by this time composers were more thoroughly trained, more ambitious, versatile, and productive and spoke a more authoritative musical language. Nevertheless it is significant that neither of the two leading figures in this generation, Loeffler and MacDowell, composed an opera. The most important dramatic composers were Converse, Hadley, and Parker.[85] Converse's *The Pipe of Desire* (Boston, 1906) was the first American opera ever to be produced at the Metropolitan (1910); it is a pleasant and tuneful score showing some impressionist influence. Another opera, *The Sacrifice*, was presented at Boston in 1911. Hadley's chief successes, in a sound conservative style, were *Azora, Daughter of Montezuma* (Chicago, 1917) and *Cleopatra's Night* (New York, 1920).

Horatio Parker's *Mona* (New York, 1912) and *Fairyland* (Los Angeles, 1915), each of which won a ten-thousand-dollar prize, are still regarded by many as the most significant American operas, important works which have been unjustly neglected. The neglect is certainly not due to any technical shortcomings of the scores, which are sound in craftsmanship, large in conception, distinguished in musical ideas, and excellent in theatrical effects. But the librettos are definitely dated: *Mona*, a sufficiently good drama in essence, is markedly romantic in plot and language, with the scene laid in medieval

[85] Frederick Shepherd Converse (1871–1940) wrote four operas (two not performed) and much orchestral and choral music.

　　Henry Kimball Hadley (1871–1937) wrote six operas, four symphonies, many overtures, and other orchestral and choral works. See biography by Boardman, and study by Berthoud.

　　Horatio William Parker (1863–1919) was, like Paine, Converse, and Hadley, of New England birth and training and studied in Germany. Most of his music is choral (oratorio, *Hora Novissima*, 1893). See Chadwick, *Horatio Parker;* Smith, "A Study of Horatio Parker," MQ XVI (1930) 153–69; and memoir by Semler.

Britain and the whole obviously owing much to *Tristan und Isolde*. *Fairyland* is one of those combinations of whimsy, symbolism, and vague pantheistic aspiration such as are found in the fairy operas of Rimsky-Korsakov or in Converse's *Pipe of Desire*. Parker's music is likewise typical of the late romantic period. *Mona* is a slightly modernized *Tristan*, with the same sort of continuous symphonic structure, system of leitmotifs, opulent harmony, chromatic melody, and avoidance of perfect cadences which characterize its model; *Fairyland* is somewhat lighter in texture and more diatonic in harmony —Wagner leavened by a dash of late Strauss. Musically, the gravest accusation that can be made against either opera is that the same things had been said before; and it may be regretted that these works had the misfortune to come at a moment when tastes in musical matters were on the verge of a radical change.

Of later American operas in a conservative style, designed for full-scale production, the most successful were two by Deems Taylor: [86] *The King's Henchman* (New York, 1927) and *Peter Ibbetson* (New York, 1931), smooth, expert works in a mild late-romantic style with modern trimmings, well molded to the taste of that large majority of the opera-going public who are pleased with expressive melodies and sensuous harmonies which pleasantly stimulate without disturbing. Other American operas at the Metropolitan have been much less enthusiastically received (for example, Richard Hageman's *Caponsacchi*, 1937).[87] A brief popular success was obtained by the Italian-born Gian-Carlo Menotti's opera buffa *Amelia Goes to the Ball* (1937).[88] Among the American operas which have been produced under respectable auspices and gone their way without leaving a mark may be mentioned Ernest Carter's *The White Bird* (Chicago, 1930), Forrest Hamilton's jazzy *Camille* (Chicago, 1930), and John

[86] Joseph Deems Taylor (b. 1885) is known for his orchestral suite *Through the Looking Glass* (1922) and for cantatas, as well as his operas which have received more performances at the Metropolitan than those of any other American composer. See study by J. T. Howard.

[87] Hageman was born in Holland in 1882 and has been active in the United States as accompanist and opera conductor since 1906. *Caponsacchi* was first performed in German translation as *Tragödie in Arezzo* at Freiburg in 1932. The libretto is from Browning's *The Ring and the Book*.

[88] Menotti was born in Italy in 1911. *Amelia,* his first opera, was performed in Philadelphia and at the Metropolitan in 1938. He composed a similar work for radio (*The Old Maid and the Thief,* 1939), a serious grand opera, *The Island God* (1942), and a chamber opera, *The Medium* (1946).

Laurence Seymour's prize-winning *In the Pasha's Garden* (New York, 1935).[89]

National scenes and subjects, as might be expected, have been frequently tried by composers. Charles Wakefield Cadman's *The Robin Woman (Shanewis)*,[90] given at the Metropolitan in 1918, uses a number of authentic Indian tunes and has an attractive, if superficial, melodic vein, but is very slight in substance and awkward in dramatic details. The same composer's *A Witch of Salem* (Chicago, 1926) has been frequently given in the United States.

The best American historical opera to date is Hanson's *Merry Mount* (New York, 1934),[91] a work incorporating many ballets and choruses in a wild, implausible story of Puritan New England. It may be the extravagance of the libretto which has interfered with the full success of *Merry Mount*, or it may be a somewhat stiff, oratorio-like, undramatic quality in much of the music. The harmonic style is generally static; the chords are built on pandiatonic principles (with occasional bitonality) and there is much use of modal effects and parallel progressions. The melodies likewise are often static, consisting of reiterated phrases within a narrow range. There are four distinct idioms: the psalmlike choruses of the Puritans; the madrigalesque worldly songs of the revelers (beginning of Act II); the beautifully sensuous love music of Bradford's aria "Rise up, my love" and the duet which is its continuation; and the bacchanalian strains for the evil spirits of the "Walpurgisnacht" ballet in Act II. The music is able, serious, and sincere; there is no compromise of principle, no writing down to a supposed lower taste of an opera audience. The whole is good enough to make one sad at the thought of what American composers might do in opera if they had more incentive to produce and more opportunity to try out their works in actual performance.

In the period following the First World War American composers, in common with those of other nationalities, produced many operas which, for lack of a better common descriptive term, may be called

---

[89] For fuller lists see Hipsher, *American Opera*, or Howard, *Our Contemporary Composers*.

[90] Cadman (1881–1946) wrote six operas and seven operettas, numerous orchestral suites, cantatas, songs, etc.

[91] Howard Hanson (b. 1896), director of the Eastman School of Music, is widely known for his symphonies, choral works, and chamber music. *Merry Mount* is his only opera. See Tuthill, "Howard Hanson," MQ XXII (1936) 140–53.

"experimental." Such a work was George Antheil's *Transatlantic* (Frankfurt, Germany, 1930),[92] which uses jazz tunes and odd mechanical effects in a fantastic, satirical plot similar to Křenek's *Jonny spielt auf*. Louis Gruenberg's *Emperor Jones* (New York, 1933),[93] based on Eugene O'Neill's play, cleverly exploits a neoprimitive orchestra with percussive drum rhythms and choral interludes in an exciting drama. Perhaps the most publicized of all American experimental operas is Virgil Thomson's *Four Saints in Three Acts* (Hartford, 1934),[94] on a libretto by Gertrude Stein, in a sophisticatedly simple musical style and with the melodic lines fitted to the text with exceptional sensitivity.

In view of the very limited opportunities for the production of large operas it is natural that in America, as in England, there is considerable interest in chamber opera of various kinds. An early work in this field is Lazare Saminsky's *Gagliarda of a Merry Plague* (New York, 1925).[95] Marc Blitzstein[96] has also produced a number of chamber operas in New York. The first of these to attract wide notice was *The Cradle Will Rock* (1937), a leftist propaganda play, alternating spoken dialogue, recitatives, and singable tunes in a cultured and clever jazz idiom. *No for an Answer* (1941) has relatively more music (including some very effective choral portions) and a wider range of characterization and feeling, though still based for the most part on the popular song style. The Juilliard Music School in New York has sponsored several chamber operas, including works by Gruenberg (*Jack and the Beanstalk*, 1931), Antheil (*Helen Retires*, 1934), Robert Russell Bennet (*Maria Malibran*, 1935), Albert Stoes-

[92] Antheil (b. 1900) has written much music for the stage and screen, three symphonies, and other orchestral and chamber works. See Pound, *Antheil and the Treatise of Harmony;* Thompson, "George Antheil," MMus VIII, No. 4 (May–June, 1931) 17–27; Wiesengrund-Adorno, critical review of *Transatlantic,* MMus VII, No. 4 (June–July, 1930) 38–41.
[93] Gruenberg (b. 1884) has written much orchestral and chamber music, but is best known for his stage works and the cantata *Daniel Jazz* (1923).
[94] Virgil Thomson (b. 1896) has written many articles and reviews and two books: *The State of Music* (1939) and *The Musical Scene* (1945): *Four Saints* is his best known composition. See Seldes, "Delight in the Theatre," MMus XI, No. 3 (March–April, 1934) 138–41.
[95] Saminsky (b. 1882) has composed five symphonies and other orchestral works; he has written many articles and two books (*Music of Our Day,* 1932). See Pisk, "Lazare Saminsky," *The Chesterian* XX (1938–39) 74–78.
[96] Blitzstein (b. 1905) has written six stage works and a number of songs and chamber pieces, besides many articles for periodicals. See Barlow, "Blitzstein's Answer," MMus XVIII, No. 2 (January–February, 1941) 81–83.

sel (*Garrick,* 1937), and Beryl Rubinstein (*The Sleeping Beauty,* 1938). Still other "school operas," suitable for use by semiprofessional or amateur groups, are Aaron Copland's *The Second Hurricane* (New York, 1937), Douglas Moore's *The Devil and Daniel Webster* (New York, 1939), Randall Thompson's *Solomon and Balkis* (Cambridge, 1942), Ernst Bacon's *A Tree on the Plains* (1942), and Normand Lockwood's *The Scarecrow* (1945).[97] As long as present conditions prevail it seems likely that the best possibilities for both the development of American opera composers and the education of audiences will be found in works of the chamber-opera type.

American operetta and comic opera may be traced from the works of the German-born Julius Eichberg, 1824–1893 (*The Doctor of Alcantara,* Boston, 1862) through Dudley Buck, 1839–1909 (*Deseret,* New York, 1880), Edgar Stillman Kelley, 1857–1944 (*Puritania,* Boston, 1892), George Whitefield Chadwick, 1854–1931 (*Tabasco,* Boston, 1894), and John Philip Sousa, 1854–1923 (*El Capitan,* Boston, 1896) to a climax in the works of Reginald de Koven, 1859–1920 (*Robin Hood,* Chicago, 1890) and Victor Herbert, 1859–1924 (*Babes in Toyland,* 1903). Both De Koven and Herbert attempted grand opera, but comparatively without success in either case (De Koven's *The Canterbury Pilgrims,* New York, 1917, and *Rip van Winkle,* Chicago, 1920; Herbert's *Natoma,* Philadelphia, 1911, and *Madeleine,* New York, 1914).

In light opera and musical comedy after the First World War the two leading figures were Jerome Kern, 1885–1945 (*Sally,* 1920) and George Gershwin, 1898–1937 (*Of Thee I Sing,* 1931). Each of these composers has written one distinguished work in more serious style: Kern's *Showboat* (1928) and Gershwin's *Porgy and Bess* (1935).[98] These widely popular works are practically American folk operas.

[97] Copland (b. 1900) is one of the best known contemporary American composers. His book *Our New Music* (1941) has a very discerning chapter on the opera music of Thomson and Blitzstein.

Moore (b. 1893) is the composer of three chamber operas and several symphonic works which have been frequently performed.

Thompson (b. 1899) is a distinguished composer of choral and symphonic music. *Solomon and Balkis* is his only opera.

Bacon (b. 1898) is a pianist, conductor, and the composer of several symphonic works.

Normand Lockwood (b. 1906) is particularly noted in the field of vocal and choral music.

[98] See review by Virgil Thomson, MMus XIII, No. 1 (November–December, 1935) 13–19.

28

Opera between Two Wars

THE MOST RECENT EVENTS ARE NOTORI-
ously the most difficult to set in historical order. This is especially the
case with music in the period from the end of the First to the beginning of the Second World War, when so many apparently immutable
principles were being called in question and when for a time it
seemed almost incumbent on every composer to invent a new style
before he could begin to write music. It was only natural that the
opera, like all other forms, should be strongly affected by these new
currents, and that a great many works of an experimental nature
should be produced, particularly where economic and social conditions were favorable for such experimental work on a full scale, as in
Germany during the 1920's and in France for a somewhat longer
period. The revival of chamber opera was also a potent factor in
encouraging new dramatic and musical devices, since chamber operas
could be produced at less financial risk, and thus serve as a kind of
laboratory for new ideas. On the other hand, there are many forces
which always tend to make opera conservative, chief of which is the
cost of production (as compared with solo, chamber, or even symphonic music) and the consequent necessity of appealing to a large
public. Though it may be true that opera is the ideal medium through
which to introduce new musical ideas to the masses,[1] yet in practice
it has usually been found that during an unsettled era the masses are
uninterested in advanced notions and prefer their opera in a more
familiar idiom. Thus during the period under consideration there
was a considerable proportion of opera in musical and dramatic
styles which did not pretend to be radical in any respect, and which
advanced beyond the styles of the immediately preceding decade
either not at all, or else only slightly and in a direction easily to be
understood by the public. Some such works we have already noticed,
such as those of Deems Taylor in the United States, Richard Strauss

[1] Cf. George Antheil, MMus VII, No. 4 (June–July 1930) 11–16, and XI, No. 2 (January–
February, 1934) 89–94.

in Germany, and in general the later operas of established older composers. But there were other men, some old, some young, who of deliberate choice wrote conservatively; and not all these are negligible figures. Let us therefore first turn our attention to the progress of what may be called "orthodox" opera in the three principal operatic countries, Italy, France, and Germany.

One of the leading composers in Italy is Franco Alfano,[2] the choice of whom to complete Puccini's *Turandot* is significant of his historical position as a continuator of the main Italian opera tradition. Alfano had become known as early as 1904 with his *Risurrezione* ("Resurrection"), but his two principal works are the heavily tragic *Leggenda di Sakuntala* (1921) and the lyrical comedy *Madonna imperia* (1927). The latter may be taken as an example of his style. It is on a charming Boccaccio-like libretto (by Arthur Rossato) with neo-Puccinian music. The voice lines alternate smoothly between melodic phrases and a most flexible, lively, and expressive arioso, supported by luscious and delicate harmonies not unlike Ravel in many respects (complex key relationships, continual chromaticism, parallelism) and with beautiful impressionistic orchestration—a perfect match for the refinedly voluptuous text (Example 123). Alfano's *L'ultimo Lord* ("The Last Lord," 1930) is in a light, vivacious comic style, with a modern scene.

The operas of Ildebrando Pizzetti[3] are less conventional than those of Alfano but nevertheless do not attempt any radical reforms. One of Pizzetti's salient characteristics is his extensive use of polyphonic choruses, especially at the dramatic climaxes. This is seen already in his first opera *Fedra* (1915; text by D'Annunzio) and likewise in *Dèbora e Jaéle* (1922). These are his two most important stage works. The solo singing in both is in a close-packed, tense recitative, with occasional short melodic fragments closely molded to the text. The orchestra furnishes continuous musical support, full textured and expertly varied in color, a mosaic of motifs but without the systematic recurrences characteristic of the old leitmotif system. The

2 Alfano (b. 1876) has composed little except opera music. See Gatti, "Franco Alfano," MQ IX (1923) 556–77; *idem,* "Recent Italian Operas," MQ XXIII (1937) 77–88; Della Corte, *Rittrato di Franco Alfano.*

3 Pizzetti (b. 1880) has composed principally choral works and incidental music for plays in addition to his eight operas. See study by Gatti; also De'Paoli, "Pizzetti's Fra Gherardo," MMus VI, No. 2 (January–February, 1929) 39–42.

MADONNA IMPERIA

Ex.123.

Alfano

Co - me u - na stol - ta fan - ciul - la   che ha so - gna - to ca -

- rez - ze....   e si sve - glia in do - lo - - - - - -

- - - - re....   Chis - sà   per - chè   o mio dol - ce ri -

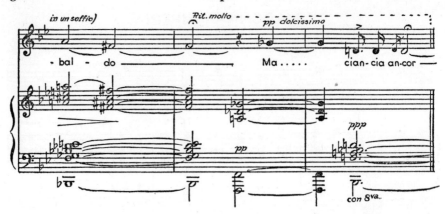

harmonies are late romantic rather than modernistic, with impressionist touches, strongly dramatic and always at high emotional tension. In *Fra Gherardo* (1928) Pizzetti attempted to introduce lyrical portions in the manner of nineteenth-century opera, but the result (perhaps partly due to the weak libretto) was a comparatively uninteresting hybrid. Of Pizzetti's later works *Orsèolo* (1935) has had some success in Italy, but not elsewhere.

A composer of decidedly prewar style was Ottorino Respighi,[4] though his best stage works were composed in the postwar period: the comic, colorful *Belfagor* (1923), *La campana sommersa* ("The Sunken Bell," 1927), the spectacular biblical ballet *Belkis, regina di Saba* (1930), the mystery play *Maria Egiziaca* (New York, 1932), and especially *La fiamma* ("The Flame," 1934) with its sumptuous orchestral texture. Ricardo Pick-Mangiagalli (b. 1862) has had some successful opera performances at Rome. The operas of Felice Lattuada (b. 1882) are conventional in the main, though the composer "distinguishes himself by an exuberance which sometimes attains its effect."[5] His *Preziose ridicole* (after Molière) was heard at the Metropolitan in 1930. Adriano Lualdi (b. 1887), experienced conductor and important musical official in Fascist Italy, wrote his most popular opera, *La figlia del re* ("The King's Daughter"), in 1922. The most prolific of younger Italian opera composers seems to be

4 Respighi (1879–1936) is best known for his symphonic poems and other instrumental works, also a few songs. He was the greatest master of orchestral color of his generation in Italy. He composed eight operas and several ballets. See biography by De Rensis.
5 G. Gatti, MMus XI, No. 4 (May–June, 1934) 216.

Lodovico Rocca (b. 1895); his best-known work, *Il dibuc* (1934), contains important choral sections.

In France the line of demarcation between prewar and postwar opera is much more clearly drawn than in either Italy or Germany. Strictly speaking, there are no important operas of a genuinely conservative type in France after the war, with the possible exception of Marcel Delannoy's (b. 1898) *Poirier de misère* (1927); there are, however, some works of a neoclassical nature which have a deceptive old-fashioned appearance, such as Henri Sauget's operetta *Le Plumet du colonel* (1925) and his opera *La Chartreuse de Parme*. Continuity with the past is generally most apparent in comic opera; some successful composers in this field were Alfred Bachelet (1864–1944) with *Quand le cloche sonnera* ("When the Clock Strikes," 1922); Charles Gaston Levadé (b. 1869) with *La Rôtisserie de la reine Pédauque* ("Queen Pédauque's Cook Shop," 1920) and *Le Peau de chagrin* ("The Shagreen Pelt," 1929); Marcel Samuel-Rousseau (b. 1882) with *Le Hulla* (1923) and *Le Bon Roi Dagobert* ("Good King Dagobert," 1927); and Arthur Honegger with *Les Aventures du roi Pausole* (1930). Perhaps the best comic operas of this period are by Jacques Ibert.[6] His *Angélique* (1927) is a witty one-act farce with spoken dialogue. The music is unpretentious, frankly of the entertainment variety, and very well adapted to this aim; it is in Ibert's scintillating epigrammatic manner, using polytonal effects, dance rhythms, and banal melodies dressed up with dissonant chords or skeleton-like harmonies, as in the chanson "Pauvre Madame Boniface" (Example 124), which is in the never-dying spirit of the old Paris vaudevilles. Ibert's later operatic works include *Le Roi d'Yvetot* (1930) and *L'Aiglon* (1937, in collaboration with Honegger).

Opera in Germany during the interwar years was strongly affected by the economic collapse of the late 1920's and the rise to power of the National Socialist regime in 1933; the former event put an end to a lush era of experimenting, and the latter officially discouraged all types of "modern" music. Therefore, German conservative composers in this period tend to divide into two groups: the first, which may be called "conservative by conviction," is made up of composers like Pfitzner, Strauss, and Schreker, whose style had already been

---

[6] Ibert (b. 1890) is noted especially for his ballets, cinema music, chamber works, and songs, as well as some half-dozen operas.

established earlier in the century; the younger group, "conservative with the blessing of the government," seems, on the basis of information at present available, to be of little importance. It includes Rudolf Wagner-Régeny (b. 1903), with two operas: *Der Günstling* ("The Favorite," 1935), a neo-Handelian work with choruses and

ANGÉLIQUE

arias, spiced with "a nice admixture of Kurt Weill"; [7] and *Die Bürger von Calais* ("The Citizens of Calais," 1939). The principal other member of this group is Werner Egk (b. 1901) with *Die Zaubergeige* ("The Magic Fiddle," 1935), a folk-opera plot with intricately rhythmed, sometimes polytonal, music; and *Peer Gynt* (1938). Among the older composers who may be said to belong to the conservative

[7] MMus XVI, No. 4 (May–June, 1939) 210.

party in this period are a few who have not been mentioned earlier. Paul Graener (1872–1944) had become known as conductor and composer before the war; his most popular opera was *Friedemann Bach* (1931). The distinguished Swiss composer Othmar Schoeck [8] is best known in opera for *Penthesilea* (1927). Paul von Klenau (b. 1883) produced a neo-Wagnerian work *Rembrandt von Rijn* in 1937. The most talented of this group is doubtless Walter Braunfels (b. 1882), whose operas, while not adventurous, have attractive melodies, good workmanship, charm, and a sense of the theatre. His best work, *Die Vögel* ("The Birds"), to his own libretto after Aristophanes, was first given in 1920. Braunfels' activity was suppressed during the Nazi regime, but for racial, not musical, reasons. The operas of Max Ettinger (b. 1874) continued the tradition of the Munich school of Thuille, Braunfels, and Waltershausen (*Frühlings Erwachen*, "Spring's Awakening," 1928). A brilliant younger composer of essentially conservative style, influenced by Strauss, Schreker, and Puccini, was Erich Wolfgang Korngold (*Die tote Stadt*, "The Dead City," 1920).[9]

We now turn to the consideration of those operas produced during the interwar period which may fairly be called modern in musical style.[10] There is no completely satisfactory method of classification in this field. Modernity may be evident to varying degrees in the different aspects of an opera: in the choice and treatment of subject, in the extent to which current social, economic, or political events are consciously reflected, in the relation between composer and audience, in the musical style itself, and in the relation between music and text. Despite the difficulties, however, some classification must be attempted unless we are willing to produce a mere chronology.

[8] On Schoeck (b. 1886) see essays by W. Schuh and H. Corrodi.

[9] Korngold (b. 1897) has produced some instrumental works, arrangements of operettas, much incidental music for plays and films, and the following operas: *Violante* and *Der Ring des Polykrates* ("Polykrates' Ring"; both 1916), *Das Wunder der Heliane* ("The Miracle of Heliana," 1927), and *Die Katrein* (1937). He is now living in the United States.

[10] Bibliography: Copland, *Our New Music* (1941); Slonimsky, *Music Since 1900* (1937); Istel, "For a Reversion to Opera," MQ X (1924) 405–37; Prunières, "The Departure from Opera," MMus III, No. 2 (January–February, 1926) 3–9; Bekker, "The Opera Walks New Paths," MQ XXI (1935) 266–78; Křenek, *Music Here and Now* (1939); *idem*, "Opera between the Wars," MMus XX, No. 2 (January–February, 1943) 102–11; Gatti, *Musicisti moderni d'Italia e di fuori* (1920); Saint-Cyr, *Musicisti italiani contemporanei* (1932); *Annuario del teatro lirico italiano*, 1940–; Bekker, *Neue Musik* (1920); Heinsheimer, "Die Umgestaltung des Operntheaters in Deutschland," *Anbruch* XV (August–September, 1933) 107–13.

Without aiming at undue rigidity, therefore, we shall consider modern opera under the following heads: (1) opera which seeks to appeal to a broad public by means of music in a popular style, subjects of topical interest, or both. (2) Opera which, to varying degrees, revives the musical forms and aesthetic of the eighteenth century or earlier periods and, in some cases, combines hitherto conventionally distinct musical forms, in a modern idiom of antiromantic tendency. (3) Opera which, while in many respects similar to the preceding type, is in a more radical or unfamiliar (for example, atonal) musical style.

1. The most striking examples of popularized modern opera are two extremely successful works produced in Germany in the late 1920's: Ernst Křenek's *Jonny spielt auf* ("Johnny Strikes Up," 1927) and Kurt Weill's *Dreigroschenoper* ("The Threepenny Opera," 1928).[11] The plot of the former work is a combination of gross realism and fantasy. The music undoubtedly owed its popularity to the exuberant rhythms and catchy tunes of the then novel jazz style which prevails throughout, spiced with enough dissonance to give audiences the comfortably superior sensation of listening to something really modernistic and daring. Viewed in cold blood nearly twenty years later, it is astonishing to realize what variety of effect was possible within the restrictions of this idiom, from the gaudily vulgar tunes of a restaurant orchestra to the moving, almost romantically conceived scene 7, and the final apotheosis of Johnny, the Negro band leader, incarnation of the vigorous new world "conquering old Europe with the dance." Needless to say, the jazz is about as genuinely American in flavor as a French ice-cream soda, but the German audiences were not aware of this, and the work altogether did not pretend to be much more than a revue, frankly aiming at popular success and deservedly enjoying it for a few years.

11 Křenek (b. 1900), a pupil of Schreker, has composed at least twelve operas and a large quantity of other music in all forms. He is now living in the United States. His opera *Tarquin* was performed at Vassar College in 1941. See his book *Music Here and Now*; also "The New Music and Today's Theatre," MMus XIV, No. 4 (May–June, 1937) 200–203; Stuckenschmidt, "Ernst Křenek," MMus XVI, No. 1 (November–December, 1938) 41–44; Weissmann, "Germany's Latest Music Dramas," MMus IV, No. 4 (May–June, 1927) 20–26.

Weill (b. 1900), after a successful career in Germany, was compelled to emigrate when the Nazis came to power. He is now living in the United States. He has written about a dozen operas and ballets, incidental music for plays, and some choral and orchestral works.

Křenek, one of the most gifted and productive of modern German opera composers, was already known to the public by three earlier works: *Der Sprung über den Schatten* ("The Leap over the Shadow," 1924), a farce operetta of variegated musical styles; and *Zwingburg* ("Dungeon Castle," 1924) and *Orpheus und Euridike* (1926), both in a dissonant, linear idiom. Three one-act operas produced at Wiesbaden in 1928 did not attain the popularity of *Jonny*. Křenek's subsequent operas come within the orbit of the Vienna school of composers and will be noticed later.

Weill's *Dreigroschenoper* makes even less pretension to eternal significance than does *Jonny*. A modern version of Gay's *Beggar's Opera*, the music consists only of a succession of German-American jazz songs, one would-be *Schlager* after another, unbearably monotonous now that the shine of novelty has worn off. Some of Weill's other stage works are more interesting and historically of greater importance. *Der Protagonist* (1926) and *Der Zar lässt sich photographieren* ("The Czar Permits Himself to Be Photographed," 1928), both surrealistic in technique, show skillful craftsmanship but lack the melodic inventiveness of *Die Dreigroschenoper*. *Aufstieg und Fall der Stadt Mahagonny* ("The Rise and Fall of the City of Mahogany," 1927, 1930) is a bitterly satirical picture of degenerate modern life, which attempts to extend the basic style of *Die Dreigroschenoper* to a longer work with continuous music. In both *Mahagonny* and *Die Bürgschaft* ("The Surety," 1932) the note of warning and revolt against evil social conditions is sounded. Weill, more than any other composer, is the inspiration of many modern American operatic works of a socially critical, satirical, or topical nature: not only Antheil's *Transatlantic*, but also the operas of Blitzstein and even Gershwin's *Of Thee I Sing* and *Porgy and Bess*. Weill, moreover, in a delicate balance between banality and poignancy, caught the mood of life at a moment in Germany when economic disaster was preparing the way for the Hitler regime which was to put a violent end to all such sensitive expression.[12] Finally, he exemplifies in his most characteristic operas the modern aesthetic view expressed by Bert Brecht, the librettist of *Mahagonny:* "Opera should be a spectacle made up of clearly definable components, rather than an illusory image of a magic super-world, and that spectacle should con-

---

12 Virgil Thomson writes of Weill's "tearful but elegant ditties about the Berlin ghetto," and claims that "Weill did for Berlin what Charpentier did for Paris." See "Most Melodious Tears," MMus XI, No. 1 (November–December, 1933) 13–17.

vey an explicitly demonstrated meaning for those beholding it, instead of being merely expensive entertainment or glorified dope." [13]

Another modern German opera may be listed here, although it is not by any means a pure example of the popular type. Max Brand's *Maschinist Hopkins* (1929; libretto by the composer) [14] is obviously influenced in its text by Eugene O'Neill and in the music to some extent by Berg's *Wozzek*. It is a realistic-expressionistic play of murder, lust, and revenge, with references to actual factory working conditions, a kind of modernized Zola-Bruneau opera. The music is extremely percussive and dissonant, underlaying dialogue of an intense, declamatory nature. In addition to ordinary spoken declamation, three distinct types of delivery are indicated: the Sprechstimme, as in Schönberg and Berg (words half sung in varying but not exactly notated pitch with exactly notated rhythm); rhythmic declamation of words on one tone level; and unarticulated vowel sounds of indefinite pitch in exactly notated rhythm. Sensational novelties of this opera were the choruses of the machines, in which these three techniques are combined. The prevailing percussive style of music gives way in the love scene (scene 5, end of Act I) to long, lyrical, neo-Straussian melodic lines, though the harmonies remain dissonant as ever. The current fad for American jazz is recognized particularly in scenes 4 and 10; the former has a song in English (words by George Antheil) by a six-man Negro jazz band; the latter makes use, among other effects, of an out-of-tune electric piano.[15] *Maschinist Hopkins* was altogether too much of its own day to have remained permanently in the repertoire, even without the "purifying" influence of National Socialism; it is interesting chiefly as being symptomatic of this peculiar period in German opera, specializing in the depiction of restless, pathological states of suffering and situations calling forth extravagantly bitter emotions.

[13] Quoted in Křenek, "Opera between the Wars," MMus XX, No. 2 (January–February, 1943) 108. See also Einstein, "German Opera, Past and Present," MMus XI, No. 2 (January–February, 1934) 65–72; and Gutman, *"Mahagonny* and Other Novelties," MMus VII, No. 4 (June–July, 1930) 32–36.

[14] Brand (b. 1892) was a pupil of Schreker. See his essay " 'Mechanische' Musik und das Problem der Oper," *Musikblätter des Anbruch* VIII (1926) 356–59. Articles on *Maschinist Hopkins* in *Signale für die musikalische Welt* LXXXVII (1929) 136–65, 1075–78; LXXXVIII (1930) 395–99; see also Thompson, "Fly-Wheel Opera," MMus VII, No. 1 (December–January 1929–30) 39–42.

[15] Cf. *Wozzek*, Act III sc. 3. Is the taste for off-pitch effects in music comparable to the taste for ripe game and certain kinds of cheese?

TWO DESIGNS FOR BERG'S "WOZZEK"

The minor operas of Paul Hindemith [16] well illustrate the popular satirical tendencies fashionable in Germany in the late 1920's. The most notable of these operas are *Hin und zurück* ("There and Back," 1927) and *Neues vom Tage* ("News of the Day," 1929). *Hin und zurück* [17] is a one-act tour de force in which the second half exactly reverses the action of the first, so that at the end the situation is exactly the same as at the beginning; the music correspondingly reverses the order of its themes and movements, but without going into the intricacies of an academic crab canon. The work is scored for an orchestra of seven wind instruments and two pianos; the music is in various styles by turns but triumphantly unified in effect nevertheless, and decidedly clever and successful in performance. *Neues vom Tage*, Hindemith's last opera to be produced in Germany, is a larger work, a witty revue about a married couple who, through their efforts to obtain evidence for a divorce, become "the news of the day," with characters so firmly established in the minds of their public that they no longer have any right of private action and cannot even drop their divorce proceedings, although they wish to. On this plot are strung several amusing episodes, including a chorus of stenographers to the rhythmic accompaniment of clacking typewriters and a bathroom scene which attracted the august disapproval of Dr. Goebbels himself. The music, like most of Hindemith in this period, is linear in texture and strongly rhythmic, well suited to the lively action. There is, of course, a jazz scene, and the final chorus is a fugue. It is unfortunate that the text is so full of topical references which have long since lost their timeliness as to make revivals of the work difficult if not impossible. One of Hindemith's most charming examples of *Gebrauchsmusik* is a children's opera, *Wir bauen eine Stadt* ("We Build a Town"), in straightforward simple melodic style, first performed at Oxford in 1931.

[16] Hindemith (b. 1895), the foremost modern German composer, has produced a dozen stage works, as well as a large quantity of other music in all forms. See his *Craft of Musical Composition*, 2 vols. (New York, Associated Music Publishers [1937–1945]); biography by H. Strobel (3d ed., 1937); Epstein, "Hindemiths Theatermusik," *Die Musik* XXIII (1931) 582–87; Blitzstein, *"Hin und Zurück* in Philadelphia," MMus V, No. 4 (May–June, 1928) 34–36; Gutman, "Tabloid Hindemith" [on *Neues vom Tage*], MMus VII, No. 1 (December, 1929–January, 1930) 34–37; Reich, "Paul Hindemith," MQ XVII (1931) 486–96.

[17] This was originally produced at Baden-Baden on the same program as Ernst Toch's *Die Prinzessin auf der Erbse* ("The Princess and the Pea"), Weill's *Mohagonny*, and Milhaud's *Enlèvement d'Europe* ("The Rape of Europa").

In the Soviet Union [18] an effort has been made, nation-wide in scope, long continued, and sponsored by official government agencies, to bring art to the masses of the people. This is an experiment which, considering all its aspects, is perhaps unique in modern times. It has definite results in all forms of music written by Soviet composers and especially in the musical and dramatic content of recent operas. One effect has been to extend the nationalist musical movement to new peoples within the orbit of Soviet Russia: thus Reinhold Glière (b. 1875), a composer of the older generation, produced at Baku in 1926 (revised version, 1934) *Shah-Senem,* an opera based on Caucasian legends and including musical elements from Turkish, Arabian, and Persian sources; Sergei Vassilenko's (b. 1872) *Son of the Sun* (Moscow, 1929), based on a story of the Boxer Rebellion, uses Chinese and Mongolian themes; Michail Gnessin (b. 1883) has spoken for the Jewish population of Russia in *The Maccabeans* and *The Youth of Abraham* (1921); Andrei Pashtchenko's *Eagles in Revolt* (Leningrad, 1923) is a revolutionary opera employing Kirghiz, Russian, and Tartar melodies; and other national groups are represented by V. A. Uspensky's *Farkhad and Shirin* (Tashkent, 1936; national Uzbek tunes),[19] S. A. Balasanian's *Revolt of Vose* (Stalinabad, 1939; Tadzik folk melodies), and Nazib Zhiganov's *The Deserter,* the "first nationalist Tartar opera." [20]

The Russian Revolution, like the French Revolution, called forth a large number of musical works on patriotic themes. Practically every Soviet composer has written program symphonies, symphonic poems, oratorios, choral odes, or the like glorifying different phases of life under the new regime. Naturally opera has not been neglected as a means for promoting Soviet ideology. Russian history has been operatically reinterpreted in the light of new doctrines; satirical, moral, or didactic dramas have condemned the abuses of the old order; life under the Marxian dispensation has been idyllically represented and the hardier revolutionary virtues glowingly extolled. The music in these works is, of course, uneven in quality; most are fundamentally conservative in style. Few, probably, are of per-

---

[18] Bibliography: Sabaneiev, *Modern Russian Composers;* Braudo, "The Russian Panorama," MMus X, No. 2 (January–February, 1933) 79–86; *idem,* "Concerts, Opera, Ballet in Russia Today," MMus X, No. 4 (May–June, 1933) 213–19; Keefer, "Opera in the Soviet," *Music Library Association Notes, Second Series* II, No. 2 (March, 1945) 110–17.
[19] Slonimsky, *Music Since 1900,* p. 406.   [20] *Ibid.,* p. 117.

manent value. So far the most enduringly popular Soviet opera, and one which apparently fully meets the ideal official requirements, is *The Quiet Don,* based on Sholokhov's novel with music by Ivan Dzerzhinsky, first performed at Leningrad in 1935.[21] The music is nationalistic, inspired by Russian folk melody (though without obvious citation of particular tunes), fairly simple in texture, and slightly modernist in some of its harmonies and rhythms.

Since his return to Russia in 1934, Sergei Prokofiev [22] has become an important influence in Soviet music. Prokofiev's early opera, *Love for Three Oranges* (Chicago, 1921), written in his facile, rhythmic, brilliant manner of those days, was very successful. A still earlier opera, *The Gambler,* prepared for performance at Petrograd in 1917, was not performed until 1929, at Brussels. As a Soviet composer, Prokofiev has produced his two most important operas: *Simeon Kotko* (Moscow, 1940), based on scenes from the life of one of the leaders in the Russian civil war and revolution; and *War and Peace,* an epical setting of Tolstoy's epical novel, completed in 1941, consisting of arias, duets, important choral sections, and mass battle scenes, in the grand tradition of old Russian opera.

Probably the best-known Soviet opera is Shostakovitch's *Lady Macbeth of Mzensk District* (Moscow, 1934), which was at first accepted by the Russian critics, made its way to the United States for a few sensational performances, and a year later was suddenly and savagely condemned in an official article in *Pravda* as "a leftist mess instead of human music . . . fidgety, screaming, neurasthenic." [23] *Lady Macbeth* has no connection with Shakespeare. Its heroine is Ekaterina, an adulterous wife who first murders her father-in-law and then collaborates with her lover in murdering her husband. The

[21] See Slonimsky, *Music Since 1900,* p. 397, for a translation of interesting analytical comments on this work by A. Ostertzov. Dzerzhinsky (b. 1909) has written other operas: *Soil Upturned* (Moscow, 1937); *Volatchaevko Days; Nadeshda Svetlova* (1944).

[22] Prokofiev (b. 1891), one of the best known abroad of all Soviet Russian composers, has written much music in nearly all instrumental and choral forms. See Slonimsky, "Sergei Prokofiev," *American Quarterly on the Soviet Union* II, No. 1 (1939) 37–44; Prokofiev, "The War Years," MQ XXX (1944) 421–27; Schlifstein, "On *War and Peace,*" MMus XX, No. 3 (March–April, 1943) 185–87; biography by Nestyev.

[23] Quoted in Slonimsky, *Music since 1900,* p. 403; see also *ibid.,* pp. 372, 389. Cf. also Shostakovitch, "My Opera, Lady Macbeth," MMus XII, No. 1 (November–December, 1934) 23–30; Rosenfeld, *Discoveries of a Music Critic.* There is a biography in English of Shostakavitch (b. 1906) by V. I. Seroff (1943). Shostakovitch's earlier satirical opera, *The Nose* (1930), was not successful.

pair is arrested and sent to Siberia with a convict gang; the lover
deserts Ekaterina for another of the women convicts; Ekaterina murders her rival by pushing her off a bridge and commits suicide by
jumping off the bridge herself. It is hard to say how much of this
story is intended to satirize bourgeois society—the scene is nineteenth-century Russia under the Czarist regime—and how much is
mere pornography (the love scenes) and perversion (the whipping
scene). The music is well suited to the action, being brutal, lusty,
strong in the suggestion of horror, cruelty, and suffering, full of tre-
mendous rhythmic drive and willful dissonance. There are many
distinct arias, some duets, and a few passages of straight recitative,
as well as the more typical long sections where the voice parts are
freely woven into a continuous orchestral texture. As in the old
Russian opera, choruses and crowd scenes are prominent. The work
is divided into four acts, with nine scenes. Within each act the
scenes are connected by means of orchestral interludes which con-
tinue and develop the preceding musical material. Very little use
is made of motifs recurring from one scene to another, but within
each scene the music is organized as a clearly planned formal unit.
Moreover, the four acts are designed like the four movements of a
symphony: I. Alternating slow and fast tempi, and ending in F
major. II. Adagio, with a few interludes in fast tempo, centering
about the key of G minor but ending on a C major chord with an
added flat seventh (that is, the dominant seventh of F); the climax
of this long act is the powerful orchestral interlude between scenes 4
and 5. III. Scherzo: comic drunken solo and a Gilbert-and-Sullivan-
esque policemen's chorus; the tonalities are varying, but prominence
is given to the key of F-sharp minor, in which the act ends. IV. Finale:
Adagio, F minor, framed by gloomy Mussorgsky-like choruses of
convicts.

As in his other music of this period, Shostakovitch excels in two
idioms: the nervously energetic presto, thin textured, erratic in tonality, rhythmically irregular, conveying an inimitable and positively
physical sensation of excitement; and the perfectly objective, long-
spun adagio, mounting with clashing contrapuntal lines to sonorous
climaxes of elemental grandeur. There is no subjective feeling in
this score; indeed, the libretto makes no place for any, except for an
occasional touch of sneering satire. The only use of national material

is in Act IV, where Ekaterina sings a grotesquely distorted version of a folk song. The music is vivid and theatrical; to hear it must be an experience one would be equally sorry either to miss or to be often obliged to repeat.

Outside Soviet Russia there appears to have been but little significant operatic composition inspired by the ideals or achievements of governments. Exception may be made, perhaps, of two Italian works glorifying the ill-fated imperialism of Mussolini. Alfredo Casella's *Il deserto tentato* ("Conquest of the Desert," 1937), a "mystery in one act," presents the adventures of a crew of a wrecked bombing plane who brave the dangers of the wilderness and eventually gain the respect and loyalty of the natives. It endeavors "to evoke the Ethiopian war, transfiguring it on an altogether unreal and mythical plane. It reflects a poetic exaltation of the civilizing mission of a great nation." [24] The music is in a rather simple oratorio-like style with many choral sections.

Another work which was conceived at least in part as a gesture of acclaim to Mussolini is Francesco Malipiero's *Giulio Cesare* (1936), based on Shakespeare's play. The vocal parts of this opera are all robust declamation of the recitativo secco type, supported by a continuous orchestral ground with distinct leading motifs. Each scene is developed over a few such motifs, woven into a texture of comparatively static harmony (slow-changing basses, frequent ostinato figures, short motifs canonically in a pandiatonic web, parallelism). The effect therefore depends on the vividness of the declamation, the directness and economy of the dramatic details, the strikingly pictorial or expressive character of the motifs themselves, and the admirable dramatic quality of the infrequent harmonic changes, which follow and underline the action most effectively. It is a style, for example, which permits a really successful musical setting of Anthony's funeral oration. The dramatic choruses in this scene and the temple chorus in Act I (with percussion accompaniment) are also excellent writing. Altogether, this is a stageworthy work, good theatre, though possibly a trifle monotonous in musical texture.

2. The second main current in modern opera may be called, in contrast to all the foregoing, neoclassical. In this type of opera, the

---

[24] From a letter of the composer, quoted in Slonimsky, *Music Since 1900*, p. 426. See also review by Einstein, MMus XV, No. 1 (November–December, 1937) 41.

subjects are generally timeless rather than timely; or if the latter, their topical significance is not stressed. The action is likely to be condensed, simplified, even stylized, so that a comparatively few significant moments stand out, with the essential interconnecting material reduced to the minimum. Composers are not inclined to appeal to their audience by recalling effects familiar in common musical experience but rather tend to pile up subtlety, novelty, and complexity. Although there are many varieties of musical style, the prevailing tone in these operas is antiromantic; the music may be pathetic or objective, intense or indifferent, monumental and stark or witty and satirical, but it is seldom sentimental. In form, these operas tend toward the eighteenth-century ideal of distinct units, the number opera. Many are in the typically modern compressed form of chamber opera; others must be designated as opera oratorio or opera ballet; still others resemble in form the medieval mystery plays.

The founders of neoclassicism were Busoni and Stravinsky. Busoni's *Doktor Faustus* (1925) is the earliest opera which exemplifies the neoclassic principles on a large scale. Stravinsky, however, had already begun a characteristic development of similar principles in three short stage works which had considerable influence. *L'Histoire du soldat* ("Story of the Soldier," Lausanne, 1918) is a ballet the action of which is explained by a narrator, with dry, percussive, metrically complex music for an orchestra of only seven players. Two burlesque one-act chamber operas, *Renard* and *Mavra,* were produced at Paris in 1922. The latter is a particularly good modern example of opera buffa; it is a farce based on a story by Pushkin, with artificially simplified characters (almost like puppets), a continuously developing symphonic background of nimble rhythm, and vocal declamation similar to that in the cantata *Les Noces* (1923). Repose and classical proportions are evident in Stravinsky's later ballet *Apollon Musagète* (1928) and the opera ballet *Persèphone* (1934). His greatest neoclassic dramatic work is the monumental Latin opera-oratorio *Oedipus Rex* (1927; original French text by Jean Cocteau, after Sophocles) for chorus, soloists, and narrator, in which the stylized, completely impersonal character of the action, words, and music often produces sublime effects. (Similar means are employed even more fittingly in the oratorio *Symphony of Psalms,* 1930.)

An important work in this period of the Paris lyric theatre is the opera ballet *Padmâvati,* words by Louis Laloy and music by Albert Roussel,[25] produced in 1923. The ancient French genius for this type of spectacle—slender plot with a large proportion of choruses and ballets—is here realized in modern style. The variety and splendor of the rhythms, the great individuality of the harmony, the exquisite finesse and good taste of the whole, are remarkable. The ballets often include wordless choruses, and this peculiar technique is developed here to a point which has probably never been excelled (see especially the Funeral Ceremony at the end of Act II). Slonimsky's notation on this work—"free from pseudo-exoticism" [26]—is ambiguous. Does it mean "having genuine exoticism"? What is genuine exoticism? If it is the free, striking, individual use of themes and harmonies which may perhaps have been suggested by hearing oriental music, and the employment of these in such a way as to create a definite feeling of the Hindu background without anywhere giving the impression of merely quoting oriental melodies for the sake of factitious local color—then the music of *Padmâvati,* like that of Roussel's earlier orchestral-choral *Evocations,* is genuinely exotic. Whether or not it is pedantically authentic is of no importance. There is no composer who more than Roussel gives the impression of complete originality. The dissonances of his music are never arbitrary, but always vital and logical. He is able to make an extremely complex and refined harmonic idiom really sound. He is a true disciple of D'Indy, but no mere copyist; in line of descent from Dukas, but with greater imaginative fire and poetic genius. One feels that here is the revelation in music of something always existing but hitherto veiled, and now made known with perfect assurance and clarity.

Another major composer of French neoclassical opera is the Swiss Arthur Honegger,[27] who became famous after his *Roi David* was

25 Roussel (1869–1937) also composed a one-act opera *La Naissance de la lyre* to a text by Théodore Reinach after Sophocles' *Ichneutai* (Paris, 1925); a comic opera *Le Testament de la tante Caroline* ("Aunt Caroline's Will," Bergamo, 1936); several ballets, incidental music, and many orchestral and chamber works. See special Roussel issue of RM (1929); Hill, *Modern French Music,* pp. 314–26; and Hoérée, *Albert Roussel.*
26 Slonimsky, *Music since 1900,* p. 236.
27 Honegger (b. 1892) is distinguished for his symphonic poems and other orchestral and chamber works, as well as for ballets, incidental music, and operas. His most recent opera is *L'Aiglon* (in collaboration with Ibert, 1937). See Tappolet, *Honegger;* review of *Judith* by Prunières, MMus III, No. 4 (May–June, 1926) 30–33.

presented, in the original dramatic version, in 1921. In *Judith* (1926), rewritten as an opera from the incidental music to René Morax's biblical drama produced in 1925, the style of *Le Roi David* was continued; fervid declamatory phrases in incisive rhythms over percussive harmonies, the progressions of which are actuated by contrapuntal, chromatically moving lines generally in contrary motion, with much use of ostinato figures. In both works the chorus is extensively used; in *Judith* it functions chiefly as a background for the soloists' singing, except for the last scene, with its strong closing fugue "Gloire au dieu tout puissant Jehovah des armées." Honegger's *Antigone* (1927) is his most important opera, to a text by Jean Cocteau "freely adapted from Sophocles." It is a continuous symphonic setting of the drama without word repetitions, arias, ballets, or any other diversionary matter. The vocal lines are constantly in a type of recitative analogous to that of Lully (that is, deriving its pace, accent, and contour immediately and in detail from the words), but of course much more varied in rhythm and melodic pattern than Lully's. An unusual feature of the declamation is the placing of first syllables on the accented beat instead of treating them in the usual way as anacruses, resulting in a singular vehemence of expression (Example 125).[28] The orchestral part is, as usual in Honegger,

ANTIGONE, sc. 4

Ex.125.   Honegger

la jus - ti - ce non plus n'im - po - se pas des lois de ce
gen- re et je ne croy-ais pas que ton de - cret put fai - re pré-va-loir le
ca-pri-ce d'un hom-me sur la ré-gle des im-mor-tels sur ces lois qui ne sont pas é-cri-tes

strongly dissonant and percussive; the effect is altogether stark, quite in keeping with the grim, tragic, swift-moving text.

The leading composer of French opera during the interwar period, one of the most productive of contemporary musicians, is Darius

[28] Cf. Honegger's foreword to the score.

Milhaud.[29] Milhaud's first big success was *Le Pauvre Matelot* ("The Poor Sailor," 1927), a short three-act play by Jean Cocteau about a sailor who, returning home rich after an absence of many years, decides to test his wife's fidelity by telling her he is a rich friend of her husband who, he says, is about to return home in utter poverty; the wife, not recognizing him, murders the supposed stranger in order to get his money for her husband. The peculiar unreality of the action is heightened by Milhaud's music, which is in a playful, intentionally banal manner, with jazzy tunes and sophisticated, dissonant harmony. Much of the same mocking spirit and the same musical characteristics are found in the three one-act *opéras minutes* composed in 1927, parodies of Greek myths in the fashion of the early eighteenth-century Théâtre de la Foire. Another comic opera, *Esther de Carpentras* (composed in 1925, produced in 1938), a modern, lightly satirical version of the biblical Esther story, is especially remarkable for the comic ensembles of Act I and the vivid crowd scenes of Act II.

[29] Milhaud (b. 1892) studied at the Paris Conservatory and has composed a large amount of music in all instrumental and vocal forms. He is now living in the United States. The following is a complete list of his operas:

TITLE AND LIBRETTIST	COMPOSED	PERFORMED
La Brebis egarée Francis Jammes	1910–1915	Opéra-Comique, December, 1923
Les Euménides Aeschylus, tr. Claudel	1917–1922	————————
Les Malheurs d'Orphée Armand Lunel	1924	La Monnaie (Brussels), 1926
Esther de Carpentras Armand Lunel	1925	Opéra-Comique, February, 1938

Three opéras minutes:
  L'Enlèvement d'Europe
  L'Abandon d'Ariane
  La Delivrance de Thesée
  Henri Hoppenot
	1927	Wiesbaden, April, 1928
		(*L'Enlèvement d'Europe* had been performed at Baden-Baden, July, 1927)

Le Pauvre Matelot Jean Cocteau	1926	Opéra-Comique, December, 1927
Christophe Colomb Paul Claudel	1928	Berlin, May, 1930
Maximilien Werfel-Hoffmann-Lunel	1930	Paris Opéra, January, 1932
La Sagesse Paul Claudel	1935	————————
Médée Madeleine Milhaud	1938	Paris Opéra, May, 1940
Bolivar Supervielle—Madeleine Milhaud	1943	————————

Milhaud's first serious opera was *Les Euménides,* composed in the years 1917–1922 to the text of Aeschylus translated by Claudel, a massive work with huge choruses, constantly polytonal in an extremely dissonant texture of blended ostinato figures. Similar technical procedures are found in *Christophe Colomb* (composed 1928),[30] one of Milhaud's principal operas. It is interesting to note the position of this work in the history of French opera. Having in mind the music of such composers as Gounod, Massenet, and Debussy, one is inclined to think of French opera music as marked chiefly by the qualities of economy, elegance, and restraint; yet it must also be remembered that Berlioz's *Troyens,* the outstanding French musical drama of the nineteenth century, was not distinguished alone by these qualities but rather by what seem to be their opposites: expansiveness, grandeur, and (on occasion) lavish expenditure of resources. *Christophe Colomb* belongs in this "grand" tradition of French opera, in the line reaching back through Berlioz to Spontini, Gluck, Rameau, and Lully. It is on a large scale: two acts and twenty-seven scenes, with ten principal soloists, thirty-five other solo parts, three speaking parts, a chorus, and orchestra reinforced by a special battery of percussion instruments. The drama is conceived in epic-allegorical form, with a Narrator and other external personages, presented in a series of tableaux which are explained, commented on, and connected by choral and spoken interludes with percussion accompaniment. There is no English term which fits this kind of work so well as the French designation *opéra sacrale;* an idea of the method will be best obtained from the Prayer of the Narrator in the prologue (spoken in rhythm, with words murmured by the chorus as a background, to a rhythmical accompaniment of percussion instruments, softly): " 'I pray to the God of all power to give me light and strength to open and explain to you the Book of the Life and Voyages of Christopher Columbus who discovered America and that land which lies beyond. For it is he who has brought together the whole Catholic world and made it one globe under the Cross. I set forth the life of this chosen man whose name signifies the Dove and the Christ-bearer, as it passed not only in time but in eternity. For it is not he alone but all men who hear the call to the other world and to that farther shore whither may it please the Divine Grace to bring us all.' Chorus (shout): 'So mote it be!' "

[30] Lopatnikoff, "*Christophe Colomb,*" MMus VII, No. 4 (June–July, 1930) 36–38.

This mystical interpretation of Christopher Columbus is always at the forefront as the various scenes in his career are unfolded. The climax of Act I is the scene of the mutiny on board Columbus' ship; this act ends with a gigantic setting (in Latin) of the Sanctus. Part II finally takes us back to the Inn at Valladolid, the exact point at which the action began after the prologue, and there is an epilogue ending with a choral Alleluia.

The music is in planar polytonal harmony, that is, with free dissonance arising from superposing motifs (often chord streams) in different tonalities, though as a rule no one motif is completely in a single key. The usual method of construction, except in the longest scenes, is to introduce one theme, establish it by ostinato-like repetition, then add successively one, two, or more themes, each of which is also usually treated in ostinato fashion. For example, scene 8 (orchestra alone) consists of three different motifs over sustained bitonal chords: the first motif is in the Aeolian mode on G-sharp with parallel sevenths and ninths, the second a chromatic series of six-four chords, and the third a melody in F-sharp minor fluctuating to F minor, while the sustained chords consist of the G major and C-sharp major triads. In the following scene there is added to all this a wordless chorus in the Hypodorian mode on E-flat with conflicting major-minor thirds in the sustaining chords (for tenors and basses). Some scenes are simpler than this, others more complex. Of course the various planes of harmony are kept distinct to some degree by the use of contrasting orchestral color, but nevertheless the total effect is one of practically unmitigated dissonance, so that the harmony is consequently static. To be sure, there is some contrast between the amount of dissonance produced by, say, two conflicting keys and that produced by a half-dozen; but these are contrasts within what is to the ordinary ear a very limited harmonic range: it is extremely difficult, if not actually impossible, to perceive distinct degrees in dissonance beyond a certain point of harmonic complexity. Compensation for all this is found, however, in the variety and vitality of Milhaud's rhythmic patterns and in the completely impersonal, spectacular, monumental effect of this type of musical construction. Moreover, when the long-continued dissonance finally resolves to a simple chord at the end of a section, the intensity of the resolution is magnified. An example of this is the great mutiny scene in Act I, where after a climax of four tonalities in the chorus and four in the orchestra (a total of seven different keys at once, one being reduplicated), the whole resolves on a closing climactic triad of B-flat major with a perfectly electrifying result. The motifs themselves, the units of the structure, are mostly short and in strongly marked rhythm. The voice lines are treated more freely as longer melodic phrases, never in the style of recitative. On occasion, special rhythmic patterns may be used, as in the Spanish dances in the scene at Queen Isabella's court (Act I, scene 7).

In 1930 Milhaud applied a similar technique to a historical opera, *Maximilien,* based on a drama by Franz Werfel. Here, however, the degree of stylization surpasses that of any previous works: action, melodies, rhythms, all are ritualistic; even church hymns and military marches are indicated in formal, antirealistic outline as parts of a tonal design rather than representations of actual happenings. But in *Médée* (composed 1938) there is less of the monumental, less dissonance, more lyricism, and more interest in the individual figures of the drama. The restrained dramatic force of the scene of the preparation of the enchantments is remarkable. Most expressive are the slow, melismatic, long lines in the soprano role of the suffering Creusa, innocent victim of Medea's cruelty (Example 126).

It appears, then, that Milhaud has recapitulated the typical course of development of composers of his generation, from the flippant-satirical (rococo) through the grandiose-formal (baroque) to the more equable and balanced (classical) style of *Médée*. It is to be hoped that his recent *Bolivar* (1943) may be widely performed, and that still other operas may be forthcoming.

One of the outstanding German serious operas of a neoclassical type is Hindemith's *Cardillac* (1926),[31] on an excellent tragic libretto by Ferdinand Lion. This is one of the best examples in this period of the revival of the principle of separate musical numbers in opera. Not only is each number a distinct, clearly organized musical unit, but the music is constructed purely according to its own laws, the themes being straightforwardly developed in the manner of a concerto, undeflected by any attempt to illustrate mere details of the text. Music and drama run parallel, but without interpenetration. The absolute, instrumental character of the music is aided by the

[31] See Willms, *Führer zur Oper Cardillac.*

prevailing texture, which is highly rhythmic and contrapuntal; the voice is treated in the eighteenth-century way as one contrapuntal line among concertizing instruments. In addition to this typical

MÉDÉE, Act III

Hindemith linear style, two other idioms are occasionally used: a kind of accompanied recitative in which the vocal declamation is set against a single rhapsodic line in the orchestra (for example, p. 131 of the piano-vocal score); and a quieter, chordal, neoromantic style which foreshadows some of Hindemith's characteristic later development (for example, the recitative and aria "Die Zeit vergeht" in Act I, scene 2). The chorus writing is vigorous, idiomatic, and effective, especially in the closing scene. Hindemith's latest dramatic work, *Mathis der Maler* ("Mathias the Painter"), was performed at Zurich in 1938.[32] It is an oratorio opera on the subject of Matthias Grünewald, the sixteenth-century German painter. In its original form it is a long, complex work holding much the same position in Hindemith's dramatic production as *Christophe Colomb* in Milhaud's and embracing a great variety of musical styles, among which suggestions of medieval modality are prominent. *Mathis* has been given a few times in concert form; the most familiar portions of the music are those arranged by the composer as an orchestral suite, which is frequently heard.

Another German work of large size, combining characteristics of both oratorio and opera, is Kaminski's *Jürg Jenatch* (1929),[33] a historical drama from the period of the Thirty Years' War. The most striking feature of this work is the extensive choral writing in very intricate polyphony, often with special acoustical and polychoral effects. The action is carried on by means of spoken dialogue combined with vocal numbers, massive tableaux, and orchestral numbers.

In Italy the distinctive modern trend is not toward opera of gigantic size but rather toward a revival of classical subjects, light ballet-like pieces, or eighteenth-century opera buffa. Thus the Orpheus theme, one of the earliest and best opera subjects, has been recently used by Malipiero (*L'Orfeide*, trilogy, 1925), Rieti (1928), and Casella (1932).[34] Malipiero's trilogy is most interesting formally:

[32] See Huth, "Forbidden Opus—Protestant," MMus XVI, No. 1 (November–December, 1938) 38–41.

[33] Heinrich Kaminski (b. 1886) is known chiefly as a choral composer. See Krieger, "Heinrich Kaminski's Drama *Jürg Jenatsch*," *Zeitschrift für Musik* C (1933) 992–95; Saminsky, "*Jürg Jenatch*," MMus VII, No. 1 (December, 1929–January, 1930) 37–39.

[34] Gian Francesco Malipiero (b. 1882), one of the most celebrated modern Italian composers, has written (in addition to many stage works) symphonies, suites, chamber music, and oratorios. His own style has doubtless been influenced by his studies of old Italian

it consists of seven short detached scenes (*sette canzone*) with a prologue and semisatirical epilogue, in which a puppet show is introduced (compare De Falla's *Retablo de Maese Pedro,* 1923). A similar
technique of short, concentrated action is found in Malipiero's *Tre
commedie goldoniani* ("Three Goldonian Comedies") of 1926, the
Komödie des Todes ("Comedy of Death," Munich, 1931), which
comprises seven scenes called by the composer "nocturnes," and *Mys-
terium Venedigs* ("Mystery [in the medieval sense] of Venice," 1932),
another trilogy. Heroic subjects and longer continuous structure are
found in his more recent operas *Giulio Cesare* (1936), *Antonio e
Cleopatra* (1938), and *Ecuba* (1941; based on Euripides). Casella has
produced an excellent comedy in *La donna serpente* ("The Ser-
pent Lady," 1932).

There are two Italian operas of an experimental type which have attracted
some attention, though they have had only a few performances: *L'aviatore
Dro* ("Aviator Dro," 1920) by the futurist composer Francesco Balilla
Pratella (b. 1880), and *Mirra* (1920) by Domenico Alaleona (1881–1928).
The former is harmonically based on the whole-tone scale, and the latter
uses "novel non-tempered scales such as a 'pentafonia' of five equal intervals." [35]

   3. The third and last principal group of modern operas might
almost be considered as a subdivision of the neoclassical school. Like
the latter, its dramatic themes are mostly nontopical and their treatment nonrealistic and nonpopular. It is set apart by the two circumstances that all its composers stem from central Europe (principally
Vienna) and that all are to a greater or lesser degree committed to the
twelve-tone (or so-called "atonal") technique of composition.[36] There
are only a few composers in this group, but their influence and importance are great in proportion to their numbers.

---

music; he is editor of the Collected Edition of Monteverdi. For a bibliography of the
numerous articles relating to Malipiero's dramatic music see Baker's *Biographical Dictionary* (4th ed.) and add: Labroca, "The Rebirth of Italian Opera," MMus IV, No. 4
(May–June 1927) 8–14; De'Paoli, "Italy's New Music of the Theatre," MMus VIII, No. 1
(November–December, 1930) 21–26.

   Vittorio Rieti (b. 1898) is best known for his chamber music; he has written a chamber
opera *Teresa nel bosco* (1933) and several ballets which have been produced by Diaghilev.

   Alfredo Casella (1883–1947), distinguished as conductor and editor, has written orchestral, chamber, and piano music. See study by L. Cortese.

35 Slonimsky, *Music Since 1900,* pp. 207, 204.
36 Cf. R. Hill, "Schoenberg's Tone-Rows and the Tonal System of the Future," MQ
XXII (1936) 14–37.

The founder and head of the school is Arnold Schönberg,[37] who has composed three operas. Two of these, *Erwartung* ("Expectation") and *Die glückliche Hand* ("The Lucky Hand"), were composed before the First World War (1909 and 1913 respectively), though not performed until 1924. Both call for a very large orchestra, usually subdivided with only a few instruments playing at any one time, and both are in the extremely dissonant, peculiar, thick Schönbergian harmonic style of the prewar period. The voice lines are wide ranged, with large, ultraexpressive intervals, occasionally going over into the Sprechstimme.[38] Both dramas are essentially subjective, and the outward scenery and action are largely symbolical; both are, in scale, rather cantatas than operas. The only character in *Erwartung* is a woman who, seeking her lover, finds only his dead body, over which she sings a long monologue, a kind of modernistic Liebestod. *Die glückliche Hand* has three soloists with a chorus of twelve voices, and uses colors symbolically in scenery, costumes, and lighting. Both in the music and in the dramatic technique, these two pieces may be regarded as forestages of Berg's *Wozzek*. Schönberg's later one-act opera, *Von Heute auf Morgen* ("From Today until Tomorrow," 1930), is completely in the twelve-tone technique, with distinct recitatives and arias, thus following the general trend of the postwar period toward the number opera.

The two operas of Schönberg's distinguished pupil Alban Berg [39] are among the most discussed works of modern times. *Wozzek*, composed in the years 1914–1922 and first performed at Berlin in December of 1925, is based on a "dramatic fragment" by Georg Büchner (1813–1837), the original twenty-five scenes being reduced by Berg to fifteen and grouped in three acts of five scenes each. Wozzek, the hero, is a representative of what he himself calls "Wir arme Leut'"

[37] Schönberg (b. 1874) has been influential as a theorist and teacher as well as through his compositions. He is now living in the United States. See Armitage (ed.), *Arnold Schoenberg;* also Stefan, "Schoenberg's Operas," MMus II, No. 1 (January, 1925) 12–15, and VII, No. 1 (December, 1929–January, 1930) 24–28; Pisk, "Schoenberg's Twelve-Tone Opera," MMus VII, No. 3 (April–May, 1930) 18–21.

[38] See musical excerpt from *Erwartung* in *Grove's Dictionary, Supplementary Volume,* p. 480.

[39] On Berg (1885–1935) see the standard biography by W. Reich and others (1937); also Berg, "A Word about *Wozzek,*" MMus V, No. 1 (November–December, 1927) 22–24; Reich, "Alban Berg's *Lulu,*" MQ XXII (1936) 383–401; *idem, "Lulu*—the Text and Music," MMus XII, No. 3 (March–April, 1935) 103–11; List, "*Lulu,* after the Premiere," MMus XV, No. 1 (November–December, 1937) 8–12.

("We poor people"), tormented by circumstances, suffering through no fault of his own, finally murdering his mistress and killing himself, driven always by forces incomprehensible to him and too strong for him to resist. Despite the date of Büchner's drama, *Wozzek* is a thoroughly typical opera of the postwar period in Germany—expressionistic, morbid, neurotic, hysterical, "charged with passionate bitterness, the fruit of shock." [40] Yet it is not merely topical; Wozzek is a universal figure, a symbol of the oppressed. All the characters and events of the opera have an unearthly quality, like a tragic puppet show, and the music supports this impression, being for the most part systematically atonal with multiple orchestras and many unusual tone effects, giving an unreal, unhuman feeling through the very strangeness of the idiom. The music is continuous throughout each act, changes of scene being accompanied by orchestral interludes. The voice parts are in flexibly rhythmed declamatory style, with exaggerated intervals; in some scenes the Sprechstimme is used, and also ordinary speech. There are leitmotifs for the principal characters, but the chief means of unity is the organization of each act in strict forms derived mostly from absolute music. Thus the five scenes of Act I are respectively a suite, rhapsody and hunting song, military march and cradlesong, passacaglia (twenty-one variations on a tone row), and rondo; Act II is a symphony in five movements: sonata form, fantasia and fugue on three themes, largo for chamber orchestra, scherzo, and rondo; Act III consists of six "inventions": on a theme (variations), a tone (pedal point), a rhythm, a six-note chord (A-sharp, C-sharp, E-sharp, G-sharp, E-flat, F-flat), a tonality (D minor), and an equal movement in eighth notes (quasi toccata). [41] Of course it is not intended that these forms shall be perceived as such during the performance of the opera; they are primarily for musical rather than dramatic purposes. In principle, the music, like that of Hindemith's *Cardillac*, runs generally parallel to the action but takes much more account of detailed nuances. However, the relation is not altogether one of details; there is a grim appropriateness, for example, in the choice of the learned passacaglia (or chaconne) form for the scene (Act I, scene 4) in which Wozzek, desperately seek-

[40] Lazare Saminsky in MMus VIII, No. 4 (May–June, 1931) 37.
[41] See W. Reich, *A Guide to . . . Wozzek*. The author is indebted also to Dr. Karl H. Eschman for additional information on this topic.

ing to earn more money for the support of his mistress and their child, submits himself to a doctor as a subject for scientific experiments. In this scene, as throughout the opera, there is a special quality of poignancy, an emotional tension, which is unmistakable though impossible to explain. All in all, *Wozzek* deserves its reputation as one of the most remarkable operas of the twentieth century, perhaps the most profound musico-dramatic creation rising out of its own peculiar moment of history.

Berg's second opera, *Lulu,* was completed in substance before the composer's death, but the orchestration had been finished only through the first two acts and a small part of the third. The first two acts, and two fragments of the third, were performed with great success at Zurich in 1937. The libretto is taken, with some cuts, from a drama in two parts by Frank Wedekind (1864–1918). The central personage, Lulu, is conceived as the incarnation of the "primal woman-spirit," and the drama is concerned with the fatal effects of her attraction for various lovers, finally ending with her own doom. Although externally occupied with the most realistic details, the work is not essentially realistic but rather an example of symbolism in modern accoutrements, often grotesque and extravagantly expressionistic, but never as abstract as Schönberg's operas. This symbolic, universal character, which *Lulu* shares with *Wozzek,* is the justification for setting such a work to a long and highly complex musical score. It is nearly impossible to form an opinion as to the effect of this opera without having actually heard and seen it on the stage. The jagged, overrealistic declamation, the alternation of singing, Sprechstimme, and spoken dialogue, the use of a silent film accompanied by orchestral music to carry on the central episode of the action, the unusual but perfectly appropriate instrumentation, and especially Berg's characteristic use of the twelve-tone technique, all over and above the strange qualities of the drama itself, make an accumulation of impressions which it is difficult to summarize. Be it said, however, that the fundamental impression is one of monumental dramatic strength, intensity of emotion controlled by form-creating intellectual power. It is all too easy to be repelled by the apparently rigid mathematical character of Berg's principles of construction. The entire music of *Lulu,* for example, is founded on a single tone row; from this are derived various themes associated with individuals of the drama in the manner of leitmotifs. The row in its primitive form (transposed) gives the opening phrase of Lulu's aria in Act II, scene 1 (Example 127). Some other principles of structure

LULU, Act II

Ex.127.   Berg

Wenn sich die Men-schen um mei-net-wil-len um-ge-bracht ha-ben

in *Lulu* have been stated by the composer: musical form types are associated with certain characters (instead of with specific scenes as in *Wozzek*); the two scenes of the second act are rigidly symmetrical and are connected by an interlude built on the principle of a crab canon, with the second half recapitulating the first half in reverse. Do such things, it may be asked, make great music? Neither their presence nor their absence does so. The issue is whether they are used as means or as ends. If they are means which effectually help to accomplish the desired end of making a musical drama, their use is justified. Whether or not this is the case with *Lulu* can be decided only when there has been more opportunity to hear and understand the work. Meanwhile, and irrespective of theoretical explanations, there can be no doubt that the music of *Lulu* owes part of its variety and effect to the manipulation of the tone row in such a way as to give at times the impression of orthodox tonality—an agreeable contrast among the multitude of other harmonic impressions.

Another opera composer of the Vienna school is Egon Wellesz.[42] His *Alkestis* (1924) is a one-act opera to a text by von Hofmannsthal, from Euripides, in which the death of Alkestis, the funeral ceremonies, the arrival of Herakles, Admetus' hospitality, and the restoration of Alkestis to life are presented in a series of broad tableaux without any unessential connecting material. The music, while it does not break entirely with conventional tonality, shows the Schönberg influence in its wide-sweeping melodic lines and dissonant harmonies. Lacking almost all dominant-tonic or other tension-release

[42] Wellesz (b. 1885) is a distinguished scholar and teacher as well as a composer (principally operas, ballets, and choral works). See Beer, "Egon Wellesz und die Oper," *Die Musik* XXIII (1931) 909–12; Redlich, "Egon Wellesz," MQ XXVI (1940) 65–75; review of *Die Bakchantinnen* by Paul Pisk, MMus IX, No. 1 (November–December, 1931) 44–45; Wellesz, "The Return to the Stage," MMus IV, No. 1 (November–December, 1926) 19–24.

patterns, it does not always escape the peril of harmonic monotony; the whole setting is, perhaps intentionally, oppressive, monolithic, of an almost forbidding austerity. The important position of the chorus in *Alkestis* is even more emphasized in *Die Bakchantinnen* (1931; text by the composer after Euripides).

The later operas of Křenek may also be numbered among the productions of the Vienna school. His *Leben des Orest* (1930),[43] a half-satirical, surrealistic treatment of the whole Orestes myth cycle, shows Křenek in a stage of transition between the early jazzlike manner of *Jonny* and a serious classical style. *Karl V*, composed before 1933 and first performed at Prague in 1938, is entirely in the twelvetone system. The nobility of style is remarkable in this work, well fitting the epic treatment of the subject. The music is somewhat similar to Wellesz's *Alkestis* but less uncompromising in its dissonances and often very expressive in melodic line.

This concludes our survey of the history of opera. As we look back over the past there is borne in upon us with irresistible force a certain feeling of futility. The thought of so much buried beauty is saddening; for it is buried for the most part beyond recall, with even less hope of resurrection than old poems or old paintings, which can at least be enjoyed without a complex mediating apparatus in the shape of instruments and performers to create the art work anew each time. We have tried to bring to the reader some idea of how these operas of the past sounded and why they were written as they were. But none of this can be more than a simple introduction. All descriptions, all analyses of forms, music, or poetry, make only a flat picture, a map, a mere diagram. The real living art can be glimpsed through the music, vividly enough perhaps in the case of a few works which still hold a place on our stage, but for all the rest only in moments of insight, and only then if we are able to cast ourselves back in imagination to the times when these operas were part of the life of men now passed away, "faded into impalpability through death, through absence, through change of manners." [44]

[43] Cf. Stuckenschmidt, "Hellenic Jazz," MMus VII, No. 3 (April–May, 1930) 22–25.
[44] James Joyce, *Ulysses* (New York, Random House, 1934) p. 186.

Bibliography

Bibliography

I

*Bibliographies, Lexicons, Guides, Histories,
and Other Works Dealing with
the Opera in General*

Aber, Adolf. Die Musik im Schauspiel, Geschichtliches und Aesthetisches. Leipzig, M. Beck, 1926.

Abert, Hermann. Grundprobleme der Operngeschichte. Leipzig, B&H, 1926.

Ademollo, Alessandro. Bibliografia della cronistoria teatrale italiana. Milano, Ricordi, 1888.

Albinati, Giuseppe. Piccolo dizionario di opere teatrali, oratori, cantati, ecc. Milano, Ricordi, 1913.

Allacci, Leone. Drammaturgia . . . accresciuta e continuata fino all' anno MDCCLV. Venezia, G. Pasquali, 1755. First published Rome, 1666.

Altmann, Wilhelm. Führer durch die einaktigen Opern, Operetten und Singspiele des Verlages Ed. Bote und G. Bock. Berlin, Bote & Bock, 1919.

—— Katalog der seit 1861 in den Handel gekommenen theatralischen Musik (Opern, Operetten, Possen, Musik zu Schauspielen, usw.); ein musikbibliographischer Versuch. Wolfenbüttel, Verlag für musikalische Kultur und Wissenschaft, 1935.

Annesley, Charles (pseud. of Charles and Anna Tittman). Home Book of the Opera, Including the Standard Opera Glass; Detailed Plots of the Celebrated Operas. New York, Tudor, 1937.

Apthorp, William Foster. The Opera Past and Present. London, John Murray, 1901.

Arnals, Alexander d'. Der Operndarsteller; Lehrgang zur musikalischen Darstellung in der Oper. Berlin, Bote & Bock, [1932].

Arundell, Dennis. "Operatic Ignorance," PMA LI (1924–25) 73–96.

Associazione dei musicologi italiana. Bolletino: catalogo delle opere musicali sino ai primi decenni del secolo XIX, Parma, 1910–11.
Catalogues of music collections by cities, under each city by libraries, under each library by forms and media, e.g. "opere teatrali."

Austin, Cecil. "Cinema Music," M&L V (1924) 177–91.

Barrenechea, Mariano Antonío. Historia estética de la música, con dos estudios mas sobre consideraciones historicas y tecnicas acerca del canto y la obra maestra del teatro melodramatico. Buenos Aires, Editorial Claridad, 1941.

Bekker, Paul. Das Operntheater. Leipzig, Quelle & Meyer, 1931.
—— Wandlungen der Oper. Zürich and Leipzig, Orell Füssli, [1934]. Translated as: The Changing Opera. [New York], W. W. Norton, [1935].
Bertrand, Paul. "Pure Music and Dramatic Music," MQ IX (1923) 545–55.
Bibliographie für Theatergeschichte 1905–1910, bearbeitet von Paul Alfred Merbach. Berlin, Selbstverlag der Gesellschaft für Theatergeschichte, 1913.
Bie, Oskar. Die Oper. Berlin, S. Fischer, 1913.
Bologna. Liceo musicale. Biblioteca. Catalogo della biblioteca del Liceo musicale di Bologna, compilato da Gaetano Gaspari. Bologna, Libreria romagnoli dell' acqua, 1890–1905. 4 vols.
Bonaccorsi, Alfredo. "L'opera in musica," RMI XXXVI (1929) 594–99.
Boston. Public Library. Allen A. Brown Collection. A Catalogue of the Allen A. Brown Collection of Books Relating to the Stage. Boston, 1919.
—— Catalogue of the Allen A. Brown Collection of Music. Boston, 1910–16. 4 vols.
British Museum. Department of Manuscripts. Catalogue of Manuscript Music in the British Museum, by Augustus Hughes-Hughes. London, 1906–1909. 3 vols.
British Museum. Department of Printed Books. Catalogue of Printed Music Published between 1487 and 1800 Now in the British Museum, by W. Barclay Squire. [London], 1912. 2 vols. The Second Supplement (1940) lists all acquisitions from 1912 to 1940 and makes corrections of the 1912 catalogue.
British Museum. Department of Printed Books. King's Music Library. Catalogue of the King's Music Iibrary, by William Barclay Squire. London, 1927–29. 3 vols.
Brockway, Wallace, and Herbert Weinstock. The Opera; a History of Its Creation and Performance, 1600–1941. New York, Simon & Schuster, 1941.
Brussels. Bibliothèque royale de Belgique. Catalogue de la bibliothèque de F. J. Fétis acquise par l'état belge. Gand, J. S. Van Doosselaere; Bruxelles, C. Muquardt; Paris, Firmin-Didot, 1877.
Brussels. Conservatoire royal de musique. Bibliothèque. Catalogue de la bibliothèque du Conservatoire royal de musique de Bruxelles . . . par Alfred Wotquenne. Bruxelles, J.-J. Coosemans, 1898– . 4 vols. Annexe[s] I, Bruxelles, O. Schepens, 1901, contains: Libretti d'opéras et d'oratorios italiens du XVIIe siècle.
Bulthaupt, Heinrich Alfred. Dramaturgie der Oper. Leipzig, B&H, 1887. 2 vols.
Bustico, Guido. Bibliografia delle storie e cronistorie dei teatri italiani. Milano, Bollettino bibliografico musicale, 1929.
Cambridge. University. Fitzwilliam Museum. Library. Catalogue of the Music in the Fitzwilliam Museum, Cambridge, by J. A. Fuller-Maitland. London, C. J. Clay, 1893.

Capell, Richard. Opera. London, E. Benn, [1930].

Capri, Antonio. Il melodramma dalle origini ai nostri giorni. Modena, Guanda, 1938.

Carducci, Edgardo. "The Tenor Voice in Europe," M&L XI (1930) 318–23.

Challis, Bennett. "The Technique of Operatic Acting," MQ XIII (1927) 630–45.

Cheney, Sheldon. The Theatre. New York, Longmans, Green, 1929.

Child, Harold. "Some Thoughts on Opera Libretto," M&L II (1921) 244–53.

Clayton, Ellen Creathorne. Queens of Song. London, Smith, Elder, 1863. 2 vols.

Contains a (worthless) "chronological list of all the operas that have been performed in Europe [!]."

Clément, Félix. Dictionnaire des opéras (dictionnaire lyrique), rev. et mis à jour par Arthur Pougin. Paris, Larousse, [1905].

Closson, Hermann. Musique et drame. Bruxelles, [Institut national belge de radiodiffusion], 1939.

[Conti, Armand de Bourbon, prince de.] Traité de la comédie et des spectacles selon la tradition de l'église, tirée des conciles & des saints pères. Paris, L. Billaine, 1669.

Curzon, Henri de. L'Evolution lyrique au théâtre dans les differents pays; tableau chronologique. Paris, Fortin, 1908.

Czech, Stany. Das Operettenbuch; ein Wegweiser durch die Operetten und Singspiele der deutschen Bühne. Dresden, E. Wulffen, [1939]. 2d ed.

Dassori, Carlo. Opere e operisti (dizionario lirico 1541–1902); elenco nominativo universale dei maestri compositori di opere teatrali, col prospetto cronologico dei lori principali lavori e catalogo alfabetico generale delle opere . . . coll' indicazione di data e di luogo della prima rappresentazione, avuto speciale reguardo al repertorio italiano. Genova, R. Istituto sordomuti, 1903.

Davidson, Gladys. Standard Stories from the Operas. London, T. W. Laurie, 1935–[40]. 2 vols.

Deditius, Annemarie. Theorien über die Verbindung von Poesie und Musik. Liegnitz, Seyffarth, 1918.

Denkmäler des Theaters; Inszenierung, Dekoration, Kostüm des Theaters. Wien, Nationalbibliothek; München, R. Piper, [1925?–30]. In twelve parts; plates (some colored) in portfolios, with explanatory text laid in. Also published as: Monumenta scenica: The Art of the Theatre. London, Batsford, 1925–31.

Dent, Edward J. "The Nomenclature of Opera," M&L XXV (1944) 132–40, 213–26.

—— Opera. New York, Penguin Books, [1940].

—— "The Translation of Operas," PMA LXI (1934–35) 81–104.

Dilla, Geraldine P. "Music Drama: An Art Form in Four Dimensions," MQ X (1924) 492–99.

Dittmar, Franz. Opernführer, ein unentbehrlicher Ratgeber für den Besuch der Oper. Leipzig, Hachmeister & Thal, [1919].

Dubech, Lucien, J. de Montbrial, and Hélène Horn-Monval. Histoire générale illustrée du théâtre. Paris, Librairie de France, 1931–34. 5 vols.

Edwards, [Henry] Sutherland. History of the Opera from Monteverdi to Donizetti. London, W. H. Allen, 1862. 2d ed.

Einstein, Alfred. "The Mortality of Opera," M&L XXII (1941) 358–66.

Eisenmann, Alexander. Das grosse Opernbuch. Stuttgart and Berlin, Deutsche Verlagsanstalt, 1923.

Elson, Arthur. A Critical History of Opera; Giving an Account of the Rise and Progress of the Different Schools, with a Description of the Master Works in Each. Boston, L. C. Page, 1901.

Elson, Louis C. "Atrocities and Humors of Opera," MQ VI (1920) 206–13.

England, Paul. Fifty Favourite Operas; a Popular Account Intended as an Aid to Dramatic and Musical Appreciation. London, G. G. Harrap, [1925].

Fink, Gottfried Wilhelm. Wesen und Geschichte der Oper; ein Handbuch für alle Freunde der Tonkunst. Leipzig, G. Wigand, 1838.

Frankenfelder, August. Historische Elemente in der Oper und ihre ästhetische Bedeutung. Würzburg, Becker, 1896.

Freedley, George, and John A. Reeves. A History of the Theatre. New York, Crown Publishers, [1941].
Includes a bibliography of 433 works, cross-indexed by country and special topics.

Fürst, Leonhard. Der musikalische Ausdruck der Körperbewegung in der Opernmusik. Miesbach, Mayr, 1932.

Galli, Amintore. Estetica della musica ossia del bello nella musica sacra, teatrale, e da concerto in ordine alla sua storia. Torino, Bocca, 1899.

Galloway, W. Johnson. The Operatic Problem. London, Long, 1902.

Gavazzeni, Gianandrea. "La poesia dell' opera in musica," RassM XI (1938) 137–62.

Gloggner, Carl. "Oper und Gesangskunst," Musikalisches Wochenblatt I (1870) 65–67, 81–82, 97–98, 113–14.

Goddard, Joseph. The Rise and Development of Opera. London, W. Reeves, 1912.

Götze, Willibald. Studien zur Formbildung der Oper. Frankfurt a.M., Brönner, 1935.

Goode, Gerald. The Book of Ballets. New York, Crown Publishers, [1939].

Grabbe, Paul. Minute Stories of the Opera. New York, Grosset & Dunlap, [1932].

Grand-Carteret, John. "Les Titres illustrés et l'image au service de la musique," RMI V (1898) 1–63, 225–80; VI (1899) 289–329; IX (1902) 557–635; XI (1904) 1–23, 191–227.

Gregor, Hans. Die Welt der Oper—die Oper der Welt. Berlin, Bote & Bock, [1931].

Gregor, Joseph. Kulturgeschichte der Oper. Wien, Gallus, 1941.

Hagemann, Carl. Oper und Szene; Aufsätze zur Regie des musikalischen Dramas. Berlin, Schuster & Loeffler, 1905.

Hansemann, Marlise. Der Klavier-Auszug von den Anfängen bis Weber. Borna, Meyen, 1943.

Hatton, A. P. "Personality in Opera," M&L XII (1931) 164–69.

Heseltine, Philip. "The Scope of Opera," M&L I (1920) 230–33.

Hirsch, Paul. Katalog der Musikbibliothek Paul Hirsch . . . Band II: Opern-Partituren. Berlin, Breslauer, 1930.

Howes, Frank. A Key to Opera. London and Glasgow, Blackie, [1939].

—— "Professor Wellesz on Opera," M&L XV (1934) 120–27.

Hussey, Dyneley. Euridice; or The Nature of Opera. London, K. Paul, 1929.

Istel, Edgar. Das Buch der Oper. Berlin, M. Hesse, [1920]. 2d ed.

—— Das Libretto; Wesen, Aufbau und Wirkung des Opernbuchs. Berlin and Leipzig, Schuster & Loeffler, 1914. Translated (revised) as: The Art of Writing Opera Librettos. New York, G. Schirmer, [1922].

—— Revolution und Oper. Regensburg, G. Bosse, 1919.

Kapp, Julius. Das Opernbuch; eine Geschichte der Oper und ein musikalisch-dramatischer Führer. Leipzig, Hesse & Becker, 1935.

Kinsky, Georg. [Geschichte der Musik in Bildern.] A History of Music in Pictures. London, J. M. Dent, [1937].

Kobbé, Gustav. The Complete Opera Book; the Stories of the Operas, together with 400 of the Leading Airs and Motives in Musical Notation. New York and London, G. P. Putnam's Sons, [1932].

Köhler, Louis. Die Melodie der Sprache in ihrer Anwendung besonders auf das Lied und die Oper. Leipzig, Weber, 1853.

Kraussold, Max. Geist und Stoff der Operndichtung; eine Dramaturgie in Umrissen. Leipzig, Strache, 1931.

Krehbiel, Henry Edward. A Book of Operas. New York, Macmillan, 1928. 2 vols. in one, combining "A Book of Operas" and "A Second Book of Operas."

Kretzschmar, Hermann. "Für und gegen die Oper," JMP XX (1913) 59–70.

—— Geschichte der Oper. Leipzig, B&H, 1919.

Kruse, Georg Richard. Reclams Opernführer. Leipzig, P. Reclam, [1937]. 7th enlarged ed. 1942, 13th ed.

Kunath, Martin. "Die Charakterologie der stimmlichen Einheiten in der Oper," ZfMw VIII (1925–26) 403–10.

—— Die Oper als literarische Form. Leipzig Dissertation, 1925.

La Laurencie, Lionel de. Inventaire critique du fonds Blancheton de la Bibliothèque du Conservatoire de Paris. Paris, E. Droz, 1930–31. 2 vols.

Loewenberg, Alfred. Annals of Opera, 1597–1940. Cambridge, W. Heffer, 1943.

Loschelder, Josef. Die Oper als Kunstform. Wien, A. Schroll, [1941].

McSpadden, Joseph Walker. Light Opera and Musical Comedy. New York, Thomas Y. Crowell, [1936].

—— Opera Synopses. New York, Thomas Y. Crowell, [1934]. 5th ed.

—— Operas and Musical Comedies. New York, Thomas Y. Crowell, 1946. A rearrangement and expansion of his two earlier books above.

Madrid. Biblioteca nacional. Departmento de manuscritos. Catálogo de las piezas de teatro. Madrid, Blass, 1934–35. 2 vols.

Manners, Charles. "The Financial Problems of National Opera," M&L VII (1926) 93–105.

Mantzius, Karl. A History of Theatrical Art in Ancient and Modern Times. London, Duckworth, 1903–21. 6 vols.

Martens, Frederick Herman. The Book of the Opera and the Ballet and History of the Opera. New York, C. Fischer, [1925].

—— A Thousand and One Nights of Opera. New York, D. Appleton, [1926].

Matthews, Brander. "The Conventions of the Music Drama," MQ V (1919) 255–63.

Mayer, Anton. Die Oper; eine Anleitung zu ihrem Verständnis. Berlin, K. Wolff, [1935].

Mayer, Ernesto Rodolfo. "Verso quali mète è diretta l' 'opera'?" RMI XLII (1938) 363–67.

Melitz, Leo L. The Opera Goers' Complete Guide. New York, Dodd, Mead, 1924.

[Mendelssohn, Felix.] The Story of a Hundred Operas. New York, Grosset & Dunlap, [1940].

Mengelberg, Curt Rudolf. "Das Musikdrama als Kunstform," Die Musik XIII (1913–14) 288–99.

Mila, Massimo. "Il concetto di musica drammatica," RassM IV (1931) 98–106.

Mnilk, Walter. Reclams Operettenführer. Leipzig, Reclam, [1937].

Neitzel, Otto. Der Führer durch die Oper des Theaters der Gegenwart. Leipzig, A. G. Liebeskind, 1890–98. 3 vols.

Newman, Ernest. More stories of Famous Operas. New York, Knopf, 1943.

—— Stories of the Great Operas and Their Composers. New York, Garden City Publishing Company, [1928]. 3 vols. in one. Both the above titles reprinted, 1946.

New York. Public Library. The Development of Scenic Art and Stage Machinery; a List of References in the New York Public Library. New York, 1920.

Nicoll, Allardyce. The Development of the Theatre. London, George C. Harrap, 1927.

O'Neill, Norman. "Music to Stage Plays," PMA XXXVII (1911) 85–102.

"Opera," in Enciclopedia universal ilustrada europea-americana ("Espasa") XXXIX, 1360–94; XXI, 1297–1300.

Ordway, Edith Bertha. The Opera Book. New York, Sully & Kleinteich, [1915].

Paris. Bibliothèque nationale. Département des imprimés. Catalogue du fonds de musique de la Bibliothèque nationale, par J. Ecorcheville. Paris, 1910–14. 8 vols.

Paris. Conservatoire national de musique et de déclamation. Bibliothèque. Catalogue bibliographique . . . avec notices et reproductions musicales des principaux ouvrages de la réserve, par J. B. Weckerlin. Paris, Firmin-Didot, 1885.

Peltz, Mary Ellis. The Metropolitan Opera Guide. New York, The Modern Library, [1939].

Percival, Robert. "Can Opera Be Made to Pay?" M&L VII (1926) 114–19.

[Pereira Peixoto d'Almeida Carvalhaes, Manoel.] Catálogo da importante biblioteca que pertencen ao . . . erudito e bibliofilo ilustre Manuel de Carvalhaes . . . organisado par Augusta Sâ da Costa. Lisboa, 1928.

Peyser, Herbert F. "Some Observations on Translation," MQ VIII (1922) 353–71.

Prod'homme, Jacques Gabriel: "Etat alphabétique sommaire des archives de l'opéra," RdM XIV (1933) 193–205.

Rabich, Ernst. Die Entwicklung der Oper. Langensalza, Beyer, 1926.

Radford, Maisie. "A Comparative Study of Indigenous Forms of Opera," M&L VII (1926) 106–13.

Radio Listener's Book of Operas. Boston, Lothrop, Lee & Shepard, [1926]. 2 vols. in one.

Refardt, Edgar. Verzeichnis der Aufsätze zur Musik in den nichtmusikalischen Zeitschriften der Universitätsbibliothek Basel abgeschlossen auf den 1. Januar 1924. Leipzig, B&H, 1925.

Renner, Hans. Die Wunderwelt der Oper; der grosse Führer durch die Oper und die klassische Operette. Berlin, Vier Falken Verlag, [1938].

Riemann, Hugo. Opern-Handbuch; Repertorium der dramatisch-musikalischen Litteratur. Leipzig, H. Seemann Nachfolger, [published in parts; 1881–1900?].

Rinaldi, Mario. L'opera in musica; saggio estetico. Roma, "Novissima," [1934].

Sanborn, Pitts. The Metropolitan Book of the Opera; Synopses of the Operas. Garden City, N.Y., Garden City Publishing Co., [1942].

Sauerlandt, Max. Die Musik in fünf Jahrhunderten der europäischen Malerei etwa 1450 bis etwa 1850. Leipzig, Langewiesche Verlag, 1922.

Schiedermair, Ludwig. "Ueber den Stand der Operngeschichte," in International Music Society, Second Congress Report (Leipzig, B&H, 1907) pp. 212–16.

Schladebach, Julius. "Geschichte der Oper bis auf Gluck," Die Wissenschaft im 19. Jahrhundert I (1856) 361.

Scholze, Johannes. Vollständiger Opernführer. Berlin, S. Mode, 1919. 4th ed. 5th ed., S. Mode, 1921. 7th ed. under the title "Opernführer," Leipzig, J. Dörner, 1935.

Schumann, Otto. Meyers Opernbuch. Leipzig, Bibliographisches Institut, [1938]. 4th ed.

Sear, H. G. "Operatic Mortality," M&L XXI (1940) 60–74.

Small, Herbert F. "On Opera," MQ IV (1918) 37–49.

Sonneck, Oscar George Theodore. "Noch etwas über Opernlexika," *Die Musik* XIII (1913–14) Qt. 4, 140–43.

Steidel, Max. Oper und Drama. Karlsruhe, G. Braun, 1923.

Stieger, Franz. "Opernkomponistinnen," *Die Musik* XIII (1913–14) Qt. 4, 270–71.

Storck, Karl G. L. Das Opernbuch. Stuttgart, Muth, 1929. 33–34th ed.

[Strangways, A. H. Fox.] "Opera and the Musician," M&L XIII (1932) 119–25.

Strantz, Ferdinand von. Opernführer. Berlin, A. Weichert, [1931].

Streatfeild, Richard Alexander. The Opera. London, G. Routledge, 1925. 5th ed.

Theatrical Designs from the Baroque through Neo-Classicism; Unpublished Material from American Private Collections. New York, H. Bittner, 1940. 3 vols.

Thompson, Oscar. Plots of the Operas, as Compiled for the International Cyclopedia of Music and Musicians. New York, Dodd, Mead, 1940.

Tommasini, Vincenzo. "Del drama lirico," RMI XXXIX (1932) 73–113.

Towers, John. Dictionary-Catalogue of Operas and Operettas Which Have Been Performed on the Public Stage. Morgantown, W. Va., Acme, [1910].

Turin. Biblioteca civica. Sezione teatrale. [Letteratura drammatica. Torino, G. B. Vassallo, 1912, 1911. 2 vols.]

United States Library of Congress. Division of Music. Catalogue of Opera Librettos Printed before 1800, prepared by Oscar George Theodore Sonneck. Washington, Government Printing Office, 1914. 2 vols.

—— Dramatic Music (Class M 1500, 1510, 1520); Catalogue of Full Scores, Compiled by E. G. T. Sonneck. Washington, Government Printing Office, 1908.

Upton, George Putnam. The Standard Light Operas. Chicago, A. C. McClurg, 1902.

—— The Standard Operas. Chicago, A. C. McClurg, 1928. New ed.

Valentin, Erich. "Dichtung und Oper; eine Untersuchung des Stilproblems der Oper," AfMf III (1938) 138–79.

Watkins, Mary Fitch. First Aid to the Opera-Goer. New York, F. A. Stokes, 1924.

Welter, Friedrich. Führer durch die Opern. Leipzig, Hachmeister & Thal, [1937].

Wichmann, Heinz. Der neue Opernführer, mit einem Anhang, Klassische Operetten. Berlin, P. Franke, 1943.

Wossidlo, Walter. Opern-Bibliothek; populärer Führer durch Poesie und Musik. Leipzig, Rühle & Wendling, [1919?].

Zopff, Hermann. Grundzüge einer Theorie der Oper. Leipzig, Arnold, 1868.

II

Works Dealing with Particular Operas,
Composers, Schools, Regions,
or Periods

Abascal Brunet, Manuel. Apuntes para la historia del teatro en Chile; la zarzuela grande. Santiago de Chile, Imprenta universitaria, 1940.

Abendroth, Walter. Hans Pfitzner. München, A. Lagen & G. Müller, 1935.

Abert, Hermann. "Die dramatische Musik," in *Herzog Karl Eugen von Württemberg und seine Zeit* I (Esslingen a. N., 1907) 555–611.

—— Gesammelte Schriften und Vorträge. Halle an der Saale, M. Niemeyer, 1929.
Contains essays on Gluck, Handel, Meyerbeer, Mozart, Noverre, Paisiello, Piccinni, Wagner, Weber, and eighteenth-century opera.

—— "Gluck und unsere Zeit," *Die Musik* XIII (1913–14) Qt. 4, 3–9.

—— "Glucks Alkestis im Stuttgarter Landestheater," ZfMw VI (1923–24) 353–61.

—— "Händel als Dramatiker," in *Haendelfestspiele (Göttinger, 1922)*. Göttingen, Turm-Verlag, 1922.

—— "Herzog Karl von Württemberg und die Musik," in *Süddeutsche Monatshefte* V (1908) Bd. 1, 548–54.

—— "Johann Christian Bach's italienische Opern und ihr Einfluss auf Mozart," ZfMw I (1918–19) 313–28.

—— "Mozart and Gluck." M&L X (1929) 256–65.

—— Niccolo Jommelli als Opernkomponist, mit einer Biographie. Halle an der Saale, M. Niemeyer, 1908.

—— "Robert Schumann's *Genoveva*," ZIMG XI (1909–10) 277–89.

—— W. A. Mozart: neubearbeitete und erweiterte Ausgabe von Otto Jahns Mozart. Leipzig, B&H, 1923–24. 6th ed. 2 vols.

—— "Zur Geschichte der Oper in Württemberg," in *III. Kongress der Internationalen Musikgesellschaft . . . Bericht* (Wien, Artaria; Leipzig, B&H, 1909) pp. 186–93.

Abraham, Gerald. "The Best of Spontini," M&L XXIII (1942) 163–71.

—— Borodin, the Composer and His Music. London, Wm. Reeves, [1927].

—— *"The Flying Dutchman:* Original Version," M&L XX (1939) 412–19.

—— A Hundred Years of Music. New York, Knopf, 1938.

—— "The Leitmotif since Wagner," M&L VI (1925) 175–90.

—— "Moussorgsky's *Boris* and Pushkin's," M&L XXVI (1945) 31–38.

—— "Nietzsche's Attitude to Wagner; a Fresh View," M&L XIII (1932) 64–74.

—— On Russian Music. New York, Scribner, 1939.

—— Studies in Russian Music. New York, Scribner, 1936.

Abry, Emile. Histoire illustrée de la littérature française . . . par E. Aubry, C. Audic, P. Crouzet. Paris, Didier, 1935. Nouvelle éd.

Achenwall, Max. Studien über die komische Oper in Frankreich im 18. Jahrhundert und ihre Beziehungen zu Molière. Eilenburg, Offenhauer, 1912.

Adaiewsky, E. "Glinka; études analytiques," RMI XI (1904) 725–60; XVII (1910) 113–29.

Adam, Adolphe. Derniers souvenirs d'un musicien. Paris, Michel Levy frères, 1859.

—— Souvenirs d'un musicien . . . précédés de notes biographiques écrites par lui-même. Paris, Calmann-Lévy, 1884.

Adam de la Halle. Œuvres complètes du trouvère Adam de la Halle, poésies et musique; publiées . . . par E. de Coussemaker. Paris, A. Durand & Pedone-Lauriel, 1872.

Adami, Giuseppe. Puccini. Milano, Fratelli Treves, [1935].

Ademollo, Alessandro. La bell' Adriana ed altre virtuose del suo tempo alla corte di Mantova; contributo de documenti per la storia della musica in Italia nel primo quarto del seicento. Città di Castello, Lapi, 1888.

—— I primi fasti del teatro di via della Pergola in Firenze (1657–1661). Milano, Ricordi, [etc., 1885].

—— I teatri di Roma nel secolo decimosettimo. Roma, L. Pasqualucci, 1888.

Adimari, Lodovico. "Satira quarta; contro alcuni vizi delle donne, e particolamente contro le cantatrice," in Satire del marchese Lodovico Adimari (Londra, Si vende in Livorno presso T. Masi e comp., 1788) pp. 183–253.

Adler, Guido. "Einleitung [to Cesti's Pomo d'oro]," DTOe, Jahrg. III, Pt. 2 (1896) v–xxvi.

—— "Euryanthe in neuer Einrichtung [von Gustav Mahler]," ZIMG V (1903–1904) 269–75.

—— Handbuch der Musikgeschichte unter Mitwirkung von Fachgenossen. Frankfurt am Main, Frankfurter Verlags-Anstalt, 1924.

—— "Die Kaiser Ferdinand III., Leopold I., Joseph I. und Karl VI. als Tonsetzer und Förderer der Musik," VfMw VIII (1892) 252–74.

—— Richard Wagner, Vorlesungen gehalten an der Universität zu Wien. München, Drei Masken Verlag, 1923. 2d ed. (first publ. 1904).

Adorján, Andor. "L'Opérette hongroise," Revue de Hongrie VI (1910) 269–80.

Alaleona, Domenico. Studi su la storia dell' oratorio musicale in Italia. Torino, Bocca, 1908.

—— "Su Emilio de' Cavalieri," La nuova musica, Nos. 113–114 (1905) 35–38, 47–50.

Alarcón, Esperanza. "La ópera en México, sus comienzos y los mexicanos autores de óperas," Boletín del instituto mexicano de musicología y folklore I (1940) 5–9.

Albert, Maurice. Les Théâtres de la foire (1660–1789). Paris, Hachette, 1900.

—— Les Théâtres des boulevards (1789–1848). [Paris?], Lecène et Oudin, 1902.

Alberti, C. E. R. Ludwig van Beethoven als dramatischer Tondichter. Stettin, 1859. ("Für Freunde der Tonkunst.")

Albrecht, Otto E. Four Latin Plays of St. Nicholas from the 12th Century Fleury Play-Book; Text and Commentary, with a Study of the Music of the Plays, and of the Sources and Iconography of the Legends. Philadelphia, University of Pennsylvania Press; London, Oxford University Press, 1935.

Aldrich, Putnam C. The Principal Agréments of the Seventeenth and Eighteenth Centuries; a Study in Musical Ornamentation. Harvard Dissertation, 1942.

Alfieri, Pietro. Notizie biografiche di Niccolò Jommelli di Aversa. Roma, Tip. delle belle arte, 1845.

Algarotti, Francesco, conte. Saggio sopra l'opera in musica. Livorno, Coltellini, 1763.

Almanach der deutschen Musikbücherei auf das Jahr 1924/25. Regensburg, Gustav Bosse, 1924.

Almanach des Spectacles. Paris, Nos. 1–43, 1874–1913.

Almeida, Renato. História da música brasileira. Rio de Janeiro, F. Briguiet, 1942. 2d. ed.

Altmann, Charlotte. Der französische Einfluss auf die Textbücher der klassischen Wiener Operette. Vienna Dissertation, 1935.

Altmann, Wilhelm. "Lortzing als dramaturgischer Lehrer," *Die Musik* XIII (1913–14) Qt. 4, 157–58.

—— "Meyerbeer-Forschungen; archivalische Beiträge aus der Registratur der Generalintendantur der Königlichen Schauspiele zu Berlin," SIMG IV (1902–1903) 519–34.

—— "Spontini an der Berliner Oper; eine archivalische Studie." SIMG IV (1902–1903) 244–92.

—— "Ur- und Erstaufführungen von Opernwerken auf deutschen Bühnen in den letzten Spielzeiten 1899/1900 bis 1924/25," in *Jahrbuch der Universal-Edition* (1926).

Altucci, Carlo. Le origini del teatro comico in Francia. Aversa, Tip. R. Catoggio, 1931.

Ambros, August Wilhelm. Geschichte der Musik, Bd. IV. Leipzig, Leuchart, 1909. 3d ed., rev. and enl. by Hugo Leichtentritt.

Anderson, Emily, ed. The Letters of Mozart and His Family Chronologically Arranged, Translated and Edited with an Introduction, Notes and Indices . . . with Extracts from the Letters of Constanze Mozart to Johann Anton André Translated and Edited by C. B. Oldman. London, Macmillan, 1938. 3 vols., paged continuously.

Andeutungen zur Geschichte der Oper. Marienwerder, A. Baumann, 1845. "Besonderer Abdruck aus dem ersten Hefte des Archivs für vaterländische Interessen pro 1845."

Andrade, Mário de. Carlos Gomez. Rio de Janeiro, Pongetti, 1939.

Anecdotes dramatiques; contenant toutes les pièces de théâtre . . . joués à Paris . . . jusq'à l'année 1775. Paris, Duchesne, 1775. 3 vols.

Anheisser, Siegfried. Für den deutschen Mozart. Emsdetten i. Westf., H. & J. Lechte, 1938.

—— "Die unbekannte Urfassung von Mozarts *Figaro*," ZfMw XV (1932–33) 301–17.

—— "Das Vorspiel zu *Tristan und Isolde* und seine Motivik," ZfMw III (1921) 257–304.

Annuario del teatro lirico italiano, 1940—. [Milano], Edizioni Corbaccio, [1940–   ].

Antcliffe, Herbert. "The British School of Music-Drama; the Work of Rutland Boughton," MQ IV (1918) 117–27.

Antheil, George. "Opera—a Way Out," MMus XI, No. 2 (January–February, 1934) 89–94.

—— "Wanted—Opera by and for Americans," MMus VII, No. 4 (June–July, 1930) 11–16.

Anthon, Carl Gustav. Music and Musicians in Northern Italy during the Sixteenth Century. Harvard Dissertation, 1943.

Anticlo, —— "Gli spiriti della musica nella tragedia greca," RMI XX (1913) 821–87.

Antonini, G. "Un episodio emotivo di Gaetano Donizetti," RMI VII (1900) 518–35.

Appia, Adolphe. La Mise en scène du drame Wagnérien. Paris, L. Chailley, 1895.

—— Die Musik und die Inscenierung; aus dem Französischen übersetzt. München, Bruckmann, 1899.

Arend, Max. "Gluck, der Reformator des Tanzes," *Die Musik* XIII (1913–14) Qt. 4, 16–22.

—— Gluck, eine Biographie. Berlin, Schuster & Loeffler, 1921.

—— "Die Ouvertüren zu Glucks *Cythère assiégée*," ZfMw IV (1921–22) 94–95.

—— "Die unter Gluck's Mitwirkung, verschollene älteste deutsche Übersetzung der *Iphigenia auf Tauris*," ZIMG VII (1905–1906) 261–67.

Arger, Jane. Les Agréments et le rhythme; leur représentation graphique dans la musique vocale française du XVIIe siècle. Paris, Rouart, Lerolle, [pref. 1917].

—— "Le Rôle expressif des 'agréments' dans l'école vocale française de 1680 à 1760," RdM I (1917–19) 215–26.

Aristotle. Aristotle's Treatise on Poetry, translated . . . by Thomas Twining. London, Payne and Son [etc.], 1789.

Armitage, Merle, ed. Arnold Schoenberg. New York, G. Schirmer, 1937.

—— ed. Igor Stravinsky; Articles and Critiques. New York, G. Schirmer, 1936.

Arnaldi, Enea, conte. Idea di un teatro nelle principali sue parte simile a' teatri antichi. Vicenza, A. Veronese, 1762.

Arnaudiès, Fernand. Histoire de l'opéra d'Alger; épisodes de la vie théâtrale algéroise, 1830–1940. Alger, V. Heintz, [1941].

Arnheim, Amalie. "Ein Beitrag zur Geschichte des einstimmigen weltlichen Kunstliedes in Frankreich im 17. Jahrhundert," SIMG X (1908–1909) 399–421.

—— "Le Devin du village von Jean-Jacques Rousseau und die Parodie Les Amours de Bastien et Bastienne," SIMG IV (1902–1903) 686–727.

Arnold, Franck T. The Art of Accompaniment from a Thorough-Bass as Practiced in the XVIIth and XVIIIth Centuries. London, Oxford University Press, 1931.

Arnold, Robert F. Das deutsche Drama. München, C. H. Beck, 1925.

Arnoldson, Mrs. Louise Parkinson. Sedaine et les musiciens de son temps. Paris, l'Entente linotypiste, 1934.

Arteaga, Stefano. Le rivoluzioni del teatro musicale italiano, dalla sua origine fino al presente. Venezia, C. Palese, 1785. 2d ed. 3 vols.

Arundell, Dennis. Henry Purcell. London, Oxford University Press, 1927.

Asenjo y Barbieri, Francisco. Cancionero musical de los siglos XV y XVI. Madrid, Tip. de los huérfanos, [1890].

Aubignac, François Hédelin, abbé d. La Pratique du théâtre. Amsterdam, J. F. Bernard, 1715. New ed. Alger, J. Carbonel, 1927.

Aubin, Léon. Le Drame lyrique; histoire de la musique dramatique en France. [Tours, édition de l' "Echo littéraire et artistique"], 1908.

Aubry, Georges Jean. La Musique française d'aujourd'hui. Paris, Perrin, 1916. Translated as: French Music of Today. London, K. Paul [etc.], 1919.

Augé-Chiquet, Mathieu. La Vie, les idées et l'œuvre de Baïf. Paris [etc.], Edouard Privat Hachette, 1909.

Augé de Lassus, Lucien. Boieldieu . . . ; biographie critique illustree. Paris, H. Laurens, [1908].

Auriac, Eugène d'. Théâtre de la foire; recueil de pièces représentées aux foires St.-Germain et St.-Laurent, précédé d'une essai historique sur les spectacles forains. Paris, Garnier frères, 1878.

Ayesterán, Lauro. Crónica de una temporada musical en el Montevideo de 1830. Montevideo, Ediciones Ceibo, 1943.

Babbitt, Irving. Rousseau and Romanticism. Boston and New York, Houghton Mifflin, 1919.

Babcock, Robert W. "Francis Coleman's 'Register of Operas,' 1712–1734," M&L XXIV (1943) 155–58. Supplemented and corrected in a letter by O. E. Deutsch, ibid. XXV (1944) 126.

Bacher, Otto. "Die deutschen Erstaufführungen von Mozarts Don Giovanni," Jahrbuch des Freien deutschen Hochstifts Frankfurt a. M. (1926) pp. 338–79. Also separately reprinted.

—— "Ein Frankfurter Szene zu Glucks Don Juan," ZfMw VII (1924–25) 570–74.

Bacher, Otto (*Cont.*). "Frankfurts musikalische Bühnengeschichte im 18. Jahrhundert. Theil I. Die Zeit der Wandertruppen (1700–1786)," *Archiv für Frankfurts Geschichte und Kunst* (1925) pp. 133–206.

—— Die Geschichte der Frankfurter Oper im 18. Jahrhundert. Frankfurt a. M., Englert und Schlosser, 1926.

—— "Ein Mozartfund," ZfMw VIII (1925–26) 226–30.

—— "Zur Geschichte der Oper auf Frankfurter Boden im 18. Jahrhundert," ZfMw VIII (1925–26) 93–102.

Bätz, Rüdiger. Schauspielmusiken zu Goethes *Faust*. Leipzig Dissertation, 1924.

Bagge, Selmar. "Robert Schumann und seine *Faust*-Scenen," in Waldersee, *Sammlung musikalischer Vorträge* (Leipzig, Graf, 1879) I, 121–40.

"Le Ballet au XIXe siècle," RM II (December, 1921; numéro special) 97–231.

Ballo, Ferdinando. Arrigo Boito. Torino, Ed. Arione, [1938].

Bannard, Yorke. "Music of the Commonwealth," M&L III (1922) 394–401.

Bapst, Germain. Essai sur l'histoire du théâtre. Paris, 1883.

Barberet, Vincent. Lesage et le théâtre de la foire. Nancy, 1887.

Barberio, Francesco. "Disavventure di Paisiello." RMI XXIII (1916) 534–58.

—— "Giovanni Paisiello tra le ire di un copista e di un innovatore," RMI XXII (1915) 301–18.

—— "Lettere inedite di Paisiello [1792–1812]," RMI XXIV (1917) 173–88.

—— "I primi dieci anni di vita artistica di Paisiello," RMI XXIX (1922) 264–76.

Barbieri, Francisco. *See* Asenjo y Barbieri.

Barclay Squire. *See* Squire, W. Barclay.

Bardi-Poswiansky, Benno. Flotow als Opernkomponist, Königsberg Dissertation, 1924.

—— Der tolle Kapellmeister; heitere Oper in 3 Akten mit Benutzung Reinhard Keiserscher Melodien. Textbuch. Berlin, Revo-Verlag, [1929].

Barini, Giorgio. "Noterelle Belliniane," RMI IX (1902) 62–71.

Barlow, Samuel. "Blitzstein's Answer," MMus XVIII, No. 2 (January–February, 1941) 81–83.

Baroni, Jole Maria. "La lirica musicale di Pietro Metastasio," RMI XII (1905) 383–406.

Barrett, William. Balfe; His Life and Work. London, Remington, 1882.

Barros Sierra, José. *"Tata Vasco* y su partitura," *Romance,* Vol. II, No. 23 (April [1941]).

Barry, C. A. "Introductory to the Study of Wagner's Comic Opera *Die Meistersinger von Nürnberg,*" PMA VII (March 7, 1881) 74–97.

Bartmuss, Arwed Waldemar. Die Hamburger Barockoper und ihre Bedeutung für die Entwicklung der deutschen Dichtung und der deutschen Bühne. Jena Dissertation, 1925.

Bartsch, Karl. Romances et pastourelles françaises des XIIe et XIIIe siècles. Leipzig, F. Vogel, 1870.

Barzun, Jacques. Darwin, Marx and Wagner; Critique of a Heritage. Boston, Little, Brown, 1941.

Bateson, F. W. English Comic Drama, 1700–1750. Oxford, Clarendon Press, 1929.

Batka, Richard. Die alt-italienische Aria; Ida Isori und ihre Kunst des Bel-Canto. Wien, H. Heller, 1912.

—— Aus der Opernwelt; Prager Kritiken und Skizzen. München, Callwey, 1907.

—— Die moderne Oper. Prag, Verlag der Lese- und Redehalle der deutschen Studenten in Prag, 1902.

Bauer, Marion. "Darius Milhaud," MQ XXVIII (1942) 139–59.

Baumann, Ken C. The Change of Style in Verdi's Operatic Work in the Interlude between *Aida* and *Otello*. Cornell A. M. Thesis, 1945.

Beare, Mary. The German Popular Play *Atis* and the Venetian Opera: a Study of the Conversion of Operas into Popular Plays, 1675–1722. Cambridge, University Press, 1938.

Beau, A. Eduard. "Die Musik im Werk des Gil Vicente," *Volkstum und Kultur der Romanen* IX (1936) 177–201.

Beaujoyeulx, Baltasar de. Balet comique de la royne, faict aux nopces de Monsieur le Duc de Ioyeuse & madamoyselle de Vaudemont sa soeur. Paris, LeRoy, Ballard & Patisson, 1682.

Beaulieu, Henri. Les Théâtres du boulevard de Crime . . . de Nicolet à Déjazet (1752–1862). Paris, H. Daragon, 1905.

Beck, Paul. "Oberschwäbische Volkstheater im 18. Jahrhundert," *Alemannia* XX (1892) 73–97.

Becker, Marta. "Der Einfluss der Philosophie Schellings auf Richard Wagner," ZfMw XIX (1931–32) 433–47.

Beckers, Paul. Die nachwagner'sche Oper bis zum Ausgang des 19. Jahrhunderts im Spiegel der Münchener Presse. Bielefeld, Beyer & Hausknecht, 1936.

Beer, Otto Fritz. "Egon Wellesz und die Oper," *Die Musik* XXIII (1931) 909–12.

—— Mozart und das Wiener Singspiel. Vienna Dissertation, 1932.

Behrend, William. "Weyse und Kuhlau; Studie zur Geschichte der dänischen Musik," *Die Musik* III, No. 22 (1904) 272–86.

Bekker, Paul. Franz Schreker; Studie zur Kritik der modernen Oper. Berlin, Schuster & Loeffler, 1919.

—— "Glucks *Alkeste* auf der Bühne," ZfMw I (1918–19) 193–96.

—— Klang und Eros. Stuttgart and Berlin, Deutsche Verlags-Anstalt, 1922.

—— Kritische Zeitbilder. Berlin, Schuster & Loeffler, 1921.

—— Das Musikdrama der Gegenwart. Stuttgart, Strecker & Schröder, 1909.

—— Neue Musik. Berlin, E. Reiss, 1920. 5th ed.

—— "The Opera Walks New Paths," MQ XXI (1935) 266–78.

Bekker, Paul (*Cont.*). Wagner; das Leben im Werke. Stuttgart, Deutsche Verlags-Anstalt, 1924. Translated as: Richard Wagner; His Life in His Works. New York, Norton, [1931].

Belaiev, Victor. Moussorgsky's *Boris Goudonov* and Its New Version. London, Oxford University Press, 1928.

Bellaigue, Camille. "Les Epoques de la musique; le grand opéra français," *Revue des deux mondes* (1906) No. 5, pp. 612–49.

—— "Les Epoques de la musique; l'opéra-comique," *Revue des deux mondes* (1905) No. 5, pp. 177–210.

—— "Les Epoques de la musique; l'opéra mélodique—Mozart," *Revue des deux mondes* (1901) No. 6, pp. 885–907.

—— "Les Epoques de la musique; l'opéra récitatif," *Revue des deux mondes* (1900) No. 6, pp. 608–38.

Bellasis, Edward. Cherubini; Memorials Illustrative of His Life. London, Burns & Oates, 1874.

Bellini, Vincenzo. Epistolario, a cura di Luisa Cambi. Verona, Mondadori, 1943.

Belluci la Salandra, Mario. Opere teatrali serie e buffe di Nicolò Piccinni. Roma, Edizioni Psalterium, 1935. For corrections, etc., see *Note d'archivio* XIII (1936) 55–58.

—— Saggio cronologico delle opere teatrali di Gaetano Latilla. Bari, 1935. Separate from *"Japigia," Rivista di arch., storica e arte.*

—— Triade musicale bitontina; . . . Logroscino, Traetta, Planelli. Bitonto, A. Amendolagene, 1935.

Beloch, Julius. "La populazione d'Italia nei secoli XVI, XVII e XVIII," *Bulletin de l'Institut international de statistique* III (1888) 1–42.

Benham, Evelyn. "A Musical Monopolist [J. B. Lully]," M&L IX (1928) 249–54.

[Benjamin, Lewis Saul.] Life and Letters of John Gay . . . by Lewis Melville [pseud.]. London, D. O'Connor, 1921.

Bennett, Howard G. "Opera in Modern Germany," MTNA XXIX (1934) 65–73.

Benvenuti, Giacomo. "Il manoscritto veneziano della *Incoronazione di Poppea*," RMI XLI (1937) 176–84.

Bérard, Jean Antoine. L'Art du chant. Paris, Dessait & Saillant, 1755.

Berend, Fritz. Nicolaus Adam Strungk. Hannover, E. Homann, [1915].

Berg, Alban. "A Word about *Wozzek*," MMus V, No. 1 (November–December, 1927) 22–24.

Berger, Arthur V. *"The Beggar's Opera,* the Burlesque, and Italian Opera," M&L XVII (1936) 93–105.

Bergmans, Paul. "Une Collection de livrets d'opéras italiens (1669–1710)," SIMG XII (1910–11) 221–34.

Berl, Paul. Die Opern Giuseppe Verdis in ihrer Instrumentation. Vienna Dissertation, 1931.

Berlioz, Hector. A Travers Chants; études musicales. Paris, Michel Lévy, 1872. 2d ed.

—— Les Grotesques de la musique. Paris, A. Bourdilliat, 1854.

—— Mémoires. Paris, Michel Lévy, 1870. Translated as: Memoirs of Hector Berlioz. New York, Tudor, [1935]. Annotated and the translation revised by Ernest Newman.

—— Les Musiciens et la musique. Paris, Calmann-Lévy, [1903].
A selection of articles from the *Journal des débats*, 1835–63.

—— Les Soirées de l'orchestre. Paris, Michel Lévy, 1852. Translated as: Evenings in the Orchestra. New York and London, Knopf, 1924. Introduction by Ernest Newman.

Bernacki, Ludwik. Teatr, dramat i muzyka za Stanislawa Augusta. Lwów, Zaktad Narodowy imiena Ussolínskich, 1925. 2 vols.

Bernet Kempers, Karel P. De Italiaansche Opera, haar Ontstaan en Ontwikkeling van Peri tot Puccini. Amsterdam, H. J. Paris, 1929.

Bernhard, Christoph. Die Kompositionslehre Heinrich Schützens in der Fassung seines Schülers Christoph Bernhard. Leipzig, B&H, 1926. Edited with an introduction by J. M. Müller-Blattau.

Bernstein, Nikolai Davidovich. Russland's Theater und Musik zur Zeit Peters des Grossen. Riga, Gizycko; Leipzig, Pabst, [1904].

Berrsche, Alexander. Kurze Einführung in Hans Pfitzners Musikdrama *Der arme Heinrich*. Leipzig, [1910].

Berthoud, Paul B. The Musical Works of Dr. Henry Hadley. New York, National Association for American Composers and Conductors, 1942.

Bertolotti, Antonio. Artisti francesi in Roma nei secoli XV, XVI e XVII. Mantua, Mondovi, 1894.

—— Musici alla corte dei Gonzaga in Mantova dal secolo XV al XVII; notizie e documenti raccolti negli Archivi Mantovani. Milano, Ricordi, [1890].

Besch, Otto. Engelbert Humperdinck. Leipzig, B&H, 1914.

Bethléem, Abbé L., and others. Les Opéras, les opéras-comiques et les opérettes. Paris, Editions de la Revue des lectures, 1926.
Critical evaluations from the standpoint of historical truthfulness, religion, and morality.

Beyle, Henri. Vie de Rossini, suivi des notes d'un dilettante. Paris, E. Champion, 1922. Preface and annotations by Henry Prunières. Translated as: Memoirs of Rossini. London, T. Hookham, 1824.

—— Vies de Haydn, de Mozart et de Métastase. Paris, H. Champion, 1914. Text established and annotated by Daniel Muller, preface by Romain Rolland.

Bie, Oscar. "Stand der Oper," *Die Neue Rundschau* XLIII, No. 2 (July–December, 1932) 124–31.

Biedenfeld, [Ferdinand, Freiherr von]. Die komische Oper der Italiener, der Franzosen und der Deutschen. Leipzig, Weigl, 1848.

Biehle, Herbert. Musikgeschichte der Stadt Bautzen. Berlin Dissertation, 1923.

Bienenfeld, Elsa. "Verdi and Schiller," MQ XVII (1931) 204–208.

Bilbao, José. Teatro Real; recuerdos de las cinco temporadas del empresario Arana. Madrid, Editorial Norma, 1936.

Billeci, A. La Bohème di Giacomo Puccini; studio critico. Palermo, Vesca, 1931.

Bitter, K[arl] H[ermann]. Die Reform der Oper durch Gluck und R. Wagner's Kunstwerk der Zukunft. Braunschweig, F. Vieweg, 1884. Critical review by H. Kretzschmar, VfMw I (1885) 227–34.

—— Mozart's Don Juan und Gluck's Iphigenia in Tauris; ein Versuch neuer Uebersetzungen. Berlin, F. Schneider, 1866.

Bitter, Werner. Die deutsche komische Oper der Gegenwart; Studien zu ihrer Entwicklung. Leipzig, Kistner & Siegel, 1932.

Bittrich, Gerhard. Ein deutsches Opernballett des siebzehnten Jahrhunderts; ein Beitrag zur Frühgeschichte der deutschen Oper. Leipzig, Frommhold & Wendler, 1931.

[Bizet, Georges.] See RdM XXII (November, 1938), special number devoted to Bizet.

Bizet, René. Une Heure de musique avec Oscar Straus. Paris, Editions cosmopolites, 1930.

Blareau, Ludovic. Histoire de la création et du développement du drame musical particulièrement en Italie, depuis l' Euridice de Peri jusqu'à l' Orfeo de Gluck. Bruxelles, Maurice Lamerten, 1921.
Superficial and uncritical.

Blaze, [François Henri Joseph], called Castil-Blaze. L'Académie impériale de musique . . . de 1645 à 1855. Paris, Castil-Blaze, 1855.

—— Chapelle-musique des rois de France. Paris, Paulin, 1832.

—— De l'opéra en France. Paris, Janet et Cotelle, 1820.

—— L'Opéra-Italien de 1548 à 1856. Paris, Castil-Blaze, 1856.

Blaze de Bury, Yetta. "The French Opera," Nineteenth Century (1890) No. 2, pp. 39–53.

Blitzstein, Marc. "Hin und Zurück in Philadelphia," MMus V, No. 4 (May–June, 1928) 34–36.

—— "The Phenomenon of Stravinsky," MQ XXI (1935) 330–47.

Blom, Eric. "The Problem of Don Giovanni," M&L XIII (1932) 381–90.

Blondel, S. "Les Castrats," La Chronique musicale IX (1875) 241–50.

Blümml, Emil Karl, and Gustav Gugitz. Alt-Wiener Thespiskarren; die Frühzeit der Wiener Vorstadtbühnen. Wien, A. Schroll, 1925.

Boardman, Herbert Russell. Henry Hadley, Ambassador of Harmony. Emory University, Georgia, Banner Press, [1932].

Boas, Hans. "Lorenzo da Ponte als Wiener Theaterdichter," SIMG XV (1913–14) 325–38.

[Bobillier, Marie.] Les Concerts en France sous l'ancien régime. Paris, Fischbacher, 1900.

——— "Grétry, sa vie et ses œuvres," in *Mémoires couronnés et autres mémoires publiés par l'Académie royale* . . . *de Belgique,* Tome XXXVI, 1884.

——— Notes sur l'histoire du luth en France. Turin, Bocca, 1899.

Böhme, Erdmann Werner. "Die frühdeutsche Oper in Altenburg," *Jahrbuch der Theaterfreunde für Altenburg und Umkreis* (1930) pp. 53 ff.

——— Die frühdeutsche Oper in Thüringen. Stadtroda in Thüringen, Richter, 1931.

——— Musik und Oper am Hofe Christians von Sachsen-Eisenberg (1677–1707). Stadtroda in Thüringen, Richter, [1930]. First published in *Mitteilungen des Geschichts- und Altertumsvereins zu Eisenberg in Thüringen,* 41. und 42. Heft (8. Band, 1. und 2. Heft, 1930).

——— "Zur Vorgeschichte der Barockoper in Altenburg," *Jahrbuch der Theaterfreunde für Altenburg und Umkreis* (1931).

Böhme, Franz Magnus. Geschichte des Tanzes in Deutschland. Leipzig, B&H, 1886. 2 vols.

Bötcher, Elmar. Goethes Singspiele *Erwin und Elmire* und *Claudine von Villa Bella* und die "opera buffa." Marburg, Elwert, 1912.

Böttger, Friedrich. Die "Comédie-Ballet" von Molière-Lully. Berlin, Funk, 1931.

Bohe, Walter. Die Wiener Presse in der Kriegszeit der Oper. Würzburg, Triltsch, 1933. Published also with the title: Wagner im Spiegel der Wiener Presse.

Bohn, [Emil?]. "Theophilus; niederdeutsches Schauspiel aus einer Handschrift des 15. Jahrhunderts," MfMg IX (1877) 3–4. Music, pp. 24–25.

Boislisle, Arthur Michel de. "Les Débuts de l'opéra français à Paris," *Mémoires de la Société de l'histoire de Paris* II (1876) 172 ff.

Boïto, Arrigo. Lettere. Roma, Società editrice "Novissima," [1932].

——— "Pensieri critici giovanili," RMI XXXI (1924) 161–98.

Boladeres Ibern, Guillermo de. Enrique Granados. Barcelona, Editorial Arte y letras, [1921].

Bollert, Werner. Aufsätze zur Musikgeschichte. Bottrop, Postberg, 1938. Contains essays on Salieri and Weigl.

——— Die Buffoopern Baldassare Galuppis. Bottrop, Postberg, 1935.

——— "Giuseppe Petrosellini quale librettista di opere," RMI XLIII (1939) 531–38.

——— "Tre opere di Galuppi, Haydn e Paisiello sul' *Mondo della luna* di Goldoni," *Musica d'oggi* XXI (1939) 265–70.

Bolte, Johannes. Die Singspiele der englischen Komödianten und ihrer Nachfolger in Deutschland, Holland und Skandinavia. Hamburg and Leipzig, L. Voss, 1893.

Bonaventura, Arnaldo. "Una celebre cantante livornese del settecento," *Musica d'oggi* VI (1924) 255–58.

——— Giacomo Puccini. Livorno, [1925].

——— "Le maggiolate," RMI XXIV (1917) 272–99.

Bonaventura, Arnaldo (*Cont.*). L'opera italiana. Firenze, Novissima enciclopedia monografia illustrata, [1928].

—— Saggio storico sul teatro musicale italiano. Livorno, R. Giusti, 1913.

—— Verdi. Paris, F. Alcan, 1923.

Bonavia, Ferrucio. Verdi. London, Oxford University Press, 1930.

Bonnefon, Paul. "Les Métamorphoses d'un opéra (lettres inédites d'Eugène Scribe)," *Revue des deux mondes* (1917) No. 5, pp. 877–99.

Bonnet, George Edgar. Philidor et l'évolution de la musique française au XVIIIe siècle. Paris, Delagrave, 1921.

[Bonnet, Jacques.] Histoire de la musique, et de ses effets. Paris, J. Cochart, 1715.

Borcherdt, Hans Heinrich. "Beiträge zur Geschichte der Oper und des Schauspiels in Schlesien bis zum Jahre 1740," *Zeitschrift für die Geschichte Schlesiens* XLIII (1909) 217 ff.

—— "Geschichte der italienischen Oper in Breslau," *Zeitschrift für die Geschichte Schlesiens* XLIV (1910) 18 ff.

Borland, John E. "French Opera before 1750," PMA XXXIII (1907) 133–57.

Borrel, Eugène. L'Interprétation de la musique française (de Lully à la révolution). Paris, F. Alcan, 1924.

——"L'Interprétation de l'ancien récitatif français," RdM XII (1931) 13–21.

—— "Les Notes inégales dans l'ancienne musique française," RdM XII (1931) 278–89.

—— "Un Paradoxe musical au XVIIIe siècle," in *Mélanges de musicologie* (Paris, Droz, 1933) pp. 217–21.

Borrelli, E. "Il Wort-Ton-Drama," RassM VII (1934) 333–43, 433–36.

Borren, Charles van den. Alessandro Scarlatti et l'esthétique de l'opéra napolitain. Paris, Editions de la Renaissance d'occident, 1921.

—— *Il ritorno d'Ulisse in patria* du Claudio Monteverdi. Bruxelles, Weissenbruch, 1925.

—— "Roma centro musicale del settecento," RMI XXXI (1924) 69–71.

Bosch, Mariano. Historia de la ópera en Buenos Aires. Buenos Aires, El Comercio, 1905.

Boschot, Adolphe. "A propos du centenaire de La Damnation de Faust," RM XXII (February–March, 1946) 11–14.

—— Le *Faust* de Berlioz. Paris, Librairie de France, 1927.

—— Hector Berlioz; une vie romantique. Paris, Plon, [1939]. Published in 1920 under title: Une Vie romantique; Hector Berlioz.

—— L'Histoire d'un romantique: Hector Berlioz. I. La Jeunesse d'un romantique . . . 1803–1831. Paris, Plon-Nourrit, 1906. II. Un Romantique sous Louis-Philippe . . . 1831–1842. Paris, Plon-Nourrit, 1908. III. Le Crépuscule d'un romantique . . . 1842–1869. Paris, Plon-Nourrit, 1913.

—— "Sur Gluck et Wagner," *Revue politique et littéraire* XXXVII (1900) 19–23.

—— La Vie et les œuvres de Alfred Bruneau. Paris, Fasquelle, [1937].

Botstiber, Hugo. Geschichte der Ouvertüre und der freien Orchesterformen. Leipzig, B&H, 1913.

Boughton, Rutland. The Death and Resurrection of the Music Festival. London, W. Reeves, [1913].

—— The Glastonbury Festival Movement. London, [Somerset Press], 1922. Reprinted from *Somerset and the Drama* [by S. R. Littlewood and others].

—— Music Drama of the Future; *Uther and Igraine,* Choral Drama . . . with Essays by the Collaborators. London, W. Reeves, 1911.

—— "A National Music Drama; the Glastonbury Festival," PMA XLIV (1917–18) 19–35.

Bourdelot, Pierre. *See* Bonnet, Jacques.

Bouvet, Charles. Spontini. Paris, Rieder, [1930].

Bowen, Catherine D. Free Artist. New York, Random House, [1939].

Bowen, Catherine D., and Barbara von Meck. "Beloved Friend." New York, Random House, 1937.

Brabec, Ernst. Richard Wagner und Friedrich Smetana. Prague Dissertation, 1937.

Brady, William S. "Operatic Opportunities for American Pupils," MTNA XXI (1926) 140–44.

Braga, Theophilo. Historia do theatro portuguez [Vol. III]; a baixa comedia e a opera, secolo XVIII. Porto, Impr. portugueza-editora, 1870–71.

Bragaglia, Anton Giulio. "Celebrazioni Marchigiane; Giacomo Torelli da Fano," *Il giornale di politica e di letteratura* X (1934) 331–62; XI (1935) 69–80.

Brancour, René. Félicien David. Paris, H. Laurens, [190–].

—— Méhul. Paris, H. Laurens, [1912].

Brand, Max. " 'Mechanische' Musik und das Problem der Oper," *Musikblätter des Anbruch* VIII (1926) 356–59.

Brandstetter, Renward. "Musik und Gesang beiden Luzerner Osterspielen," *Der Geschichtsfreund* XL (1885) 145–68.

Braudo, Eugen. "Concerts, Opera, Ballet in Russia Today," MMus X, No. 4 (May–June, 1933) 213–19.

—— "The Russian Panorama," MMus X, No. 2 (January–February, 1933) 79–86.

Braun, Lisbeth. "Die Balletkomposition von Joseph Starzer," SzMw XIII (1926) 38–56.

Braunstein, Josef. Beethovens Leonore-Ouvertüren; eine historisch-stilkritische Untersuchung. Leipzig, B&H, 1927.

—— "Gibt es zwei Fassungen von der Ouvertüre Leonore Nr. 2?" ZfMw IX (1926–27) 349–60.

Bravo, F. Suarez. "La Musique à Barcelone: *Los Pireneos* de F. Pedrell," ZIMG III (1901–02) 231–39.

Brazil. Ministerio da educação e saude. Relação das opéras de autores brasileiros por Luiz Heitor Corrêa de Azevedo. Rio de Janeiro, Serviço gráfico do Ministerio da educação e saude, 1938. (Coleção brasileira de teatro. Série D: Estudos sobre teatro. Vol. II.)

Brenon, Algernon. "Giuseppe Verdi," MQ II (1916) 130–62.

Breville, Pierre de, and H. Gauthier-Villars. *Fervaal;* étude thématique et analytique. Paris, A. Durand, 1897.

Bricqueville, Eugène de. Le Livret d'opéra français de Lully à Gluck. Bruxelles, 1888.

Brindejont-Offenbach, Jacques. Offenbach, mon grand-père. Paris, Plon, 1940.

Brinkmann, Hennig. Zum Ursprung des liturgischen Spieles. Bonn, F. Cohen, 1929.

Brockt, Johannes. "Verdi's Operatic Choruses," M&L XX (1939) 309–12.

Brosses, Charles de. Lettres familières sur l'Italie. Paris, Firmin-Didot, 1931. Introduction and notes by Yvonne Bezard.

Brown, John. Letters on the Italian Opera. London, T. Cadell, 1791. 2d ed.

Brownlow, Jane. "The Bardi Coterie," PMA XXII (1896) 111–27.

Brück, Paul. "Glucks *Orpheus und Euridike*," AfMw VII (1925) 436–76.

Brückner, Fritz. Georg Benda und das deutsche Singspiel. Leipzig, B&H, 1904. Also SIMG V (1903–04) 571–621.

—— "Zum Thema 'Georg Benda und das Monodram,'" SIMG VI (1904–05) 496–500.

Brüggemann, Fritz. Bänkelgesang und Singspiel vor Goethe. Leipzig, Reclam, 1937.

Bruger, Hans. Glucks dramatische Instrumentationskunst und ihre geschichtlichen Grundlagen. Teil 1: Glucks italienischen Werke (einschliesslich der Wiener Reformopern). Heidelberg Dissertation, 1922.

Brukner, Fr. *Die Zauberflöte;* unbekannte Handschriften und seltene Drucke aus der Frühzeit Mozarts Oper. Wien, Gilhofer & Rauschburg, 1934.

Bruneau, Alfred. Massenet. Paris, Delagrave, 1934.

—— La Musique française; rapport sur la musique en France du XIIIe au XXe siècles; la musique à Paris en 1900. Paris, E. Fasquelle, 1901.

—— Musiques d'hier et de demain. Paris, Bibliothèque Charpentier, 1900.

—— La Vie et les œuvres de Gabriel Fauré. Paris, Charpentier & Fasquelle, 1925.

Brunswick, Mark. "Beethoven's Tribute to Mozart in *Fidelio*," MQ XXXI (1945) 29–32.

Brusa, Filippo. "Il *Nerone* di Arrigo Boito," RMI XXXI (1924) 392–443.

Bruyr, José. Grétry. Paris, Rieder, [1931].

Bücken, Ernst. Der heroische Stil in der Oper. Leipzig, Kistner & Siegel, 1924.

Bukofzer, Manfred. "The *Book of the Courtier* on Music," MTNA XXXVIII (1944) 230–35.

Burckhardt, Jakob. The Civilization of the Period of the Renaissance in Italy. London, C. K. Paul, 1878. 2 vols.

Burney, Charles. A General History of Music from the Earliest Ages to the Present Period. London, Printed for the Author, 1776. Also: 2d ed., with critical and historical notes by Frank Mercer. London, Foulis; New York, Harcourt, Brace, 1935.

—— Memoirs of the Life and Writings of the Abate Metastasio; in Which Are Incorporated Translations of His Principal Letters. London, G. G. and J. Robinson, 1796. 3 vols.

—— The Present State of Music in France and Italy. London, T. Becket, 1771.

—— The Present State of Music in Germany, the Netherlands, and United Provinces. London, T. Becket, 1773. 2 vols.

Buschkötter, Wilhelm. "Jean François Le Sueur; eine Biographie," SIMG XIV (1912–13) 58–154.

Busi, Leonida. Benedetto Marcello. Bologna, N. Zanichelli, 1884.

Busne, Henry de. "*Ariane et Barbe-bleue* de M. Paul Dukas," MM III (1907) 465–71.

Busoni, Ferruccio. Entwurf einer neuen Aesthetik der Tonkunst. Leipzig, Insel-Verlag, [19—]. Translated as: Sketch of a New Esthetic of Music. New York, G. Schirmer, 1911.

[——] "Nota bio-bibliografica su Ferruccio Busoni," RassM XIII (1940) 82–88.

—— Über die Möglichkeiten der Oper und über die Partitur des *Doktor Faust*. Leipzig, B&H, 1926.

—— Von der Einheit der Musik. Berlin, M. Hesse, [1923].

Bustico, Guido. "Un librettista antiromantico (Angelo Anelli)," RMI XXVIII (1921) 53–81.

—— Pier Alessandro Guglielmi, musicista. Massa, Medici, 1898.

—— "Saggio di una bibliografia di libretti musicali di Felice Romani," RMI XIV (1907) 229–84.

—— "Saverio Mercadante a Novara," RMI XXVIII (1921) 361–96.

—— "Gli spettacoli musicali al 'Teatro Novo' di Novara (1779–1873)," RMI XXV (1918) 84–103, 202–48; "Nuovo contributo," RMI XXVI (1919) 615–52.

Caccini, Giulio. Le nuove musiche; riproduzione dell' edizione dell' 1601. Roma, Raccolte Claudio Monteverdi (R. Mezzetti), 1930.

Cahn-Speyer, Rudolf. Franz Seydelmann als dramatischer Komponist. Leipzig, B&H, 1909.

Callegari, Matelda. "Il melodramma e Pietro Metastasio," RMI XXVI (1919) 518–44; XXVII (1920) 31–59, 458–76.

Calmus, Georgy. "Die *Beggar's Opera* von Gay und Pepusch," SIMG VIII (1906–1907) 286–335.

—— "Drei satirisch-kritische Aufsätze von Addison über die italienische Oper in England," SIMG IX (1907–08) 131–45, 448.

—— Die ersten deutschen Singspiele von Standfuss und Hiller. Leipzig, B&H, 1908.

—— Zwei Opernburlesken aus der Rokokozeit. Berlin, Liepmannssohn, 1912. Contents: *Télémaque* (Lesage), *The Beggar's Opera* (Gay and Pepusch).

Calvocoressi, Michel D. *"Boris Goudonov,"* MM IV (1908) 61–78.

—— Glinka. Paris, H. Laurens, [1911?].

—— *"Le Mariage,* par Moussorgsky," MM IV (1908) 1284–90.

—— Masters of Russian Music, by M. D. Calvocoressi and Gerald Abraham. New York, Knopf, 1936.

—— Moussorgsky. Paris, F. Alcan, 1921. 3d ed. Translated as: Musorgsky, the Russian Musical Nationalist. London, K. Paul; New York, Dutton, 1919.

—— Moussorgsky. London, Dent, 1946.

—— "Moussorgsky's Musical Style," MQ XVIII (1932) 530–46.

—— "L'orchestrazione autentica dal *Boris Godunof,"* RassM I (1928) 633–39.

—— "La vera *Kovanscina* di Mussorgski," RassM V (1932) 166–75.

—— "Il vero e completo *Boris Godunof,"* RassM I (1928) 217–25.

—— Vincent d'Indy, *L'Etranger;* le poème, analyse thématique de la partition. Paris, Editions du Courrier musical, [1903].

Cametti, Alberto. "Alcuni documenti inediti su la vita di Luigi Rossi," SIMG XIV (1912–13) 1–26.

—— Christina di Svezia, l'arte musicale e gli spettacoli teatrali in Roma. Roma, Tipografia Romano Mezzetti, 1931.

—— "Critiche e satire teatrali romane del '700," RMI IX (1902) 1–35.

—— "Donizetti a Roma; con lettere e documenti inediti," RMI XI (1904) 761–88; XII (1905) 1–39, 515–54, 689–713; XIII (1906) 50–90, 522–45, 616–55; XIV (1907) 301–32.

—— "Il *Guglielmo Tell* e le sue prime rappresentazioni in Italia," RMI VI (1899) 580–92.

—— "Leonardo Vinci e i suoi drammi in musica al Teatro delle Dame 1724–30," *Musica d'oggi* (1924) No. 10, pp. 297–99.

—— La musica teatrale a Roma cento anni fa: Il *Corsaro* di Pacini. Roma, Mezzetti, 1931.

—— La musica teatrale a Roma cento anni fa: *Olivo e Pasquale* di Donizetti. Roma, A. Manuzio, 1928.

—— Un poeta melodrammatico romano . . . Jacopo Ferretti. Milano, Ricordi, [1898].

—— "Saggio cronologico delle opere teatrali (1754–1794) di Nicolò Piccinni," RMI VIII (1901) 75–100.

—— Il teatro di Tordinona, poi di Apollo. Tivoli, A. Chicca, 1939.

Campardon, Emile. L'Académie royale de musique au XVIIIe siècle. Paris, Berger-Levrault, 1884. 2 vols.

—— Les Comédiens du roi de la troupe italienne. Paris, Berger-Levrault, 1880. 2 vols.

—— Les Spectacles des foires . . . depuis 1595 jusqu'à 1791. Paris, Berger-Levrault, 1877. 2 vols.

Canal, Pietro. Dalla musica in Mantova. Venezia, Presso la segreteria del R. Istituto, 1881.

Cantillon, Arthur. Essai sur les symboles de la tétralogie Wagnerienne. Mons, Imprimerie générale, 1911.

Canudo, Ricciotto. "Le Drame musical contemporain," MM III (1907) 1185–92; IV (1908) 56–60.

—— "L'Esthétique de Verdi et la culture musicale italienne," MM III (1907) 719–37.

Capell, Richard. "Dame Ethel Smyth's Operas at Covent Garden," *Monthly Musical Record* LIII (1923) 197–98.

Capri, Antonio. Musica e musicisti d'Europa dal 1800 al 1938. Milano, Hoepli, 1939. 2d ed.

—— Il seicento musicale in Europa. Milano, Hoepli, 1933.

—— Il settecento musicale in Europa. Milano, Hoepli, 1936.

—— Verdi, uomo e artista. Milano, Ed. ufficio concerti, 1939.

Carey, Clive. "The Problem of *Don Giovanni* Again," M&L XIV (1933) 30–35.

Carlez, Jules. Catel. Caen, H. Delesques, 1894.

—— Grimm et la musique de son temps. Caen, Le Blanc-Hardel, 1872.

—— L'Œuvre d'Auber. Caen, Le Blanc-Hardel, 1874.

—— Un Opéra biblique au XVIIIe siècle. Caen, Le Blanc-Hardel, 1879.

—— Pacini et l'opéra italien. Caen, H. Delesques, 1888.

—— Pierre et Thomas Corneille librettistes. N.p., n.d.

—— La Sémiramis de Destouches. Caen, H. Delesques, 1892.

Carlyle, Thomas. "The Opera," in *Critical and Miscellaneous Essays* (New York, Scribner, 1904) IV, 397–403.

Carmena y Millán, Luis. Crónica de la ópera italiana en Madrid desde el año 1738 hasta nuestros dias. Madrid, M. Minuesa de los Rios, 1878.

Carmody, Francis J. Le Repertoire de l'opéra-comique en vaudevilles de 1708 à 1764. Berkeley, California, University of California Press, 1933.

Carner, Mosco. "The Erotic Element in Puccini," MQ XXII (1936) 45–67.

—— "Puccini's Early Operas," M&L XIX (1938) 295–307.

Carreras y Bulbena, José Rafael. Domenech Terradellas. Barcelona, F. X. Altés, 1908.

Carson, Wm. G. B. St. Louis Goes to the Opera, 1837–1941. St. Louis, The Missouri Historical Society, 1946.

Casella, Alfredo, ed. *La favola di Orfeo,* opera in un atto di Messer Angelo Ambrogini detto "Poliziano." Milano, Carisch, [1934].

Castiglione, Baldassare, conte. Il libro del cortegiano. Firenze, Heredi di Philippo di Giunta, 1528. Translated by Thomas Hoby as: The Courtier. [New York], The National Alumni, [1907].

Castil-Blaze, see Blaze.

Castro, Enio de Freitas e. Carlo Gomes. Pôrto Alegre, A. Nação, 1941.

Catelani, Angelo. Delle opere di Alessandro Stradella esistente nell' archivio musicale della R. Biblioteca Palatina di Modena. Modena, C. Vincenzi, 1866.

Cauchie, Maurice. "The High Lights of French Opéra Comique," MQ XXV (1939) 306–12.

Cavalli, Francesco. Venti arie tratte dai drami musicali di Francesco Cavalli. Wien-Triest, Verlag Schmiedel (Mozarthaus), 1909.

Cecil, George. "Impressions of Opera in France," MQ VII (1921) 314–30.

—— "Monte Carlo: Opéra de Luxe," MQ IX (1923) 65–71.

Celani, Enrico. "Canzoni musicale del secolo XVII," RMI XII (1905) 109–150.

—— "Musica e musicisti in Roma (1750–1850)," RMI XVIII (1911) 1–63; XX (1913) 33–88.

Cellamare, Daniele. Mascagni e la Cavalleria visti da Cerignola. Roma, Filli Palombi, 1941.

Cernicchiaro, Vincenzo. Storia della musica nel Brasile dai tempi coloniali sino ai nostri giorni. Milano, Fratelli Riccioni, 1926.

Cesari, Gaetano, and others. Antonio Bartolomeo Bruni, musicista cuneese (1751–1821). Torino, S. Lattes, 1931.

Chadwick, George. Horatio Parker. New Haven, Yale University Press, 1921.

Challis, Bennett. "Opera Publics of Europe; Impressions and Reminiscences," MQ XII (1926) 564–79.

Chamberlain, Houston Stewart. Das Drama Richard Wagners. Leipzig, B&H, 1921. 6th ed. First published 1892. Translated as: The Wagnerian Drama. London and New York, John Lane, 1915.

—— Die Grundlagen des neunzehnten Jahrhunderts. München, F. Bruckmann, 1912. 10th ed. First published 1900. Translated as: Foundations of the Nineteenth Century. München, F. Bruckmann, 1911.

—— Richard Wagner. München, F. Bruckmann, [1936]. 9th ed. First published 1896. English translation: London, Dent, 1900.

Chambers, E. K. The Medieval Stage. London, Oxford University Press, 1903. 2 vols.

Champigneulle, Bernard. "L'Influence de Lully hors de France," RM XXII (February–March, 1946) 26–35.

Chase, Gilbert. A Guide to Latin-American Music. Washington, D.C., Government Printing Office, 1945.

—— The Music of Spain. New York, Norton, [1941].

—— "Origins of the Lyric Theater in Spain," MQ XXV (1939) 292–305.

—— "Some Notes on Afro-Cuban Music and Dancing," Inter-American Monthly I, No. 8 (December, 1942) 32–33.

Chatfield-Taylor, H. C. Goldoni; a Biography. New York, Duffield, 1913.

Chavarri, Eduardo López. Historia de la música. Barcelona, Imprenta elzeviriana, 1929. 3d ed.

Chevaillier, Lucien. "Le Récit chez Monteverdi," RHCM X (1910) 284–94.

Chop, Max. August Bungert. Leipzig, H. Seemann Nachfolger, 1903.

—— E. N. v. Reznicek. Wien, Leipzig, Universal-Edition, [1920].

Chorley, Henry F. Music and Manners in France and Germany. London, Longmans, 1844.

—— Thirty Years' Musical Recollections. New York, Knopf, 1926.

Chouquet, Gustave. Histoire de la musique dramatique en France. Paris, Firmin Didot, 1873.

Chrysander, Friedrich. "Adonis; Oper von Reinhard Keiser," AMZ XIII (1878) 65–70, 81–87, 97–101.

—— "Eine englische Serenata von J. Sigismund Kusser um 1710," AMZ XIV (1879) 408–12, 417–22.

—— "Der erste Entwurf der Bassarie 'Nasce al bosco' in Händel's Oper Ezio (1732)," AMZ XIV (1879) 641–46.

—— "Die Feier des zweihundertjährigen Bestandes der Oper in Hamburg," AMZ XIII (1878) 113–15, 129–32, 145–48.

—— "Geschichte der Braunschweig-Wolfenbüttelschen Capelle und Oper vom XVI. bis zum XVIII. Jahrhundert," Jahrbücher für musikalische Wissenschaft I (1863) 147–286.

—— ["Geschichte der Hamburger Oper"], AMZ XII–XV (1877–80):
   "Die erste Periode," AMZ XII (1877) 369–486 passim
   "Die zweite Periode," AMZ XIII (1878) 289–442 passim
   ". . . unter . . . J. S. Kusser 1693–1696," AMZ XIV (1879) 385–408 passim
   ". . . vom Abgange Kusser's bis zum Tode Schott's," AMZ XIV (1879) 433–534 passim
   ". . . unter der Direction von Reinhard Keiser (1703–1706)," AMZ XV (1880) 17–87 passim.

—— G. F. Händel. Leipzig, B&H, 1858–67. 3 vols.

—— "Ludovico Zacconi als Lehrer des Kunstgesanges," VfMw VII (1891) 337–96; IX (1893) 249–310; X (1894) 531–67.

—— "Mattheson's Verzeichniss Hamburgischer Opern von 1678 bis 1728, gedruckt im Musikalischen Patrioten, mit seinen handschriftlichen Fortsetzungen bis 1751, nebst Zusätzen und Berichtigungen," AMZ XII (1877) 198–282, passim.

—— "Musik und Theater in Mecklenburg," Archiv für Landeskunde in den Grossherzogthümern Mecklenburg IV (1854) 105–25, 258–80, 346–79.

—— "Neue Beiträge zur mecklenburgischen Musikgeschichte," Archiv für Landeskunde in den Grossherzogthümern Mecklenburg VI (1856) 666–82.

—— "Die Oper Don Giovanni von Gazzaniga und von Mozart," VfMw IV (1888) 351–435.

Chrysander, Friedrich (*Cont.*). "Reinhard Keiser," in *Allgemeine deutsche Biographie* XV (1882) 540–51.

—— "Spontini nach Mitteilungen von Caroline Bauer und H. Marschner," AMZ XIV (1879) 259–64, 274–80, 289–93.

—— "Ueber die Unsittlichkeiten in unseren Operntexten," AMZ XIV (1879) 257–59, 273–74, 305–308.

—— ". . . über Wagners Tannhäuser," ZIMG V (1903–1904) 208–19.

Cinquante Ans de musique française de 1874 à 1925. Paris, Librairie de France, [1925]. Ed. by L. Rohozinski.

Civita, A. Ottavio Rinuccini e il sorgere del melodramma in Italia. Mantova, Manuzio, 1900.

Clark, George Norman. The Seventeenth Century. Oxford, Clarendon Press, 1929.

Clarke, Henry Leland. "Cambert, Lully, and Blow." Unpublished essay.

—— Dr. John Blow (1649–1708), Last Composer of an Era. Harvard Dissertation, 1947.

Clément, Félix. "Liturgie, musique et drama du moyen age," *Annales archéologiques* VII (1847) 303–20; VIII (1848) 36–48, 77–87, 304–11; IX (1849) 27–40, 162–74; X (1850) 154–60; XI (1851) 6–15.

Coeuroy, André. "Further Aspects of Contemporary Music," MQ XV (1929) 547–73.

—— La Musique française moderne. Paris, Delagrave, 1922.

—— "Nouveau Visages de l'opéra," RM (February, 1928) 7–16.

—— *La Tosca* de Puccini. Paris, Mellottée, [1922?].

—— "Wagner et le ballet," RM II (December, 1921) 206–13.

Cohen, Alex. "Ernest Bloch's *Macbeth*," M&L XIX (1938) 143–48.

Cohen, Gustave. Histoire de la mise en scène dans le théâtre réligieux français du moyen age. Paris, Champion, 1926. New ed.

Cohen, Hermann. Die dramatische Idee in Mozarts Operntexten. Berlin, Cassirer, 1916.

Colles, H. C. "Philip Napier Miles," M&L XVII (1936) 357–67.

Collet, Henri. Albeniz et Granados. Paris, F. Alcan, 1929. New ed.

—— *Samson et Dalila* de C. Saint-Saëns. Paris. Mellottée, [1922].

Colombani, A. L'opera italiana nel secolo XIX. Milano, ed. Corriere della Sera, 1900.

Colomb de Batines. Bibliografia delle antiche rappresentazioni italiane sacre e profane, stampate nei secoli XV e XVI. Firenze, Società tip., 1852. Additions by E. Narducci in *Il bibliofilo* III (1882) 73–74, 87–88.

Colson, J. B. Manuel dramatique. Bordeaux, chez l'auteur, 1817.

Combarieu, Jules. Histoire de la musique. Paris, A. Colin, 1920. 3d ed. 3 vols.

—— "Histoire du théâtre lyrique," RHCM VII (1907) 581–97; VIII (1908) 1–594 *passim*; IX (1909) *passim*; X (1910) *passim*.

—— "J.-J. Rousseau et le mélodrame," RHCM I (1901) 273–77.

—— "L'Opéra-comique d'hier et d'aujourd'hui," RHCM VII (1907) 549–63.

Comte, Charles, and Paul Laumonier. "Ronsard et les musiciens du XVIe siècle," *Revue d'histoire littéraire de la France* VII (1900) 341–81.

Conrad, Leopold. Mozarts Dramaturgie der Oper. Würzburg, Triltsch, 1943.

Conrat, Hugo J. "La musica in Shakespeare," RMI X (1903) 646–69; XI (1904) 35–54.

[Contant d'Orville, André Guillaume.] Histoire de l'opéra bouffon. Amsterdam and Paris, Grangé, 1768. 2 vols.

Cooper, Martin. "Charles Gounod and His Influence on French Music," M&L XXI (1940) 50–59.

—— Georges Bizet. London and New York, Oxford University Press, 1938.

—— Gluck. New York, Oxford University Press, 1935.

Coopersmith, J[acob] M[aurice]. [1.] An Investigation of Georg Friedrich Händel's Orchestral Style. [2.] A Thematic Index of the Printed Works of Händel. Harvard Dissertation, 1932. 12 vols.

—— "The Libretto of Handel's *Jupiter in Argos*," M&L XVII (1936) 289–96.

Copland, Aaron. Our New Music. New York, Whittlesey, [1941].

Coradini, Francesco. Antonio Maria Abbatini e d. Lorenzo Abbatini; notizie biografiche. Arezzo, Scuola tipografica aretina, 1922.

—— Brevi notizie sul musicista aretino Giovanni Apolloni. Arezzo, Scuola tipografica aretina, 1922.

—— "P. Antonio Cesti; nuove notizie biografiche," RMI XXX (1923) 371–88.

Corbet, August. Het muziekdrama in de XVIe en XVIIe eeuwen in Italie gezien in het licht van H. Wölfflin's *Kunstgeschichtliche Grundbegriffen;* ein bijdrage tot de theorie van het parallelisme in de kunst. Antwerpen, De Sikkel, 1936.

Corder, Frederick. "The Works of Sir Henry Bishop," MQ IV (1918) 78–97.

Cornelissen, Thilo. C. M. v. Webers *Freischütz* als Beispiel einer Opernbehandlung. Berlin, Matthiesen, 1940.

Cornelius, Carl Maria. Peter Cornelius, der Wort- und Tondichter. Regensburg, G. Bosse, [1925].

Cornelius, Peter. Literarische Werke. Leipzig, B&H, 1904–05. 4 vols.

Cornet, J. Die Oper in Deutschland und das Theater der Neuzeit. Hamburg, O. Meissner, 1849.

Correa de Azvedo, L. H. "Carlos Gomes; sua verdadeira posição no quadro da ópera italiana no sec. XIX e na evolução da musica brasileira," *Boletin latino-americano de música* III (1937) 83–87.

Corrodi, Hans. "Othmar Schoeck's *Massimilla Doni,*" M&L XVIII (1937) 391–97.

Cortese, Louis. Alfredo Casella. Genova, Orfini, [1935].

Cortese, Nino. "Un' autobiografia inedita di Giovanni Paisiello," RassM III (1930) 123–35. Following is Paisiello's autobiography.

Cortolezis, Fritz. "Gedanken über eine stilgerechte Aufführung des *Fidelio,*" Neues Beethoven Jahrbuch III (1926) 93–102.

Costa, Alessandro. "Schopenhauer e Wagner," RMI XXXIX (1932) 1–12.

Cotarelo y Mori, Emilio, ed. Colección de entremeses, loas, bailes, jácaras y mojingangas desde fines del siglo XVI á mediados del XVII. Madrid, Bailly-Baillière, 1911.

—— Historia de la zarzuela o sea El drama lírico en España, desde su origen a fines del siglo XIX. Madrid, Tipografía de Archivos, 1934.

—— Orígenes y establecimento de la ópera en España hasta 1800. Madrid, Tip. de la "Revista de arch.," [etc.], 1917.

Coussemaker, Edmond de. Drames liturgiques du moyen âge. Rennes, H. Vatar, 1860; Paris, Lib. archéologique de V. Didron, 1861.

Cowen, Sir Frederic Hymen. My Art and My Friends. London, E. Arnold, 1913.

Croce, Benedetto. I teatri di Napoli, secolo XV–XVIII. Napoli, L. Pierro, 1891.

Crocioni, Giovanni. L'Alidoro o dei primordi del melodramma. Bologna, L. Parma, 1938.

Crocker, Eunice. The Instrumental Ensemble Canzona. Radcliffe Dissertation, 1943.

Crowder, C. Fairfax. "Neglected Treasures in Handel's Operas," M&L II (1921) 135–48.

Cucuel, Georges. Les Créateurs de l'opéra-comique français. Paris, F. Alcan, 1914.

—— "La Critique musicale dans les 'revues' du XVIIIe siècle," L'Année musicale II (1912) 127–203.

—— "Giacomo Casanova e la musica," RMI XXXVI (1929) 446–65.

—— "Notes sur la comédie italienne de 1717 à 1789," SIMG XV (1913–14) 154–66.

—— "Les Opéras de Gluck dans les parodies du XVIIIe siècle," RM III, No. 5 (1922) 201–21; No. 6, pp. 51–68.

—— "Sources et documents pour servir à l'histoire de l'opéra-comique en France," L'Année musicale III (1913) 247–82.

Cui, César. La Musique en Russie. Paris, Fischbacher, 1880.

Cummings, William H. "The Lord Chamberlain and Opera in London, 1700 to 1741," PMA XL (1914) 37–72.

—— "Matthew Locke, Composer for the Church and Theatre," SIMG XIII (1911–12) 120–26.

Curiel, Carlo Leone. Il teatro S. Pietro di Trieste, 1690–1801. [Milano], Archetipographia di Milano, 1937.

Curzon, Henri de. Ernest Reyer. Paris, Perrin, 1924.

—— Felipe Pedrell et Les Pyrénées. Paris, Fischbacher, 1902.

—— Grétry. Paris, Laurens, [1907].

—— La Légende de Sigurd. Paris, Fischbacher, [1889].

—— Léo Delibes. Paris, G. Legouix, 1926.

—— "L'Opéra en 1843; mémoire du directeur Léon Pillet," RdM II (1920–21) 223–33.

—— "Les Opéras-comiques de Boieldieu," RM XIV (November, 1933) 249–63.

Czech, Stan. Franz Lehár; Weg und Werk. Berlin, Werk-Verlag, 1942.

Dacier, Emile. *"Les Caractères de la danse;* histoire d'un divertissement pendant la première moitié du XVIIIe siècle," RHCM V (1905) 324–35, 365–67.

—— "Une Danseuse française à Londres au début du XVIIIe siècle," MM III (1907) 437–63, 746–65.

—— "L'Opéra au XVIIIe siècle; les premières représentations du *Dardanus* de Rameau," RHCM III (1903) 163–73.

Daffner, Hugo. Friedrich Nietzsches Rundglossen zu Bizets *Carmen.* Regensburg, Bosse. 1938.

Dahms, Walter. "The 'Gallant' Style of Music," MQ XI (1925) 356–72.

Damerini, Adelmo. "Un precursore italiano di Gluck: Tommaso Traetta," *Il pianoforte* (July, 1927).

—— "Tommaso Traetta; cenni biografici," *Bollettino bibliografico musicale* II (July, 1927) 1–13.

Damrosch, Walter. My Musical Life. New York, Scribner, 1923.

D'Ancona, Alessandro. Origini del teatro italiano. Torino, E. Loescher, 1891. 2d ed. 2 vols.

Dandelot, Arthur. Evolution de la musique de théâtre depuis Meyerbeer jusqu'à nos jours. Paris, Flammarion, 1927.

D'Angeli, Andrea. Benedetto Marcello, vita e opere. Milano, Fratelli Bocca, 1940.

—— Commemorazione di Gio. Batta Pergolesi. Padova, L. Penada, 1936.

Daninger, Josef G. Sage und Märchen im Musikdrama; eine ästhetische Untersuchung an der Sagen- und Märchenoper des 19. Jahrhunderts. Prag, Hoffmanns Witwe, 1916.

Da Ponte, Lorenzo. Memorie. Nuova-Jorca, Lorenzo e Carlo Da Ponte, 1823. 2 vols. Translated, with introduction and notes, by L. A. Sheppard, Boston, Houghton Mifflin, 1929. Translated by Elisabeth Abbott, edited and annotated by Arthur Livingston, Philadelphia, J. B. Lippincott, 1929. Other editions: Bari, G. Laterza, 1918 (Italian); Paris, Henri Jonquières, 1931 (French; includes previously unpublished letters to Casanova; preface and notes by Raoul Vèze).

—— Storia compendiosa della vita di Lorenzo Da Ponte scritta di lui medesimo. New York, Riley, 1807.

D'Arienzo, Nicola. "Le origini dell' opera comica," RMI II (1895) 597–628; IV (1897) 421–59; VI (1899) 473–95; VII (1900) 1–33.

Daube, Otto. Siegfried Wagner und die Märchenoper. Leipzig, Deutscher Theater-Verlag, M. Schleppegrell, [1936].

Dauriac, Lionel. "Herbert Spencer et Meyerbeer," ZIMG V (1903–1904) 103–109.

—— "Un Problème d'esthétique Wagnérienne," MM IV (1908) 50–55.

Davari, Stefano. "Notizie biografiche del distinto maestro di musica Claudio Monteverdi," *Atti e memorie della R. Accademia Virgiliana di Mantova* X (1884–85) 79–183.

Davey, Henry. History of English Music. London, Curwen, [1921]. 2d ed., revised.

David, Ernest. Les Opéras du juif Antonio José da Silva. Paris, A. Wittersheim, 1880.

De Angelis, Alberto. "Cantanti italiani del secolo XIX: Erminia e Giuseppe Frezzolini," RMI XXXII (1925) 438–54.

—— "Musica e musicisti nell' opera di G. d'Annunzio," RMI XLIII (1939) 275–301.

—— "Il teatro farnese di Parma," RMI XLIII (1939) 364–82.

Debussy, Claude. Monsieur Croche, anti dilettante. Paris, Dorbon-aîné, 1921.

De' Calzabigi, Ranieri. "Dissertazione . . . su le poesie drammatiche del Sig. Abate Pietro Metastasio," in *Poesie del Signor Abate Pietro Metastasio* (Parigi, Vedova Quillan, 1755–69) I, xix–cciv.

—— Risposta . . . alla critica ragionatissima delle poesie drammatiche del C. de' Calsabigi, fatta del baccelliere D. Stefan Arteaga. Venezia, Curti, 1790.

Decsey, Ernst. Franz Lehár. München, Drei Masken-Verlag, 1930. 2d ed.

—— Hugo Wolf. Berlin, Schuster & Loeffler, [1919]. 3d-6th ed., revised.

—— Johann Strauss. Stuttgart, Berlin, Deutsche Verlags-Anstalt, 1922.

Dedekind, Constantin Christian. Heilige Arbeit über Freud und Leid der alten und neuen Zeit in Music-bekwehmen Schau-Spielen (9) ahngewendet. Dreszden, 1676.

—— Neue geistliche Schauspiele (5) bekwehmet zur Musik. [Dresden], 1670.

De Dominicis, Giulia. "Roma centro musicale nel settecento," RMI XXX (1923) 511–28.

De Donno, Alfredo. Mascagni nel 900 musicale. Roma, Casa del libro, [1935].

—— Modernità di Mascagni. Roma, Pinciana, 1931.

De Eisner-Eisenhof, A. "Giuseppe Weigl; una biografia," RMI XI (1904) 459–83.

Degey, Maurice. Les Echos imprévus de la mort de Grétry. Liège, Editions de la Vie wallonne, 1938.

Della Corte, Andrea. "Appunti sull' estetica musicale di Pietro Metastasio," RMI XXVIII (1921) 94–119.

—— ed. Canto e bel canto (Tosi e Mancini). Torino, G. B. Paravia, [1933].

—— "Cimarosa nel '99 e nella fortuna postuma," RassM IX (1936) 280–83.

—— "La drammaturgia nella *Semiramide* di Rossini," RassM XI (1938) 1–6.

—— Figuras y motivas de lo opera bufa italiano. Buenos Aires, La revista de musica, 1928.

—— Un Italiano all' estero, Antonio Salieri. Torino, G. B. Paravia, [1936].

—— "Nel II centenario della morte di Pergolesi; *Il geloso schernito e Il maestro di musica*," RassM IX (1936) 202–208.

—— "Notizie di Gaetano Pugnani musicista torinese (1731–1798)," *Rassegna mensile municipale "Torino"* (1931) pp. 26–39.

—— L'opera comica italiana nel 1700. Bari, G. Laterza, 1923. 2 vols.

—— Paisiello; con una tavola tematica. L'estetica musicale di P. Metastasio. Torino, Fratelli Bocca, 1922.

—— Piccinni (settecento italiano); con frammenti musicali inediti e due ritratti. Bari, G. Laterza, 1928.

—— Rittrato di Franco Alfano. Torino, G. B. Paravia, [1935].

—— "Tragico e comico nell' opera veneziana della seconda parte del seicento," RassM XI (1938) 325–33.

—— Tre secoli di opera italiana. Torino, Arione, [1938].

Della Torre, Arnaldo. Saggio di una bibliografia delle opere intorno a Carlo Goldoni (1793–1907). Firenze, Alfani e Venturi, 1908.

Delmas, Marc. Gustave Charpentier et le lyrisme français. Paris, Delagrave, 1931.

Demarquez, Suzanne. "Un Voyageur français et la musique italienne au XVIIIe siècle," RM, numéro spécial, "La Musique dans les pays Latins" (February–March, 1940) pp. 125–33.

De Napoli, Giuseppe. "Niccolò Piccinni nel secondo centenario della nascità," RMI XXXV (1928) 209–18.

—— La triade melodrammatica altamurana: Giacomo Tritto, 1733–1824; Vincenzo Lavigna, 1776–1836; Saverio Mercadante, 1795–1870. Milano, Rosio e Fabe, 1932.

Denizard, Marie. "La Famille française de Lully," MM VIII, No. 5 (1912) 1–14.

Dent, Edward J. "Alessandro Scarlatti," PMA XXX (1904) 75–90.

—— Alessandro Scarlatti, His Life and Works. London, E. Arnold, 1905.

—— "The *Amfiparnaso* of Orazio Vecchi," *Monthly Musical Record* XXXVI (1906) 50–52, 74–75.

—— "The Baroque Opera," MA I (1909–10) 93–107.

—— "A Best-Seller in Opera," M&L XXII (1941) 139–54.

—— "Busoni's *Doctor Faust*," M&L VII (1926) 196–208.

—— "Ensembles and Finales in 18th Century Italian Opera," SIMG XI (1909–10) 543–69; XII (1910–11) 112–38.

—— Ferrucio Busoni; a Biography. London, Oxford University Press, 1933.

—— Foundations of English Opera. Cambridge (England), University Press, 1928.

—— "Giuseppe Maria Buini," SIMG XIII (1911–12) 329–36.

—— Handel. London, Duckworth, [1934].

Dent, Edward J. (*Cont.*). "Handel on the Stage," M&L XVI (1935) 174–87.

—— "Hans Pfitzner," M&L IV (1923) 119–32.

—— "Italian Opera in the Eighteenth Century, and Its Influence on the Music of the Classical Period," SIMG XIV (1912–13) 500–509.

—— "Leonardo Leo," SIMG VIII (1906–1907) 550–66.

—— Mozart's Operas; a Critical Study. London, Chatto & Windus; New York, McBride, Nast, 1913.

—— Mozart's Opera *The Magic Flute;* Its History and Interpretation. Cambridge, W. Heffer, 1911.

—— "The Musical Interpretation of Shakespeare on the Modern Stage," MQ II (1916) 523–37.

—— "Notes on Leonardo Vinci," MA IV (1912–13) 193–201.

—— "Notes on the *Amfiparnaso* of Orazio Vecchi," SIMG XII (1910–11) 330–47.

—— "The Operas of Alessandro Scarlatti," SIMG IV (1902–1903) 143–56.

—— The Rise of the Romantic Opera. (The Messenger Lectures at Cornell University, 1937–38.) Typescript, 256 pp.

—— "The Romantic Spirit in Music," PMA LIX (1932–33) 85–102.

—— "Translating *Trovatore,* M&L XX (1939) 7–20.

De' Paoli, Domenico. Claudio Monteverdi. Milano, Hoepli, 1945.

—— "*Diane ed Endimione* di Alessandro Scarlatti," RassM XIII (1940) 139–46.

—— "Italian Chamber Cantatas," MA II (1911) 142–53, 185–99.

—— "Italy's New Music of the Theatre," MMus VIII, No. 1 (November–December, 1930) 21–26.

—— "*Orfeo* and *Pelléas,*" M&L XX (1939) 381–98.

—— "Pizzetti's *Fra Gherardo,*" MMus VI, No. 2 (January–February, 1929) 39–42.

De Rensis, Raffaello. Ercole Bernabei. Roma, tip. Sociale, 1920.

—— Ermanno Wolf-Ferrari, la sua vita d'artista. Milano, Fratelli Treves, 1937.

—— Musica italiana in Francia; la riforma intitolata a Gluck. Roma, Casa editrice "Musica," 1916.

—— "Un musicista diplomatico del settecento: Agostino Steffani," *Musica d'oggi* III, No. 5 (May, 1921) 129–32.

—— Ottorino Respighi. Torino, Paravia, [1935].

—— Primo Riccitelli: *I compagnacci;* guida attraverso la commedia e la musica. Milano, Bottega di poesia, 1923.

Desastre, Jean. Carlo Broschi; kuriose Abenteuer eines Sopranisten. Zürich, Bürdecke & Herwig, 1903.

[Desboulmiers, Jean Auguste Julien.] Histoire anecdotique et raisonée du théâtre italien, depuis son rétablissement en France jusqu'à l'année 1769. Paris, Lacombe, 1769. 7 vols.

—— Histoire du théâtre de l'opéra-comique. Paris, Lacombe, 1769. 2 vols.

Desderi, Ettore. "Le tendenze attuali della musica; il teatro," RMI XXXVIII (1931) 247–77.

Desessarts, Nicolas Toussaint Lemoyne. Les Trois Théâtres de Paris, ou abrégé historique de l'établissement de la Comédie Françoise, de la Comédie Italienne & de l'Opéra, Paris, Lacombe, 1777.

Desnoiresterres, Gustave. Gluck et Piccinni, 1774–1800. Paris, Didier, 1875. 2d ed.

Destranges, Etienne. Le Chant de la cloche, de Vincent d'Indy; étude analytique. Paris, Tresse et Stock, 1890.

—— L'Etranger de M. Vincent d'Indy; étude analytique et thématique. Paris, Fischbacher, 1904.

——L'Evolution musicale chez Verdi; Aida—Othello—Falstaff. Paris, Fischbacher, 1895.

—— Fervaal de Vincent d'Indy: étude thématique et analytique. Paris, A. Durand, 1896.

—— Messidor d'A. Bruneau; étude analytique et critique. Paris, Fischbacher, 1897.

—— L'Œuvre théâtral de Meyerbeer; étude critique. Paris, Fischbacher, 1893.

—— L'Ouragan d'Alfred Bruneau; étude analytique et thématique. Paris, Fischbacher, 1902.

—— Le Rêve d'Alfred Bruneau; étude thématique et analytique. Paris, Fischbacher, 1896.

Deutsch, Otto Erich. Das Freihaustheater auf der Wieden, 1787–1801. Wien-Leipzig, Deutsche Verlag für Jugend und Volk Gesellschaft, [1937].

—— Mozart und die Wiener Logen; zur Geschichte seiner Freimaurer-Kompositionen. Wien, Wiener Freimaurer-Zeitung, 1932.

De Vito, M. S. L'origine del dramma liturgico. Milano, Dante Alighieri, [1939?]

Dickinson, Alan Edgar Frederic. The Musical Design of The Ring. London, Oxford University Press, 1926.

Diderot, Denis. Le Neveu de Rameau; satyre publiée pour la première fois sur le manuscrit original autographe. Paris, Plon, Nourrit, 1891.

Dieckmann, Karin. De Braut von Messina auf der Bühne im Wandel der Zeit. Helsingfors Dissertation, 1935.

Dietz, Max. Geschichte des musikalischen Dramas in Frankreich während der Revolution bis zum Directorium (1787 bis 1795). Wien, Groscher & Blaha, 1885. 2d ed., Leipzig, B&H, 1893.

Di Giacomo, Salvatore. Il conservatorio dei poveri di Gesu Cristo e quello di S. M. di Loreto. Palermo, Sandron, 1928.

—— Il conservatorio di Sant' Onofrio a Capuana e quello di S. M. della Pietà dei Turchini. Napoli, Sandron, 1924. ("I quattro antichi conservatorii di Napoli MDXLIII–MDCCC.")

[Ditters] von Dittersdorf, Karl. Karl von Dittersdorfs Lebensbeschreibung; seinem Sohne in die Feder diktiert. Leipzig, B&H, 1801. Translated as: The Autobiography of Karl von Dittersdorf. London, R. Bentley, 1896. Modern German editions: Leipzig, Reclam, 1909 (Istel); Regensburg, G. Bosse, [ca. 1940] (E. Schmitz); Leipzig, Staackmann, 1940 (Loets).

Dobronić, A. "A Study of Jugoslav Music," MQ XII (1926) 56–71.

"Documents historiques: les origines de l'opéra en France," RHCM VIII (1908) 562–64.

Doebner, Richard, ed. Briefe der Königin Sophie Charlotte von Preussen und der Kurfürstin Sophie von Hannover an hannoversche Diplomaten. Leipzig, S. Hirzel, 1905.
  Contains letters to Agostino Steffani.

Donath, Gustav. "Florian Gassmann als Opernkomponist," SzMw II (1914) 34–211.

Donati Petteni, Giuliano. Donizetti. Milano, Fratelli Treves, 1930.

Doni, Giovanni Battista. Compendio del trattato de' generi e de' modi della mvsica. Roma, A. Fei, 1635.
  Abstract of a larger work which was never published. Portions of this work are quoted in Solerti's Origini under the title "Trattato della musica scenica."

—— Lyra Barberina ΑΜΦΙΧΟΡΔΟΣ; accedunt eiusdem opera, pleaque nondum edita ad veterem musicam illustrandam pertinentia. Florentiae typis Caesareis, 1763. 2 vols.

Doran, John. 'Mann' and Manners at the Court of Florence, 1740–1786; Founded on the Letters of Horace Mann to Horace Walpole. London, R. Bentley, 1876. 2 vols.

Dorn, Heinrich. Aus meinem Leben. Berlin, B. Behr, 1870–1886. 7 vols.

—— Gesetzgebung und Operntext (eine Schrift für Männer); zeitgemässe Betrachtungen. Berlin, Schlesinger, 1879.

Draper, John W. Eighteenth Century English Aesthetics; a Bibliography. Heidelberg, C. Winter, 1931.

Dresden, Sem. Het Muziekleven in Nederland sinds 1880. Amsterdam, Uitgeversmaatschlappy "Elsevier," 1923.

Du Bled, Victor. "Le Ballet de l'opéra," RM II (December, 1921) 191–205.

DuBos, Jean Baptiste. Critical Reflections on Poetry, Painting and Music. London, J. Nourse, 1748. 3 vols. Translated from the French 5th ed. Originally published anonymously, Paris, 1719.

Ducannès–Duval, G. "L'Opéra à Bordeaux en 1784," RdM XXI (1937) 82–83.

Dufrane, Louis. Gossec. Paris, Fischbacher, 1927.

Du Gérard, N. B. Tables alphabetique & chronologique de pieces representées sur l'ancien Theatre italien, depuis son etablissement jusqu'en 1697. Paris, Prault, 1750.

Duhamel, Raoul. "Eugène Delacroix et la musique," RMI XLIII (1939) 35–54, 333–56.

—— "Ferdinand Herold," RM XIV (November, 1933) 278–90.

—— "Quelques Maîtres de l'opéra-comique au XIXe siècle," RM XIV (November, 1933) 291–302.

[Dukas, Paul.] RM numéro spécial (May–June, 1936) contains articles on Dukas' operas.

Dumesnil, Maurice. Claude Debussy, Master of Dreams. New York, Ives Washburn, [1940].

—— "Gabriel Dupont, Musician of Normandy," MQ XXX (1944) 441–47.

Dumesnil, René. Le Don Juan de Mozart. Paris, Editions musicales de la librairie de France, 1927.

—— "Le Livret et les personnages de Don Giovanni," RM No. 4 (February, 1927) 118–28.

Du Moulin-Eckart, Richard Maria Ferdinand. Wahnfried. Leipzig, Kistner & Siegel, 1925.

Dunhill, Thomas F. Sullivan's Comic Operas; a Critical Appreciation. New York, Oxford University Press; London, Edw. Arnold, 1928.

Dupré, Henri. Purcell. Paris, Alcan, 1927. Translated, New York, Knopf, 1928.

Du Tillet, Jacques. "A propos du drame lyrique; une lettre de M. Camille Saint-Saëns," Revue politique et littéraire (July 3, 1897) pp. 27–30.

"Early Elizabethan Stage Music," MA I (1909–10) 30–40; IV (1912–13) 112–17.

Ebert, Alfred. Attilio Ariosti in Berlin (1697–1703). Leipzig, Giesecke & Devrient, 1905.

Eckermann, Johann Peter. Gespräche mit Goethe. Berlin, Bong, [1916]. 2 vols.

Ecorcheville, Jules. "Corneille et la musique," Courrier musical IX (1906) 405–12, 438–49. Also separate: Paris, Fortin, 1906.

—— De Lulli à Rameau, 1690–1730; l'esthétique musicale. Paris, Fortin, 1906.

—— "Lully gentilhomme et sa descendance," MM VII No. 5 (1911) 1–19; No. 6, pp. 1–27; No. 7, pp. 36–52.

Edgar, Clifford B. "Mozart's Early Efforts in Opera," PMA XXXII (1906) 45–58.

—— "A Résumé of Mozart's Early Operas," ZIMG VII (1905–1906) 460–64.

Edwards, Henry Sutherland. The Life of Rossini. London, Hurst & Blackett, 1869.

—— Rossini and His School. New York, Scribner & Welford, 1881.

Egert, Paul. Peter Cornelius. Berlin, B. Hahnefeld, [ca. 1940].

Ehrenhaus, Martin. Die Operndichtung der deutschen Romantik; ein Beitrag zur Geschichte der deutschen Oper. Einleitung und I. Teil. Breslau, F. Hirt, 1911. (Breslauer Beiträge zur Literaturgeschichte, Heft 29 [New Series 19].)

Ehrhard, Auguste. "La Danse à l'opéra en 1834; les debuts de Fanny Elssler," Bulletin de la société des amis de l'université de Lyon XIX (1906) 61–81.

Ehrichs, Alfred. Giulio Caccini. Leipzig, Hesse & Becker, 1908.

Eichborn, Hermann. Die Trompete in alter und neuer Zeit. Leipzig, B&H, 1881.

Einstein, Alfred. "Agostino Steffani," *Kirchenmusikalisches Jahrbuch* XXIII (1910) 1–36.

—— "Agostino Steffani," *Neue Musik-Zeitung* XLIX (1928) 316–19.

—— "Ein Bericht über den Turiner Mordanfall auf Alessandro Stradella," in *Festschrift Adolf Sandberger* (Müchen, Zierfuss, 1918) pp. 135–37.

—— "Concerning Some Recitatives in *Don Giovanni*," M&L XIX (1938) 417–25.

—— "Das erste Libretto des *Don Giovanni*," *Acta musicologica* IX (1937) 149–50.

—— "Firenze prima della monodia," RassM VII (1934) 253.

—— "German Opera, Past and Present," MMus XI, No. 2 (January–February, 1934) 65–72.

—— Gluck. London, Dent; New York, E. P. Dutton, [1936].

—— "The Greghesca and the Giustiniana of the Sixteenth Century," *Journal of Renaissance and Baroque Music* I (1946) 19–32.

—— "Die mehrstimmige weltliche Musik von 1450–1600," in Adler, *Handbuch der Musikgeschichte* (Frankfurt a.M., Frankfurter Vertags-Anstalt, 1924) pp. 358–73.

—— "Mozart et l'opéra-bouffe à Salzburg," RdM XXI (1937) 1–4.

—— "Mozart e Tarchi; un episodio della storia delle *Nozze di Figaro*," RassM VIII (1935) 269–72.

—— Mozart, His Character, His Work. New York and London, Oxford University Press, 1945.

—— "L'opera tedesca d'oggi," RassM V (1932) 26–37.

—— "Richard Wagners *Liebesverbot;* zur Aufführung am Münchner National-Theater (24. März 1923)," ZfMw V (1922–23) 382–86.

—— "Ein Schüler Gluck's," *Acta musicologica* X (1938) 48–50.

—— "Die Text-Vorlage zu Mozart's *Zaide*," *Acta musicologica* VIII (1936) 30–37.

—— "Eine unbekannte Arie der Marcelline," ZfMw XIII (1930–31) 200–205.

—— "Vincenzo Bellini," M&L XVI (1935) 325-32.

Eisenschmidt, Joachim. Die szenische Darstellung der Opern Georg Friedrich Händels auf der Londoner Bühne seiner Zeit. Wolfenbüttel and Berlin, Kallmeyer, 1940.

Eitner, Robert, ed. "Das älteste bekannte deutsche Singspiel, *Seelewig*, von S. G. Staden, 1644," MfMg XIII (1881) 53–147.

—— "Benedetto Marcello," MfMg XXIII (1891) 187–94, 197–211.

—— "Die deutsche komische Oper," MfMg XXIV (1892) 37–92.

—— "Der Generalbass des 18. Jahrhunderts," MfMg XII (1880) 151–54.

—— "Johann Philipp Krieger," MfMg XXIX (1897) 114–17.

[——] "Die Quellen zur Entstehung der Oper," MfMg XIII (1881) 10–15, 21–28.

Ellinger, Georg. "Händel's *Admet* und seine Quelle," VfMw I (1885) 201–24.

Ellinwood, Leonard. "The *Conductus*," MQ XXVII (1941) 165–204.

Ellis, W. Ashton. "Richard Wagner's Prose," PMA XIX (1892) 13–33.

Elson, Louis C. The History of American Music. New York, Macmillan, 1925. Revised to 1925 by Arthur Elson.

Emmanuel, Maurice. *Pelléas et Mélisande* de Debussy; étude et analyse. Paris, Mellottée, [1925?].

Engel, Carl. "Die Wagnerdämmerung," MQ XIV (1928) 438–55.

Engel, Gustav. "Eine mathematisch-harmonische Analyse des *Don Giovanni* von Mozart," VfMw III (1887) 491–560.

Engelfred, Abele. *"Enoch Arden* di Riccardo Strauss," RMI VI (1899) 176–84.

—— *"Hulda* . . . di Cesare Franck," RMI II (1895) 312–23.

Engelke, Bernhard. "Aus den entscheidenden Entwicklungsjahren der Opéra-comique," in *Festschrift Arnold Schering* (Berlin, A. Glas, 1937) pp. 51–60.

—— Musik und Musiker am Gottorfer Hofe. Bd. 1. Die Zeit der englischen Komödianten (1590–1627). Breslau, Hirt, 1930.

Engländer, Richard. "Domenico Fischietti als Buffokomponist in Dresden," ZfMw II (1919–20) 321–52, 399–442.

—— "Dresden und die deutsche Oper im letzten Drittel des 18. Jahrhunderts," ZfMw III (1920–21) 1–21.

—— "Das Ende der *opera seria* in Dresden: Naumanns *Clemenza di Tito* 1769," *Neues Archiv für Sächsische Geschichte und Altertumskunde* XXXIX (1918) 311–29.

—— Johann Gottlieb Naumann als Opernkomponist. Leipzig, B&H, 1922.

—— Joseph Martin Kraus und die Gustavianische Oper. Uppsala, Almqvist & Wiksell; Leipzig, O. Harrassowitz, [1943].

—— "Die Opern Joseph Schusters," ZfMw X (1927–28) 257–91.

—— "Paërs *Leonora* und Beethovens *Fidelio*," *Neues Beethoven Jahrbuch* IV (1930) 118–32.

—— "Il *Paride* in musica (1662) di G. A. Bontempi," *Note d'archivio* XVII (1940) 39–53.

—— "The Sketches for *The Magic Flute* at Upsala," MQ XXVII (1941) 343–55.

—— "Zur Frage der *Dafne* (1671) von G. A. Bontempi und M. G. Peranda," *Acta musicologica* XIII (1941) 59–77.

—— "Zur Musikgeschichte Dresdens gegen 1800," ZfMw IV (1921–22) 199–241.

Engler, Günther. Verdis Anschauung vom Wesen der Oper. Breslau, Stenzel, 1938.

Enzinger, Moriz. Die Entwicklung des Wiener Theaters vom 16. zum 19. Jahrhundert. Berlin, Gesellschaft für Theatergeschichte, 1918–19. 2 vols.

Epstein, Peter. "Dichtung und Musik in Monteverdi's *Lamento d'Arianna*," ZfMw X (1927–28) 216–22.

—— "Paul Hindemiths Theatermusik," *Die Musik* XXIII (May, 1931) 582–87.

—— "Zur Rhythmisierung eines Ritornells von Monteverdi," AfMw VIII (1926) 416–19.

Epstein, Th. *Don Giovanni* von Mozart. Frankfurt a. M., Offenbach a. M., Andre, 1870.

Ernst, Alfred. "Les Motifs du *Héros* dans l'œuvre de R. Wagner," RMI I (1894) 657–77.

—— L'Œuvre dramatique de Berlioz. Paris, Levy, 1884.

—— "*Thaïs* . . . de J. Massenet," RMI I (1894) 296–306.

Esbert, C. L. R. "Hans Sachs," M&L XVII (1936) 59–61.

Eschweiler, Hans-Georg. Klara Ziegler; ein Beitrag zur Theatergeschichte des 19. Jahrhunderts. Rostock Dissertation, 1935.

Ettler, Carl. "Bibliographie des œuvres de Meyerbeer," RHCM IV (1904) 436–44.

Euting, Ernst. Zur Geschichte der Blasinstrumente im 16. und 17. Jahrhundert. Berlin, A. Schulze, 1899.

Evans, Edwin. Tchaikovsky. New York, E. P. Dutton, 1935. New ed., revised by E. Blom.

Evans, Herbert Arthur, ed. English Masques. London, Glasgow, Blackie & Son, 1897.

Evans, Willa McClung. Ben Jonson and Elizabethan Music. Lancaster, Pa., Lancaster Press, 1929.

Evelyn, John. Diary. London, J. M. Dent, 1907. 2 vols.

Färber, Sigfrid. Das Regensburger Fürstlich Thurn und Taxissche Hoftheater und seine Oper 1760–1786. [Regensburg], Pustet, 1936.

Faller, H. Die Gesangskoloratur in Rossinis Opern und ihre Ausführung. Berlin, Triltsch & Huther, 1935.

Fano, Fabio, ed. La camerata fiorentina; Vincenzo Galilei. Milano, Ricordi, 1934. (Istituzioni e monumenti dell' arte musicale italiana, Vol. IV.)

—— "*Norma* nella storia del melodramma italiano," RassM VIII (1935) 315–26.

Fassini, Sesto. "Gli albori del melodramma italiano a Londra," *Giornale storico della letteratura italiana* LX (1912) 340–76.

—— "Il melodramma italiano a Londra ai tempi del Rolli," RMI XIX (1912) 35–74, 575–636.

—— Il melodramma italiano a Londra nella prima metà del settecento. Turin, Bocca, 1914.

[Fauré, Gabriel Urbain.] *See* RM, numéro spécial (October, 1922).

[——] "Gabriel Fauré; note biografiche," *Bollettino bibliografico musicale* V, No. 3 (March, 1930) 5–[17].

Faustini-Fasini, Eugenio. "Gli astri maggiori del 'bel canto' Napoletano," *Note d'archivio* XII (1935) 297–316.

—— "Documenti paisielliani inediti," *Note d'archivio* XIII (1936) 105–27.

—— G. B. Pergolesi attraverso i suoi biografi e le sue opere. Milano, Ricordi, 1900.

—— "Leonardo Leo e la sua famiglia," *Note d'archivio* XIV (1937) 11–18.

—— Opere teatrali, oratori e cantate di Giovanni Paisiello (1764–1808); saggio storico-cronologico. Bari, Laterza, 1940.

Favart, Charles Simon. Memoires et correspondances littéraires, dramatiques et anecdotiques. Paris, L. Collin, 1808. 3 vols.

—— Théâtre. Paris, DuChesne, 1763–[77]. 10 vols.

Favre, G. Boieldieu. Paris, Droz, 1944–45. 2 vols.

Fedeli, Vito. "Dal *Cavaliere Ergasto* alla *Molinarella*," RMI XVIII (1911) 357–81.

—— "*La Molinarella* di Piccinni," SIMG XIII (1911–12) 302–21, 507.

—— "Un' opera sconosciuta di Pergolesi?" SIMG XII (1910–11) 139–50.

Fehr, Max. Apostolo Zeno, 1668–1750, und seine Reform des Operntextes. Zürich, A. Tschopp, 1912.

—— "Pergolesi und Zeno," SIMG XV (1913–14) 166–68.

—— "Zeno, Pergolesi und Jommelli," ZfMw I (1918–19) 281–87.

Fellerer, Karl Gustav. Beiträge zur Musikgeschichte Freisings. Freising, Freising. Tagbl., 1926.

—— "Max von Droste-Hülshoff," AfMf II (1937) 160–72.

Fellmann, Hans Georg. Die Böhmsche Theatergruppe und ihre Zeit. Leipzig, L. Voss, 1928.

Fellowes, E. H. "The Philidor Manuscripts," M&L XII (1931) 116–29.

Ferand, Ernst. Die Improvisation in der Musik. Zürich, Rhein-Verlag, [1938].

Ferrari, A. Rodigino; le convenienze teatrali; analisi della condizione presente del teatro musicale italiano. Milano, Redaelli, 1843.

Ferrari Nicolay, Mauricio. "En torno a *Las Vírgenes del Sol*, la nueva opera argentina," *Estudios* (Buenos Aires) Año 29, tomo 62 (1939) 29–46.

Fétis, Edouard. Les Musiciens belges, tome premier. Bruxelles, Ajamar, n.d.

Filippi, Joseph de. Parallèle des principaux théâtres modernes de l'Europe et des machines théâtrales françaises, allemandes et anglaises. Paris, Lévy, 1870. 2 vols.

Finck, Henry T. Richard Strauss. Boston, Little, Brown, 1917.

Findeisen, Nicholas. "The Earliest Russian Operas," MQ XIX (1933) 331–40.

—— "Die Entwicklung der Tonkunst in Russland in der ersten Hälfte des 19. Jahrhunderts," SIMG II (1900–1901) 279–302.

—— "Die Oper in Russland," ZIMG I (1899–1900) 367–75.

Finney, Gretchen Ludke. "Chorus in *Samson Agonistes*," *Publications of the Modern Language Association of America* LVIII (1943) 649–64.

Finney, Gretchen Ludke (*Cont.*). "*Comus*, Dramma per Musica," *Studies in Philology* XXXVII (1940) 483–500; also separate.

Fiorda Kelly, Alfredo. Cronología de las óperas, dramas líricos, oratorios, himnos, etc. cantados en Buenos Aires. Buenos Aires, Riera, 1934.

Fischer, Georg. Marschner-Erinnerungen. Hannover and Leipzig, Hahn, 1918.

—— Musik in Hannover. Hannover, Hahn, 1903. 2d enlarged edition of his Opern und Concerte im Hoftheater zu Hannover bis 1866.

Fleischer, Oskar. "Napoleon Bonaparte's Musikpolitik," ZIMG III (1901–02) 431–40.

Flemming, Willi. Geschichte des Jesuitentheaters in den Landen deutscher Zunge. Berlin, Gesellschaft für Theatergeschichte, 1923.

—— ed. Die Oper. Leipzig, Reclam, 1933. (Deutsche Literatur; Sammlung literarischer Kunst- und Kulturdenkmäler in Entwicklungsreihen . . . Reihe Barock; Barockdrama. Bd. 5.)

Floch, Siegfried. Die Oper seit Richard Wagner. Köln, Fulda, 1904.

Flögel, Bruno. "Studien zur Arientechnik in den Opern Händels," *Händel-Jahrbuch* II (1929) 50–156.

Flood, W. H. Grattan. "The *Beggar's Opera* and Its Composers," M&L III (1922) 402–406.

—— "Quelques Précisions nouvelles sur Cambert et Grabu à Londres," RM IX (August, 1928) 351–61.

—— William Vincent Wallace; a memoir. Waterford, "The Waterford News," 1912.

Florence, Italy. R. Istituto musicale. Atti dell' accademia del R. Istituto musicale di Firenze, Anno XXXIII; commemorazione della riforma melodrammatica. Firenze, Galletti e Cocci, 1895.

Florimo, Francesco. La scuola musicale di Napoli e i suoi conservatori. Napoli, V. Morano, 1880–1882. 4 vols. 2d ed.

Flotow, Rosa. Friedrich von Flotow's Leben von seiner Wittwe. Leipzig, B&H, 1892.

Flower, Newman. George Frederic Handel; His Personality and His Times. Boston and New York, Houghton Mifflin, 1923.

Foerster-Nietzsche, Elizabeth. "Wagner and Nietzsche; the Beginning and End of Their Friendship," MQ IV (1918) 466–89.

Fondi, Enrico. "Il sentimento musicale di Vittorio Alfieri," RMI XI (1904) 484–99.

—— La vita e l'opera letteraria del musicista Benedetto Marcello. Roma, W. Modes, 1909.

Fonseco Benevides, Francisco da. O real theatro de S. Carlos de Lisboa, desde a sua funação em 1793 até á actualidade. Lisboa, Castro Irmão, [1883].

Font, Auguste. Favart, l'opéra-comique et la comédie-vaudeville aux XVIIe et XVIIIe siècles. Paris, Fischbacher, 1894.

Fontana, Francesco. "Vita di Benedetto Marcello," in *Estro poetico-armonico parafrasi sopra le primi venticinque salmi, poesia di Girolamo Asconio Giustiniani, musica di Benedetto Marcello* (Venezia, Sebastiano Valle, 1803), I, 1–48.

Forsyth, Cecil. Music and Nationalism; a Study of English Opera. London, Macmillan, 1911.

Fouque, Octave. "Le Sueur comme prédécesseur de Berlioz," in *Les Révolutionnaires de la musique* (Paris, Calmann-Lévy, 1882) pp. 1–183.

Fraccaroli, Arnaldo. La vita di Giacomo Puccini. Milan, Ricordi, 1925.

Fraguier, Marguerite-Marie de. Vincent d'Indy; souvenirs d'une élève. Paris, Jean Naert, 1933.

Franklin, Benjamin. "The Ephemera; an Emblem of Human Life," in *The Writings of Benjamin Franklin,* edited by Albert Henry Smith (New York, Macmillan, 1907) VII, 206–209.

Frati, Lodovico. "Antonio Bernacchi e la sua scuola di canto," RMI XXIX (1922) 443–91.

—— "Attilio Ottavio Ariosti," RMI XXXIII (1926) 551–57.

—— "Un impresario teatrale del settecento e la sua biblioteca," RMI XVIII (1911) 64–84.

—— "Metastasio e Farinelli," RMI XX (1913) 1–30.

—— "Musica e balli alla corte dei Pico della Mirandola," RMI XXV (1918) 249–58.

—— "Musicisti e cantanti bolognesi del settecento," RMI XXI (1914) 189–202.

—— "Per la storia della musica in Bologna nel secolo XVII," RMI XXXII (1925) 544–65.

—— "Satire di musicisti," RMI XXII (1915) 560–66.

—— "Torquato Tasso in musica," RMI XXX (1923) 389–400.

Freisauff, Rudolf von. Mozart's *Don Juan,* 1787–1887. Salzburg, H. Kerber, 1887.

"The *Freischütz* in London, 1824," ZIMG XI (1909–10) 251–54.

Fremy, Edouard. Origines de l'Académie française: l'Académie des derniers Valois. Paris, E. Leroux, [1887].

Frensdorf, Victor Egon. Peter Winter als Opernkomponist. Erlangen, Junge, 1908.

Frere, Walter Howard, ed. The Winchester Troper, from Mss. of the Xth and XIth Centuries, with Other Documents Illustrating the History of Tropes in England and France. London, [Printed for the Henry Bradshaw Society by Harrison and Sons], 1894.

Freund, Hans and Wilhelm Reinking. Musikalisches Theater in Hamburg; Versuch über die Dramaturgie der Oper. Hamburg, Hans Christians, 1938.

Friedländer, Max. "Deutsche Dichtung in Beethovens Musik," JMP XIX (1912) 25–48.

Friedländer, Max (*Cont.*). Das deutsche Lied im 18. Jahrhundert. Stuttgart and Berlin, Cotta, 1902. 3 parts in 2 vols.

Friedrich, Gerhard. Die deutsche und italienische Gestaltung des Falstaff-Stoffes in der Oper. Habelschwerdt, Groeger, 1941.

Friedrich, Julius. Claus Schall als dramatischer Komponist. Herchenbach, Wanne-Eickel, 1930.

Fröhlich, Willi. Jean Paul's Beziehungen zur Musik. Frankfurt Dissertation, 1922.

Frost, Henry F. "Some Remarks on Richard Wagner's Music Drama *Tristan und Isolde*," PMA VIII (1882) 147–67.

Fuchs, Albert. "Wieland et l'esthétique de l'opéra," *Revue de littérature comparée* X (1930) 608–33.

Fuchs, Marianne. Die Entwicklung des Finales in der italienischen Opera Buffa vor Mozart. Vienna Dissertation, 1932.

Fürstenau, Moritz. "Maria Antonia Walpurgis, Kurfürstin von Sachsen; eine biografische Skizze," MfMg XI (1879) 167–81.

—— "Die Oper *Antiope* und die Bestellungen des Kurfürstlich Sächsischen Vicekapellmeisters Nicolaus Adam Strunck und des Hofpoeten Stefano Pallavicini," MfMg XIII (1881) 1–6.

—— "Eine theologische Zeitschrift des 17. Jahrhunderts über Castraten und Oper; Johann Samuel Adami," *Musikalisches Wochenblatt* I (1870) 241–43.

—— "Zur Don Juan-Literatur," MfMg II (1870) 41–47.

—— Zur Geschichte der Musik und des Theaters am Hofe zu Dresden. Dresden, R. Kuntze, 1861–62. 2 parts.

Fuller-Maitland, John Alexander. The Age of Bach and Handel. Oxford, Clarendon Press, 1902. 2d ed., London, Oxford University Press, 1931. (Oxford History of Music, Vol. IV.)

—— The Music of Parry and Stanford. Cambridge, W. Heffer, 1934.

Gaartz, Hans. Die Opern Heinrich Marschners. Leipzig, B&H, 1912.

Gagey, Edmond M. Ballad Opera. New York, Columbia University Press, 1937.

Gál, Hans. "A Deleted Episode in Verdi's *Falstaff*," *Music Review* II (1941) 266–72.

Galilei, Vincenzo. Dialogo della musica antica, et della moderna. Fiorenza, G. Marescotti, 1581. Facsimile reprint, Roma, R. Accademia d'Italia, 1934.

Galindo, Miguel. Nociones de historia de la música mejicana, tomo 1. Colima, Tip. de "El dragón," 1933.

Galli, Amintore. Umberto Giordano nell' arte e nella vita. Milano, E. Sonzogno, 1915.

Gallusser, Rita. Verdis Frauengestalten. Zürich Dissertation, 1936.

[Galluzzi, Riguccio.] Istoria del granducato di Toscana sotto il governo della casa Medici. Firenze, Stamperia di R. del Vivo, 1781. 5 vols. New ed., Firenze, 1822. 11 vols.

Gandolfi, Riccardo. "Appunti di storia musicale; Cristofano Malvezzi—Emilio de' Cavalieri," *Rassegna nazionale* XV (November, 1893) 297–306.

—— "Cinque lettere inedite di Giuseppe Verdi," RMI XX (1913) 168–72.

Gaspari, Gaetano. "Dei musicisti Bolognesi al XVII secolo e delle loro opere a stampa," *Atti e memorie della R. R. Deputazione di storia patria per le provincie dell'Emilia, Nuova serie* III (1878) 1–24.

Gastoué, Amadée. "Gossec et Gluck à l'opéra de Paris: le ballet final *d'Iphigénie en Tauride*," RdM XVI (1935) 87–99.

—— "Nicolò Piccinni et ses opéras à Paris," *Note d'archivio* XIII (1936) 52–54.

Gatti, Carlo. Il Teatro alla Scala rinnovato; le prime quattro stagioni. Milano, Fratelli Treves, 1926.

Gatti, Guido Maria. *Le Barbier de Seville* de Rossini; étude historique et critique, analyse musicale. Paris, P. Mellottée, [1924?].

—— "Boito's *Nero*," MQ X (1924) 596–621.

—— "Franco Alfano," MQ IX (1923) 556–77.

—— "Gabriele D'Annunzio and the Italian Opera Composers," MQ X (1924) 263–88.

—— Ildebrando Pizzetti. Torino, G. B. Paravia, [1934].

—— "Ildebrando Pizzetti," MQ IX (1923) 96–121, 271–86.

—— "Malipiero and Pirandello at the Opera," MMus XI, No. 4 (May-June, 1934) 213–16.

—— Musicisti moderni d'Italia e di fuori. Bologna, Pizzi, 1920.

—— "Recent Italian Operas," MQ XXIII (1937) 77–88.

—— "The Stage Works of Ferruccio Busoni," MQ XX (1934) 267–77.

—— "Two *Macbeths*: Verdi—Bloch," MQ XII (1926) 22–31.

—— "The Works of Giacomo Puccini," MQ XIV (1928) 16–34.

Gatti-Casazza, Giulio. Memories of the Opera. New York, Charles Scribner's Sons, 1941.

Gaudier, Charles. *Carmen* de Bizet; étude historique et critique, analyse musicale. Paris, P. Mellottée, [1922].

Gautier, Léon. Histoire de la poésie liturgique au moyen âge: les tropes. Paris, V. Palmé, 1886.

Gautier, Théophile. Les Beautés de l'opéra. Paris, Soulié, 1845.

—— Histoire de l'art dramatique en France depuis vingt-cinq ans. Paris, Magnin, Blanchard, 1858–59. 6 vols.

Gavazzeni, Gianandrea. "Donizetti e l' *Elisir d'amore*," RassM VI (1933) 44–50.

—— "Karol Szymanowski e il *Re Ruggero*," RassM X (1937) 409–15.

Gay, John. The Beggar's Opera. London, De la Mare Press, 1905.

Gaye, Phoebe Fenwick. John Gay; His Place in the 18th Century. London, Collins, 1938.

Gedenkschrift für Hermann Abert. Halle an der Saale, M. Niemeyer, 1928. Contains essays on Sailer, G. C. Wagenseil, and French Opera.

Geffcken, Johannes. "Die ältesten Hamburgischen Opern," *Zeitschrift des Vereines für Hamburgische Geschichte* III (1851) 34–55.

Geiringer, Karl. Haydn; a Creative Life in Music. New York, W. W. Norton, 1946.

—— "Haydn as an Opera Composer," PMA LXVI (1939–40) 23–30.

—— Joseph Haydn. Potsdam, Athenaion, [1932].

Genest, Émile. L'Opéra-comique connu et inconnu. Paris, Fischbacher, 1925.

Gentili, Alberto. "La raccolta Mauro Foà nella Biblioteca Nazionale di Torino," RMI XXXIV (1927) 356–68.

George, André. Arthur Honegger. Paris, C. Aveline, 1926.

—— *Tristan et Isolde* de Richard Wagner; étude historique et critique, analyse musicale. Paris, Mellottée, [1929].

Georges, Horst. Das Klangsymbol des Todes im dramatischen Werk Mozarts. Wolfenbüttel-Berlin, G. Kallmeyer, 1937.

Gerber, Rudolf. Der Operntypus Johann Adolf Hasses und seine textlichen Grundlage. Leipzig, Kistner & Siegel, 1925.

Gerigk, Herbert. "Das alte und das neue Bild Rossinis," ZfMw XVI (1934) 26–32.

Gérold, Théodore. L'Art du chant en France au XVIIe siècle. Strasbourg, G. Fischbach, 1921.

—— La Musique au moyen age. Paris, Champion, 1932.

Gettemann, H. "*Sniégourotchka* opéra de M. Rimsky-Korsakoff," RHCM VIII (1908) 137–43, 179–87, 213–16.

Geulette, Thomas Simon. Notes et souvenirs sur le théâtre-italien au XVIIIe siècle. Paris, E. Praz, 1938.

Gherardi, Evaristo, compiler. Le Théâtre italien de Gherardi. Amsterdam, M. C. le Cene, 1721. 6 vols. 5th ed.

Ghisi, Federico. I canti carnascialeschi nelle fonti musicali del XV e XVI secolo. Firenze-Roma, L. S. Olschki, 1937.

—— Del "Fuggilotio musicale" di Giulio Romano (Caccini); saggio critico. Roma, De Santis, 1934.

—— Feste musicali della Firenze Medicea. Firenze, Vallecchi, 1939.

Giani, Romualdo. "Il *Nerone* di Arrigo Boito," RMI VIII (1901) 861–1006.

Giazotto, Remo. Il melodramma a Genova nei secoli 17 & 18; con gli elenchi completi dei titoli, dei musicisti, dei poeti e degli attori di quei componomenti rappresentati fra il 1652 e il 1771 ai teatri detti "Del Falcone" e "Da S. Agostino." Genova, A cura dell' ente del Teatro Carlo Felice, 1941.

Gilman, Lawrence. Aspects of Modern Opera. London, John Lane; New York, Dodd, Mead, 1924.

—— Debussy's *Pelléas et Mélisande,* a Guide to the Opera. New York, G. Schirmer, 1907.

—— Wagner's Operas. New York, Toronto, Farrar & Rhinehart, [1937].

Gilse van der Pals, Nikolai van. N. A. Rimsky-Korssakow: Opernschaffen nebst Skizze über Leben und Wirken. Paris-Leipzig, W. Bessel, 1929.

Ginisty, Paul. Le Melodrama. Paris, L. Michaud, [1910].

Giraldi, Romolo. Giovanni Battista Pergolese. Roma, Laziale, 1936.

Glareanus, Henricus. Dodecachordon. Leipzig, B&H, 1888. Translated and transcribed by Peter Bohn. Originally published 1547.

Glasenapp, Carl Friedrich. Das Leben Richard Wagners. Leipzig, B&H, 1904–11. 6 vols. 4th ed. Translated as: The Life of Richard Wagner. London, Paul, Trench & Trübner, 1900–1908. 6 vols.

—— Siegfried Wagner und seine Kunst. Leipzig, B&H, 1911.

—— Siegfried Wagner und seine Kunst. Neue Folge. I. Schwartzschwanenreich (Leipzig, B&H, 1913); II. Sonnenflammen (Leipzig, B&H, 1919).

—— Versuch einer thematischen Analyse der Musik zu Siegfried Wagner's Kobold. Leipzig, M. Brockhaus, 1904.

Gluck, Christoph Willibald, Ritter von. "Correspondance inédite," MM X, No. 11 (1914) 1–16.

—— "Vier Gluck-Briefe," Die Musik XIII (1913–14) Qt. 4, 10–15.

Gluck-Jahrbuch. Jahrgang I–IV (1913, 1915, 1917, 1918). Leipzig, B&H. Ed. by H. Abert.

Gmeyner, Alice. Die Opern M. A. Caldaras. Vienna Dissertation, 1935.

Gnirs, Anton. Hans Heiling. Karlsbad, Heinich, 1931.

Goddard, Scott. "Editions of Boris Goudonov," M&L X (1929) 278–86.

Godet, Robert. En Marge de Boris Godounof; notes sur les documents iconographiques de l'édition Chester. Paris, F. Alcan, 1926.

Goldberg, Isaac. The Story of Gilbert and Sullivan. New York, Simon & Schuster, 1928.

Goldmark, Karl. Erinnerungen aus meinem Leben. Wien, Rikola, 1922. Translated as: Notes from the Life of a Viennese Composer. New York, A. and C. Boni, 1927.

Goldoni, Carlo. Mémoires. Paris, Veuve Duchesne, 1787. 3 vols. Translated as: Memoirs of Goldoni. London, H. Colburn, 1814. 2 vols.

Goldschmidt, Hugo. "Cavalli als dramatischer Komponist," MfMg XXV (1893) 45–48, 53–58, 61–111.

—— "Das Cembalo im Orchester der italienischen Oper der zweiten Hälfte des 18. Jahrhunderts," in Festschrift Liliencron (Leipzig, B&H, 1910) pp. 87–92.

—— "Claudio Monteverdi's Oper: Il ritorno d'Ulisse in patria," SIMG IX (1907–1908) 570–92.

—— "Francesco Provenzale als Dramatiker," SIMG VII (1905–1906) 608–34.

—— "Die Instrumentalbegleitung der italienischen Musikdramen in der ersten Hälfte des XVII. Jahrhunderts," MfMg XXVII (1895) 52–62.

—— Die italienische Gesangsmethode des XVII. Jahrhunderts und ihre Bedeutung für die Gegenwart. Breslau, Schlesische Buchdruckerei, 1890. 2d ed., Breslau, S. Schottlaender, 1892.

Goldschmidt, Hugo (*Cont.*). Die Lehre von der vokalen Ornamentik, erster Band: das 17. und 18. Jahrhundert bis in die Zeit Glucks. Charlottenburg, P. Lehsten, 1907.

—— "Monteverdi's *Ritorno d'Ulisse*," SIMG IV (1902–1903) 671–76.

—— Die Musikästhetik des 18. Jahrhunderts und ihre Beziehungen zu seinen Kunstschaffen. Zürich, Rascher, 1915. *See also* review by A. Schering, ZfMw I (1918–1919) 298–308.

—— "Die Reform der italienischen Oper des 18. Jahrhunderts und ihre Beziehungen zur musikalischen Aesthetik," in *III. Kongress der Internationalen Musikgesellschaft . . . Bericht* (Wien, Artaria; Leipzig, B&H, 1909) pp. 196–207.

—— Studien zur Geschichte der italienischen Oper im 17. Jahrhundert. Leipzig, B&H, 1901–1904. 2 vols. Review by R. Rolland, RHCM II (1902) 20–29.

—— "Verzierungen, Veränderungen und Passaggien im 16. und 17. Jahrhundert," MfMg XXIII (1891) 111–26.

—— "Zur Geschichte der Arien- und Symphonie-Formen," MfMg XXXIII (1901) 61–70.

Gómez, Julio. "Don Blas de Laserna; un capítolo de la historia del teatro lirico español," *Archivo y museo al ayuntamicuto de Madrid* (1925–26).

Gorer, R. "Weber and the Romantic Movement," M&L XVII (1936) 13–24.

Goslich, Siegfried. Beiträge zur Geschichte der deutschen romantischen Oper zwischen Spohrs *Faust* und Wagners *Lohengrin*. Leipzig, Kistner & Siegel, 1937.

Gottsched, Johann Christoph. Nöthiger Vorrath zur Geschichte der deutschen dramatischen Dichtkunst oder Verzeichniss aller deutschen Trauer-Lust- und Sing-Spiele, die im Druck erschienen von 1450 bis zur Hälfte des jetzigen Jahrhunderts. Leipzig, J. M. Teubner, 1757–65. 2 vols.

—— Versuch einer kritischen Dichtkunst vor die Deutschen. Leipzig, B. C. Breitkopf, 1730. 2d ed., 1737.

Goudar, Ange. Le Brigandage de la musique italienne. 1777.

[Goudar, Mme. Sara.] De Venise, remarques sur la musique & la danse. Venise, C. Palese, 1773.

Gounod, Charles François. Autobiographical Reminiscences, with Family Letters and Notes on Music. London, W. Heinemann, 1896.

—— Mémoires d'un artiste. Paris, Calmann Lévy, 1896. 5th ed. Translated as: Memoirs of an Artist. New York, Rand, McNally, 1895.

—— Mozart's *Don Giovanni;* a Commentary. London, R. Cocks, 1895. Translated from the 3d French ed.

Graf, Herbert. The Opera and Its Future in America. New York, W. W. Norton, [1941].

—— Richard Wagner als Regisseur. Vienna Dissertation, 1925.

Gramisch, Lore. Die Erscheinungsformen des melodramatischen Stils im 19. Jahrhundert. Vienna Dissertation, 1936.

Grannis, Valleria Belt. Dramatic Parody in Eighteenth Century France. New York, Institute of French Studies, 1931.

Grattan Flood, *see* Flood, William Henry Grattan.

Gray, Alan. "Purcell's Dramatic Music," PMA XLIII (1916–17) 51–62.

Gray, Cecil. "Pietro Raimondi," *Music Review* I (1940) 25–35.

—— "Vincenzo Bellini," M&L VII (1926) 49–62.

Greene, Harry Plunket. Charles Villiers Stanford. London, E. Arnold, [1935].

Grégoir, Edouard. Bibliothèque musicale populaire. Bruxelles, Schott, 1877–79. 3 vols.

—— Des Gloires de l'opéra et la musique à Paris. Bruxelles, Schott, 1878. 3 vols.

—— Littérature musicale. Bruxelles, Schott, 1872–76. 4 vols.

—— Panthéon musical populaire. Bruxelles, Schott, 1876–77. 6 vols.

Gregor, Joseph. Richard Strauss. München, R. Piper, [1939].

—— Weltgeschichte des Theaters. [Zürich], Phaidon, [1933].

Grétry, André Ernest Modeste. Mémoires, ou essais sur la musique. Paris, Imprimerie de la république, [1797]. 3 vols. First published 1789.

—— Oèuvres complètes; reflexions d'un solitaire. Bruxelles-Paris, Von Oest, 1919–22. 4 vols.

Greulich, Martin. Beiträge zur Geschichte des Streichinstrumentenspiels im 16. Jahrhundert. Saalfeld, Günther, [1934?].

Griepenkerl, Wolfgang Robert. Die Oper der Gegenwart. Leipzig, Hinrich, 1847.

Griggs, John C. "The Influence of Comedy upon Operatic Form," MQ III (1917) 552–61.

Grimm, Friedrich Melchior, Freiherr von. Correspondance littéraire, philosophique et critique. Paris, Garnier, 1877–82. 16 vols. Contains "Lettre sur Omphale," XVI, 287–309.

—— Le Petit Prophète de Boemischbroda. Paris, 1753.

Grisson, Alexandra Carola. Ermanno Wolf-Ferrari, autorisierte Lebensbeschreibung. Regensburg, Bosse, 1941.

Groppo, Antonio. Catalogo di tutti i drammi per musica recitati ne' teatri di Venezia dall' anno 1637 sin all' anno presente 1745. Venezia, A. Groppo, [1745?].

Gros, Etienne. Philippe Quinault. Paris, E. Champion, 1926.

Grosheim, Georg Christoph. Selbstbiographie. Hamburg, Cassel, F. Settnick, 1925. Ed. by Georg Heinrichs.

[Grosley, Pierre Jean.] New Observations on Italy and Its Inhabitants. London, L. Davis & C. Reymers, 1769. 2 vols.

Gross, Rolf. Joseph Hartmann Stuntz als Opernkomponist. Würzburg, Triltsch, 1936.

Grout, Donald J. "German Baroque Opera," MQ XXXII (1946) 574–87.

—— "The 'Machine' Operas," *Bulletin of the Fogg Museum of Art, Harvard University* IX, No. 5 (November, 1941) 100–103.

Grout, Donald J. (*Cont.*). "The Music of the Italian Theatre at Paris, 1682–1697," in *Papers of the American Musicological Society, Annual Meeting, 1941 . . . Edited by Gustave Reese* (Printed by the Society [cop. 1946]), pp. 158–70.

—— The Origins of the Opéra-comique. Harvard Dissertation, 1939.

—— "Seventeenth Century Parodies of French Opera," MQ XXVII (1941) 211–19, 514–26.

—— "Some Forerunners of the Lully Opera," M&L XXII (1941) 1–25.

Grovlez, Gabriel. "Jacques Offenbach; a Centennial Sketch," MQ V (1919) 329–37.

Grüel, C. Aufschlüsse über die Bedeutung des angeblich Schikaneder'schen Textes zu Mozart's *Zauberflöte*. Magdeburg, Creutz, 1868.

Güttler, Hermann. Königsbergs Musikkultur im 18. Jahrhundert. Kassel, Bärenreiter, [1929].

Gui, Vittorio. "Arlecchino," RassM XIII (1940) 30–37.

Guiet, René. L'Evolution d'un genre: le livret d'opéra en France de Gluck à la révolution (1774–1793). Northampton, Mass., Smith College, Dept. of Modern Languages, 1936.

Guingené, Pierre Louis. Notice sur la vie et les ouvrages de Nicolas Piccini. Paris, Panckoucke, [1801].

Gutman, Hans. "*Mahagonny* and Other Novelties," MMus VII, No. 4 (June–July, 1930) 32–36.

—— "Tabloid Hindemith," MMus VII, No. 1 (December, 1929–January, 1930) 34–37.

Guy, Henri. Bibliographie critique du trouvère Adan de le Hale. Paris, A. Fontemoing, [1900].

—— Essai sur la vie et les œuvres littéraires du trouvère Adan de le Hale. Paris, Hachette, 1898.

Haas, Robert A. Afführungspraxis der Musik. Wildpark-Potsdam, Athenaion, [1931].

—— "Beitrag zur Geschichte der Oper in Prag und Dresden," *Neues Archiv für Sächsische Geschichte und Altertumskunde* XXXVII (1916) 68–96.

—— "Gioseppe Zamponis *Ulisse nell' isola di Circe*," ZfMw III (1920–21) 385–405.

—— Gluck und Durazzo im Burgtheater. Zürich, Amalthea, 1925.

—— "Josse de Villeneuves Brief über den Mechanismus der italienischen Oper von 1756," ZfMw VII (1924–25) 129–63.

—— Die Musik des Barocks. Potsdam, Athenaion, [1934].

—— "Die Musik in der Wiener deutscher Stegreifkomödie," SzMw XII (1925) 1–64.

—— "Teutsche Comedie Arien," ZfMw III (1920–21) 405–15.

—— "Die Wiener Ballet-Pantomime im 18. Jahrhundert und Glucks *Don Juan*," SzMw X (1923) 3–36.

—— "Der Wiener Bühnentanz von 1740 bis 1767," JMP XLIV (1937) 77–93.

—— "Wiener deutsche Parodieopern um 1730," ZfMw VIII (1925–26) 201–25.

—— Die Wiener Oper. Wien-Budapest, Eligius, 1926.

—— "Zur Neuausgabe von Claudio Monteverdis *Il ritorno d'Ulisse in patria*," SzMw IX (1922) 3–42.

—— "Zur Wiener Balletpantomime um den *Prometheus*," *Neues Beethoven Jahrbuch* II (1925) 84–103.

Haberl, Franz X. "Johann Mattheson; biographische Skizze," *Caecilien Kalender* (1885) 53–60.

Habets, Alfred. Alexandre Borodine, d'après la biographie et la correspondance publiées par M. Wladimir Stassof. Paris, Fischbacher, 1893. Translated as: Borodin and Liszt. London, Digby, Long, [1895].

Haböck, Franz. Die Gesangskunst der Kastraten; erster Notenbuch A. Die Kunst des cavaliere Carlo Broschi Farinelli. B. Farinellis berühmte Arien. Wien, Universal, [1923].

—— Die Kastraten und ihre Gesangskunst. Stuttgart, Deutsche Verlags-Anstalt, 1927.

Hackett, Karleton. "The Possibilities of Opera in America," MTNA IV (1909) 52–60.

Hadow, Sir William Henry. Studies in Modern Music, Second Series. New York, Macmillan, [1923]. 10th ed.

Händel-Festspiele . . . 1922; veranstaltet vom Universitätsbund. Göttingen, W. H. Lange, 1922. Contains essays on Handel by H. Abert and O. Hagen.

Händel-Jahrbuch. Leipzig, B&H, 1928–.

Hänsler, Rolf. Peter Lindpainter als Opernkomponist. Stuttgart-Caunstadt, Kirchoff, [1930].

Hagen, Oskar. "Die Bearbeitung der Händelschen *Rodelinde* und ihre Uraufführung am 26. Juni 1920 in Göttingen," ZfMw II (1919–20) 725–32.

Halévy, François. Derniers Souvenirs et portraits. Paris, M. Lévy, 1863.

—— Souvenirs et portraits. Paris, M. Lévy, 1861.

Hall, Raymond. "The *Macbeth* of Bloch," MMus XV, No. 4 (May–June, 1938) 209–15.

Halle. Stadtarchiv. Georg Friedrich Händel, Abstammung und Jugendwelt. Halle, Gebauer-Schwetschke, 1935.

Halusa, Karl. Hans Pfitzners musikdramatisches Schaffen. Vienna Dissertation, 1929.

Hamilton, Edith. "The Greek Chorus, Fifteen or Fifty?" *Theatre Arts Monthly* XVII (1933) 459.

Hamilton, Mrs. Mary (Neal). Music in Eighteenth Century Spain. Urbana, The University of Illinois, 1937.

Hampe, Theodor. Die Entwicklung des Theaterwesens in Nürnberg von der 2. Hälfte des 15. Jahrhunderts bis 1806. Nürnberg, J. L. Schrag, 1900.

Handbook of Latin American Studies. Cambridge, Mass., Harvard University Press, 1936–.

Handschin, Jacques. Igor Stravinsky. Zürich and Leipzig, Hug, 1933.

—— "Das Weinachts-Mysterium von Rouen als musikgeschichtliche Quelle," *Acta musicologica* VII (1935) 97–110.

Hanslick, Eduard. Die moderne Oper; Kritiken und Studien. Berlin, A. Hofmann, 1875. This is also the title of a series of books by Hanslick, the respective subtitles and dates of which are as follows: I. Die moderne Oper, 1875; II. Musikalische Stationen, 1880; III. Aus dem Opernleben der Gegenwart, 1884; IV. Musikalische Skizzenbuch, 1888; V. Musikalisches und Litterarisches, 1889; VI. Aus dem Tagebuche eines Musikers, 1892; VII. Fünf Jahre Musik (1891–1895), 1896; VIII. Am Ende des Jahrhunderts (1895–1899), 1899; IX. Aus neuer und neuester Zeit, 1900.

—— Vom Musikalisch-Schönen; ein Beitrag zur Revision der Aesthetik der Tonkunst. Leipzig, R. Weigel, 1854.

Harászti, Emil. Béla Bartók, His Life and Works. Paris, The Lyrebird Press, [1938].

—— La Musique hongroise. Paris, Laurens, 1933.

—— "Le Problème du Leit-motiv," RM IV (August, 1923) 35–37.

Harcourt, Eugène d'. La Musique actuelle en Allemagne et Autriche-Hongrie. Paris, Durdilly, [1908].

—— La Musique actuelle en Italie. Paris, Durdilly, [1907].

[Harsdörffer, Georg Philipp.] Frauenzimmer Gesprechspiele so bey ehr- und tugendliebenden Gesellschaften mit nutzlicher Ergetzlichkeit beliebet und geübet werden mögen. Nürnberg, W. Endtern, 1643–57. 8 vols.

Hartmann, Fritz. Sechs Bücher Braunschweigischer Theatergeschichte. Wolfenbüttel, J. Zwissler, 1905.

Hasse, Max. Der Dichtermusiker Peter Cornelius. Leipzig, B&H, 1922–23. 2 vols.

—— Peter Cornelius und sein *Barbier von Bagdad*. Leipzig, B&H, 1904.

Hasselberg, Felix. *Der Freischütz;* Friedrich Kinds Operndichtung und ihre Quellen. Berlin, Dom Verlag, 1921.

Hausegger, Siegmund von. Alexander Ritter; ein Bild seines Characters und Schaffens. Berlin, Marquardt, [1907].

Haweis, Hugh Reginald. Music and Morals. New York, Harper, 1872.

Hawkins, John. A General History of the Science and Practice of Music. London, T. Payne, 1776. 5 vols.

[——?] Memoirs of the Life of Sig. Agostino Steffani. [London? 17—.]

Hédouin, Pierre. Gossec, sa vie et ses ouvrages. Paris, Prignet, 1852.

—— Mosaique; peintres—musiciens— . . . à partir du 15e siècle jusqu'à nos jours. Paris, Heugel, 1856.

—— *Richard Coeur-de-Lion* de Grétry. Boulogne, Birlé-Morel, 1842.

Hegel, Georg Wilhelm Friedrich. Sämtliche Werke. Stuttgart, F. Fromann, 1927. Contains (Vols. 12–14): "Vorlesungen über die Aesthetik."

Heger, Theodore E. The Function and Type of Music in the English Dramatic Theater of the Early 18th Century. Michigan A.M. Dissertation 1939.

Heinemann, Franz. "Schillers *Wilhelm Tell* in der Musikgeschichte des 19. Jahrhunderts," *Zeitschrift für Bücherfreunde* XI, No. 2 (1907) 321–38.

Heinichen, Johann David. Der General-Bass in der Composition. Dresden, bey dem Autor, 1728. A revised ed. of his Neu erfundene und gründliche Anweisung (Hamburg, B. Schiller, 1711.)

Heinrich, Viktor. Komik und Humor in der Musik. Vienna Dissertation, 1931.

Heinrichs, Georg. *See* Grosheim, Georg Christoph.

Heinse, Wilhelm. Hildegard von Hohenthal. Berlin, Vossischen Buchhandlung, 1795–96. 3 vols.

Heinsheimer, Hans. "Die Umgestaltung des Operntheaters in Deutschland," *Anbruch* XV (August/September, 1933) 107–13.

Helfert, W. "Zur Geschichte des Wiener Singspiels," ZfMw V (1922–23) 194–209.

Hellberg (-Kupfer), Geerd. Richard Wagner als Regisseur. Berlin, Gesellschaft für Theatergeschichte, 1942.

Hellmer, Elmund, ed. *Der Corregidor* von Hugo Wolf. Wien, Hugo Wolf Verein; Berlin, S. Fischer, 1900.

Hellouin, Frédéric. Gossec et la musique française à la fin du XVIIIe siècle. Paris, A. Charles, 1903.

—— Un Musicien oublié; Catel. Paris, Fischbacher, 1910.

Henderson, William James. "A Note on Floridity," MQ II (1916) 339–48.

—— Some Forerunners of the Italian Opera. London, John Murray, 1911.

Henseler, Anton. Jakob Offenbach. Berlin-Schöneberg, M. Hesse, 1930.

Herford, Charles. "Jonson," in *Dictionary of National Biography* X (1917) 1069–79.

Hernried, Robert. "Hugo Wolf's *Corregidor* at Mannheim," MQ XXVI (1940) 19–30.

—— "Hugo Wolf's 'Four Operas,' " MQ XXXI (1945) 89–100.

Herre, Max. Franz Danzi; ein Beitrag zur Geschichte der deutschen Oper. Munich Dissertation, 1930.

Heseltine, Philip. Frederick Delius. London, John Lane, [1923].

Hess, Heinz. Zur Geschichte des musikalischen Dramas im Seicento; die Opern Alessandro Stradellas. Leipzig, B&H, 1906. (PIMG, 2. Folge, Heft 3.)

Heuberger, Richard. Im Foyer; gesammelte Essays über das Opernrepertoire der Gegenwart. Leipzig, H. Seemann, 1901.

—— Musikalische Skizzen. Leipzig, H. Seemann, 1901.

Heulhard, Arthur. La Foire Saint-Laurent; son histoire et ses spectacles. Paris, A. Lemerre, 1878.

—— Jean Monnet. Paris, A. Lemerre, 1884.

Heuss, Alfred. "Carl Heinrich Graun's *Montezuma*," ZIMG VI (1904–1905) 71–75.

—— "Das dämonische Element in Mozarts Werken," ZIMG VII (1906) 175–86.

—— "Gluck als Musikdramatiker," ZIMG XV (1913–14) 274–91.

—— "Graun's *Montezuma* und seine Herausgabe durch Albert Mayer-Reinach," MfMg XXXVII (1905) 67–71.

—— Die Instrumental-Stücke des *Orfeo* und die venetianischen Opern-Sinfonien. Leipzig, B&H, 1903. (Both parts of this work were published independently in SIMG IV.)

—— "Mozarts *Idomeneo* als Quelle für *Don Giovanni* and *Die Zauberflöte*," ZfMw XIII (1930–31) 177–99.

—— "Verdi als melodischer Charakteristiker," ZIMG XV (1913–14) 63–72.

—— "Zu Umlauf's Singspiel: *Die Bergknappen*," ZIMG XIII (1911–12) 164–71.

Hey, Julius. Richard Wagner als Vortragsmeister 1864–1876; Erinnerungen. Leipzig, B&H, 1911.

Heyden, Otto. Das Kölner Theaterwesen im 19. Jahrhundert. Emsdetten, Lechte, 1939.

Hill, Edward Burlingame. Modern French Music. Boston and New York, Houghton Mifflin, 1924.

Hill, Richard S. "Concert Life in Berlin, Season 1943–44," *Music Library Association Notes, Second Series* I, No. 3 (June, 1944) 13–33.

—— "Schoenberg's Tone-Rows and the Tonal System of the Future," MQ XXII (1936) 14–37.

Hiller, Johann Adam. Johann Adam Hiller. Leipzig, C. F. W. Siegel, [1915].

Hiltebrandt, Philipp. Preussen und die römische Kurie. Berlin, Bath, 1910. Vol. I: Die vorfriderizianische Zeit (1625–1740).

Himonet, André. *Lohengrin* . . . étude historique et critique, analyse musicale. Paris, Mellottée, [1925].

—— *Louise* de Charpentier; étude historique et critique, analyse musicale. Paris, Mellottée, [1922].

Hipsher, Edward E. American Opera and Its Composers. Philadelphia, T. Presser, [1927].

Hirsch, Franz. Die Oper und der Literaturgeist; ein Wort zu Operntextreform. Leipzig, Voigt, 1868.

Hirsch, R. Mozart's *Schauspieldirektor;* musikalische Reminiscenzen. Leipzig, Matthis, 1859.

Hirschberg, Eugen. Die Enzyklopädisten und die französische Oper im 18. Jahrhundert. Leipzig, B&H, 1903. *See also* review by A. Heuss, ZIMG V (1903–1904) 280–87.

Hirschfeld, Robert. "Mozart's *Zaide* in der Wiener Hofoper," ZIMG IV (1902–1903) 66–71.

—— "Oper in Wien [1857–1900]," ZIMG I (1899–1900) 264–67.

Hirt, Giulio C. "Autografi di G. Rossini," RMI II (1895) 23–35.

Hirtler, Franz. Hans Pfitzners *Armer Heinrich* in seiner Stellung zur Musik des ausgehenden 19. Jahrhunderts. Würzburg, K. Triltsch, 1940.

Hirzel, Bruno. "Operatic Italy in 1770—by an Eyewitness," MTNA V (1910) 219–31.

—— "Der Text Wagner's *Liebesverbot* nach der Handschrift in Washington," SIMG XIII (1911–12) 348–82.

Hitzig, Wilhelm. Georg Friedrich Händel, 1685–1759; sein Leben in Bildern. Leipzig, Bibliographisches Institut, [1935].

Hjelmborg, Bjørn. "Une Partition de Cavalli," *Acta Musicologica* XVI–XVII (1944–45) 39–54.

Hodermann, Richard. Georg Benda. Coburg, H. Wechsung, 1895.

—— Geschichte des Gothaischen Hoftheaters 1725–1779. Hamburg, L. Voss, 1894.

Hodik, Fritz. Das Horn bei Richard Wagner. Innsbruck Dissertation, 1937.

Höffding, Harold. Jean Jacques Rousseau and His Philosophy. New Haven, Yale University Press; London, Oxford University Press, 1930. Translated from the 2d Danish ed.

Högg, Margarete. Die Gesangskunst der Faustina Hasse und das Sängerinnenwesen ihrer Zeit in Deutschland. Königsbrück i. Sa., Pabst, 1931.

Hoérée, Arthur. Albert Roussel. Paris, Rieder, 1938.

Hoffmann, Ernst Theodor Amadeus. Sämtliche Werke. Leipzig, M. Hesse, 1900. 15 vols.

—— Musikalische Novellen und Aufsätze; vollständige Gesamtausgabe, herausgegeben und erläutert von Dr. Edgar Istel. Regensburg, G. Bosse, [1921?]. 2 vols.

Hoffmann, Rudolf Stephan. Franz Schreker. Leipzig, E. P. Tal, 1921.

Hoffmann von Fallersleben, August Heinrich. In dulci jubilo . . . ein Beitrag zur Geschichte der deutschen Poesie. Hannover, C. Rümpler, 1854.

—— Unsere volkstümlichen Lieder. Leipzig, W. Engelmann, 1900. 4th ed.

Hoffmeister, Karel. Antonín Dvořák. London, John Lane, 1928. Ed. and translated by Rosa Newmarch.

Hofmannsthal, Hugo von. "Ce que nous avons voulu en écrivant *Ariane à Naxos* et *Le Bourgeois Gentilhomme,*" MM VIII, Nos. 9–10 (1912) 1–3.

Hogarth, George. Memoirs of the Musical Drama. London, R. Bentley, 1838. 2 vols. New ed. as: Memoirs of the Opera in Italy, France, Germany, and England. London, R. Bentley, 1851. 2 vols.

Hohenemser, R. Luigi Cherubini. Leipzig, B&H, 1913.

Hol, Joan C. *"L'Amfiparnaso* e *Le veglie di Siena,"* RMI XL (1936) 3–22.

—— "Horatio Vecchi et l'évolution créatrice," in *Gedenkboek Dr. D. F. Scheurleer* ('s-Gravenhage, Nijhoff, 1925) pp. 159–67.

Hol, Joan C. (*Cont.*). Horatio Vecchi's weltliche Werke. Leipzig, Heitz, 1934.

—— "*Le Veglie di Siena* de Horatio Vecchi," RMI XLIII (1939) 17–34.

Holbrooke, Josef. Contemporary British Composers. London, C. Palmer, [1925].

Holl, Karl. Carl Ditters von Dittersdorfs Opern für das wiederhergestellte Johannisberger Theater. Heidelberg, C. Winter, 1913.

Holländer, Hans. "Hugo von Hofmannsthal als Opernlibrettist," *Zeitschrift für Musik* XCVI (1929) 551–54.

—— "Leoš Janáček and His Operas," MQ XV (1929) 29–36.

Holst, Imogen. Gustav Holst. London, Oxford University Press, 1938.

Holzer, Ludmilla. "Die komische Opern Glucks," SzMw XIII (1926) 3–37.

Hoover, Kathleen O'Donnell. "Gustave Charpentier," MQ XXV (1939) 334–50.

—— "Verdi's *Rocester*," MQ XXVIII (1942) 505–13.

"*Hortus musarum* de Pierre Phalèse, deuxième partie (1553)," in *Chansons au luth et airs de cour français du XVIe siècle* (Paris, E. Droz, 1934).

Howard, John Tasker. "The Hewitt Family in America," MQ XVII (1931) 25–39.

—— Our American Music. New York, Thomas Y. Crowell, [1939]. 3d ed., 1946.

—— Our Contemporary Composers. New York, Thomas Y. Crowell, 1941.

—— Studies of Contemporary American Composers: Deems Taylor. New York, J. Fischer, 1927.

Howes, Frank. The Dramatic Works of Ralph Vaughan Williams. London, Oxford University Press, 1937.

Hübner, O. Richard Strauss und das Musikdrama. Leipzig, [Pabst], 1910. 2d ed.

Hughes, Charles W. "John Christopher Pepusch," MQ XXXI (1945) 54–70.

[Hunold, Christian Friedrich.] Die allerneueste Art, zur reinen und galanten Poesie zu gelangen. Hamburg, G. Liebernickel, 1707.

—— "Gesellschaftliche Verhältnisse in der Oper zu Anfang des achtzehnten Jahrhunderts," AMZ [New Series] XV (1880) 753–58, 769–73, 785–90.

—— Theatralische, galante und geistliche Gedichte. Hamburg, G. Liebernickel, 1706.

Hussey, Dyneley. "Beethoven as a Composer of Opera," M&L VIII (1927) 243–52.

—— "Casanova and *Don Giovanni*," M&L VIII (1927) 470–72.

—— "Nationalism and Opera," M&L VII (1926) 3–16.

Hutcheson, Ernest. A Musical Guide to the Richard Wagner *Ring of the Nibelung*. New York, Simon & Schuster, 1940.

Hutchings, A. J. B. "The Unexpected in Mozart," M&L XX (1939) 21–31.

Huth, Arno. "Forbidden Opus—Protestant," MMus XVI, No. 1 (November–December, 1938) 38–41.

Huygens, Constantijn. Correspondance et œuvre musical. Leyden, W. J. A. Jonckbloet, 1882.

Iacuzzi, Alfred. The European Vogue of Favart; the Diffusion of the Opéra-Comique. New York, Institute of French Studies, 1932.

Iglesias, Ignasi. Enric Morera; estudi biografie. Barcelona, Artis, [1921].

Inch, Herbert Reynolds. A Bibliography of Glinka. [New York, 1935.] Typewritten; available in the Music Division of the New York Public Library.

Indy, Vincent d'. César Franck. Paris, F. Alcan, 1906. Translated: New York, John Lane, 1910.

—— Richard Wagner et son influence sur l'art musical français. Paris, Delagrave, 1930.

Ingegneri, Angelo. Della poesia rappresentativa e del modo di rappresentare le favole sceniche. Ferrara, V. Baldini, 1598.

Irvine, David. Parsifal and Wagner's Christianity. London, H. Grevel, 1899.

Irving, William Henry. John Gay, Favorite of Poets. Durham, N.C., Duke University Press, 1940.

Iselin, Isaak. Pariser Tagebuch 1752. Basel, Benno Schwabe, 1919.

Istel, Edgar. "Act IV of Les Huguenots," MQ XXII (1936) 87–97.

—— "Beethoven's Leonora and Fidelio," MQ VII (1921) 226–51.

—— Bizet und Carmen. Stuttgart, J. Engelhorn, 1927.

—— Die Blütezeit der musikalischen Romantik in Deutschland. Leipzig, B. G. Teubner, 1909. 2d ed., 1921.

—— "Einiges über Georg Benda's 'akkompagnierte' Monodramen," SIMG VI (1904–1905) 179–82.

—— Die Entstehung des deutschen Melodramas. Berlin, Schuster & Loeffler, 1906.

—— "Felipe Pedrell," MQ XI (1925) 164–91.

—— "For a Reversion to Opera," MQ X (1924) 405–37.

—— "Fünf Briefe Spohrs an Marschner," in Festschrift . . . Liliencron (Leipzig, B&H, 1910) pp. 110–15.

—— "A Genetic Study of the Aida Libretto," MQ III (1917) 34–52.

—— "German Opera Since Richard Wagner," MQ I (1915) 260–90.

—— "Gluck's Dramaturgy," MQ XVII (1931) 227–33.

—— "Hermann Goetz," ZIMG III (1901–1902) 177–88.

—— "Isaac Albeniz," MQ XV (1929) 117–48.

—— Die komische Oper; eine historisch-ästhetische Studie. Stuttgart, C. Grüninger, [1906].

—— Das Kunstwerk Richard Wagners. Leipzig, B. G. Teubner, 1918.

—— "Meyerbeer's Way to Mastership," MQ XII (1926) 72–109.

—— Die moderne Oper vom Tode Wagners bis zum Weltkrieg. Leipzig, B. G. Teubner, 1915. 2d ed., 1923.

—— "Mozart's Magic Flute and Freemasonry," MQ XIII (1927) 510–27.

—— "The Othello of Verdi and Shakespeare," MQ II (1916) 375–86.

Istel, Edgar (*Cont.*). "Peter Cornelius," MQ XX (1934) 334–43.

—— "Rossini: a Study," MQ IX (1923) 401–22.

—— Studien zur Geschichte des Melodrams. I. Jean Jacques Rousseau als Komponist seiner lyrischen Szene *Pygmalion.* Leipzig, B&H, 1901. (PIMG, Beihefte, Heft I.)

Jachimecki, Zdzislaw. "Karol Szymanowski," MQ VIII (1922) 23–37.

—— "Karol Szymanowski," *Slavonic and East European Review* XVII (July, 1938) 174–85.

—— "Stanislaus Moniuszko," MQ XIV (1928) 54–62.

Jacob, Heinrich Eduard. Johann Strauss, Father and Son. [New York], Greystone Press, 1940.

—— Johann Strauss und das neunzehnte Jahrhundert. Amsterdam, Querido Verlag, 1937.

Jacob, Walter, ed. Leo Blech; ein Brevier. Hamburg-Leipzig, Prisman-Verlag, [1931].

Jacobs, Reginald. Covent Garden, Its Romance and History. London, Simpkin, 1913.

Jacobsohn, Fritz. Hans Gregors komische Oper, 1905–1911. Berlin, Oesterheld, [1911].

Jäger, Erich. "Gluck und Goethe," *Die Musik* XIII (1913–14) Qt. 4, 131–39.

Jahn, Otto. W. A. Mozart. Leipzig, B&H, 1905–1907. 2 vols. 4th ed. Translated as: Life of Mozart. London, Novello, Ewer, 1882. 3 vols. (From the 2d German ed., 1867.) *See also* Abert, Hermann.

Janowitzer, Erwin. Peter Cornelius als Opernkomponist. Vienna Dissertation, 1921.

Jansen, Albert. Jean-Jacques Rousseau als Musiker. Berlin, Reimer, 1884.

Jansen, Lothar. Studien zur Entwicklungsgeschichte der Oper in Italien, Frankreich, und Deutschland. Bonn Dissertation, 1914.

Jardillier, Robert. Pelléas. Paris, C. Aveline, 1927.

Jaspert, Werner. Johann Strauss. Berlin, Werk Verlag, [1939].

Jean-Aubry, G. "A Romantic Dilettante: Emile Deschamps (1791–1871)," M&L XX (1939) 250–65.

Jenny, Ernst. "Das alte Basler Theater auf dem Blömlein," *Basler Jahrbuch* (1908) 1–68.

Jensen, Wilhelm. Spontini als Opernkomponist. Berlin Dissertation, 1920.

Jeri, A. Mascagni. Milano, Garzanti, 1940. 2d ed.

Jersild, Jorgen. "Le Ballet d'action italien du 18e siècle au Danemark," *Acta musicologica* XIV (1942) 74–93.

Johnson, Harold Edgar. Iphigenia in Tauris as the Subject for French Opera. Cornell Dissertation (A.M.) 1939.

Jouvin, B[enoît Jean Baptiste]. Hérold, sa vie et ses œuvres. Paris, Au Ménestrel, Heugel, 1868.

Jubinal, Achille, ed. Mystères inédits du quinzième siècle. Paris, Téchener, 1837. 2 vols.

Jullien, Adolphe. "Ambroise Thomas," RMI III (1896) 358–66.

—— "A Propos de la mort de Charles Gounod," RMI I (1894) 60–67.

—— La Cour et l'opéra sous Louis XVI. Paris, Didier, 1878.

—— "Hector Berlioz," RMI I (1894) 454–82.

—— Hector Berlioz, sa vie et ses œuvres. Paris, Librairie de l'Art, 1888.

—— Musiciens d'aujourd'hui. Paris, Librairie de l'Art, 1892–94. 2 vols.

—— La Ville et la cour au XVIIIe siècle. Paris, E. Rouveyre, 1881.

Jungk, Klaus. Tonbildliches und Tonsymbolisches in Mozarts Opern. Berlin, Triltsch & Huther, 1938.

Junk, Victor. Die Bedeutung der Schlusskadenz im Musikdrama. Leipzig, L. Doblinger, [1926].

—— Goethe's Fortsetzung der Zauberflöte. Berlin, Duncker, 1899.

Junker, Hermann. "Zwei 'Griselda'-Opern," in Festschrift Adolf Sandberger (München, Zierfuss, 1918) pp. 51–64.

Kaestner, Erwin. Das Opernproblem und seine Lösung bei Mozart. Jena, Neuenhahn, 1932.

Kaestner, Rudolf. Johann Heinrich Rolle. Kassel, Bärenreiter, 1932.

Kalbeck, Max. Opern-Abende. Berlin, "Harmonie," 1898.

—— "Zu Scheidemantels Don Juan-Uebersetzung," Die Musik XIII (1913–14) Qt. 4, 67–72.

Kalisch, Alfred. "Impressions of Strauss's Elektra," ZIMG X (1908–1909) 198–202.

Kapp, Julius. Franz Schreker. München, Drei Masken, 1921.

—— 185 Jahre Staatsoper. Berlin, Atlantic-Verlag, 1928.

—— Geschichte der Staatsoper Berlin. Berlin, M. Hesse, 1937. New ed., 1942.

—— Meyerbeer. Berlin, Schuster & Loeffler, [1920]. 8th ed., 1930.

—— Richard Wagner. Berlin, M. Hesse, 1929. 32d ed.

—— Richard Wagner und die Berliner Oper. Berlin-Schöneberg, M. Hesse, 1933.

—— Die Staatsoper Berlin 1919 bis 1925. Stuttgart, Deutsche Verlags-Anstalt, [1925].

—— 200 Jahre Staatsoper im Bild. Berlin, M. Hesse, 1942.

Karasowski, Maurycy. Rys historyczny opery polskiéj. Warszawa, M. Glücksberga, 1859.

Karstädt, Georg. "Zur Geschichte des Zinken und seiner Verwendung in der Musik des 16.–18. Jahrhunderts," AfMf II (1937) 385–432.

Kastner, Emerich. Bibliotheca Beethoveniana; Versuch einer Beethoven-Bibliographie. Leipzig, B&H, 1913.

—— Die dramatischen Werke R. Wagner's; chronologisches Verzeichnis der ersten Aufführungen. Leipzig, B&H, 1899. 2d ed.

Kaul, Oskar. Geschichte der Würzburger Hofmusik im 18. Jahrhundert. Würzburg, Becker, 1924.

—— "Die musikdramatischen Werke des Würzburgischen Hofkapellmeisters Georg Franz Wassmuth," ZfMw VII (1924–25) 390–408, 478–500.

Keefer, Lubov. "Opera in the Soviet," *Music Library Association Notes, Second Series* II, No. 2 (March, 1945) 110–17.

Keeton, A. E. "Elgar's Music for *The Starlight Express,*" M&L XXVI (1945) 43–46.

Keller, Otto. Franz von Suppé. Leipzig, R. Wöpke, 1905.

—— "Gluck-Bibliographie," *Die Musik* XIII (1913–14) Qt. 4, 23–37, 85–91.

—— Karl Goldmark. Leipzig, H. Seemann, [1901].

—— Die Operette in ihrer geschichtlichen Entwicklung. Wien, Stein-Verlag, 1926.

Keller, Otto. Wolfgang Amadeus Mozart; Bibliographie und Ikonographie. Berlin, Gebrüder Paetel, 1927.

Kelly, Alfredo. *See* Fiorda Kelly, Alfredo.

Kelly, Michael. Reminiscences of the King's Theatre. London, H. Colburn, 1826. 2 vols.

Kenney, Charles Lamb. A Memoir of Michael William Balfe. London, Tinsley, 1875.

Kidson, Frank. *The Beggar's Opera,* Its Predecessors and Successors. Cambridge, The University Press, 1922.

Kienzl, Wilhelm. Meine Lebenswanderung. Stuttgart, J. Engelhorn, 1926.

Kiesewetter, R[aphael] G[eorg], Edler von Wiesenbrunn. Schicksale und Beschaffenheit des weltlichen Gesanges. Leipzig, B&H, 1841.

Killer, Hermann. Albert Lortzing. Potsdam, Athenaion, 1938.

—— Die Tenorpartien in Mozarts Opern. Kassel, Bärenreiter, 1929.

Kindem, Ingeborg Eckhoff. Den norske operas historie. Oslo, E. G. Mortensen, 1941.

Kinkeldey, Otto. "Luzzasco Luzzaschi's Solo-Madrigale mit Klavierbegleitung," SIMG IX (1907–1908) 538–65.

—— Orgel und Klavier in der Musik des 16. Jahrhunderts. Leipzig, B&H, 1910.

Kinsky, Georg. "Glucks Reisen nach Paris," ZfMw VIII (1925–26) 551–66.

Kirby, Percival R. "The Kettle-drums; an Historical Survey," M&L IX (1928) 34–43.

—— "A 13th Century Ballad Opera," M&L XI (1930) 163–71.

Kisch, Eve. "Rameau and Rousseau," M&L XXII (1941) 97–114.

Kitzig, Berthold. "Briefe Carl Heinrich Grauns," ZfMw IX (1926–27) 385–405.

Klages, Richard. Johann Wolfgang Franck. Hamburg, 1937.

Kleefeld, Wilhelm. "Hessens Beziehungen zur alten deutschen Oper," *Vom Rhein; Monatsschrift des Altertumsvereins für die Stadt Worms* IV (1905) 15.

—— Landgraf Ernst Ludwig von Hessen-Darmstadt und die deutsche Oper. Berlin, Hofmann, 1904.

—— "Das Orchester der Hamburger Oper 1678–1738," SIMG I (1899–1900) 219–89.

Klein, Herman. "Albéniz's Opera *Pepita Jiménez,*" *Musical Times* LIX (March, 1918) 116–17.
—— The Golden Age of Opera. London, George Routledge, 1933.
—— "The Vienna Hofoper," M&L XIV (1933) 239–46.
Klein, John W. "Alfredo Catalani," MQ XXIII (1937) 287–94.
—— "Bizet's Early Operas," M&L XVIII (1937) 169–75.
—— "Boito and His Two Operas," M&L VII (1926) 73–80.
—— "Nietzsche and Bizet," MQ XI (1925) 482–505.
—— "Verdi and Boito," MQ XIV (1928) 158–71.
—— "Verdi's Italian Contemporaries and Successors," M&L XV (1934) 37–45.
—— "Wagner and His Operatic Contemporaries," M&L IX (1928) 59–66.
Kling, H. "Caron de Beaumarchais et la musique," RMI VII (1900) 673–97.
—— "Le Centenaire d'un compositeur suisse célèbre: Louis Niedermeyer," RMI IX (1902) 830–59.
—— "Goethe et Berlioz," RMI XII (1905) 714–32.
—— "Helmine de Chézy," RMI XIV (1907) 25–39.
Klob, Karl Maria. Beiträge zur Geschichte der deutschen komischen Oper. Berlin, "Harmonie," [1903].
—— Die komische Oper seit Lortzing. Berlin, "Harmonie," [1905].
—— Die Oper von Gluck bis Wagner. Ulm, H. Kerler, 1913.
Kloiber, Rudolf. Die dramatischen Ballette von Christian Cannabich. Munich Dissertation, 1927.
Knappe, Heinrich. Friedrich Klose. München, Drei Masken, 1921.
Knopf, Kurt. Die romantische Struktur des Denkens Richard Wagners. Jena, G. Neuenhahn, 1932.
Knudsen, Hans. "Das Posener Theater unter Franz Wallner," *Zeitschrift der historischen Gesellschaft für die Provinz Posen* XXVI (1911) 225–42.
[Koch, Lajos.] Karl Goldmark. Budapest, Hauptstädtische Hausdruckerei, 1930.
Koch, Max. Richard Wagner. Berlin, E. Hofmann, 1907–18. 3 vols.
Köchel, Ludwig, Ritter von. Chronologisch-thematisches Verzeichnis sämtlicher Tonwerke Wolfgang Amade Mozarts. Leipzig, B&H, 1937. 3d ed., revised by Alfred Einstein.
—— Johann Josef Fux. Vienna, A. Hölder, 1872.
—— Die kaiserliche Hofmusikkapelle in Wien von 1543 bis 1867. Wien, Beck, 1869.
Koechlin, Charles. Gabriel Fauré. Paris, F. Alcan, 1927. 2d ed.
Kohut, Adolph. Auber. Leipzig, Reclam, 1895.
Kolodin, Irving. The Metropolitan Opera, 1883–1938. New York, Oxford University Press, 1939. Revised ed.
Komorzyński, Egon von. Emmanuel Schikaneder. Berlin, B. Behr, 1901.

Komorzyński, Egon von *(Cont.)*. "Lortzings *Waffenschmied* und seine Tradition," *Euphorion* VIII (1901) 340–50.

—— "Streit um den Text der *Zauberflöte*," *Alt-Wiener Kalender* (1922) 79–105.

Korngold, Julius. Deutsches Opernschaffen der Gegenwart. Wien, Rikola, 1922.

—— Die romanische Oper der Gegenwart. Wien, Rikola, 1922.

Kracauer, Siegfried. Orpheus in Paris. New York, Knopf, 1938. First published as: Jacques Offenbach und das Paris seiner Zeit. Amsterdam, de Lange, 1937.

Kramer, Margarete. Beiträge zu einer Geschichte des Affektenbegriffes in der Musik von 1550–1700. Halle Dissertation, 1924.

Kraus, Ludwig. Das deutsche Liederspiel in den Jahren 1800–1830. Halle Dissertation, 1921.

Krause, Christian Gottfried. Abhandlung von der musikalischen Poesie. Berlin, J. F. Voss, 1752.

Krauss, Rudolf. Das Stuttgarter Hoftheater von den ältesten Zeiten bis zur Gegenwart. Stuttgart, J. B. Metzler, 1908.

—— "Das Theater," in *Herzog Karl Eugen von Württemberg und seine Zeit* (Esslingen a. N., 1907) I, 481–554.

Krebs, Carl. Dittersdorfiana. Berlin, Gebrüder Paetel, 1900.

Krehbiel, Henry. Music and Manners in the Classical Period. New York, Scribner, 1899.

Kreidler, Walter. Heinrich Schütz und der Stile concitato von Claudio Monteverdi. Cassel, Bärenreiter, 1934.

Křenek, Ernst. Music Here and Now. New York, W. W. Norton, [1939].

—— "The New Music and Today's Theatre," MMus XIV, No. 4 (May–June, 1937) 200–203.

—— "Opera between the Wars," MMus XX, No. 2 (January–February, 1943) 102–111.

—— "Problemi di stile nell' opera," RassM VII (1934) 199–202.

—— "Zur musikalischen Bearbeitung von Monteverdis *Poppea*," *Schweizerische Musikzeitung* LXXVI (1936) 545–55.

Kretzschmar, Hermann. "Allgemeines und Besonderes zur Affektenlehre," JMP XVIII (1911) 63–77; XIX (1912) 65–78.

—— "Aus Deutschlands italienischer Zeit," JMP VIII (1901) 45–61.

—— "Beiträge zur Geschichte der venetianischen Oper," JMP XIV (1907) 71–81; XVII (1910) 61–71; XVIII (1911) 49–61.

—— "Die *Correspondance littéraire* als musikgeschichtliche Quelle," JMP X (1903) 77–92; also in his *Gesammelte Aufsätze* II, 210–25.

—— "Einige Bemerkungen über den Vortrag alter Musik," JMP VII (1900) 53–68.

—— Gesammelte Aufsätze über Musik und anderes. Leipzig, F. W. Grunow, 1910–[11]. 2 vols.

—— Geschichte des neuen deutschen Liedes; I. Teil: von Albert bis Zelter. Leipzig, B&H, 1911.

—— "Giuseppe Verdi," JMP XX (1913) 43–58.

—— "Hasse über Mozart," ZIMG III (1901–1902) 263–65.

—— "Monteverdi's *Incoronazione di Poppea*," VfMw X (1894) 483–530.

—— "Mozart in der Geschichte der Oper," JMP XII (1905) 53–71.

—— "Die musikgeschichtliche Bedeutung Simon Mayrs," JMP XI (1904) 27–41.

—— "Peter Cornelius," in Waldersee, *Sammlung musikalischer Vorträge* (Leipzig, B&H, 1879–98) II, 225–60.

—— "Ueber das Wesen, das Wachsen und Wirken Richard Wagners," JMP XIX (1912) 49–64.

—— "Ueber die Bedeutung von Cherubinis Ouvertüren und Hauptopern für die Gegenwart," JMP XIII (1906) 75–91.

—— "Die venetianische Oper und die Werke Cavalli's und Cesti's," VfMw VIII (1892) 1–76.

—— "Zum Verständnis Glucks," JMP X (1903) 61–76.

—— "Zwei Opern Nicolo Logroscinos," JMP XV (1908) 47–68.

Kreuzhage, Eduard. Hermann Goetz. Leipzig, B&H, 1916.

Krieger, Erhard. "Heinrich Kaminski's Drama *Jürg Jenatsch*," *Zeitschrift für Musik* C (1933) 992–95.

Krieger, Ludwig. Die sozialische Lage der Theatermusiker. Heidelberg, Schulze, 1913.

Krienitz, Willy. Richard Wagner's *Feen*. München, G. Müller, 1910.

Krogh, Torben Thorberg. "Reinhard Keiser in Kopenhagen," in *Musikwissenschaftliche Beiträge; Festschrift für Johannes Wolf* (Berlin, Breslauer, 1929).

—— Zur Geschichte des dänischen Singspiels im 18. Jahrhundert. København, Levin & Munksgaard, 1924.

Krohn, Ilmari. "Puccini: *Butterfly*," in *Gedenkboek D. F. Scheurleer* ('s Gravenhage, Nijhoff, 1925) pp. 181–90.

Kroll, Erwin. Carl Maria von Weber. Potsdam, Athenaion, [1934].

—— Ernst Theodor Amadeus Hoffmann. Leipzig, B&H, 1923.

Krone, Walter. Wenzel Müller. Berlin, Ebering, 1906.

Krott, Rudolfine. Die Singspiele Schuberts. Vienna Dissertation, 1921.

Kroyer, Theodor. Anfänge der Chromatik im italienischen Madrigal des XVI. Jahrhunderts. Leipzig, B&H, 1902. (PIMG, Beihefte, IV.)

—— "Die circumpolare Oper," JMP XXVI (1919) 16–33.

Krüger, Karl Joachim. Hugo von Hofmannsthal und Richard Strauss. Marburg Dissertation, 1935.

Krüger, Viktor. Die Entwicklung Carl Maria von Webers in seinen Jugendopern *Abu Hassan* und *Silvana*. Vienna Dissertation, 1907.

Kruse, Georg Richard. Albert Lortzing. Berlin, "Harmonie," 1899.

—— Hermann Goetz. Leipzig, Reclam, [1920].

—— "Meyerbeers Jugendopern," ZfMw I (1918–19) 399–413.

—— Otto Nicolai. Berlin, Verlag "Berlin-Wien," [1911].

Kruse, Georg Richard (*Cont.*). "Otto Nicolai's italienische Opern," SIMG XII (1910–1911) 267–96.

Kuckuk, Ludwig. Peter Winter als deutscher Opernkomponist. Heidelberg Dissertation, 1924.

Kufferath, Maurice. *"Fervaal* . . . di V. d'Indy," RMI IV (1897) 313–27.

—— *Fidelio* de L. van Beethoven. Paris, Fischbacher, 1913.

—— *La Flûte enchantée* de Mozart. Paris, Fischbacher, 1914.

Kuhn, Max. Die Verzierungskunst in der Gesangs-Musik des 16.–17. Jahrhunderts (1535–1650). Leipzig, B&H, 1902. (PIMG, Beiheft 7.)

Kurth, Ernst. "Die Jugendopern Glucks bis *Orfeo*," SzMw I (1913) 193–277.

—— Romantische Harmonik und ihre Krise in Wagners *Tristan*. Berlin, M. Hesse, 1923. 2d ed.

Kutscher, Artur. Vom Salzburger Barocktheater zu den Salzburger Festspielen. Düsseldorf, Pflugscher-Verlag, 1939.

Kuznitzky, Hans. "Weber und Spontini in der musikalischen Anschauung von E. T. A. Hoffmann," ZfMw X (1927–28) 292–99.

Labroca, Mario. "The Rebirth of Italian Opera," MMus IV, No. 4 (May–June, 1927) 8–14.

Lach, Robert. "Das mittelaltleriche Musikdrama im Spiegel der Kunstgeschichte," in *Festschrift Adolph Koczirz* (Wien, Strache, [1930]) pp. 17–20.

—— "Sebastian Sailers *Schöpfung* in der Musik," *Akademie der Wissenschaften in Wien, Denkschriften,* 60. Band, 1. Abhandlung (1917).

Lacroix, Paul. Ballets et mascarades de cour, de Henri III à Louis XIV (1581–1652). Geneva, J. Gay, 1868–70. 6 vols.

Lafontaine, H. C. de. "Richard Wagner," PMA XVI (1890) 63–78.

Lafont du Cujala. "Réflexions sur l'état actuel de la musique dramatique en France," *Mercure de France* (February, 1782) pp. 38–44.

Lajarte, Théodore de. Bibliothèque musicale du théâtre de l'opéra. Paris, Librairie des bibliophiles, 1878. 2 vols.

—— Curiosités de l'opéra. Paris, Calmann Lévy, 1883.

Lalande, Joseph Jérôme Lefrançais de. Voyage d'un françois en Italie, fait dans les années 1765 & 1766. A Venise, et se trouve à Paris chez Desaint, 1769. 8 vols.

La Laurencie, Lionel de. "André Campra, musicien profane; notes biographiques," *Année musicale* III (1913) 153–205.

—— "Une Convention commerciale entre Lully, Quinault et Ballard en 1680," RdM II (1920–21) 176–82.

—— Les Créateurs de l'opéra français. Paris, F. Alcan, 1930. New ed.

—— "Les Débuts de Viotti comme directeur de l'opéra en 1819," RdM V (1924) 110–22.

—— "Deux Imitateurs français des bouffons: Blavet et Dauvergne," *Année musicale* II (1912) 65–125.

—— "Un Emule de Lully: Pierre Gautier de Marseille," SIMG XIII (1911–12) 39–69, 400.

—— "La Grande Saison italienne de 1752; les bouffons," MM VIII, No. 6

(1912) 18–33; Nos. 7–8, pp. 13–22. Also separate as: Les Bouffons (1752–1754). Paris, Publications de la Revue SIM, 1912.

—— "Leclair; une assertion de Fétis; Jean-Marie Leclair l'ainé à l'orchestre de l'Opéra," RHCM IV (1904) 496–503.

—— Lully. Paris, F. Alcan, 1911.

—— "Un Musicien dramatique du XVIIIe siècle français: Pierre Guedron," RMI XXIX (1922) 445–72.

—— "Un Musicien italien en France à la fin du XVIIIe siècle," RdM XII (1931) 268–77.

—— "Notes sur la jeunesse d'André Campra," SIMG X (1908–1909) 159–258. Also separate: Leipzig, B&H, 1909.

—— "L'Opéra français au XVIIe siècle; la musique," RM VI (January, 1925) 26–43.

—— "Un Opéra inédit de M.-A. Charpentier: La Descente d'Orphée aux enfers," RdM X (1929) 184–93.

—— "L'Orfeo nell' inferni d'André Campra," RdM IX (1928) 129–33.

—— Orphée de Gluck; étude et analyse. Paris, Mellottée, 1934.

—— "Les Pastorales en musique au XVIIe siècle en France avant Lully et leur influence sur l'opéra," in International Musical Society, 4th Congress Report (London, Novello, 1912) pp. 139–46.

—— "Quelques documents sur Jean-Philippe Rameau et sa famille," MM III (1907) 541–614.

—— "Rameau et les clarinettes," MM IX, No. 2 (1913) 27–28.

—— "Rameau et son gendre," MM VII, No. 2 (1911) 12–23.

Laloy, Louis. "Le Drame musical moderne," MM I (1905) 8–16, 75–84, 169–77, 233–50.

—— "Les Idées de Jean-Philippe Rameau sur la musique," MM III (1907) 1144–59.

Lamm, Max. Beiträge zur Entwicklung des musikalischen Motivs in den Tondramen Richard Wagners. Vienna Dissertation, 1932.

Lamy, Félix. Jean-François le Sueur. Paris, Fischbacher, 1912.

Landi, Antonio. Il commodo, commedia d'Antonio Landi con i suoi intermedi [etc.]. Firenze, I. Giunti, 1566. The intermedi are by G. B. Strozzi the elder. Earlier ed. 1539.

Landormy, Paul Charles René. Faust de Gounod. Paris, P. Mellottée, [1922].

—— "Gabriel Fauré," MQ XVII (1931) 293–301.

—— "Maurice Ravel," MQ XXV (1939) 430–41.

—— "Vincent d'Indy," MQ XVIII (1932) 507–18.

Láng, Paul Henry. "Background Music for Mein Kampf," Saturday Review of Literature XXVIII, No. 3 (January 20, 1945) 5–9.

—— "Haydn and the Opera," MQ XVIII (1932) 274–81.

—— The Literary Aspects of the History of the Opera in France. Cornell Dissertation, 1935.

—— Music in Western Civilization. New York, W. W. Norton, [1941].

Lange, Francisco Curt. "Leon Ribeiro," *Boletin latino-americano de musica* III (1937) 519–36.

Langlois, Jacques. Camille Saint-Saëns. Moulins, Crépin-Leblond, 1934.

[Lardin, Jules.] *Zémire et Azor* par Grétry; quelques questions à propos de la nouvelle falsification de cet opéra. Paris, Moëssard et Jousset, 1846.

La Roche, Charles. Antonio Bertali als Opern- und Oratorienkomponist. Vienna Dissertation, 1919.

La Rotella, Pasquale. Niccolo Piccinni. Bari, Cressati, 1928.

Larsen, Jens Peter. Die Haydn-Ueberlieferungen. Kopenhagen, Munksgaard, 1939.

La Salandra. *See* Belluci La Salandra.

La Tour, Georges Imbart de. "La Mise en scène d' *Hippolyte et Aricie*," MM IV (1908) 247–71.

Laue, Hellmuth. Die Operndichtung Lortzings. Bonn am Rhein, L. Röhrscheid, 1932.

Lavignac, Albert. Le Voyage artistique à Bayreuth. Paris, C. Delagrave, 1900. 4th ed. Translated as: The Music Dramas of Richard Wagner and His Festival Theatre in Bayreuth. New York, Dodd, Mead, 1904.

Lavoix, Henri. "Les Opéras madrigalesques," *Revue et gazette musicale* XLIV (1877) 307–309, 323–24, 331–32.

Lawrence, William John. "Early Irish Ballad Opera and Comic Opera," MQ VIII (1922) 397–412.

—— "The Early Years of the First English Opera House," MQ VII (1921) 104–17.

—— The Elizabethan Playhouse and Other Studies. Philadelphia, J. B. Lippincott, 1912.

—— "The English Theatre Orchestra: Its Rise and Early Characteristics," MQ III (1917) 9–27.

—— "Foreign Singers and Musicians at the Court of Charles II," MQ IX (1923) 217–25.

—— "Marionette Operas," MQ X (1924) 236–43.

—— "Notes on a Collection of Masque Music," M&L III (1922) 49–58.

Lebègue, Raymond. Le Mystère des Actes des Apôtres. Paris, Champion, 1929.

[Le Blond, Gaspard Michel, ed.] Mémoires pour sevir à l'histoire de la révolution opérée dans la musique par M. le Chevalier Gluck. Naples and Paris, Bailly, 1781.

[Le Cerf de La Viéville, Jean Laurent, seigneur de Freneuse.] Comparaison de la musique italienne et de la musique françoise. Bruxelles, F. Foppens, 1704–1706. 3 vols. Also forms Vols. 2–4 of Jacques Bonnet's Histoire de la musique et de ses effets. Amsterdam, J. Royer, 17—.

[Leclercq, Louis.] Les Décors, les costumes, et la mise en scène au XVIIe siècle, 1615–1680, par Ludovic Celler [pseud.]. Paris, Liepmannssohn & Dufour, 1869.

Lee, Vernon. *See* Paget, Violet.

Lehmann, Lilly. Studien zu *Fidelio*. Leipzig, B&H, 1904.

Lehner, Walter. "Franz Xaver Süssmayr als Opernkomponist," SzMw XVIII (1931) 66–96.

Leib, Walter. Joseph Huber; Beitrag zur Geschichte der circumpolaren Oper. Heidelberg Dissertation, 1923.

Leichtentritt, Hugo. Händel. Stuttgart-Berlin, Deutsche Verlags-Anstalt, 1924.

—— "Handel's Harmonic Art," MQ XXI (1935) 208–23.

—— Music, History, and Ideas. Cambridge, Mass., Harvard University Press, 1938.

—— "On the Prologue in Early Opera," MTNA XXXI (1936) 292–99.

—— Reinhard Keiser in seinen Opern. Berlin, Tessarotypie-Actien-Gesellschaft, 1901.

—— "Schubert's Early Operas," MQ XIV (1928) 620–38.

—— *See also:* Ambros, August Wilhelm. Geschichte der Musik.

Leist, Friedrich. "Geschichte des Theaters in Bamberg bis zum Jahre 1862," *Berichte des historischen Vereins zu Bamberg* LV (1893) 1–283.

Lejeune, Caroline. "Opera in the Eighteenth Century," PMA XLIX (1922–23) 1–20.

Lengl, Georg. Die Genesis der Oper. München, Mössl, 1936.

Lenzewsky, Gustav. "Friedrich der Grosse als Komponist des Singspiels *Il Re pastore*," *Schriften des Vereins für die Geschichte Berlins* XXIX (1912) 20.

Leo, Giacomo. Leonardo Leo, celebre musicista del secolo XVIII, ed il suo omonimo Leonardo Leo di Corrado; nota storica. Napoli, Cozzolino, 1901.

—— Leonardo Leo . . . e le sue opere musicali. Napoli, Melfi & Joele, 1905.

Leo, Sophie Augustine. "Musical Life in Paris (1817–1848)," MQ XVII (1931) 259–71, 389–403.

Leoni, Carlo. Dell'arte e del teatro nuovo di Padova; racconto anecdotico. Padova, Sacchetto, 1873.

Lepel, Felix von. Die Dresdner Oper als Weltkulturstätte. Dresden, Spohr, 1942.

[Le Prévost d'Exmes, François.] Lully, musicien. [Paris, 1779.]

[Léris, Antoine de.] Dictionnaire portatif des théâtres. Paris, C. A. Jombert, 1754. Another ed., 1763.

Leroy, L. Archier. Wagner's Music Drama of *The Ring*. London, N. Douglas, [1925].

Lert, Ernst. Mozart auf dem Theater. Berlin, Schuster & Loeffler, 1918.

Le Sage, Alain René. Le Théâtre de la foire, ou l'Opéra-comique. Paris, P. Gandouin, 1724–37. 10 vols.

Lespês, Léo. Les Mystères du grand-opéra. Paris, Maresq, 1843.

Leti, Giuseppe, and Louis Lachat. L'Esotérisme à la scène; *La Flûte en-chantée, Parsifal, Faust*. Annecy, L. Dépollier, 1935.

Leux, Irmgard. Christian Gottlob Neefe. Leipzig, Kistner & Siegel, 1925.

—— "Ueber die 'verschollene' Händel-Oper *Hermann von Balcke*," AfMw VIII (1926) 441–51.

Levi, Vito. "Un grande operista italiano (Antonio Smareglia, 1854–1929)," RMI XXXVI (1929) 600–15.

Levinson, André. "Notes sur le ballet au XVIIe siècle; les danseurs de Lully," RM VI (January, 1925) 44–55.

Lieboldt, J. "Der Verbleib der alten Hamburger Operndekoration *Der Tempel Salomonis*," *Mitteilungen des Vereins für Hamburgische Ge-schichte* XIII (1890) 128–29.

Liliencron, Rochus, Freiherr von. "Die Chorgesänge des lateinischen-deutschen Schuldramas im 16. Jahrhundert," VfMw VI (1890) 309–87.

[Limojon de St. Didier, Alexandre Toussaint.] La Ville et la république de Venise. Paris, G. de Luyne, 1680. Translated as: The City and Repub-lick of Venice. London, C. Brome, 1699.

Lindner, Ernst Otto. Die erste stehende deutsche Oper. Berlin, Schlesinger, 1855. 2 vols.

—— Zur Tonkunst; Abhandlungen. Berlin, I. Guttentag, 1864. Contains essays on the rise of opera, Vittorio Loreto, and *The Beggar's Opera*.

List, Kurt. "*Lulu*, after the Premiere," MMus XV, No. 1 (November-December, 1937) 8–12.

Liuzzi, Fernando. "Drammi musicali dei secoli XI–XIV," *Studi medievali, nuova serie* III (1930) 82–109.

—— "L'espressione musicale nel dramma liturgico," *Studi medievali, nuova serie* II (1929) 74–109.

Livermore, Ann. "The Spanish Dramatists and Their Use of Music," M&L XXV (1944) 140–49.

Livingston, Arthur. Lorenzo da Ponte in America. Philadelphia, Lippin-cott, 1930.

Lockspeiser, Edward. Debussy. London, J. M. Dent; New York, E. P. Dut-ton, [1936].

—— "Musorgsky and Debussy," MQ XXIII (1937) 421–27.

Lockwood, Elisabeth M. "Some Old-Fashioned Music," M&L XII (1931) 262–70.

Loëb, Harry Brunswick. "The Opera in New Orleans," *Louisiana Histori-cal Society, Proceedings and Reports* IX (1916) 2941.

Loehner, Ermanno von. "Carlo Goldoni e le sue memorie," *Archivio veneto* XXIII (1881) 45–65; XXIV (1882) 5–27.

Loewenberg, Alfred. "*Bastien and Bastienne* Once More," M&L XXV (1924) 176–81.

—— "Gluck's *Orfeo* on the Stage," MQ XXVI (1940) 311–39.

—— "Lorenzo da Ponte in London," *Music Review* IV (1943) 171–89.

—— "Paisiello's and Rossini's *Barbiere di Siviglia*," M&L XX (1939) 157–67.

Loisel, Joseph. *Manon* de Massenet; étude historique et critique, analyse musicale. Paris, Mellottée, [1922].

Long des Clavières, P. "Lettres inédites de A. E. M. Grétry," RMI XXI (1914) 699–727.

—— "Les *Réflexions d'un solitaire* par A. E. M. Grétry," RMI XXVI (1919) 565–614.

Loomis, Roger Sherman, ed. The Romance of Tristram and Ysolt by Thomas of Britain. New York, Columbia University Press, 1931. Revised ed.

Lopatnikoff, Nikolai. "*Christophe Colomb* [by Milhaud]," MMus VII, No. 4 (June–July, 1930) 36–38.

López Chavarri, *see* Chavarri, Eduardo López.

Lorenz, Alfred Ottokar. Alessandro Scarlatti's Jugendoper. Augsburg, Benno Filser, 1927. 2 vols.

—— "Alessandro Scarlattis Opern und Wien," ZfMw IX (1926–27) 86–89.

—— "Das Finale in Mozarts Meisteropern," *Die Musik* XIX (June, 1927) 621–32.

—— Das Geheimnis der Form bei Richard Wagner. Berlin, M. Hesse, 1924–33. 4 vols.

Lortzing, Gustav Albert. Gesammelte Briefe. Regensburg. G. Bosse, [1913]. New, enlarged ed.

Loschelder, Josef. Das Todesproblem in Verdis Opernschaffen. Stuttgart, Deutsche Verlagsanstalt, 1938.

Lote, Georges. "La Déclamation du vers français à la fin du XVIIe siècle," *Revue de phonétique* II (1912) 313–63.

Lothar, Rudolf, [and Julius Stern]. 50 Jahre Hoftheater; Geschichte der beiden Wiener Hoftheater unter der Regierungszeit des Kaisers Franz Josef I. Wien, Steyermühl, [1898].

Louis, Rudolf. Die deutsche Musik der Gegenwart. München, G. Müller, 1909. 3d ed., 1912.

—— Hans Pfitzners *Die Rose vom Liebesgarten*. München, C. A. Seyfried, 1904.

Lowe, George. Josef Holbrooke and His Work. London, K. Paul [etc.]; New York, E. P. Dutton, 1920.

Lozzi, C. "Brigida Banti, regina del teatro lirico nel secolo XVIII," RMI XI (1904) 64–76.

—— "La musica e specialmente il melodramma alla Corte Medicea," RMI IX (1902) 297–338.

Lualdi, Adriano. "Arrigo Boito, un' anima," RMI XXV (1918) 524–49.

—— "Claudio Debussy, la sua arte e la sua parabola," RMI XXV (1918) 271–305.

—— "Il *Principe Igor* de Borodine," RMI XXIII (1916) 115–39.

Luciani, Sebastiano Arturo. "Domenico Scarlatti," RassM XI (1938) 460–72; XII (1939) 20–31, 61–74.

—— La rinascita del dramma: saggio sul teatro di musica. Roma, Ausonia, 1922.

Lucianus Samosatensis. Lucian; with an English Translation by A. M. Harmon. London, W. Heinemann; New York, Macmillan, 1913–36. Contains "On the Dance," V, 209–89.

Lütge, Wilhelm. "Zu Beethovens Leonoren-Ouvertüre Nr. 2," ZfMw IX (1926–27) 235–36.

Lüthge, Kurt. Die deutsche Spieloper. Braunschweig, W. Piepenschneider, 1924.

Lugli, A. Il melodramma, l'ultima geniale creazione del rinascimento. Milano, A. Ballardi, 1921.

Luin, E. J. "Giovanni Ferrandini e l'apertura del Teatro Residenziale a Monaco nel 1745," RMI XXXIX (1932) 561–66.

Lully et l'opéra français. RM, numéro spécial, Vol. VI (January, 1925).

Lunelli, R. Un' opera in musica, la morte di un vescovo ed una bega consolare nel 1800. Trient, Artigrafiche Tridentum, 1923.

Lupo, Bettina. "Scene e persone musicale dell' Amfiparnaso," RassM XI (1938) 445–59.

Lusson, A. L. Projet d'un théâtre d'opéra définitif pour la ville de Paris en remplacement de l'opéra provisoire. Paris, Gratiot, 1846.

Lutze, G. Aus Sonderhausens Vergangenheit. III. Band. Sonderhausen, Fr. Aug. Eupel, 1919.

Lynn, Thelma. César Franck; a Bio-bibliography. New York, 1934. Typescript. Available at the New York Public Library.

Mably, Gabriel Bonnot de. Lettres à Madame la Marquise de P . . . sur l'opéra. Paris, Didot, 1741.

Macchetta, Mrs. Blanche Roosevelt (Tucker). Verdi: Milan and Othello . . . by Blanche Roosevelt. London, Ward & Downey, 1887.

MacCormack, Gilson. "Weber in Paris," M&L IX (1928) 240–48.

MacFarren, Sir George Alexander. "The Lyrical Drama," PMA VI (1880) 125–40.

Maclean, Charles. "La Princesse Osra [by Herbert Bunning] and Der Wald [by Ethel Smyth]," ZIMG III (1901–1902) 482–88.

McMullen, Edward Wallace. The Earliest Operatic Adaptations of Shakespeare. Columbia Dissertation (A.M.), 1939.

Maddalena, E. "Libretti del Goldoni e d'altri," RMI VII (1900) 739–45.

Maecklenburg, Albert. "Der Fall Spontini-Weber," ZfMw VI (1923–24) 449–65.

—— "Verdi and Manzoni," MQ XVII (1931) 209–18.

Magnani, Giuseppe. Antonio Salieri. [Legnano], Edito a cura del commune di Legnano e di un comitato cittadino, 1934.

Magni-Dufflocq, Enrico. "Domenico Cimarosa, note biografiche," Bollettino bibliografico musicale V (1930) 5–15.

Maier, Johann Christoph. Beschreibung von Venedig. Leipzig, J. A. Barth, 1795. 4 vols. 2d ed.

Maine, Basil. *"Don Juan de Mañara;* Goossens' New Opera," *The Chesterian* XVI (1935–36) 5–10.

[Mainwaring, John.] Memoirs of the Life of the Late George Frederic Handel. London, R. & J. Dodsley, 1760.

Maione, Italo. "Tasso-Monteverdi; *Il combattimento di Tancredi e Clorinda,"* RassM III (1930) 206–15.

Maisch, W. Puccinis musikalische Formgebung, untersucht an der Oper *La Bohême.* Neustadt a. d. Aisch, Schmidt, 1934.

Malherbe, Charles Théodore. Auber; biographie critique. Paris, H. Laurens, [1911].

—— "Le Centenaire de Donizetti et l'exposition de Bergamo," RMI IV (1897) 707–29.

—— "Un Précurseur de Gluck; le comte Algarotti," RHCM II (1902) 369–74, 414–23.

Malipiero, Gian Francesco. Claudio Monteverdi. Milano, Treves, 1929.

—— "Claudio Monteverdi of Cremona," MQ XVIII (1932) 383–96.

—— "Orchestra e orchestrazione," RMI XXIII (1916) 559–69; XXIV (1917) 89–114.

Mandalari, M. T. "Gradi della evoluzione drammatica nel *Ballo in Maschera* di Verdi," RassM XII (1931) 277–87.

Mann, Thomas. Leiden und Grösse der Meister. Berlin, S. Fischer, 1935. A condensed English translation of the essay on Wagner in this volume is found in Mann's *Freud, Goethe, Wagner* (New York, Knopf, 1937).

—— Pfitzners *Palestrina.* Berlin, S. Fischer, 1919.

Manschunger, Kurt. Ferdinand Kauer. Vienna Dissertation, 1929.

Mantica, Francesco, ed. Prime fioriture del melodramma italiano. Roma, Casa editrice Claudio Monteverdi, 1912–30. 2 vols.

Manuel, Roland. Manuel de Falla. Paris, "Cahiers d'art," 1930.

—— Maurice Ravel et son œuvre dramatique. Paris, Librairie de France, 1928.

Mapleson, James Henry. The Mapleson Memoirs, 1848–1888. London, Remington, 1888. 2d ed. 2 vols.

Marangoni, Guido, and Carlo Vanbianchi. "La Scala," studie e richerche; note storiche e statistiche (1906–20). Bergamo, Istituto italiano d'arti grafiche, 1922.

Marcello, ——. "La prima rappresentazione del *Guglielmo Tell* a Parigi," RMI XVI (1909) 664–70.

[Marcello, Benedetto.] Il teatro alla moda, osia metodo sicuro, e facile per ben comporre, & esequire l'Opere Italiane in Musica all' uso moderno. [Venezia], Borghi di Belisania per A. Licante, [*ca.* 1720]. Among the numerous later editions the following may be cited: Venezia, Tip. dell' Ancora, 1887; Milano, Bottega di Poesia, 1927; French translation ("Le Théâtre à la mode au XVIIIe siècle") Paris, Fischbacher, 1890; German translation ("Das Theater nach der Mode") München and Berlin, G. Müller, [1917].

Marchant, Annie d'Armond. "Carlos Gomes, Great Brazilian Composer," *Bulletin of the Pan American Union* LXX (1936) 767–76.

Marchesan, Angelo. Della vita e delle opere di Lorenzo Da Ponte. Treviso, Turazza, 1900.

Mariani, Renato. "L'ultimo Puccini," RassM IX (1936) 133–40.

Mariani, Valerio. "Ricordando Sabbatini e Torelli scenografi marchigiani," *Rassegna Marchigiana* XII (1934) 193–207.

Maria y Campos, Armando de. Una temporada de opera italiana en Oaxaca. Mexico, Ediciones populaires, 1939.

Marix-Spire, Thérèse. "Gounod and His First Interpreter, Pauline Viardot. Part I," MQ XXXI (1945) 193–211.

Mark, Jeffrey. "Dryden and the Beginnings of Opera in England," M&L V (1924) 247–52.

—— "The Jonsonian Masque," M&L III (1922) 358–71.

Marpurg, Friedrich Wilhelm. Anleitung zur Musik überhaupt und zur Singkunst besonders. Berlin, A. Wever, 1763.

—— Historisch-kritische Beiträge zur Aufnahme der Musik. Berlin, G. A. Lange, 1754–62. 5 vols.

Marsan, Jules. La Pastorale dramatique en France à la fin du XVIe et au commencement du XVIIe siècle. Paris, Hachette, 1905.

Martens, Frederick H. "Music Mirrors of the Second Empire," MQ XVI (1930) 415–34, 563–87.

Martens, Heinrich. Das Melodram. Berlin, Vieweg, 1932. (Music.)

Martersteig, Max. Das deutsche Theater im 19. Jahrhundert. Leipzig, B&H, 1924.

Martienssen, C. A. *"Holger Danske,* Oper von Fr. L. Ae. Kunzen," ZIMG XIII (1911–12) 225–32.

Martin, Henriette. "La 'Camerata' du Comte Bardi et la musique florentine du XVIe siècle," RdM XIII (1932) 63–74, 152–61, 227–34; XIV (1933) 92–100, 141–51.

Martineau, René. Emmanuel Chabrier. Paris, Dorbon, [1910].

Marx, Adolf Bernhard. Gluck und die Oper. Berlin, O. Janke, 1863. 2 vols.

Mason, James Frederick. The Melodrama in France from the Revolution to the Beginning of Romantic Drama. Johns Hopkins Dissertation, 1911. Chapter I published: Baltimore, J. H. Furst, 1912.

Massenet, Jules. Mes Souvenirs. Paris, P. Lafitte, [1912]. Translated as: My Recollections. Boston, Small, Maynard, [1919].

Masson, Paul-Marie. *"Les Fêtes vénitiennes* de Campra," RdM XIII (1932) 127–46, 214–26.

—— "Les Idées de Rousseau sur la musique," SIM *Revue musical* VIII, No. 6 (1912), 1–17; Nos. 7–8, pp. 23–32.

—— "Lullistes et Ramistes," *L'Année musicale* I (1911) 187–211.

—— "Musique italienne et musique française," RMI XIX (1912) 519–45.

—— L'Opéra de Rameau. Paris, Laurens, 1930.

—— "Rameau and Wagner," MQ XXV (1939) 466–78.

Mathis, Alfred. "Stefan Zweig as Librettist and Richard Strauss," M&L XXV (1944) 163–76, 226–45.

Mattei, Saverio. Memorie per servire alla vita di Metastasio. Colle, A. M. Martini, 1785.

Mattfeld, Julius. A Hundred Years of Grand Opera in New York, 1825–1925; a Record of Performances. New York, The New York Public Library, 1927.

Matthes, Wilhelm. "Paul von Klenau," Blätter der Staatsoper XX (1940) 5–14.

Mattheson, [Johann]. Grundlage einer Ehrenpforte. Hamburg, In Verlegung des Verfassers, 1740. New ed., Berlin, L. Liepmannssohn, 1910.

—— Mithridat, wider den Gift einer welschen Satyre, genannt: la musica. Hamburg, Geissler, 1749.

—— Der musikalische Patriot. Hamburg, 1728.

—— Das neu-eröffnete Orchestre. Hamburg, B. Schillers Wittwe, 1713.

—— Die neueste Untersuchung der Singspiele. Hamburg, C. Herold, 1744.

—— Der vollkommene Capellmeister. Hamburg, C. Herold, 1739.

Maugars, André. "Response faite à un curieux sur le sentiment de la musique d'Italie, écrite à Rome le premier octobre 1639 . . . in deutscher Uebersetzung mitgetheilt von W. J. von Wasialewski," MfMg X (1878) 1–9, 17–23.

Maurer, Julius. Anton Schweitzer als dramatischer Komponist. Leipzig, B&H, 1912. (PIMG, 2. Folge, Heft XI.)

Maxton, Willy. Johann Theile. Tübingen Dissertation, 1927.

Mayer, Ludwig K. "Eine Vorwebersche 'Preciosa'-Musik," AfMf I (1936) 223–27.

Mayer-Reinach, Albert. "Carl Heinrich Graun als Opernkomponist," SIMG I (1899–1900) 446–529.

—— "Zur Herausgabe des Montezuma von Carl Heinrich Graun in den Denkmälern deutscher Tonkunst," MfMg XXXVII (1905) 20–31.

Mayer-Serra, Otto. Panorama de la música mexicana desde la independencia hasta la actualidad. [México], El Colegio de México, [1941].

Maylender, Michele. Storia delle accademie d'Italia. Bologna, L. Cappelli, [1926–30]. 5 vols.

Medicus, Lotte. Die Koloratur in der italienischen Oper des 19. Jahrhunderts. Zürich, Wetzikon & Rüti, 1939.

Meinardus, Ludwig. "Johann Mattheson und seine Verdienste um die deutsche Tonkunst," in Waldersee, Sammlung musikalischer Vorträge (Leipzig, B&H, 1879–98) I, 215–72.

Meissner, August Gottlieb. Bruchstücke zur Biographie J. G. Naumann's. Prag, K. Barth, 1803–1804. 2 vols.

Menantes (pseud.) *See* Hunold, Christian Friedrich.

Ménestrier, Claude François. Des Ballets anciens et modernes. Paris, R. Guignard, 1682.

Mennicke, Karl. Hasse und die Gebrüder Graun als Sinfoniker. Leipzig, B&H, 1906.

—— "Johann Adolph Hasse; eine biographische Skizze," SIMG V (1903–1904) 230–44, 469–75.

Merbach, Paul Alfred. "Briefwechsel zwischen Eduard Devrient und Julius Rietz," AfMw III (1921) 321–60.

—— "Parodien und Nachwirkungen von Webers *Freischütz*," ZfMw II (1919–20) 642–55.

—— "Das Repertoire der Hamburger Oper 1718–1750," AfMw VI (1924) 354–72.

Mercure de France. Paris. 1672–1820.

Mercure françois, Le. Paris, J. Richer, 1612–48. 25 vols.

Merlo, G. M. "L'arte di Arrigo Boito e il valore di *Nerone*," RassM VIII (1935) 126–32.

Merlo, Johann. "Zur Geschichte des Kölner Theaters im 18. und 19. Jahrhundert," *Annalen des historischen Vereins für den Niederrhein* L (1890) 145–219.

Mersenne, Marin. Harmonie universelle. Paris, S. Cramoisy, 1636–37.

Metastasio, Pietro. Dramas and Other Poems, Translated from the Italian by John Hoole. London, Otridge, 1800.

—— Lettere. Firenze, Della rosa, 1787–89. 4 vols.

—— Lettere disperse e inedite, Vol. I. Bologna, N. Zanichelli, 1883.

—— Opere. Padova, G. Foglierini, 1811–12. 17 vols.

—— *See also* Burney, *Memoirs*.

Mielsch, Rudolf. "*Dafne,* die erste deutsche Oper," *Die Musik* XIX (May, 1927) 586–91.

Mies, Paul. "Ueber die Behandlung der Frage im 17. und 18. Jahrhundert," ZfMw IV (1921–22) 286–304.

Migot, Georges. Jean-Philippe Rameau et le génie de la musique française. Paris, Delagrave, 1930.

Mila, Massimo. "Jacopo Peri," RassM VI (1933) 214–27.

—— Il melodramma di Verdi. Bari, G. Laterza, 1933.

Milizia, Francesco. Trattato completo, formale e materiale del teatro. Venezia, Pasquali, 1794.

Minor, Jakob. Christian Felix Weisse. Innsbruck, Wagner, 1880.

Miragoli, Livia. Il melodramma italiano nell' ottocento. Roma, P. Maglione & C. Strini, [1924].

Mirow, Franz. Zwischenaktsmusik und Bühnenmusik des deutschen Theaters in der klassischen Zeit. Berlin, Gesellschaft für Theatergeschichte, 1927.

Misson, Maximilien. A New Voyage to Italy. London, R. Bonwicke, 1714. 2 vols.

Mitjana y Gordón, Rafael. Histoire du développement du théâtre dramatique et musical en Espagne des origines au commencement du XIXe siècle. Uppsala, Almqvist & Wiksell, 1906.

—— "La Musique en Espagne," in Lavignac, *Encyclopédie de la musique* (Paris, Delagrave, 1920) Pt. I, Vol. IV, 1913–2351.

Mizler [von Kolof], Lorenz [Christoph]. Neu eröffnete musikalische Bibliothek. Leipzig, Im Verlag des Verfassers, 1739–54. 4 vols.

Moberg, Carl Allan. "Un Compositeur oublié de l'école de Lully: Jean Desfontaines," RdM X (1929) 5–9.

—— "Essais d'opéras en Suède, sous Charles XII," in *Mélanges de musicologie* (Paris, Droz, 1933) pp. 123–32.

Mohr, Albert Richard. Frankfurter Theaterleben im 18. Jahrhundert. Frankfurt a. M., W. Kramer, 1940.

Moller, Johannes. Cimbria literata. Havniae, G. E. Kisel, 1744. 3 vols.

Molmenti, P[ompeo] G[herardo]. La storia di Venezia nella vita privata dalle origini alla caduta della repubblica. Bergamo, Istituto italiano d'arti grafiche, 1905–1908. 3 vols.

Monaldi, Gino. "A proposito del centenario di Vincenzo Bellini," RMI IX (1902) 72–78.

—— Cantanti evirati celebri del teatro italiano. Roma, Ausonia, 1920.

—— I teatri di Roma negli ultimi tre secoli. Napoli, R. Ricciardi, 1928.

Monaldi, Guido. Vincenzo Bellini. Milan, Sonzogno, [1935].

Mone, Franz Joseph, ed. Altdeutsche Schauspiele. Quedlinburg and Leipzig, G. Basse, 1841.

—— Schauspiele des Mittelalters. Karlsruhe, C. Macklot, 1846. 2 vols.

Monnet, Jean. Mémoires. Paris, Louis-Michaud, [1884].

Monnier, Philippe. Venise au XVIIIe siècle. Paris, Perrin, 1907. Translated as: Venice in the Eighteenth Century. London, Chatto & Windus, 1910.

Monographien moderner Musiker. Leipzig, C. F. Kahnt, 1906–1909. 3 vols.

Montagu, Lady Mary [Pierrepont] Wortley. The Letters and Works of Lady Mary Wortley Montagu. London, Bickers, [1861]. 2 vols.

—— Letters to and from Pope. In Alexander Pope, *Works* (London, Longman, 1847) VII, 27–119.

Montagu-Nathan, Montagu. Glinka. London, Constable, 1916.

—— A History of Russian Music. London, W. Reeves, [1914]. 2d ed., 1918.

—— Moussorgsky. London, Constable, 1916.

—— Rimsky-Korsakof. London, Constable, 1916.

[Monteverdi, Claudio.] *See* special number of RassM II (October, 1929).

Moore, Edward C. Forty Years of Opera in Chicago. New York, H. Liveright, 1930.

Moos, Paul. Richard Wagner als Aesthetiker. Berlin and Leipzig, Schuster & Loeffler, 1906.

Mooser, Robert Aloys. Contribution à l'histoire de le musique russe; l'opéra-comique français en Russie au XVIIIe siècle. Genève, L'auteur, 1932.

Mooser, Robert Aloys (*Cont.*). "Un Musicien espagnol en Russie à la fin du XVIIIe siècle [Martin i Soler]," RMI XL (1936) 432–49.

Morgan [Sydney (Owenson)], Lady. The Life and Times of Salvator Rosa. London, 1824. 2 vols.

Morphy, G., compiler. Les Luthistes espagnoles du XVIe siècle. Leipzig, B&H, 1902. 2 vols.

Mortari, Virgilio. "L' *Oca del Cairo* di W. A. Mozart," RMI XL (1936) 477–81.

Mosel, Ignaz Franz, Edler von. Ueber das Leben und die Werke des Anton Salieri. Wien, J. B. Wallishausser, 1827.

—— Versuch einer Aesthetik des dramatischen Tonsatzes. Wien, A. Strauss, 1813. New ed., München, Lewy, 1910, with introduction and notes by Eugen Schmidt.

Moser, Hans Joachim. Christoph Willibald Gluck. Stuttgart, Cotta, 1940.

—— Geschichte der deutschen Musik. Stuttgart and Berlin, J. G. Cotta, 1920–24. 3 vols.

—— "Giuseppe Verdi," RassM XII (1939) 149–58.

—— "Kleine Beiträge zu Beethovens Liedern und Bühnenwerken," *Neues Beethoven Jahrbuch* II (1925) 43–65.

Moser, Max. Richard Wagner in der englischen Literatur des 19. Jahrhunderts. Bern, Stämpfli, 1938.

Mountford, J. F. "Greek Music in the Papyri and Inscriptions," in J. Powell and E. Barber, *New Chapters in the History of Greek Literature, Second Series* (London, Oxford University Press, 1929) pp. 146–83.

Moutoz, A. Rossini et son *Guillaume Tell*. Paris, A. Pilon, 1872.

[Mozart, Wolfgang.] Ausstellung die Zauberflöte; Mozarthaus, Katalog. Salzburg, Mozarteum, 1928.

Mozart-Jahrbuch, ed. by Abert. München, Drei Masken, 1923–29. 3 vols. (suspended 1925–28).

Müller, Erich H. "Isaak Iselins *Pariser Tagebuch* als musikgeschichtliche Quelle," ZfMw VII (1924–25) 545–52.

Müller-Blattau, Joseph. Georg Friedrich Händel. Potsdam, Athenaion, [1933].

—— "Gluck und die deutsche Dichtung," JMP XLV (1938) 30–52.

—— Hans Pfitzner. Potsdam, Athenaion, 1940.

Müller-Hartmann, Robert. "Wieland's and Gluck's Versions of the *Alkestis*," *Journal of the Warburg Institute* II (October, 1938) 176–77.

Münzer, G. Heinrich Marschner. Berlin, "Harmonie," 1901.

Muffat, Georg. Suavioris harmoniae instrumentalis hyporchematicae florilegium I. Augustae Vindelicorum, Typis Jacobi Koppmayr, 1695. Reprinted in DTOe, Vol. 2.

—— Florilegium secundum. Passovii, Typis Georgij Adam Höller, 1698. Reprinted in DTOe, Vol. 4.

Muller, Daniel. Leoš Janáček. Paris, Rieder, [1930].

Munter, Friedrich. Ludwig Thuille. München, Drei Masken, 1923.

Muratori, Lodovico Antonio. Della perfetta poesia italiana, spiegata e dimostrata con varie osservazioni. Venezia, S. Colete, 1724. Contains: Lib. III, Cap. V (Vol. II, pp. 30–45) "De' difetti, che possono osservarsi ne' moderni Drammi." Refutation of Muratori's criticisms is undertaken by Johann Mattheson in his Neueste Untersuchung der Singspiele.

Musatti, Cesare. "Drammi musicali di Goldoni e d' altri tratti dalle sue commedie," Ateneo Veneto XXI (1898) 51–60. Also separate: Venezia, Fratelli Visentini, 1898.

Musik und Bild; Festschrift Max Seiffert. Kassel, Bärenreiter, 1938.

Myers, Robert Manson. "Mrs. Delany: An Eighteenth-Century Handelian," MQ XXXII (1946) 12–36.

Nacamuli, Guido Davide. Discorso commemorativo su Antonio Smareglia. Trieste, Giuliana, 1930.

Nagel, Willibald. "Die Chöre aus Philargyrus von Petrus Dasypodius," MfMg XXI (1889) 109–12.

—— "Daniel Purcell," MfMg XXX (1898) 47–53.

—— "Deutsche Musiker des 18. Jahrhunderts im Verkehr mit J. Fr. A. v. Uffenbach," SIMG XIII (1911–12) 69–106.

—— "Das Leben Christoph Graupner's," SIMG X (1908–1909) 568–612.

—— "Die Musik in den schweitzerischen Dramen des 16. Jahrhunderts," MfMg XXII (1890) 67–83.

Napoli-Signorelli, Pietro. Storia critica dei teatri antichi e moderni. Napoli, V. Orsino, 1787–90. 6 vols. A later ed., 1813, 10 vols.

Narciss, Georg Adolf. Studien zu den Frauenzimmergesprächspielen Georg Philipp Harsdörfers. Leipzig, H. Eichblatt, 1928.

Nardi, Piero. Vita di Arrigo Boito. Verona, Mondadori, 1942.

Nathan, Hans. Das Rezitativ der Frühopern Richard Wagners. Berlin, Dobrin, 1934.

Navarra, Ugo. Nel tricentenario del teatro lirico 1637–1937; grande inchiesta particolare sulle condizioni odierne della scena melodrammatica. Milano, Alba, 1937.

Naylor, Bernard. "Albert Lortzing," PMA LVIII (1931–32) 1–13.

Naylor, Edward Woodall. "Music and Shakespeare," MA I (1909–10) 129–48.

—— Shakespeare and Music. London, J. M. Dent, [1931].

—— "Verdi and Wagner," PMA XX (1893) 1–10.

Nef, Karl. Zur Geschichte der deutschen Instrumentalmusik in der 2. Hälfte des 17. Jahrhunderts. Leipzig, B&H, 1902. (PIMG, Beiheft V.)

—— "Zur Instrumentation im 17. Jahrhundert," JMP XXXV (1929) 33–42.

Negri, Francesco. La vita di Apostolo Zeno. Venezia, Alvisopoli, 1816.

Neisser, Arthur. Servio Tullio, eine Oper aus dem Jahre 1685 von Agostino Steffani. Leipzig, C. G. Röder, 1902.

Nejedlý, Zdeněk. Frederick Smetana. London, G. Bles, [1924].

—— J. B. Foerster. V Praze, M. Urbánek, 1910.

Neretti, Luigi. L'importanza civile della nostra opera in musica. Firenze, Tipografia cooperativa, 1902.

Neri, Achille. "Gli intermezzi del Pastor fido," *Giornale storico della letteratura italiana* XI (1888) 405–15.

Nestyev, Israel. Sergei Prokofiev: His Musical Life . . . Translated by Rose Prokofieva. New York, Knopf, 1946.

Nettl, Paul. "Beitrag zur Geschichte des deutschen Singballets," ZfMw VI (1923–24) 608–20.

—— "Casanova and Music," MQ XV (1929) 212–32.

—— "An English Musician at the Court of Charles VI," MQ XXVIII (1942) 318–28.

—— "Exzerpte aus der Raudnitzer Textbüchersammlung," SzMw VII (1920) 143–44.

—— Mozart und die königliche Kunst. Berlin, Wunder, 1932.

—— "Zur Geschichte der kaiserlichen Hofkapelle von 1636–1680," SzMw XVI (1929) 70–85; XVII (1930) 95–104; XVIII (1931) 23–35; XIX (1932) 33–40.

Neues Beethoven Jahrbuch. Augsburg, B. Filser, 1924–. Articles relevant to opera will be found separately listed under the names of the following authors: Cortolezis, Engländer, Haas, Moser, Unger, Waltershausen.

Neuhaus, Max. "Antonio Draghi," SzMw I (1913) 104–92.

Neumann, Egon. Die Operetten von Johann Strauss. Vienna Dissertation, 1919.

Newman, Ernest. Gluck and the Opera. London, B. Dobell, 1895.

—— Hugo Wolf. London, Methuen, [1907].

—— The Life of Richard Wagner. New York, Knopf, 1933–46. 4 vols.

—— Richard Strauss. London and New York, J. Lane, 1908.

Newmarch, Rosa. The Music of Czechoslovakia. London, Oxford University Press, 1942.

—— "New Works in Czechoslovakia; Janáček and Novák," *The Chesterian* XII (July, 1931) 213–19.

—— The Russian Opera. New York, E. P. Dutton, [1914].

—— Tchaikovsky, His Life and Works. New York, J. Lane, 1900.

—— "Tchaikovsky's Early Lyrical Operas," ZIMG VI (1904–1905) 29–34.

Nicolai, Otto. Tagebücher. Leipzig, B&H, 1892. Edited, with biographical notes, by B. Schröder.

—— Tagebücher, soweit erhalten zum ersten Male vollständig herausgeben von Prof. Dr. Wilhelm Altmann. Regensburg, G. Bosse, 1937.

Nicolai, Paul. Der Ariadne-Stoff in der Entwicklungsgeschichte der deutschen Oper. Viersen, J. H. Meyer, 1919.

Nicoll, Allardyce. A History of Early Eighteenth Century Drama, 1700–1750. Cambridge, The University Press, 1925.

—— A History of Restoration Drama, 1660–1700. Cambridge, The University Press, 1940. 3d ed.

—— "Italian Opera in England; the First Five Years," *Anglia* XLVI (1922) 257–81.

Niecks, Frederick. "Historical Sketch of the Overture," SIMG VII (1905–1906) 386–90.

Nietan, Hanns. Die Buffoszenen der spätvenezianischen Oper (1680 bis 1710). Halle Dissertation, 1925.

Nietzsche, Friedrich. Gesammelte Werke. München, Musarion, 1920–29. 23 vols. Contains: "Die Geburt der Tragödie," Vol. 3; "Jenseits von Gut und Böse," Vol. 15; "Der Fall Wagner," "Nietzsche contra Wagner," Vol. 17.

Niggli, Arnold. "Faustina Bordoni-Hasse," in Waldersee, *Sammlung musikalischer Vorträge* (Leipzig, B&H, 1879–98) II, 261–318.

—— "Giacomo Meyerbeer," in Waldersee, *Sammlung musikalischer Vorträge* (Leipzig, B&H, 1879–98) V, 287–324.

Nilsson, Kurt. Die Rimsky-Korssakoffsche Bearbeitung des *Boris Godunoff* von Mussorgskii als Objekt der vergleichenden Musikwissenschaft. Münster, Buschmann, 1937.

Nin [y Castellano], J[oachin]. Sept Chansons picaresques espagnoles anciennes, librement harmonisées et précédées d'une étude sur les classiques espagnols du chant. Paris, M. Eschig, 1926.

—— Septs Chants lyriques espagnols anciens, librement harmonisés et précédés d'une étude sur les classiques espagnols du chant. Paris, M. Eschig, 1926.

Noack, Friedrich. "Die Musik zu der molièreschen Komödie *Monsieur de Pourceaugnac* von Jean Baptiste de Lully," in *Festschrift für Johannes Wolf* (Berlin, Breslauer, 1929) pp. 139–47.

—— "Die Opern von Christoph Graupner in Darmstadt," in *Bericht über den I. Musikwissenschaftlichen Kongress der Deutschen Musikgesellschaft* (Leipzig, B&H, 1926) pp. 252–59.

Nodot, ——. "Le Triomphe de Lully aux Champs-Elysées," RM VI (January, 1925) 89–106. First printing of Bibliothèque de l'Arsenal ms. 6.542, pp. 260 ff.

Nohl, Ludwig. Die Zauberflöte; Betrachtungen über Bedeutung der dramatischen Musik in der Geschichte des menschlichen Geistes. Frankfurt a. M., Schneider, 1862.

Nolhac, Pierre, and Angelo Solerti. Il viaggio in Italia di Enrico III, re di Francia, e le feste a Venezia, Ferrara, Mantova, e Torino. Torino, L. Roux, 1890.

Nordau, Max. Entartung. Berlin, Duncker, 1893. 2 vols. Translated as: Degeneration. New York, D. Appleton, 1895.

Norman, Gertrude. A Consideration of Seicento Opera with Particular Reference to the Rise of the Neapolitan School. Columbia Dissertation (A. M.), 1937.

Nosek, Vladimir. The Spirit of Bohemia; a Survey of Czechoslovak History, Music, and Literature. London, G. Allen & Unwin, [1926].

Nouveau Théâtre italien, Le. Paris, Briasson, 1733–1753. New ed.

Noyes, Robert Gale. Ben Jonson on the English Stage, 1660–1776. Cambridge, Mass., Harvard University Press, 1935.

—— "Contemporary Musical Settings of the Songs in Restoration Dramatic Operas," *Harvard Studies and Notes in Philology and Literature* XX (1938) 99–121.

Nuitter. *See* Truinet.

Nungezer, Edwin. Dictionary of Actors and Other Persons Associated with the Public Representations of Plays in England before 1642. New Haven, Yale University Press; London, Oxford University Press, 1929.

Nuovo, Antonio. Tommaso Traetta. Bitonto, A. Amendolagine, 1938.

Odendahl, Laurenz. Friedrich Heinrich Himmel. Bonn, P. Rost, 1917.

Oesterlein, Nikolaus. Katalog einer Wagner-Bibliothek. Leipzig, B&H, 1882–95. 4 vols.

Offenbach, Jacques. Offenbach en Amérique; notes d'un musicien en voyage. Paris, Calmann Lévy, 1877.

Ohrmann, Fritz. "Max Brands Oper *Maschinist Hopkins*," *Signale für die musikalische Welt* LXXXVIII (1930) 395–99.

Olivier, Jean Jacques (pseud.) Les Comédiens français dans les cours d'Allemagne au XVIIIe siècle. Paris, Société française d'imprimerie et de libraire, 1901–1905. Series 1–4.

Ollone, Max d'. "Gounod et l'opéra-comique," RM XIV (November, 1933) 303–308.

O'Neill, Norman. "Music to Stage Plays in England," SIMG XIII (1911–12) 321–28.

Opel, Julius Otto. "Die erste Jahrzehnte der Oper in Leipzig," *Neues Archiv für sächsische Geschichte und Altertumskunde* V (1884) 116–141.

"Opera as It Is—and May Be," general title of several articles in M&L IV (1923) 85 ff.

"L'Opéra-comique au XIXe siècle," RM XIV (November, 1933) 241–312.

Opieński, Henryk. La Musique polonaise. Paris, Gebethner & Wolff, 1929.

—— "Les Premiers Opéras polonais considérés dans leur rapports avec la musique de Chopin," RdM X (1929) 92–98.

"Origen y progressos de las tonadillas que se cantan en los Coliseos de esta Corte," *Memorial literario, instructivo y curioso de la corte de Madrid* XII (1787) 169–80.

[Origny, Abraham Jean Baptiste Antoine d'.] Annales du théâtre-italien. Paris, Duchesne, 1788. 3 vols.

Orlandini, Giuseppe. "Domenico Cimarosa e la musica nella seconda civiltà latina," *Rivista bolognese* II [?] (1868) 933–47, 1005–24.

Orsini, Giovanni. Pietro Mascagni e il suo *Nerone*. Milano, A.&G. Carisch, 1935.

Ortigue, Joseph Louis d'. Le Balcon de l'opéra. Paris, Renduel, 1833.

—— De l'école musicale italienne. Paris, Au dépôt central des meilleures productions de la presse, 1839. Second edition in 1840 entitled: Du théâtre-italien et son influence sur le goût musical français.

Ottzen, Curt. Telemann als Opernkomponist. Berlin, E. Ebering, 1902. 2 vols. See review by Oskar Fleischer, ZIMG III, 497.

Oven, A. H. E. von. "Das erste städtische Theater zu Frankfurt am Main," in *Neujahrsblatt des Vereins für Geschichte und Altertumskunde zu Frankfurt am Main* (1872).

Pagano, Luigi. "Arrigo Boito: l' artista," RMI XXXI (1924) 199–234.

—— "*Dèbora e Jaéle* di Ildebrando Pizzetti," RMI XXX (1923) 47–108.

[Paget, Violet.] Studies of the Eighteenth Century in Italy. London, W. Satchell, 1880. "By Vernon Lee" (pseud.).

Pahlen, Kurt. Das Rezitativ bei Mozart. Vienna Dissertation, 1929.

Paisiello, Cavalier Giovanni. "Saggio del corso dei travagli musicali del cavaliere Giovanni Paisiello," RassM III (1930) 124–35.

Palmer, John. "Gesture and Scenery in Modern Opera," MQ II (1916) 314–30.

Pannain, Guido. "Il *Dottor Faust*," RassM XIII (1940) 20–29.

—— "Rossini nel *Guglielmo Tell*," RMI XXXI (1924) 473–506.

—— "Saggio sulla musica a Napoli nel secolo XIX," RMI XXXV (1928) 198–208, 331–42; XXXVI (1929) 197–210; XXXVII (1930) 231–42; XXXVIII (1931) 193–206; XXXIX (1932) 51–72.

—— "Vincenzo Bellini," RassM VIII (1935) 1–13, 100–110, 174–88, 237–44.

Panoff, Peter. "Der nationale Stil N. A. Rimsky-Korsakows," AfMw VIII (1926) 78–117.

Pardo Pimentel, Nicolas. La opera italiana. Madrid, Aguado, 1851.

Parente, Alfredo. "Note sull' estetica musicale contemporanea in Italia," RassM III (1930) 289–310.

[Parfaict, François.] Dictionnaire des théâtres de Paris. Paris, Lambert, 1756. 7 vols.

—— Histoire de l'ancien théâtre italien depuis son origine en France, jusqu'à sa suppression en l'année 1697. Paris, Lambert, 1753.

—— Mémoires pour servir à l'histoire des spectacles de la foire. Paris, Briasson, 1743.

Paris, Luis. Museo-archivo teatral (Madrid); catálogo provisional. Madrid, Yagües, 1932.

Parisini, G. Musica e balli in Faenza nel 1745. Faenza, Lega, 1935.

Parker, D. C. "A View of Giacomo Puccini," MQ III (1917) 509–16.

Parodies du nouveau théâtre italien . . . avec les airs gravés, Les. Paris, Briasson, 1738. New ed.

Parolari, Cornelio. "Giambattista Velluti," RMI XXXIX (1932) 263–98.

Parry, Sir C[harles] Hubert H[astings]. The Music of the Seventeenth Century. London, Oxford University Press, 1938. 2d ed. (The Oxford History of Music, Vol. III.)

—— "The Significance of Monteverde," PMA XLII (1915–16) 51–67.

Pastor, Ludwig, Freiherr von. The History of the Popes, from the Close of the Middle Ages. Vols. 29, 30, 31. London, Kegan Paul, 1938–40.

Pastura, Francesco. "Due frammenti della *Beatrice di Tenda* di Bellini," RassM VIII (1935) 327–34.

Patterson, Frank. "Fifty Years of Opera in America," MTNA XXIII (1928) 176–85.

Paulig, Hans. Peter Cornelius und sein *Barbier von Bagdad;* ein stilkritischer Vergleich der Originalpartitur mit der Bearbeitung von Felix Mottl. Cologne Dissertation, 1923.

Pavan, Giuseppe. Contributo alla storia del teatro musicale; il dramma più musicato; l'*Artaserse* del Metastasio. Cittadella, Tip. Sociale, 1917.

Pearce, Charles E. "Polly Peachum": the Story of *Polly* and *The Beggar's Opera*. London, S. Paul, [1923].

Pearson, Hesketh. Gilbert and Sullivan; a Biography. New York, Harper, 1935.

Pedrell, Felipe. Cancionero musical popular español. Valls, E. Castells, [1918–22]. 4 vols.

—— "L'Eglogue *La Forêt sans amour* de Lope de Vega, et la musique et les musiciens du théâtre de Calderón," SIMG XI (1909–1910) 55–104.

—— "La Festa d'Elche ou le drame lyrique liturgique La Mort et l'assomption de la Vierge," SIMG II (1900–1901) 203–52.

—— Jornadas de arte (1841–1891). Paris, Ollendorf, 1911.

—— "La Musique indigène dans le théâtre espagnol du XVIIe siècle," SIMG V (1903) 46–90.

—— Orientaciones (1892–1902); continuaciò de Jornadas de arte. Paris, Ollendorf, 1911.

—— Por nuestra música; algunas observaciones sobre la magna cuestión de una escuela lírico nacional. Barcelona, Heurich, 1891.

—— Teatro lírico español anterior al siglo XIX. La Coruña, Berea, [1897–] 1898. 5 vols.

Peiser, Karl. Johann Adam Hiller. Leipzig, Gebrüder Hug, 1894.

Pelicelli, Nestore. "Musicisti in Parma dal 1800 al 1860," *Note d'archivio* XII (1935) 213–22, 317–63; XIII (1936) 180–97.

—— "Musicisti in Parma nel secolo XVIII; la musica alla corte di Parma nel 1700," *Note d'archivio* XI (1934); XII (1935) 27–42, 82–92.

Pellisson, Maurice. Les Comédies-ballets de Molière. Paris, Hachette, 1914.

Peña y Goñi, Antonio. La ópera española y la música dramática en España en el siglo XIX. Madrid, El Liberal, 1881.

Pepys, Samuel. The Diary of Samuel Pepys. London, G. Bell; New York, Harcourt, Brace, 1924–26. 8 vols.

Pereira Peixoto d'Almeida Carvalhaes, Manoel. Inês de Castro; na opera e na choregraphia italianas. Lisboa, Castro Irmão, 1908, 1915. 2 vols.

—— Marcos Portugal na sua musica dramatica. Lisboa, Castro Irmão, 1910.

Perinello, C. "L' *Amfiparnaso* di Horatio Vecchi," RMI XLI (1937) 1–23.

Perrault, Charles. Les Hommes illustres qui ont paru en France pendant ce siècle. Paris, A. Dezallier, 1696.

Perrino, Marcello. Nouvelle Methode de chant . . . précédé . . . de la vie de Benedetto Marcello . . . d'une notice sur les usages du théâtre en Italie. Paris, Ebrard, 1839. Originally published as: Osservazioni sul canto. Napoli, Stampa reale, 1810.

Peterson-Berger, Olof Wilhelm. "The Life Problem in Wagner's Dramas," MQ II (1916) 658–68.

—— Peterson-Berger recensioner; glimtar och skuggor ur Stockholms musik värld 1896–1923. Stockholm, Ahlén & Åkerlund, 1923.

—— Richard Wagner als Kulturerscheinung. Leipzig, B&H, 1917. Review by R. Hohenemser ZfMw I, 683–84.

—— "The Wagnerian Culture Synthesis," MQ VII (1921) 45–56.

Petzet, Walter. *"Maschinist Hopkins," Signale für die musikalische Welt* LXXXVII (1929) 1363–65.

Peyser, Herbert F. "Some Fallacies of Modern Anti-Wagnerism," MQ XII (1926) 175–89.

—— *"Tristan,* First-Hand," MQ XI (1925) 418–36.

Pfitzner, Hans Erich. Gesammelte Schriften. Augsburg, B. Filser, 1926. 3 vols.

—— Vom musikalischen Drama; gesammelte Aufsätze. München and Leipzig, Süddeutsche Monatshefte, 1915.

Pfordten, Hermann, Freiherr von der. Carl Maria von Weber. Leipzig, Quelle & Meyer, [1918].

Phalèse. *See* Hortus musarum.

Piccioli, Giuseppe. Composizioni di antichi autori bolognesi. Bologna, Bongiovanni, 1933.

Pierre, Constant. Les Hymnes et chansons de la révolution; aperçu général et catalogue avec notes historiques, analytiques et bibliographiques. Paris, Imprimerie nationale, 1904.

Pincherle, Marc. "Antonio Vivaldi; essai biographique," RdM XI (1930) 161–70, 265–81.

Pinetti, Gian Battista. Teatro Donizetti (già Riccardi); la stagione d'opera alla fiera d'agosto; cronistoria illustrata dal 1784 al 1936. Bergamo, Sesa, 1937.

Piovano, Francesco. "A propos d'une recente biographie de Léonard Leo," SIMG VIII (1906–1907) 70–95, 336.

—— "Baldassare Galuppi; note bio-bibliografiche," RMI XIII (1906) 676–726; XIV (1907) 333–65; XV (1908) 233–74.

—— "Elenco cronologico delle opere (1757–1802) di Pietro Guglielmi," RMI XII (1905) 407–46.

—— "Notizie storico-bibliografiche sulle opere di Pietro Guglielmi (Guglielmini) con appendice su Pietro Guglielmi," RMI XVI (1909) 243–70, 475–505, 785–820; XVII (1910) 59–90, 376–414, 554–89, 822–77. This is about the son, Pietro Carlo Guglielmi, 1763–1817.

—— "Un Opéra inconnu de Gluck," SIMG IX (1907–1908) 231–81, 448.

Pirker, Max. Die Zauberflöte. Wien, Wiener literarischer Anstalt, 1920.

Pirro, André. Descartes et la musique. Paris, Fischbacher, 1907.

—— Schütz. Paris, F. Alcan, 1913.

Pisk, Paul A. "Lazare Saminsky," *The Chesterian* XX (1938–39) 74–78.

—— "Schönberg's Twelve-Tone Opera," MMus VII, No. 3 (April–May, 1930) 18–21.

Pistorelli, L. "Due melodrammi inediti di Apostolo Zeno," RMI III (1896) 261–74.

—— "I melodrammi giocosi del Casti," RMI II (1895) 36–56, 449–72; IV (1897) 631–71.

Piton, Alexis. "Les Origines du mélodrame français à la fin du XVIIIe siècle," Revue d'histoire littéraire (1911) pp. 256–96.

Pizzetti, Ildebrando. "Ariadne et Barbebleue . . . de Paul Dukas," RMI XV (1908) 73–112.

—— "L'arte di Verdi: spiriti e forme," RassM X (1937) 201–206.

—— "Il Faust della leggenda, del poema e del dramma musicale," RMI XIII (1906) 1–49.

—— "Pelléas et Mélisande . . . Debussy," RMI XV (1908) 350–63.

—— ed. Vincenzo Bellini. Milan, Fratelli Treves, [1936].

Planelli, Antonio. Dell' opera in musica. Napoli, D. Campo, 1772.

Plümicke, Carl Martin. Entwurf einer Theatergeschichte von Berlin. Berlin and Stettin, F. Nicolai, 1781.

Pohl, Karl Ferdinand. Joseph Haydn. Leipzig, B&H, 1878–1927. 3 vols. in 2.

Pohl, Richard. "Richard Wagner," in Waldersee, Sammlung musikalischer Vorträge (Leipzig, B&H, 1879–98) V, 121–98.

Poladian, Sirvart. Handel as an Opera Composer. Cornell Dissertation, 1946.

Policastro, Guglielmo. Vincenzo Bellini. Catania, Studio editoriale moderno, 1935.

Poliziano, Angelo Ambrogini, known as. Le stanze, l'Orfeo e le rime. Firenze, G. Barbèra, 1863.

—— Orfeo. See Casella, Alfred.

Polko, Elise. Die Bettler-Oper. Hannover, Rümpler, 1863. 3 vols.

Pollatschek, Walter. Hofmannsthal und die Bühne. Frankfurt Dissertation, 1924.

Pompeati, Arturo. "Il Parini e la musica," RMI XXXVI (1929) 556–74.

Pompei, Edoardo. Pietro Mascagni. Roma, Editrice nazionale, 1912.

Ponz de Leon, Giuseppe. "Il dramma lirico nell' arte di Pizzetti," RMI XLIII (1939) 539–44.

Potter, John. The Theatrical Review; or, New Companion to the Playhouse; Containing a Critical and Historical Account of Every Tragedy, Comedy, Opera, Farce &c Exhibited at the Theatres during the Last Season. London, S. Crowder, 1772. 2 vols.

Pougin, Arthur. Adolphe Adam. Paris, G. Charpentier, 1877.

—— Auber; ses commencements, les origines de sa carrière. Paris, Pottier de Lalaine, 1873.

—— "Bernardo Mengozzi," RMI XXV (1918) 176–201, 323–44.

—— Boieldieu. Paris, Charpentier, 1875.

—— "Les Dernières Années de Spontini," RMI XXIX (1922) 54–80, 236–63.

—— Un Directeur d'opéra au dix-huitième siècle; l'opéra sous l'ancien régime; l'opéra sous la révolution. Paris, Fischbacher, 1914.

—— F. Halévy, écrivain. Paris, A. Clauden, 1865.

—— "Gounod écrivain," RMI XVII (1910) 590–627; XVIII (1911) 747–68; XIX (1912) 239–85, 637–95; XX (1913) 453–86, 792–820.

—— Herold. Paris, H. Laurens, [1906].

—— Jean-Jacques Rousseau musicien. Paris, Fischbacher, 1901.

—— Madame Favart, étude théâtrale, 1727–1772. Paris, Fischbacher, 1912.

—— "Massenet," RMI XIX (1912) 916–85.

—— Méhul. Paris, Fischbacher, 1893. 2d ed.

—— Molière et l'opéra-comique. Paris, J. Baur, 1882.

—— Monsigny et son temps. Paris, Fischbacher, 1908.

—— Musiciens français du XVIIIe siècle; Dezèdes. Paris, N. Chaix, 1862.

—— "Notice sur Méhul par Cherubini," RMI XVI (1909) 750–71.

—— L'Opéra-comique pendant la révolution de 1788 à 1801. Paris, A. Savine, 1891.

—— "L'Orchestre de Lully," Le Ménestrel LXII (1896) 44–45, 59–60, 67–68, 76, 83–84, 91–92, 99–100.

—— "Les Origines de l'opéra français: Cambert et Lully," Revue d'art dramatique Année 6, tome XXI (1891) 129–55.

—— "La Première Salle Favart et l'opéra-comique 1801–1838," Le Ménestrel LX (1894) and LXI (1895), passim.

—— Les Vrais Créateurs de l'opéra français, Perrin et Cambert. Paris, Charvay, 1881.

—— William-Vincent Wallace. Paris, A. Ikelmer, 1866.

Pound, Ezra Loomis. Antheil and the Treatise of Harmony. Chicago, P. Covici, 1927.

Preibisch, Walter. "Quellenstudien zu Mozart's Entführung aus dem Serail; ein Beitrag zur Geschichte der Türkenoper," SIMG X (1908–1909) 430–76.

Prendergast, Arthur H. "The Masque of the Seventeenth Century," PMA XXIII (1897) 113–31.

Pretzsch, Paul. Die Kunst Siegfried Wagners. Leipzig, B&H, 1919.

Previtali, F. "Turandot [Busoni]," RassM XIII (1940) 38–46.

Pribram, Alfred Francis. Materialen zur Geschichte der Preise und Löhne in Oesterreich. Bd. I. Wien, C. Ueberreuter, 1938.

Prochazka, R. Mozart in Prag. Prag, G. Neugebauer, 1899.

Prod'homme, Jacques Gabriel. "Austro-German Musicians in France in the Eighteenth Century," MQ XV (1929) 171–95.

—— "Chabrier in His Letters," MQ XXI (1935) 451–65.

—— "Les Dernières Représentations du Devin du village (mai–juin 1829)," RM VII (August, 1926) 118–25.

—— "Les Deux Benvenuto Cellini de Berlioz," SIMG XIV (1912–13) 449–60.

—— "Deux Collaborateurs italiens de Gluck: Raniero de Calzabigi e Giuseppe D'Affligio," RMI XXIII (1916) 33–65, 201–18.

—— "The Economic Status of Musicians in France until the French Revolution," MQ XVI (1930) 83–100.

Prod'homme, Jacques Gabriel (*Cont.*). "A French Maecenas of the Time of Louis XV: M. de la Pouplinière," MQ X (1924) 511–31.

—— "Gluck's French Collaborators," MQ III (1917) 249–71.

—— Gounod. Paris, Delagrave, [1911]. 2 vols.

—— "*Léonore ou l'amour conjugal,* de Bouilly et Gaveaux," SIMG VII (1905–1906) 636–39.

—— "Lettres de G. Verdi à Léon Escudier," *Bulletin de la Société union musicologique* V (1925) 7–28.

—— "Lettres de Gluck et à propos de Gluck (1776–1787)," ZIMG XIII (1911–12) 257–65.

—— "Lettres inédites de G. Verdi à Léon Escudier," RMI XXXV (1928) 1–28, 171–97, 519–52.

—— "Marie Fel (1713–1794)," SIMG IV (1902–1903) 485–518.

—— "Miscellaneous Letters by Charles Gounod," MQ IV (1918) 630–53.

—— "A Musical Map of Paris," MQ XVIII (1932) 608–27.

—— "La Musique à Paris de 1753 à 1757, d'après un manuscrit de la Bibliothèque de Munich," SIMG VI (1904–1905) 568–87.

—— "Notes sur deux librettistes français de Gluck: du Roullet et Moline (d'après des documents inédits)," ZIMG VII (1905–1906) 12–15.

—— L'Opéra (1669–1925). Paris, Delagrave, 1925.

—— "*Le Page inconstant;* ballet anacréontique . . . sur la musique de Mozart," RdM XVI (1935) 205–12.

—— "A Pastel by La Tour: Marie Fel," MQ IX (1923) 482–507.

—— "Pierre Corneille et l'opéra français," ZIMG VII (1905–1906) 416–21.

—— "Pierre de Jélyotte (1713–1797)," SIMG III (1901–1902) 686–717.

—— "The Recent Fiftieth Anniversary of the 'New Opera'," MQ XII (1926) 13–21.

—— "Rosalie Levasseur, Ambassadress of Opera," MQ II (1916) 210–43.

—— "Rossini and His Works in France," MQ XVII (1931) 110–37.

—— "Spontini et Ch. Gounod," ZIMG XI (1909–10) 325–28.

—— "Two Hundred and Fifty Years of the Opéra (1669–1919)," MQ V (1919) 513–37.

—— "Unpublished Letters from Verdi to Camille du Locle," MQ VII (1921) 73–103.

—— "Wagner and the Paris Opéra: Unpublished Letters (February–March, 1861)," MQ I (1915) 216–31.

—— "Wagner, Berlioz and Monsieur Scribe; Two Collaborations That Miscarried," MQ XII (1926) 359–75.

—— "The Works of Weber in France (1824–1926)," MQ XIV (1928) 366–86.

Prokofiev, Sergei. "The War Years," MQ XXX (1944) 421–27.

"Prospetto cronologico delle opere di Gaetano Donizetti," RMI IV (1897) 736–43.

Prota-Giurleo, Ulisse. Alessandro Scarlatti, "il Palermitano" (la patria & la famiglia). Napoli, L'autore, 1926.

—— La grande orchestra del Teatro S. Carlo nel settecento (da documenti inediti). Napoli, L'autore, 1927.

—— Musicanti napoletani alla corte di Portogallo nel 700. Napoli, Elzevira, 1925.

—— Nicola Logroscino, "il dio dell' opera buffa." Napoli, L'autore, 1927.

Provenzal, Dino. La vita e le opere di Lodovico Adimari. Rocca S. Casciano, L. Cappelli, 1902.

Prunières, Henry. "L'Académie royale de musique et de danse," RM VI (January, 1925) 3–25.

—— Le Ballet de cour en France avant Benserade et Lully. Paris, H. Laurens, 1914.

—— Cavalli et l'opéra vénitien au XVIIe siècle. Paris, Rieder, [1931].

—— Claudio Monteverdi. Paris, F. Alcan, 1924.

—— "Défense et illustration de l'Opéra-comique," RM XIV (November, 1933) 243–47.

—— "De l'interpretation des agréments du chant aux XVIIe et XVIIIe siècles," RM XIII (May, 1932) 329–44.

—— "The Departure from Opera," MMus III, No. 2 (January–February, 1926) 3–9.

—— "Honegger's Judith," MMus III, No. 4 (May–June, 1926) 30–33.

—— "Jean de Cambefort," Année musicale II (1912) 205–26.

—— "La Jeunesse de Lully (1632–62)," MM V (1909) 234–42, 329–53.

—— "Lecerf de la Viéville et l'esthétique musicale classique au XVIIe siècle," MM IV (1908) 619–54.

—— "Lettres et autographes de Lully," MM VIII (1912) 19–20.

—— "I libretti dell' opera veneziana nel secolo XVII," RassM III (1930) 441–48.

—— Lully. Paris, H. Laurens, 1909.

—— "Lully and the Académie de Musique et de Danse," MQ XI (1925) 528–46.

—— "Lully, fils de meunier," MM VIII (1912) 57–61.

—— "Monteverdi's Venetian Operas," MQ X (1924) 178–92.

—— "Les Musiciens du Cardinal Antonio Barberini," in Mélanges de musicologie (Paris, Droz, 1933) pp. 117–22.

—— "Notes sur la vie de Luigi Rossi (1598–1653)," SIMG XII (1910–11) 12–16.

—— "Notes sur les origines de l'ouverture française," SIMG XII (1910–11) 565–85.

—— "Notes sur une partition faussement attribuée à Cavalli: L'Eritrea (1686)," RMI XXVII (1920) 267–73.

—— L'Opéra italien en France avant Lulli. Paris, E. Champion, 1913. Review by R. Rolland, MM X, No. 5 (1914) 6–15.

—— "Les Premières Ballets de Lully," RM XII (June, 1931) 1–17.

—— "Recherches sur les années de jeunesse de J. B. Lully," RMI XVII (1910) 646–54.

Prunières, Henry (*Cont.*). "Les Représentations du *Palazzo d'Atlante* à Rome (1642) d'après des documents inédits," SIMG XIV (1912–13) 218–26.

—— "Ronsard et les fêtes de cour," RM V (May, 1924) 27–44.

—— "Stendhal and Rossini," MQ VII (1921) 133–55.

—— La Vie et l'œuvre de Claudio Monteverdi. Paris, Librairie de France, 1926. 2d ed., 1931. Translated as: Monteverdi; His Life and Works. London, J. M. Dent, 1926.

—— La Vie illustre et libertine de Jean-Baptiste Lully. Paris, Plon-Nourrit, [1929].

Puccini, Giacomo Epistolario. Milano, A. Mondadori, 1928. Translated as: Letters of Giacomo Puccini. Philadelphia and London, J. B. Lippincott, 1931.

Pültz, Wilhelm. Die Geburt der deutschen Oper; Roman um Carl Maria v. Weber. Leipzig, v. Hase & Koehler, [1939].

Pulver, Jeffrey. "The Intermezzi of the Opera," PMA XLIII (1916–17) 134–63.

Pupino-Carbonelli, Giuseppe. Paisiello. Napoli, Tocco, 1908.

Pure, Michel de. Idée des spectacles anciens et nouveaux. Paris, M. Brunet, 1668.

Puttman, Max. "Zur Geschichte der deutschen komischen Oper von ihren Anfängen bis Dittersdorf," *Die Musik* III (1903–1904) Qt. 4, 334–49, 416–28.

Quadrio, Francesco Saverio, abate. Della storia e della ragione d'ogni poesia. Bologna, F. Pisarri, 1739–49. 4 vols.

Quantz, Johann Joachim. Versuch einer Anweisung die Flöte traversiere zu spielen. Leipzig, C. F. Kahnt, 1906. Originally published Berlin, J. F. Voss, 1752.

Quinault, Philippe. Théâtre. Paris, Compagnie des Libraires, 1739. 5 vols.

Quittard, Henri. "Les Années de jeunesse de J. P. Rameau," RHCM II (1902) 61–63, 100–14, 152–70, 208–18.

—— "*Le Bucheron,* opéra comique de Philidor," RHCM VII (1907) 421–24.

—— "*Ernelinde,* de Philidor," RHCM VII (1907) 469–74.

—— "L' *Hortus musarum* de 1552–53 et les arrangements de pièces polyphoniques pour voix seule et luth," SIMG VIII (1906–1907) 254–85.

—— "L'Orchestre de l' *Orfeo,*" RHCM VII (1907) 380–89, 412–18.

—— "La Première Comédie française en musique," *Bulletin français de la SIM.* IV (1908) 378–96, 497–537.

—— "*Le Sorcier,* opéra comique de Philidor," RHCM VII (1907) 537–41.

—— "Le Théorbe comme instrument d'accompagnement," *Bulletin français de la SIM.* (1910) 221–37, 362–84.

Raab, Leopold. Wenzel Müller. Boden bei Wien, Verein der N.-Oe. Landesfreunde in Boden, 1928.

Raabe, Peter. Kulturwille im deutschen Musikleben. Regensburg, G. Bosse, [1936].

—— Die Musik im dritten Reich. Regensburg, G. Bosse, [1935].

Rabany, Charles. Carlo Goldoni; le théâtre et la vie en Italie au XVIIIe siècle. Paris, Berger-Levrault, 1896.

Rabich, Franz. Richard Wagner und die Zeit. Langensalza, Beyer, 1925.

Raccolta di melodrammi giocosi scritti nel secolo XVIII. Milano, Soc. tip. dei classici italiani, 1826.

Raccolta di melodrammi serj scritti nel secolo XVIII. Milano, Soc. tip. dei classici italiani, 1822. 2 vols.

Radet, Edmond. Lully, homme d'affaires, propriétaire et musicien. Paris, L. Allison, [1891].

Radiciotti, Giuseppe. "L'arte di G. B. Pergolesi," RMI XVII (1910) 916–25.

—— "Due lettere inedite di G. Rossini e la sua definitiva partenza da Bologna," RMI XXXII (1925) 206–12.

—— "La famosa lettera al Cicognara non fu scritta dal Rossini," RMI XXX (1923) 401–407.

—— Gioacchino Rossini. Tivoli, A. Chicca, 1927. 3 vols.

—— Pergolesi. Milano, Fratelli Treves, [1935].

—— "Primi anni e studi di Gioacchino Rossini," RMI XXIV (1917) 145–72, 418–48.

—— "Il Signor Bruschino ed il Tancredi di G. Rossini," RMI XXVII (1920) 231–66.

Raeli, V. "The Bi-Centenary of Tommaso Traetta," The Chesterian VIII (1926–27) 217–23.

—— "Tommaso Traetta," Rivista nazionale di musica (March, 1927).

Raff, Joachim. Die Wagnerfrage. Braunschweig, Vieweg, 1854.

[Raguenet, François.] Défense du parallèle des Italiens et des François en ce qui regarde la musique et l'opéra. Paris, C. Barben, 1705.

—— Paralele des Italiens et des François en ce qui regarde la musique et les opéras. Paris, J. Moreau, 1602 [i.e. 1702]. Translated as: A Comparison between the French and Italian Musick and Opera's . . . to Which Is Added a Critical Discourse upon Opera's in England. London, W. Lewis, 1709. German translation with notes in Mattheson's Critica Musica (Hamburg, 1722).

Raimund, Ferdinand. Die Gesänge der Märchendramen in den ursprünglichen Vertonungen. Wien, A. Schrall, 1924. (Vol. VI of his collected works.)

Rau, Carl August. Loreto Vittori. München, Verlag für moderne Musik, [1916].

Rauber, A. Die Don Juan Sage im Lichte biologischer Forschung. Leipzig, Georgi, 1898.

Rauh, Adam. Heinrich Dorn als Opernkomponist. Neustadt a. d. Aisch, Schmidt, 1939.

Raupp, Wilhelm. Eugen d'Albert. Leipzig, Koehler & Amelang, [1930].

—— Max von Schillings. Hamburg, Hanseatische Verlagsanstalt, [1935].

[Ravel, Maurice.] See the two special issues of RM: April, 1925; December, 1938.

Rayner, Robert Macey. Wagner and *Die Meistersinger*. London, Oxford University Press, 1940.

Rebois, Henri. La Renaissance de Bayreuth de Richard Wagner à son fils Siegfried. Paris, Fischbacher, 1933. Contains "Lettres de Siegfried Wagner."

Redlich, Hans F. "Egon Wellesz," MQ XXVI (1940) 65–75.

—— "Monteverdi-Renaissance," *Atlantis* VIII (1936) 768.

—— "Notationsprobleme in Cl. Monteverdis *Incoronazione di Poppea*," *Acta musicologica* X (1938) 129–32.

—— "*L'oca del Cairo*," *Music Review* II (1941) 122–31.

—— "Sull' edizione moderna delle opere di Claudio Monteverdi," RassM VIII (1935) 23–41.

—— "Zur Bearbeitung von Monteverdis *Orfeo*," *Schweizerische Musikzeitung* LXXVI (1936) 37–42, 74–80.

Reese, Gustave. Music in the Middle Ages. New York, W. W. Norton, [1940].

Refardt, Edgar. "Die Musik der Basler Volksschauspiele des 16. Jahrhunderts," AfMw III (1921) 199.

Regli, Francesco. Dizionario biografico dei più celebri poeti ed artisti melodrammatici . . . in Italia dal 1800 al 1860. Torino, E. Dalmazzo, 1860.

Reiber, Kurt. Volk und Oper; das Volkstümliche in der deutschen romantischen Oper. Würzburg, Triltsch, 1942.

Reich, Willi. Alban Berg. Vienna, H. Reichner, [1937].

—— "Alban Berg's *Lulu*," MQ XXII (1936) 383–401.

—— A Guide to Alban Berg's *Wozzek*. [New York, League of Composers, 1931.]

—— "*Lulu*—the Text and Music," MMus XII, No. 3 (March–April, 1935) 103–11.

—— "Paul Hindemith," MQ XVII (1931) 486–96.

Reicha, Antoine. Art du compositeur dramatique. Paris, A. Farrenc, 1832. 2 vols.

Reichardt, Johann Friedrich. Ueber die deutsche comische Oper. Hamburg, C. E. Bohn, 1774.

Reichel, Eugen. "Gottsched und Johann Adolph Scheibe," SIMG II (1900–1901) 654–68.

Reiff, A. "Die Anfänge der Oper in Spanien, mit Textproben," *Spanien, Zeitschrift für Auslandskunde* Jahrgang I, Heft 3 (1919).

—— "Ein Katalog zu den Werken von Felipe Pedrell," AfMw III (1921) 86–97.

Reimers, Dagmar. Geschichte des Rigaer deutschen Theaters von 1782–1822. Posen, A. Meyer, 1942.

Reina, Calcedonio. Il cigno catanese: Bellini. Catania, "Etna," 1935.

Reinach, Théodore. La Musique grècque. Paris, Payot, 1926.

Reipschläger, Erich. Schubaur, Danzi und Poissl als Opernkomponisten. Berlin-Mariendorf, H. Wegner, 1911.

Rellstab, Ludwig. "Die Gestaltung der Oper seit Mozart," *Die Wissenschaft im 19. Jahrhundert* II (1856) 361.

[Rémond de Saintmard, Toussaint.] Reflexions sur l'opéra. La Haye, J. Neaulme, 1741.

Rendell, E. D. "Some Notes on Purcell's Dramatic Music, with Especial Reference to the *Fairy Queen*," M&L I (1920) 135–44.

Reuter, Fritz. "Die Entwicklung der Leipziger, insbesondere italienischen Oper bis zum siebenjährigen Krieg," ZfMw V (1922–23) 1–16.

——— Die Geschichte der deutschen Oper in Leipzig am Ende des 17. und am Anfang des 18. Jahrhunderts (1693–1720). Leipzig Dissertation, 1923.

"Revue der Revueen: zum 200. Geburtstag von Chr. W. Gluck," *Die Musik* XIII (1913–14) Qt. 4, 223–27, 276–78.

Revue Wagnérienne. Paris, 1885–88.

Reyer, i.e., Louis Etienne Ernest Rey. Notes de musique. Paris, Charpentier, 1875. 2d ed.

——— Quarante Ans de musique. Paris, Calmann Lévy, [1909].

Reyher, Paul. Les Masques anglais. Paris, Hachette, 1909.

Ricca, Vincenzo. Il centenario della *Norma;* Vincenzo Bellini. Catania, N. Gianotta, 1932.

Ricci, Corrado. Vita barocca. Milano, L. F. Cogliati, 1904.

Ricci, Vittorio. "Un melodramma ignoto della prima metà del '600: *Celio di Baccio Baglioni e di Niccolò Sapiti*," RMI XXXII (1925) 51–79.

Riccoboni, Luigi. Reflexions historiques et critiques sur les differens théâtres de l'Europe. Paris, J. Guérin, 1738.

Richard, Pierre. "Stradella et les Contarini; épisode des moeurs vénitiennes au XVIIe siècle," *Le Ménestrel* XXXII (1864–65), XXXIII (1865–66), *passim.*

Richebourg, Louisette. Contribution à l'histoire de la "Querelle des Bouffons." Paris, Nizet, 1937.

Richter, Carl Ludwig. Zdenko Fibich. Prag, F. A. Urbánek, 1900.

Riedel, Emil. Schuldrama und Theater. Hamburg, L. Voss, 1885.

Riedinger, Lothar. "Karl von Dittersdorf als Opernkomponist," SzMw II (1914) 212–349.

Rieger, Erwin. Offenbach und seine Wiener Schule. Wien, Wiener literarischer Anstalt, 1920.

Riehl, Wilhelm Heinrich. Musikalische Characterköpfe. Stuttgart, Cotta, 1899. 2 vols.
 Contains essays on Spontini, W. Müller, K. Kreutzer, Lortzing, and other opera composers of the early nineteenth century.

——— Zur Geschichte der romantischen Oper. Berlin, Weltgeist-Bücher, [1928].

Riemann, Hugo. "*Basso ostinato* und *Basso quasi ostinato;* eine Anregung," in *Festschrift Liliencron* (Leipzig, B&H, 1910) pp. 193–202.

Riesemann, Oskar von. Monographien zur russischen Musik. München, Drei Masken, 1923–26. 2 vols. Vol. II, Modest Petrowitsch Mussorgski, translated as: Moussorgsky. New York, Tudor, 1935.

Riesenfeld, Paul. "Die Romantik der neuen Sachlichkeit," Signale für die musikalische Welt LXXXVII (1929) 1075–78.

Riess, Otto. "Johann Abraham Peter Schulz' Leben," SIMG XV (1913–14) 169–270.

Rietzler, W. Hans Pfitzner und die deutsche Bühne. München, Piper, 1917.

Rimsky-Korsakov, Nikolai. My Musical Life. New York, Knopf, 1923. Translated from the revised second Russian edition.

Rinaldi, Mario. Antonio Vivaldi. Milano, Istituto d'alta cultura, [1943].

—— Musica e verismo. Roma, Fratelli de Santis, [1932].

—— "Valori drammatici e musicali del Simon Boccanegra di Verdi," RassM VIII (1935) 42–53.

Rinuccini, Giovanni Battista. Sulla musica e sulla poesia melodrammatica italiana del secolo XIX. Lucca, L. Guidotti, 1843.

Ritscher, Hugo. Die musikalische Deklamation in Lully's Opernrezitativen. Berlin Dissertation, 1925.

Ritter, A. G. "Die musikalischen Chöre des Chr. Th. Walliser zur Tragödie Andromeda," MfMg I (1869) 134–41.

Ritter, Frédéric Louis. Music in America. New York, Scribner, 1883.

Rivalta, Camillo. Giuseppe Sarti. Faenza, F. Lega, 1928.

Robert, Paul-Louis. "Correspondance de Boieldieu," RMI XIX (1912) 75–107; XXII (1915) 520–59.

Roberti, Giuseppe. "La musica in Italia nel secolo XVIII secondo le impressioni di viaggiatori stranieri," RMI VII (1900) 698–729; VIII (1901) 519–59.

Robinson, Percy. Handel and His Orbit. London, Sheratt & Hughes, 1908.

—— "Handel up to 1720: a New Chronology," M&L XX (1939) 55–63.

Rockstro, William Smyth. The Life of George Frederick Handel. London, Macmillan, 1883.

Roethe, Gustav. "Zum dramatischen Aufbau der Wagnerschen Meistersinger," Akademie der Wissenschaften, Berlin; Sitzungsberichte (Jahrgang 1919) pp. 673–708.

Röttger, Heinz. Das Formproblem bei Richard Strauss. Berlin, Junker & Dünnhaupt, 1937.

Rogers, Francis. "Adolphe Nourrit," MQ XXV (1939) 11–25.

—— "America's First Grand Opera Season," MQ I (1915) 93–101.

—— "Handel and Five Prima Donnas," MQ XXIX (1943) 214–24.

—— "Henriette Sontag in New York," MQ XXVIII (1942) 100–104.

—— "The Male Soprano," MQ V (1919) 413–25.

—— "Sophie Arnould (1740–1803)," MQ VI (1920) 57–61.

—— "Victor Maurel," MQ XII (1926) 580–601.

Rogge, Hendrik Cornelis. "De opera te Amsterdam," Oud Holland V (1887) 177, 241–62.

—— "De opvoeringen van Mozarts *Don Juan* in Nederland," *Tijdschrift der Vereeniging voor Nord-Nederlands Muziekgeschiedenis* II (1887) 237–77.

Rognoni, Luigi. Un' opera incompiuta di Mozart: *L' oca del Cairo;* a proposito di una ricostruzione. Milano, Bocca, 1937.

Rokseth, Yvonne. "Antonia Bembo, Composer to Louis XIV," MQ XXIII (1937) 147–67.

Rolandi, Ulderico. "*Il Ciclope:* dramma harmonica con musica di D. Lorenzo Ratti (Roma: 1628)," *Note d'archivio* X (1933) 253–60.

—— "Didascalie sceniche in un libretto dell' *Euridice* del Rinuccini (1600)," RMI XXXIII (1926) 21–27.

—— Il librettista del *Matrimonio segreto:* Giovanni Bertati. Trieste, C. Reali, 1926.

—— Quattro poeti ed un compositore alle prese . . . per un libretto d'opera (*Il bravo* di S. Mercadante). Roma, A. Marchesi, 1931.

Roland-Manuel. *See* Manuel, Roland.

Rolland, Romain. "L'Autobiographie d'un illustre oublié: Telemann," in *Voyage musical au pays du passé* (Paris, Eduard-Joseph, 1919).

—— "Le Dernier Opéra de Gluck: *Echo et Narcisse* (1779)," RHCM III (1903) 212–15.

—— "*L'Etranger* de Vincent d'Indy," RMI XI (1904) 129–39.

—— "Gluck, une révolution dramatique," *Revue de Paris* (1904) No. 3, pp. 736–72.

—— Haendel. Paris, F. Alcan, 1910. Translated as: Handel. London, K. Paul, 1916.

—— "Les Maîtres de l'opéra; recueil de musique inédite du XVIIe et du XVIIIe siècle," RHCM III (1903) 40–41, 178–79.

—— "Métastase, précurseur de Gluck," MM VIII, No. 4 (1912) 1–10.

—— Musiciens d'aujourd'hui. Paris, Hachette, 1912. 5th ed. Translated as: Musicians of Today. New York, Holt, 1915. 2d ed.

—— Musiciens d'autrefois. Paris, Hachette, 1924. 9th ed. Translated as: Some Musicians of Former Days. London, K. Paul, 1915.
Contains essays on Gluck, Grétry, Mozart, Lully, L. Rossi, and the beginnings of opera.

—— "Notes sur l' *Orfeo* de Luigi Rossi et sur les musiciens italiens à Paris, sous Mazarin," RHCM I (1901) 225–36, 363–72.

—— "L'Opéra populaire à Venise; Francesco Cavalli," MM II, No. 1 (1906) 61–70, 151–60.

—— "Les Origines de l'opéra et les travaux de M. Angelo Solerti," RHCM III (1903) 127–29, 280–82.

—— Les Origines du théâtre lyrique moderne; histoire de l'opéra en Europe avant Lully et Scarlatti. Paris, E. Thorin, 1895. New ed. Paris, E. de Boccard, 1931.

—— "La Première Représentation du *Sant Alessio* de Stefano Landi en 1632, à Rome, d'après le journal manuscrit de Jean Jacques Bouchard," RHCM II (1902) 29–36, 74–75.

Rolland, Romain (*Cont.*). "La Représentation d' *Orféo* à Paris et l'opposition religieuse et politique à l'opéra," RHCM I (1901) 10–17.

Roncaglia, Gino. L'ascensione creatrice di Giuseppe Verdi. Firenze, G. C. Sansoni, 1940.

—— Le composizioni di Alessandro Stradella esistenti presso la R. Biblioteca Estense di Modena. Milano, Bocca, 1942.

—— Il melodioso settecento italiano. Milano, Hoepli, 1935. Contains examples of music by Galuppi, Paisiello, Cimarosa, A. M. Bononcini, and T. Giordani.

—— La rivoluzione musicale italiana (secolo XVII). Milano, G. Bolla, 1928.

Ronga, Luigi. "Scarlatti fra due epoche," *Musicista* VII (1940) 57–61.

Roosevelt, Blanche. *See* Macchetta.

Rosa, Salvator. "La musica," in Mattheson, *Mithridat* (Hamburg, Geissler, 1749) pp. i–lvi, with German translation.

Roscoe, P. C. "Arne and *The Guardian Outwitted*," M&L XXIV (1943) 237–45.

Rosenfeld, Ernst. Johann Baptist Schenk als Opernkomponist. Vienna Dissertation, 1921.

Rosenfeld, Paul. Discoveries of a Music Critic. New York, Harcourt, Brace, [1936].

Rosenthal, Karl. "Ueber Volksformen bei Mozart; ein Beitrag zur Entwicklung der Vokalformen von 1760 bis 1790," SzMw XIV (1927) 5–32.

Rosenzweig, Alfred. Zur Entwicklungsgeschichte des Strauss'schen Musikdramas. Vienna Dissertation, 1923.

Ross, Erwin. Deutsche und italienische Gesangsmethode; erläutert auf Grund ihrer geschichtlichen Gegensätzlichkeit im achtzehnten Jahrhundert. Kassel, Bärenreiter, 1928.

[Rossi, Bastiano de'.] Descrizione dell' apparato e degli intermedi fatti per la commedia rappresentata in Firenze nelle nozze de' serenissimi Don Ferdinando Medici, e Madama Cristina di Loreno, gran duchi di Toscana. Firenze, A. Padouani, 1589.

Rossi-Doria, Gastone. "Opera," in *Enciclopedia italiana* XXV (1935) 390–404.
Valuable for the sixteenth century and Italian opera generally.

—— "Il teatro musicale di G. F. Malipiero," RassM II (1929) 354–64.

Rossmayer, Richard. Konradin Kreutzer als dramatischer Komponist. Vienna Dissertation, 1928.

Roth, Hermann. "Händels Ballettmusiken," *Neue Musik-Zeitung* XLIX (1928) 245–52.

—— "Händels Ballettoper *Ariodante;* zur deutscher Uraufführung," ZfMw IX (1926–27) 159–67.

—— "Zur Karlsruher Einrichtung von Händels *Tamerlan*," ZfMw V (1922–23) 380–82.

Rothschild, James, Baron de, ed. Le Mistère du Viel Testament. Paris, Firmin Didot, 1878–91. 6 vols.

Rousseau, Jean Jacques. Dictionnaire de musique. Amsterdam, M. M. Rey, 1768. Vol. II, Amsterdam, M. M. Rey, 1779. Translated as: A Complete Dictionary of Music. London, J. Murray, 1779.

—— Œuvres complètes. Paris, P. Dupont, 1823–26. 25 vols. Contains "Confessions," Vols. 14–16; writings on music, Vols. 11–13.

Roustan, Marius. Les Philosophes et la société française au XVIIIe siècle. Paris, Hachette, 1911.

Royer, Louis. Bibliographie stendhalienne. Paris, Champion, 1931.

Rubinstein, Anton. Erinnerungen aus fünfzig Jahren, 1839–1889. Leipzig, B. Senff, 1895. Translated from the Russian.

Rubsamen, Walter. "Political and Ideological Censorship of Opera," in *Papers of the American Musicological Society, Annual Meeting, 1941 . . . Edited by Gustave Reese* (Printed by the Society [cop. 1946]), pp. 30–42.

Rudhart, Franz Michael. Geschichte der Oper am Hofe zu München . . . Erster Theil: die italienische Oper von 1654–1787. Freising, F. Datterer, 1865.

Rühlmann, Franz. Richard Wagner und die deutsche Opernbuehne. Kiel Dissertation, 1925.

Rusca, Paolo. "Studi critici sul *Tristano e Isotta*," RMI XIX (1912) 286–314.

—— "Il *Tannhäuser* nella vita e nell' arte di Riccardo Wagner," RMI XXI (1914) 675–98.

Russo, Joseph Louis. Lorenzo da Ponte, Poet and Adventurer. New York, Columbia University Press, 1922.

Russo, Luigi. Metastasio. Bari, G. Laterza, 1921.

Sabaneiev, Leonid Leonidovitch. Geschichte der russischen Musik. Leipzig, B&H, 1926.

—— Modern Russian Composers. Translated by Joffe. New York, International Publishers, [1927].

—— "Remarks on the Leitmotif," M&L XIII (1932) 200–206.

Sabbatini, Nicola. Pratica di fabricar scene, e machine ne' teatri. Ravenna, Pietro de Paoli, 1638. New ed. German ed. as: Anleitung Dekorationen und Theatermaschinen herzustellen. Weimar, Gesellschaft der Bibliophilen, 1926. Ed. by Willi Flemming.

Sacchi, Giovenale. Vita del cavaliere Don Carlo Broschi. Vinegia, Coleti, 1784.

Sachs, Curt. "Die Ansbacher Hofkapelle unter Markgraf Johann Friedrich (1672–86)," SIMG XI (1909–10) 105–37.

—— Die Musik der Antike. Potsdam, Athenaion, [1928].

—— Musik und Oper am kurbrandenburgischen Hofe. Berlin, J. Bard, 1910.

—— "The Road to Major," MQ XXIX (1943).

Sachs, Edwin O., and E. A. E. Woodrow. Modern Opera Houses and Theatres. London, B. T. Batsford, 1896–98. 3 vols.

Saint-Cyr, Mario. Musicisti italiani contemporanei . . . prima serie.
Roma, De Santis, [1932?].

Saint-Evremond, Charles de Marguetel de St. Denis, Seigneur de. Œuvres
meslées. Londres, Tonson, 1709. 3 vols. 2d ed. Contains "Sur les opera,"
II, 214–22; "Les Opera, comedie," II, 223–92; "A Monsieur Lulli," III,
106–107.

Saint-Foix, Georges de. "La Conclusion de l'ouverture de Don Juan," RdM
V (1924) 169–72.

—— "Le Livret de Così fan tutte," RdM XI (1930) 43–97.

—— "Les Maîtres de l'opéra bouffe dans la musique de chambre à Londres," RMI XXXI (1924) 507–26.

—— "Le Théâtre à Salzbourg en 1779–80," RdM XVI (1935) 193–204.

—— "Sammartini et les chanteurs de son temps," RMI XLIII (1939) 357–
63.

St. John-Brenon, Algernon. "Giuseppe Verdi," MQ II (1916) 130–62.

Saint-Saëns, Charles Camille. Portraits et souvenirs. Paris, Société d'édition
artistique, [1900]. Translated as: Musical Memories. Boston, Small, Maynard, [1919].

Salazar, Adolfo. Juan del Encina y la música en el primitivo teatro español.
Mexico, D.F., 1940. (Bóletin de musicologia y folklore, January, 1940.)

—— La música contemporánea en España. Madrid, Ediciones La Nave,
[1930].

——La música en el primitivo teatro español, anterior a Lope de Vega y
Calderón. México, A. Salazar, [1942?].

Salburg, Edith, Gräfin. Ludwig Spohr. Leipzig, Koehler & Amelang, [1936].

Salcedo, Angel S. Tomás Bretón. Madrid, Imprenta clásica española, 1924.

Saldívar, Gabriel. Historia de la música en México (épocas precortesiana
y colonial). Mexico, "Cvltvra," 1934.

Saldoni, Baltasar. Diccionario biográfico-bibliográfico de efemérides de
músicos españoles. Madrid, D. Antonio Perez Dubrull, 1868–81. 4 vols.

Salerno, F. Le donne Pucciniane. Palermo, A. Trimarchi, 1929.

Salvioli, Giovanni. Bibliografia universale del teatro drammatico italiano.
Volume primo. Venezia, [1894–] 1903. A-Czarina only; no more published.

[——] Saggio bibliografico relativo ai melodrammi di Felice Romani [per]
Luigi Lianovosani [pseud.]. Milano, Ricordi, [1878].

[——] Serie cronologica delle opere teatrali, cantate ed oratori del maestro
Giovanni Comm. Pacini. Milano, Ricordi, 1875.

[——] I teatri musicali di Venezia nel secolo XVII. Milano, Ricordi, [1879].

Salza, Abd-el-kader. "Drammi inediti di Giulio Rospigliosi," RMI XIV
(1907) 473–508.

Samazeuilh, Gustave. Paul Dukas. Paris, A. Durand, 1913.

Saminsky, Lazare. *"Jürg Jenatch,"* MMus VII, No. 1 (December, 1929–January, 1930) 37–39.

—— "More about *Faustus,"* MMus V, No. 1 (November–December, 1927) 38–39.

—— Music of Our Day. New York, T. Y. Crowell, [1939]. New ed.

Sandberger, Adolf. "Beziehungen der Königin Christine von Schweden zur italienischen Oper und Musik, insbesondere zu M. A. Cesti; mit einem Anhang über Cestis Innsbrucker Aufenthalt," *Bulletin de la Société union musicologique* V (1925) 121–73.

—— "Rossiniana," ZIMG IX (1907–1908) 336–45.

—— "Tommaso Traëtta," DTB XIV, No. 1 (1913) xii–xc.

—— "Zu den literarischen Quellen von Richard Wagners *Tannhäuser,"* in *Gedenkboek* . . . *Scheurleer* ('s Gravenhage, Nijhoff, 1925) pp. 267–69.

—— "Zur Geschichte der Oper in Nürnberg in der 2. Hälfte des 17. und zu Anfang des 18. Jahrhunderts," AfMw I (1918) 84–107.

—— "Zur venezianischen Oper," JMP XXXI (1924) 61–70; XXXII (1925) 53–63.

Sanders, Paul F. Moderne nederlandsche Componisten. s'Gravenhage, Kruseman, [1930].

Sartori, Claudio. "Franco Faccio e venti anni di spettacoli di fiera al Teatro Grande di Brescia," RMI XLII (1938) 64–77, 188–203, 350–62.

Sassi, Romualdo. "Lettere inedite di Gaspare Spontini," *Note d'Archivio* XII (1935) 165–83.

Saunders, William. "The American Opera," M&L XIII (1932) 147–55.

—— "National Opera, Comparatively Considered," MQ XIII (1927) 72–84.

Saussine, Henri de. "L'Harmonie Bellinienne," RMI XXVII (1920) 477–82.

Savaron, Jean. Traitté contre les masques. Paris, Perier, 1611. 3d ed.

Saviotti, Alfredo. "Feste e spettacoli nel seicento," *Giornale storico della letteratura italiana* XLI (1903) 542–77.

Scarlatti, Gli: Alessandro, Francesco, Pietro, Domenico, Giuseppe; note e documenti sulla vita e sulle opere. Siena, Ticci Poligrafico, 1940.

Schäfer, Karl. Das Opernschaffen Siegfried Wagners. Vienna Dissertation, 1936.

Schaeffner, André. Igor Stravinsky. Paris, Rieder, [1931].

Schall, Heinrich. Beiträge zur Entwicklungsgeschichte der Oper mit besonderer Berücksichtigung der deutschen in neuerer Zeit. Bonn, J. Bach, 1898.

Schatz, Albert. "Giovanni Bertati," VfMw V (1889) 231–71.

Scheibe, Johann Adolf. Critischer Musikus. Leipzig, B. C. Breitkopf, 1745. New ed.

Schemann. Ludwig. Cherubini. Stuttgart, Deutsche Verlags-Anstalt, 1925.

Schemann, Ludwig (*Cont.*). "Cherubinis dramatisches Erstlingsschaffen," *Die Musik* XVII (June, 1925) 641–47.

Schenk, Erich. Johann Strauss. Potsdam, Athenaion, 1940.

Schenk, Johann Baptist. ["Autobiographische Skizze"], SzMw XI (1924) 75–85.

Scherillo, Michele. L'opera buffa napoletana durante il settecento; storia letteraria. [Milano], R. Sandron, [1917]. 2d ed. First published as: Storia letteraria dell' opera buffa napolitana dalle origini al principio del secolo XIX. Napoli, R. Università, 1883.

——— "La prima commedia musicale a Venezia," *Giornale storico della letteratura italiana* I (1883) 230–59.

Schering, Arnold. Aufführungspraxis alter Musik. Leipzig, Quelle & Meyer, 1931.

——— Geschichte des Instrumentalkonzerts. Leipzig, B&H, 1927. 2d ed.

——— Geschichte des Oratoriums. Leipzig, B&H, [1911].

——— Musikgeschichte Leipzigs. Leipzig, Kistner & Siegel, 1926. 3 vols.

——— "Zur Geschichte des begleiteten Sologesangs im 16. Jahrhundert," ZIMG XIII (1911–12) 190–96.

——— "Zur Geschichte des italienischen Oratoriums im 17. Jahrhundert," JMP X (1903) 31–44.

——— "Zwei Singspiele des Sperontes," ZfMw VII (1924–25) 214–20.

Scheurleer, D. F. "Ein marionetten-theater te Amsterdam 1696," *Tijdschrift der Vereeniging voor Noord Nederlands muziekgeschiedenis* IX, No. 3 (1912) 147–53.

Schiedermair, Ludwig. "Die Anfänge der Münchener Oper," SIMG V (1903–1904) 442–68.

——— "Eine Autobiographie Pietro Generalis," in *Festschrift Liliencron* (Leipzig, B&H, 1910) pp. 250–53.

——— Bayreuther Festspiele im Zeitalter des Absolutismus. Leipzig, C. F. Kahnt, 1908.

——— Beiträge zur Geschichte der Oper um die Wende des 18. und 19. Jahrhunderts. Leipzig, B&H, 1907–1910. 2 vols.

——— "Briefe Johann Philipp Käfers," in *Festschrift Adolf Sandberger* (München, Zierfuss, 1918) pp. 121–28.

——— "Briefe . . . an Simon Mayr," SIMG VIII (1906–1907) 615–29.

——— ed. Die Briefe W. A. Mozarts und seiner Familie. München, G. Müller, 1914.

——— Die deutsche Oper. Leipzig, Quelle & Meyer, 1930. 2d ed., Bonn, Dümmler, 1940.

——— "Die Oper an den badischen Höfen des 17. und 18. Jahrhunderts," SIMG XIV (1912–13) 191–207, 369–449, 510–50.

——— "I sensali del teatro," SIMG VI (1904–1905) 589–94.

——— "Ueber Beethovens *Leonore*," ZIMG VIII (1906–1907) 115–26.

——— "Ein unbekannter Opernentwurf für Beethoven," *Neues Beethoven Jahrbuch* VII (1937) 32–36.

—— "Zur Geschichte der frühdeutschen Oper," JMP XVII (1910) 29–43.

Schild, M. Die Musikdramen Ottavio Rinuccinis. Würzburg, Mayr, 1933.

Schletterer, Hans Michael. Das deutsche Singspiel von seinen ersten Anfängen bis auf die neueste Zeit. Leipzig, B&H, [1863?].

—— Die Entstehung der Oper. Nördlingen, C. H. Beck, 1873.

—— "Giovanni Battista Pergolesi," in Waldersee, *Sammlung musikalischer Vorträge* (Leipzig, B&H, 1879–98) II, 139–78.

—— "Ludwig Spohr," in Waldersee, *Sammlung musikalischer Vorträge* (Leipzig, B&H, 1879–98) III, 127–62.

—— "Die Opernhäuser Neapels," MfMg XIV (1882) 175–81, 183–89; XV (1883) 12–19.

—— Vorgeschichte und erste Versuche der französischen Oper. Berlin, R. Damköhler, 1885. (Vol. III of his Studien zur Geschichte der französischen Musik.)

—— Zur Geschichte dramatischer Musik und Poesie in Deutschland. Augsburg, Schlosser, 1863.

Schlifstein, S. "On *War and Peace*," MMus XX, No. 3 (March–April, 1943) 185–87.

Schloezer, Boris Fedorovich. Igor Stravinsky. Paris, C. Aveline, 1929.

—— "The Operatic Paradox," MMus IV, No. 1 (November–December, 1926) 3–8.

Schmid, Anton. Christoph Willibald Ritter von Gluck. Leipzig, F. Fleischer, 1854.

Schmid, Otto. Carl Maria von Weber und seine Opern in Dresden. [Dresden?, Selbstverlag des Verfassers, 1922.]

—— Die Heimstätten der sächsischen Landestheater. Dresden, A. Waldheim, [19—?].

—— Richard Wagner; Gedanken über seine Ideale und seine Sendung. Langensalza, Beyer, 1920.

—— Das sächsische Königshaus in selbstschöpferischer musikalischer Bethätigung (Musik am sächsischen Hofe). Leipzig, B&H, 1900.

Schmidt, Friedrich. Das Musikleben der bürgerlichen Gesellschaft Leipzigs im Vormärz (1815–1848). Langensalza, Beyer, 1912.

Schmidt, Gustav Friedrich. "Die älteste deutsche Oper in Leipzig am Ende des 17. und Anfang des 18. Jahrhunderts," in *Festschrift Adolf Sandberger* (München, Zierfuss, 1918) pp. 209–57.

—— Die frühdeutsche Oper und die musikdramatische Kunst Georg Caspar Schürmann's. Regensburg, G. Bosse, 1933. 2 vols.

—— "Johann Wolfgang Francks Singspiel *Die drey Töchter Cecrops*," AfMf IV (1939) 257–316.

—— Neue Beiträge zur Geschichte der Musik und des Theaters am Herzoglichen Hofe zu Braunschweig-Wolfenbüttel. München, W. Berntheisel, 1929.

Schmidt, Gustav Friedrich (*Cont.*). "Zur Geschichte, Dramaturgie und Statistik der frühdeutschen Oper (1627–1750)," ZfMw V (1922–23) 582–97, 642–65; VI (1923–24) 129–57, 496–530.

Schmidt, Heinrich. Johann Mattheson, ein Förderer der deutschen Tonkunst, im Lichte seiner Werke. Leipzig, B&H, 1897.

Schmidt, Immanuel. "Ueber Ben Jonson's Maskenspiele," *Archiv für das Studium der neueren Sprachen* XXVII (1860) 55–90.

Schmidt, Leopold. Zur Geschichte der Märchenoper. Halle a.d.S., O. Hendel, 1895.

Schmidt, Ludwig. "Briefe von und über Carl Maria von Weber," ZIMG III (1901–1902) 93–99.

Schmitz, Arnold. "Monodien der Kölner Jesuiten aus der ersten Hälfte des 17. Jahrhunderts," ZfMw IV (1921–22) 266–85.

Schmitz, Eugen. "Antonio Brunelli als Monodist," ZIMG XI (1909–10) 383–86.

—— "Eugen d'Albert als Opernkomponist," *Hochland* VI, No. 2 (1909) 464–71.

—— Geschichte der weltlichen Solo-Kantate. Leipzig, B&H, 1914.

—— "Louis Spohr's Jugendoper *Alruna*," ZIMG XIII (1911–12) 293–99.

—— Richard Strauss als Musikdramatiker. München, Lewy, 1907.

—— "Zu Mozarts *Bastien und Bastienne*," *Hochland* IX, No. 2 (1912) 607–11.

—— "Zur Frühgeschichte der lyrischen Monodie Italiens im 17. Jahrhundert," JMP XVIII (1911) 35–48.

—— "Zur Geschichte des italienischen Continuo-Madrigals im 17. Jahrhundert," SIMG XI (1909–10) 509–28.

—— "Zur Geschichte des Leitmotivs in der romantischen Oper," *Hochland* IV, No. 2 (1907) 329–43.

—— "Zur musikgeschichtlichen Bedeutung der Harsdörfferschen 'Frauenzimmergesprächspiele'," in *Festschrift . . . Liliencron* (Leipzig, B&H, 1910) pp. 254–77.

Schnapp, Friedrich. "Robert Schumann's Plan for a Tristan-Opera," MQ X (1924) 485–91.

Schneider, Constantin. "Franz Heinrich von Biber als Opernkomponist," AfMw VIII (1926) 281–347.

—— "Die Oratorien und Schuldramen Anton Cajetan Adlgassers," SzMw XVIII (1931).

Schneider, Louis. Les Maîtres de l'opérette française: Offenbach. Paris, Perrin, 1923.

—— Massenet. Paris, L. Carteret, 1908. Revised ed., without illustrations and documents, Paris, Charpentier, 1926.

—— Un Précurseur de la musique italienne aux XVIe et XVIIe siècles: Claudio Monteverdi. Paris, Perrin, 1921.

Schneider, Ludwig. Geschichte der Oper und des königlichen Opernhauses in Berlin. Berlin, Duncker & Humblot, 1852.

Schneider, Max. Die Anfänge des Basso Continuo und seiner Bezifferung. Leipzig, B&H, 1918.

—— "Die Begleitung des Secco-Rezitativs um 1750," *Gluck-Jahrbuch* III (1917) 88–107.

—— "Zur Geschichte des begleiteten Sologesangs," *Festschrift Hermann Kretzschmar zum 70. Geburtstage überreicht von Kollegen, Schülern, und Freunden.* (Leipzig, C. F. Peters, 1918), pp. 138–40.

Schnerich, Alfred. "Wie sahen die ersten Vorstellungen von Mozart's *Don Juan* aus?" ZIMG XII (1910–11) 101–108.

Schoenemann, Otto. "Der Sündenfall und Marienklage; zwei niederdeutsche Schauspiele," MfMg VII (1875) 129–39, 145–57.

Scholes, Percy. The Puritans and Music in England and New England. London, Oxford University Press, 1934.

Scholz, Hans. "Hektor Berlioz zum 50. Todestage," ZfMw I (1918–19) 328–51.

—— Johann Sigismund Kusser. Leipzig, Röder, 1911.

Schopenhauer, Arthur. Sämmtliche Werke. Leipzig, Brockhaus, 1922–23. 6 vols.

Schott, Eberhardt. Zur Soziologie der Bühne; die Oper im Jahrzehnte 1901/02–1910/11. Typescript only.

Schramm, Erich. "Goethe und Diderots Dialog *Rameaus Neffe*," ZfMw XVI (1934) 294–307.

Schreiber, Irmtraud. Dichtung und Musik der deutschen Opernarien 1680–1700. Bottrop i. W., Postberg, 1934.

Schubert, Karl. Spontinis italienische Schule. Strassburg, Heitz, [1932].

Schünemann, Georg. Geschichte der deutschen Schulmusik. Leipzig, Kistner & Siegel, 1928.

—— "Mendelssohns Jugendopern," ZfMw V (1922–23) 506–45.

—— "Eine neue *Tristan*-Handschrift zu Richard Wagners 125. Geburtstag," AfMf III (1938) 129–37.

Schütze, Johannn Friedrich. Hamburgische Theatergeschichte. Hamburg, J. P. Treder, 1794.

Schuh, Willi. Othmar Schoeck. Zürich, Hug, [1934].

Schultz, William Eben. Gay's *Beggar's Opera;* Its Content, History, and Influence. New Haven, Yale University Press, 1923.

—— "The Music of the *Beggar's Opera* in Print, 1728–1923," MTNA XIX (1934) 87–99.

Schulze, Walter. Die Quellen der Hamburger Oper (1678–1738). Hamburg-Oldenburg, G. Stalling, 1938.

Schuré, Edouard. Le Drame musicale. Paris, Didier, 1886. 2 vols.

Schwan, Wilhelm Bernhard. Die opernästhetischen Theorien der deutschen klassischen Dichter. Bonn Dissertation, 1928.

Schwartz, Rudolf. "Zur Geschichte der liederlosen Zeit in Deutschland," JMP XX (1913) 13–27.

Schwarz, Max. "Johann Christian Bach," SIMG II (1900–1901) 401–54.

Schwerké, I. "Paul Dukas; a Brief Appreciation," MQ XIV (1928) 403–12.

Schwietering, Julius. "Ueber den liturgischen Ursprung des mittelalterlichen geistlichen Spiels," *Zeitschrift für deutsche Altertum* LXII (1925) 1–20.

Scudo, Pierre. Le Chevalier Sarti. Paris, Hachette, 1857. (Previously in *Revue des deux mondes*, 1854–56.)

—— "Pergolèse et *La serva padrona*," *Revue des deux mondes* XXXII, No. 41 (September 1, 1862) 226–30.

Scuola veneziana, La (secoli XVI–XVIII), note e documenti. Siena, Libreria editrice Ticci, 1941. Contains articles on Cavalli, G. B. Bassani, Caldara, and Marcello.

Sear, H. G. "Charles Dibdin: 1745–1814," M&L XXVI (1945) 61–65.

Segnitz, Eugen. "Anselmo Feuerbach e Riccardo Wagner," RMI XIII (1906) 437–50.

—— Goethe und die Oper in Weimar. Langensalza, Beyer, 1908.

—— "La musica nel romanticismo tedesco," RMI XV (1908) 500–18.

Seidl, Roberto. Carlos Gomes. Rio de Janeiro, [Imprensa moderna], 1935.

Seiffert, Max. "J.A.P. Schultz' 'dänische' Oper," AfMw I (1918–19) 422–23.

—— "Zur Biographie Joh. Adolph Hasse's," SIMG VII (1905–1906) 129–31.

Seilhamer, George Overcash. History of the American Theatre. Philadelphia, Globe Printing House, 1888–91. 3 vols.

Seldes, Gilbert. "Delight in the Theatre," MMus XI, No. 3 (March–April, 1934) 138–41.

—— "Jazz Opera or Ballet?" MMus III, No. 2 (January–February, 1926) 10–16.

Seligmann, Herbert Wolff. Beiträge zur Geschichte der Bühne der opera seria. Bonn Dissertation, 1924.

Selva, Blanche. Déodat de Séverac. Paris, Delagrave, 1930.

Semler, Isabel Parker. Horatio Parker; a Memoir for His Grandchildren Compiled from Letters and Papers. New York, Putnam, 1942.

Seré, Octave. Musiciens français d'aujourd'hui. Paris, Mercure de France, 1911.

Serov, Victor Ilyitch. Dmitri Shostakovitch. New York, Knopf, 1943.

Servières, Georges. Edouard Lalo. Paris, H. Laurens, [1925].

—— Emmanuel Chabrier. Paris, F. Alcan, 1912.

—— Gabriel Fauré. Paris, H. Laurens, 1930.

—— La Musique française moderne. Paris, G. Havard, 1897.

—— "Le 'Wagnerisme' de C. Saint-Saëns," RMI XXX (1923) 223–44.

Settecento italiano, Il. Milan-Roma, Bestetti & Tumminelli, 1932. 2 vols.

Sharp, Geoffrey. "*Don Giovanni*: Some Observations," *Music Review* IV (1943) 45–52.

Shaw, George Bernard. London Music in 1888–89 as Heard by Corno di Bassetto. New York, Dodd, Mead, 1937.

—— The Perfect Wagnerite. New York, Brentano's, 1909.

Shedlock, J. S. "The Correspondence between Wagner and Liszt," PMA XIV (1888) 119–43.

Sherwin, Oscar. Mr. Gay; Being a Picture of the Life and Times of the Author of the *Beggar's Opera.* New York, John Day, 1929.

Shostakovitch, Dmitri. "My Opera, *Lady Macbeth of Mtzensk,*" MMus XII, No. 1 (November–December, 1934) 23–30.

Sievers, Heinrich. Die lateinischen liturgischen Osterspiele der Stiftskirche St. Blasien zu Braunschweig. Wolfenbüttel, Georg Kallmeyer, 1936.

—— 250 Jahre Braunschweigisches Staatstheater, 1690–1940. Braunschweig, Appelhans, 1941.

Silbert, Doris. "Francesca Caccini, Called La Cecchina," MQ XXXII (1946) 50–62.

Silin, Charles I. Benserade and His Ballets de Cour. Baltimore, Johns Hopkins Press, 1940.

Silva, G. Silvestri. Illustri musicisti calabresi: Leonardo Vinci. Genova, Tip. Nazionale, [1935].

Silva, Lafayette. Historia do teatro brasileiro. Rio de Janeiro, Ministério da educaçiõ e saude, 1938.

Simon, Alicja. "Grétry au Théâtre national de Varsovie," in *International Society for Musical Research, First Congress, Report* (Burnham, Plainsong and Medieval Music Society, [1930]).

Simon, James. Faust in der Musik. Leipzig, C. F. W. Siegel, [1906].

Sincero, Dino. *"Boris Godounow* al teatro Alla Scala di Milano," RMI XVI (1909) 385–94.

—— "Da *Tannhäuser* a *Parsifal,*" RMI XXI (1914) 122–26.

Sittard, Josef. "Gioachimo Antonio Rossini," in Waldersee, *Sammlung musikalischer Vorträge* (Leipzig, B&H, 1879–98) IV, 385–433.

—— "Reinhard Keiser in Württemberg," MfMg XVIII (1886) 3–12.

—— Zur Geschichte der Musik und des Theaters am württembergischen Hofe. Stuttgart, W. Kohlhammer, 1890–91. 2 vols.

Skilton, Charles Sanford. "American Opera," MTNA XX (1925) 112–18.

Slanina, Ernst Alfred. Die Sakralszenen der deutschen Oper des frühen 19. Jahrhunderts. Bochum-Langendreer, Pöppinghaus, 1935.

Slawik, Friedrich. Die Jugendopern Richard Wagners und ihre Beziehungen zu den späteren Meisterwerken. Vienna Dissertation, 1928.

Slonimsky, Nicolas. Music of Latin America. New York, Thomas Y. Crowell, 1945.

—— Music Since 1900. New York, Norton, [1937].

—— "Sergei Prokofiev; His Status in Soviet Music," *American Quarterly on the Soviet Union* II, No. 1 (1939) 37–44.

Smareglia, Ariberto. Vita ed arte di Antonio Smareglia. [Lugano, C. Mazzuconi, 1932.]

Smareglia, Mario, compiler. Antonio Smareglia nella storia del teatro melodrammatico italiano dell' ottocento attraverso critiche e scritti raccolti da Mario Smareglia. Pola, Smareglia, [1934].

Smith, David Stanley. "A Study of Horatio Parker," MQ XVI (1930) 153–69.

Smits van Waesberghe, Jos. Muziek en drama in de Middeleeuwen. Amsterdam, Bigot & Van Rossum, 1942.

Smythe, Dame Ethel. Impressions That Remained; Memoirs. New York, Knopf, 1946. First published London, New York [etc.], Longmans, Green, 1919. 2 vols.

Soleinne, Martineau de. Bibliothèque dramatique. Paris, Administration de l'Alliance des arts, 1843–45. 7 vols. *See also:* Tableau générale du catalogue (Paris, Administration de l'Alliance des arts, 1845); and Table des pièces du théâtre décrites dans le catalogue . . . par Charles Brunet publiée par Henri de Rothschild (Paris, D. Morgand, 1914).

Solerti, Angelo. Gli albori del melodramma. Milano, R. Sandron, [1905]. 3 vols.

—— "Un balletto musicato da Claudio Monteverdi," RMI XI (1904) 24–34.

—— ed. Ferrara e la corte Estense nella seconda metà del secolo decimosesto; i discorsi di Annibale Romei, gentiluomo ferrarese. Città di Castello, S. Lapi, 1891.

—— "Feste musicale alla Corte di Savoia nella prima metà del secolo XVII," RMI XI (1904) 675–724.

—— Laura Guidiccioni ed Emilio de' Cavalieri; i primi tentativi del melodramma," RMI IX (1902) 797–829.

—— "Lettere inedite sulla musica di Pietro della Valle a G.B. Doni ed una Veglia drammatica-musicale del medesimo," RMI XII (1905) 271–338.

—— Musica, ballo e drammatica alla corte Medicea dal 1600 al 1637. Firenze, R. Bemporad, 1905.

—— compiler and ed. Le origini del melodramma; testimonianze dei contemporanei. Torino, Fratelli Bocca, 1903.

—— "Precedenti del melodramma," RMI X (1903) 207–33, 466–84.

—— "Primi saggi del melodramma giocoso," RMI XII (1905) 814–38; XIII (1906) 91–112.

—— "I rappresentazioni musicali di Venezia dal 1571 al 1605," RMI IX (1902) 503–58.

—— "Un viaggio in Francia di Giulio Caccini," RMI X (1903) 707–11.

—— Vita di Torquato Tasso. Torino, Roma, E. Loescher, 1895. 3 vols.

Solvay, Lucien. L'Evolution théâtrale. Bruxelles and Paris, G. van Oest, 1922. 2 vols.

—— Notice sur Jean Blockx. Bruxelles, Hayez, 1920.

Somerset, H. V. F. "Giovanni Paisiello," M&L XVIII (1937) 20–35.

—— "Jean Jacques Rousseau as a Musician," M&L XVII (1936) 37–46, 218–24.

Somiglio, Carlo. "Del teatro reale d'opera in Monaco di Baviera e del suo repertorio," RMI V (1898) 721–53.

Sommer, Hans. "Die Oper *Ludwig der Fromme* von Georg Caspar Schürmann," MfMg XIV (1882) 48–51, 53–55.

—— "Zur Schürmann'schen Oper *Ludovicus Pius*," MfMg XXIV (1892) 137–39.

Sondheimer, Robert. "Gluck in Paris," ZfMw V (1922–23) 165–75.

Sonette, Jean Jacques, pseud. *See* Goudar, Ange.

Sonneck, Oscar George Theodore. A Bibliography of Early Secular American Music (Eighteenth Century). Washington, D.C., The Library of Congress, Music Division, 1945.

—— "Ciampi's *Bertoldo, Bertoldino e Cacasenno* and Favart's *Ninette à la cour*," SIMG XII (1911) 525–64.

—— "*Dafne*, the First Opera," SIMG XV (1913–14) 102–10.

—— "A Description of Alessandro Striggio and Francesco Corteccia's Intermedi *Psyche and Amore*, 1565," MA III (1911) 40.

—— "Die drei Fassungen des Hasse'schen *Artaserse*," SIMG XIV (1912–13) 226–42.

—— Early Concert Life in America. Leipzig, B&H, 1907.

—— Early Opera in America. New York, G. Schirmer, [1915].

—— "Foot-note to the Bibliographical History of Grétry's Operas," in *Gedenkboek . . . Scheurleer* ('s Gravenhage, Nijhoff, 1925) pp. 321–36.

—— Francis Hopkinson, the First American Poet-Composer. Washington, D.C., Printed for the Author by H. L. McQueen, 1905.

—— "*Il Giocatore*," MA IV (1912–13) 160–74.

—— "Heinrich Heine's Musical Feuilletons," MQ VIII (1923) 119–59, 273–95, 435–68.

—— Miscellaneous Studies in the History of Music. New York, Macmillan, 1921. Contains "*Caractacus* Not Arne's *Caractacus*," "Ciampi's *Bertoldo, Bertoldino e Cacasenno* and Favart's *Ninette à la cour;* a Contribution to the History of the Pasticcio," "A Description of Alessandro Striggio and Francesco Corteggia's Intermedi: *Psyche and Amor*, 1565," "Early American Opera," and "A Preface."

—— "La nuova rappresentazione del *D. Giovanni* di Mozart a Monaco," RMI III (1896) 741–55.

Sooper, Frances O. "The Music of Dittersdorf," M&L XI (1930) 141–45.

Soriano Fuertes, Mariano. Historia de la musica española. Madrid, Martin y Salazar; Barcelona, Narciso Ramírez, 1856–59. 4 vols.

Soubies, Albert. Histoire de l'opéra-comique; la seconde Salle Favart 1840–[1887]. Paris, E. Flammarion, 1892–93. 2 vols.

—— Histoire du théâtre-lyrique 1851–1870. Paris, Fischbacher, 1899.

—— Le Théâtre-italien de 1801 à 1913. Paris, Fischbacher, 1913.

Soubies, Albert, and Henri de Curzon. Documents inédits sur le *Faust* de Gounod. Paris, Fischbacher, 1912.

Specht, Richard. E. N. v. Reznicek. Leipzig, E. P. Tal, 1923.

—— Giacomo Puccini. Berlin-Schöneberg, M. Hesse, [1931]. English translation: New York, Knopf, 1933.

Specht, Richard (*Cont.*). Julius Bittner. München, Drei Masken, 1921.

—— Richard Strauss, *Die Frau ohne Schatten;* thematische Einführung. Berlin, Fürstner, 1919.

—— Richard Strauss und sein Werk. Leipzig, P. Tal, 1921. 2 vols.

—— Das Wiener Operntheater; von Dingelstedt bis Schalk und Strauss. Wien, P. Knepler, 1919.

Spectator, The (London, 1711–1714). London and Toronto, J. M. Dent, 1919–26. 4 vols.

Speer, Daniel. Grund-richtiger, kurtz, leicht und nöthiger Unterricht der musikalischen Kunst. Ulm, G. W. Kühnen, 1687.

Spencer, H. "Meyerbeer," RMI X (1903) 126–28.

Speziale, G. "Ancora per Paisiello," RassM IV (1931) 1–16.

Spinelli, Alessandro Giuseppe. Bibliografia goldoniana. Milano, Dumolard, 1884.

Spinner, Leopold. Das Rezitativ in der romantischen Oper bis Wagner. Vienna Dissertation, 1931.

Spitta, Philipp. "Die älteste Faust-Oper und Goethe's Stellung zur Musik," in his *Zur Musik* (Berlin, Paetel, 1892) pp. 199–234.

—— "Jessonda," in his *Zur Musik* (Berlin, Paetel, 1892) pp. 237–66.

—— Johann Sebastian Bach. Leipzig, B&H, 1930. 4th ed. 2 vols.

—— "Rinaldo di Capua," VfMw III (1877) 92–121.

Spitz, Charlotte. "Eine anonyme italienische Oper um die Wende des 17. zum 18. Jahrhundert," ZfMw II (1919–20) 232–35.

—— Antonio Lotti in seiner Bedeutung als Opernkomponist. Borna–Leipzig, Noske, 1918.

—— "Die Entwickelung des 'stilo recitativo'," AfMw III (1921) 237–44.

—— "Die Opern *Ottone* von G. F. Händel (London 1722) und *Teofane* von A. Lotti (Dresden 1719); ein Stilvergleich," in *Festschrift Adolf Sandberger* (München, Zierfuss, 1918) pp. 265–71.

Spohr, Louis. Louis Spohr's Selbstbiographie. Cassel and Göttingen, Wigand, 1860–61. 2 vols. English translation: London, Reeves & Turner, 1878.

Spontini, G. "Lettere inedite," *Note d'archivio* IX (1932) 23–40.

Squire, William Barclay. "Gluck's London Operas," MQ I (1915) 397–409.

—— "An Index of Tunes in the Ballad-Operas," MA II (1910–1911) 1–17.

—— "J. W. Franck in England," MA III (1911–1912) 181–90.

—— "The Music of Shadwell's *Tempest*," MQ VII (1921) 565–78.

—— "An Opera under Innocent X," in *Gedenkboek . . . Scheurleer* ('s Gravenhage, Nijhoff, 1925) pp. 65–71.

—— "Purcell's Dramatic Music," SIMG V (1903–1904) 489–564.

Stählin, Karl. Aus den Papieren Jacob von Stählins. Königsberg, Ost-Europa-Verlag, 1926.

Stals, Georgs. Das lettische Ballett der Rigaer Oper. Riga, Kadilis, 1943.

Stanley, Albert Augustus. "Cesti's *Il Pomo d'Oro*," MTNA I (1906) 139–49.

Stasov, Vladimir Vasil'evich. Russkiia i inostrannyia opery ispolniavshiasia na Imperatorskikh Teatrakh v Rosii v XVIII-m'i XIX-m stoletiiakh. St. Petersburg, 1898.

Statisticus [pseud.]. "Notes sur l'histoire de l'Opéra," RHCM III (1903) 277–79.

Stauder, Wilhelm. "Johann André; ein Beitrag zur Geschichte des deutschen Singspiels," AfMf I (1936) 318–60. Also separate: Leipzig, B&H, 1936.

Stebbins, Lucy Poate, and Richard Poate Stebbins. Enchanted Wanderer; the Life of Carl Maria von Weber. New York, G. P. Putnam, [1940].

Stefan, Paul. Anton Dvořák. New York, Greystone, [1941]. Translated and rearranged from the German edition, which was based on the authoritative four-volume biography by Otakar Sourck.

—— Das neue Haus; ein Halbjahrhundert Wiener-Opernspiel und was voranging. Wien and Leipzig, E. Strache, 1919.

—— "Schoenberg's Operas," MMus II, No. 1 (January, 1925) 12–15.

—— "Schönberg's Operas," MMus VII, No. 1 (December, 1929–January, 1930) 24–28.

—— Die Wiener Oper; ihre Geschichte von den Anfängen bis in der neueste Zeit. Wien, Augartenverlag, 1932.

—— Die Zauberflöte; Herkunft, Bedeutung, Geheimnis. Wien, Reichner, 1937.

Steglich, Rudolf. "Das deutsche Händelfest in Leipzig," ZfMw VII (1924–25) 587–92.

—— "Göttinger Händelfestspiele 1924," Zeitschrift für Musik XCI (1924) 496–98.

—— "Göttinger Händel-Opern Festspiele 1927," Zeitschrift für Musik XCIV (1927) 424–26.

—— "Das Händelfest in Münster (2. bis 5. Dezember 1926)," ZfMw IX (1926–27) 290–93.

—— "Die Händel-Opern-Festspiele in Göttingen," ZfMw III (1920–21) 615–20.

—— "Händels Oper Rodelinde und ihre neue Göttinger Bühnenfassung," ZfMw III (1920–21) 518–34.

—— "Händels Saul in szenischer Darstellung," Zeitschrift für Musik XC (1923) Heft XVII, pp. 15–17.

—— "Händels Xerxes und die Göttinger Händel-Opern-Festspiele 1924," ZfMw VII (1924–25) 21–33.

—— "Händel und die Gegenwart," Zeitschrift für Musik XCII (1925) 333–38.

—— "Die neue Händel-Opern-Bewegung," Händel-Jahrbuch I (1928) 71–158.

—— "Schütz und Händel," Zeitschrift für Musik LXXXIX (1922) 478–80.

—— "Ueber die gegenwärtige Krise der Händelpflege," ZfMw X (1927–28) 632–41.

Steigman, B. M. "The Great American Opera," M&L VI (1925) 359–67.

—— " 'Nicht mehr Tristan'," MQ VII (1921) 57–67.

Steinitzer, Max. Zur Entwicklungsgeschichte des Melodrams und Mimodrams. Leipzig, C. F. W. Siegel, [1919].

Stendhal [pseud.]. *See* Beyle, Henri.

Stenhouse, May. The Character of the Opera Libretto according to Quinault. Columbia Dissertation (A.M.), 1920.

Sternfeld, Frederick W. "Some Russian Folk Songs in Stravinsky's *Petrouchka*," *Music Library Association Notes, Second Series* II, No. 2 (March, 1945) 95–107.

Stier, Ernst. "Georg Caspar Schürmann," *Die Musik* III, No. 2 (1903–1904) 107–11.

Stier-Somlo, Helene. Das Grimmsche Märchen als Text für Opern und Spiele. Berlin and Leipzig, de Gruyter, 1926.

Storz, Walter. Der Aufbau der Tänze in den Opern und Balletts Lully's vom musikalischen Standpunkte aus betrachtet. Göttingen, Dieterischen Universitäts-Buchdruckerei, 1928.

Stoullig, E. Les Annales du théâtre et de la musique. Paris, Ollendorf, 1899.

Strasser, Stefan. "Susanna und die Gräfin," ZfMw X (1927–28) 208–16.

Strauss, Franz, ed. Richard Strauss Briefwechsel mit Hugo von Hofmannsthal. Wien, Zsolnay, 1926. Translated as: Correspondence between Richard Strauss and Hugo von Hofmannsthal 1907–1918. New York, Knopf, 1927.

Stravinsky, Igor. Chroniques de ma vie. Paris, Denoël & Steele, [1935]. Translated as: Chronicles of My Life. London, V. Gollancz, 1936.

—— Poétique musicale sous forme de six leçons. Cambridge, Mass., Harvard University Press, 1942.

—— *See* RM, numéro spécial (May–June, 1939).

Streatfeild, Richard Alexander. Handel. New York, John Lane, 1909.

—— "Handel, Rolli, and Italian Opera in London in the Eighteenth Century," MQ III (1917) 428–45.

—— Musiciens anglais contemporains. Paris, Editions du temps présent, 1913.

Strelitzer, Hugo. Meyerbeers deutsche Jugend-Opern. Münster Dissertation, 1922.

Strobel, Heinrich. "Die Opern von E. N. Méhul," ZfMw VI (1923–24) 362–402.

—— Paul Hindemith. Mainz, Melosverlag, B. Schotts Söhne, 1937. 3d ed.

Strüver, Paul. Die cantata da camera Alessandro Scarlattis. Munich Dissertation, 1924.

Stuckenschmidt, H. H. "Ernst Křenek," MMus XVI, No. 1 (November–December, 1938), 41–44.

—— "Hellenic Jazz," MMus VII, No. 3 (April–May, 1930) 22–25.

—— "Opera in Germany Today," MMus XIII, No. 1 (November–December, 1935) 32–37.

Subirá, José. Enrique Granados. Madrid, [Z. Ascasíbar], 1926.
—— "Les Influences françaises dans la Tonadilla madrilène du XVIIIe siècle," in *Mélanges de musicologie* (Paris, Droz, 1933) pp. 209–16.
—— Los maestros de la tonadilla escénica. Barcelona, Editorial Labor, 1933.
—— La música en la casa de Alba. Madrid, ["Sucesores de Rivadeneyra"], 1927.
—— El operista español d. Juan Hidalgo. Madrid, Bermejo, 1934.
—— La participación musical en el antiguo teatro español. Barcelona, Disputación provincial, 1930.
—— "Le Style dans la musique théâtrale espagnole," *Acta musicologica* IV (1932) 67–75.
—— La tonadilla escénica. Madrid, Tipografía de archivos, 1928–30. 3 vols.
—— Tonadillas teatrales inéditas. Madrid, Tipografía de archivos, 1932.
Supplément aux parodies du théâtre italien. Paris, Duchesne, 1765. New ed.
Swalin, Benjamin F. "Purcell's Masque in *Timon of Athens*," in *Papers of the American Musicological Society, Annual Meeting, 1941* . . . *Edited by Gustave Reese* (Printed by the Society [cop. 1946]), pp. 112–24.
Swan, Alfred J. "Moussorgsky and Modern Music," MQ XI (1925) 271–80.
Swanepoel, Pieter. Das dramatische Schaffen Henry Purcells. Vienna Dissertation, 1926.
Symonds, John Addington. The Renaissance in Italy: Italian Literature. New York, H. Holt, 1882. 2 vols.
Szametz, Ralph. Hat Mozart eine Psychose durchgemacht? Frankfurt Dissertation, 1936.
Tabanelli, Nicola. "Oriani e la musica," RMI XLII (1938) 325–43, 495–505.
Tanner, Richard. Johann David Heinichen als dramatischer Komponist. Leipzig, B&H, 1916.
Tappolet, Willy. Arthur Honegger. Zürich and Leipzig, Gebrüder Hug, 1933. French ed., Neuchâtel, Editions de la Baconnière, [1939].
Tasso, Torquato. Opere. Pisa, Capuro, 1821–32. 33 vols.
Taubert, Otto. "*Daphne*, das erste deutsche Operntextbuch," in *Programm des Gymnasiums zu Torgau* (Torgau, Fr. Lebinsky, 1879).
Taut, Kurt. "Verzeichnis des Schrifttums über Georg Friedrich Händel," *Händel-Jahrbuch* VI (1933).
Taylor, Sedley. The Indebtedness of Handel to the Works by Other Composers; a Presentation of Evidence. Cambridge, University Press, 1906.
Tchaikovsky, Peter Ilyitch. Diaries; Translated from the Russian with Notes by Wladimir Lakond. New York, Norton, 1945.
—— Life and Letters. London, J. Lane, 1906. Ed. from the Russian by Rosa Newmarch.
Teatro italiano antico. Milano, 1808–12. 10 vols.

Tebaldini, Giovanni. "Felipe Pedrell ed il dramma lirico spagnuolo," RMI IV (1897) 267–98, 494–524. Also separate: Torino, Bocca, 1897.

—— "Giuseppe Persiani e Fanny Tacchinardi; memorie ed appunti," RMI XII (1905) 579–91.

—— "Telepatia musicale; a proposito dell' *Elettra* di Richard Strauss," RMI XVI (1909) 400–412.

Teneo, Martial. "Les Chefs-d'œuvre du chevalier Gluck à l'Opéra de Paris," RHCM VIII (1908) 109–16.

—— "Le Chevalier de Malte ou la reine de Chypre," ZIMG VIII (1906–1907) 352–54.

—— "La Détresse de Niccola Piccinni," RHCM VIII (1908) 237–44, 279–81.

—— "Jacques Offenbach d'après des documents inédits," MM VII, No. 12 (1911) 1–35.

—— "Jacques Offenbach: His Centenary," MQ VI (1920) 98–117.

—— "Pierre Montan Bertons," RHCM VIII (1908) 389–97, 416–24, 493.

—— "Un Spectacle à la cour," MM I (1905) 480–86.

Tenschert, Roland. "Die Kadenzbehandlung bei Richard Strauss," ZfMw VIII (1925–26) 161–82.

—— Mozart; ein Leben für die Oper. Wien, Frick, 1941.

—— "Die Ouvertüren Mozarts," *Mozart-Jahrbuch* II (1924).

—— "Versuch einer Typologie der Richard Strausschen Melodik," ZfMw XVI (1934) 274–93.

Ternant, Andrew de. "French Opera Libretti," M&L XI (1930) 172–76.

Terry, Charles Stanford. Johann Christian Bach. London, Oxford University Press, 1929.

Tessier, André. "Berain, créateur du pays d'opéra," RM VI (January, 1925) 56–73.

—— "Les Deux Styles de Monteverdi," RM III, No. 8 (June, 1922) 223–54.

—— "Giacomo Torelli a Parigi e la messa in scena delle *Nozze di Peleo e Teti* di Carlo Caproli," RassM I (1928) 573–90.

—— "L'*Orontée* de Lorenzani et l'*Orontea* du Padre Cesti," RM IX, No. 8 (1928) 169–86.

—— "Quelques notes sur Jean Desfontaines," RdM X (1929) 9–16.

—— "Robert Cambert à Londres," RM IX (December, 1927) 101–22.

Teutsche Arien, welche auf dem Kayserlich-privilegierten Wienerischen Theatro in unterschiedlich producirten Comoedien, deren Titeln hier jedesmahl beygerucket, gesungen worden; Codex ms. 12706–12709 der Wiener Nationalbibliothek. Wien, E. Strache, 1930.

Thayer, Alexander Wheelock. The Life of Ludwig van Beethoven. New York, The Beethoven Association, [1921]. Ed. by H. E. Krehbiel.

Theater-Kalendar auf das Jahr . . . (Reichard). Gotha, Vols. 1–25, 1775–1800.

Theatro comico portuguez, ou Collecção das operas portuguezas, que se representárão na casa do theatro público do Bairro Alto di Lisboa. Lisboa, S. T. Ferreira, 1787–92. 4 vols.

Thomas, Eugen. Die Instrumentation der *Meistersinger von Nürnberg* von Richard Wagner. Wien, Universal, [1907]. 2 vols. 2d ed.

Thomas, L. P. "Les Strophes et la composition du Sponsus," *Romania* LV (1929) 45–112.

—— "La Versification et les leçons douteuses du Sponsus," *Romania* LIII (1927) 43–81.

Thomas of Britain. The Romance of Tristram and Ysolt. *See* Loomis, Roger Sherman, ed.

Thompson, Herbert. Wagner and Wagenseil. London, Oxford University Press, 1927.

Thompson, Oscar. Debussy, Man and Artist. New York, Dodd, Mead, 1937.

—— "Fly-Wheel Opera," MMus VII, No. 1 (December, 1929–January, 1930) 39–42.

—— "If Beethoven Had Written *Faust,*" MQ X (1924) 13–20.

Thompson, Randall. "George Antheil," MMus VIII, No. 4 (May–June, 1931) 17–27.

Thomson, Virgil. "George Gershwin," MMus XIII, No. 1 (November–December, 1935) 13–19.

—— "Most Melodious Tears," MMus XI, No. 1 (November–December, 1933) 13–17.

—— The Musical Scene. New York, Knopf, 1945.

—— The State of Music. New York, W. Morrow, 1939.

Thorp, Willard, ed. Songs from the Restoration Theatre. Princeton, Princeton University Press, 1934.

Thouret, Georg. "Einzug der Musen und Grazien in die Mark," *Hohenzollern-Jahrbuch* IV (1900) 192–230.

Thrane, Carl. Danske Komponister. Copenhagen, Forlagsbureaunet, 1875.

—— "Sarti in Kopenhagen," SIMG III (1901–1902) 528–38.

Tibaldi Chiesa, Mary. Cimarosa e il suo tempo. [Milano], A. Garzanti, [1939].

Tiby, Ottavio. *L'incoronazione di Poppea* di Claudio Monteverdi. Firenze, A. Vallecchi, 1937.

Tiersot, Julien. "Auber," RM XIV (November, 1933) 265–78.

—— "Bizet and Spanish Music," MQ XIII (1927) 566–81.

—— "Charles Gounod; a Centennial Tribute," MQ IV (1918) 409–39.

—— "Les Choeurs d' *Esther* de Moreau," RHCM III (1903) 35–40.

—— Un Demi-siècle de musique française. Paris, Alcan, 1918.

—— "Edouard Lalo," MQ XI (1925) 8–35.

—— "Etude sur *Don Juan* de Mozart," *Le Ménestrel* LXII (1896) 399–411 *passim;* LXIII (1897) 1–139 *passim.*

—— "Etude sur *Orphée* de Gluck." *Le Ménestrel* LXII (1896) 273–386 *passim.*

—— "Gluck and the Encyclopædists," MQ XVI (1930) 336–57.

Tiersot, Julien (*Cont.*). "Gounod's Letters," MQ V (1919) 40–61.

—— "Hector Berlioz and Richard Wagner," MQ III (1917) 453–92.

—— Histoire de la chanson populaire en France. Paris, Plon, Nourrit, 1889. Contains (Part III, Chapter IV) "La Mélodie populaire au théâtre."

—— Jean-Jacques Rousseau. Paris, Alcan, 1912.

—— "Lettres de musiciens écrites en français du XVe au XXe siècle," RMI XVII (1910)–XXI (1914); XXIII (1916); XXIX (1922)–XXX (1923); XXXIII (1926)–XXXIV (1927); XXXVI (1929)–XXXVIII (1931), *passim*.

—— La Musique dans la comédie de Molière. Paris, La Renaissance du livre, [1922].

—— "La Musique de J.-J. Rousseau," MM VIII, No. 6 (1912) 34–56.

—— "La Musique des comédies de Molière à la Comédie-française," RdM VI (1922) 20–28.

—— "Rameau," MQ XIV (1928) 77–107.

—— "Ronsard et la musique de son temps," SIMG IV (1902–1903) 70–142.

—— "L'ultima opera di Gluck, *Eco e Narciso*," RMI IX (1902) 264–96.

Till, Theodor. Die Entwicklung der musikalischen Form in Richard Wagners Opern und Musikdramen, von der Ouvertüre (Vorspiel) und deren Funktionsvertretern aus betrachtet. Vienna Dissertation, 1930.

Tintelnot, Hans. Die Entwicklungsgeschichte der barocken Bühnendekoration in ihren Wechselbeziehungen zur bildenden Kunst. Berlin, Mann, 1938.

Tirabassi, Antonio. "The Oldest Opera: Belli's *Orfeo Dolente*," MQ XXV (1939) 26–33.

Tirabassi, M. A. "Introduction à l'étude de la parabole des vierges sages et des vierges folles," *Annales de la Société R. d' archéologie de Bruxelles* XXXII (1926) 15.

Tiraboschi, Girolamo. Storia della letteratura italiana. Roma, L. P. Salvioni, 1782–97. 10 vols.

Titon du Tillet, [Evrard]. Le Parnasse françois. Paris, J. B. Coignard, 1732–[43]. 2 vols., paged continuously.

Tittmann, Julius. Kleine Schriften zur deutschen Literatur und Kulturgeschichte. Göttingen, Dieterischen Buchhandlung, 1847.

Törnblom, Folke H. "Opera [in Sweden]," *Theatre Arts* XXIV (1940) 597–600.

Toffani, Giuseppe, ed. Storia letteraria d'Italia: il cinquecento. Milano, Vallardi, 1929. 3d ed.

Tolksdorf, Cäcilie. John Gays *Beggar's Opera* und Bert Brechts *Dreigroschenoper*. Rheinberg, Rhl., Sattler & Koss, 1934.

Tolón, Edwin T., and Jorge A. González. Operas cubanas y sus autores. Habana, [Imprenta Ucar, García], 1943.

Tommasini, Oreste. "Pietro Metastasio e lo svolgimento del melodramma italiano," in *Scritti di storia e critica* (Roma, E. Loescher, 1891) pp. 153–222.

Tommasini, Vincenzo. "L'opera di Riccardo Wagner e la sua importanza nella storia dell' arte e delle cultura," RMI IX (1902) 113–47, 422–41, 694–716.

Tonelli, Luigi. Il teatro italiano dalle origini ai giorni nostri. Milano, Modernissima, 1924.

Toni, Alceo. "Sul basso continuo e l'interpretazione della musica antica," RMI XXVI (1919) 229–64.

Torchi, Luigi. "L'accompagnamento degli istrumenti nei melodrammi italiani della prima metà del seicento," RMI I (1894) 7–38; II (1895) 666–71.

—— "Canzoni ed arie italiane ad una voce nel secolo XVII," RMI I (1894) 581–656.

—— "Consuelo di A. Rendano," RMI X (1903) 564–80.

—— "L'esito del concorso Sonzogno; le tre opere rappresentate al 'Teatro Lirico' di Milano," RMI XI (1904) 516–49.

—— "Germania, di G. Franchetti," RMI IX (1902) 377–421.

—— "Ghismonda, opera in tre atti di Eugenio D'Albert," RMI III (1896) 526–61.

—— "Guglielmo Ratcliff . . . di Pietro Mascagni," RMI II (1895) 287–311.

—— "Iris . . . di Pietro Mascagni," RMI VI (1899) 71–118.

—— "Oceana di A. Smareglia," RMI X (1903) 309–66.

—— "L'opera di Giuseppe Verdi e i suoi caretteri principali," RMI VIII (1901) 279–325.

—— "The Realistic Italian Operas," in Famous Composers and Their Works, New Series (Boston, J. B. Millet, [1900]) I, 183.

—— "R. Schumann e le sue 'Scene tratte dal Faust di Goethe'," RMI II (1895) 381–419, 629–65.

—— "Salome di Riccardo Strauss," RMI XIV (1907) 113–56.

—— "Studi di orchestrazione; l' Anello del Nibelunge di Riccardo Wagner," RMI XX (1913) 347–53; XXI (1914) 509–12, 768–75.

—— "Tosca, di G. Puccini," RMI VII (1900) 78–114.

—— "La vita nuova di E. Wolf-Ferrari," RMI X (1903) 712–36.

Torrefranca, Fausto. "Arrigo Boito," MQ VI (1920) 532–52.

—— "Il 'grande stregone' Giacomo Torelli e la scenografia del seicento," Scenario III (1934) 473–80.

—— "La nuova opera di Riccardo Strauss," RMI XIX (1912) 986–1031.

—— "L'officina dell' opera," RassM III (1930) 136–46.

—— "Opera as a 'Spectacle for the Eye'," MQ I (1915) 436–52.

—— "La prima opera francese in Italia? (l'Armida di Lulli, Roma 1690)," in Festschrift für Johannes Wolf (Berlin, Breslauer, 1929) pp. 191–97.

—— "Il Rosencavalier di R. Strauss," RMI XVIII (1911) 147–79.

—— "R. Strauss e l' Elektra," RMI XVI (1909) 335–84.

Torri, Luigi. "Il primo melodramma a Torino," RMI XXVI (1919) 1–35.

—— "Saggio di bibliografia Verdiana," RMI VIII (1901) 379–407.

Tosi, Pietro Francesco. Opinioni de' cantori antichi, e moderni, o sieno Osservazioni sopra il canto figurato. [Bologna, L. dalla Volpe, 1723.] Translated as: Observations on the Florid Song; or, Sentiments on the Ancient and Modern Singers. London, J. Wilcox, 1742. Later English editions: 1743, 1906, 1926.

Tottmann, Albert. Mozart's *Zauberflöte*. Langensalza, Beyer, 1908. Makes use of C. Grüel's "Aufschlüsse über die Bedeutung des angeblich Schikanederschen Textes zu Mozart's Zauberflöte," Magdeburg, 1868.

Touchard-Lafosse, G. Chroniques secrètes et galantes de l'opéra depuis 1667 jusqu'en 1845. Paris, Lachapelle, 1846. 4 vols.

Tovey, Donald Francis. "Christopher Willibald Gluck (1714–1787) and the Musical Revolution of the Eighteenth Century," in *The Heritage of Music,* ed. Hubert J. Foss (London, Oxford University Press, 1934) II, 69–117.

—— Essays in Musical Analysis, III: The Concerto. London, Oxford University Press, 1936.

Toye, Francis. Giuseppe Verdi. London, W. Heinemann; New York, Knopf, 1931.

—— "Is Musical Reservation Justifiable?" MQ I (1915) 118–28.

—— Rossini, a Study in Tragi-Comedy. New York, Knopf, 1934.

—— "Verdi," PMA LVI (1929–30) 37–53.

Trend, John Brande. "The Mystery of Elche," M&L I (1920) 145–57.

—— A Picture of Modern Spain. New York, Houghton Mifflin, 1921.

Trenkle, J. B. "Ueber süddeutsche geistliche Schulkomödien," *Freiburger Diöcesan-archiv* II (1866) 131–76.

Trilogia *Los Pireneos* y la critica, La. Barcelona, Oliva, 1901.

Trocki, Ladislas von. Die Entwickelung der Oper in Polen. Leipzig, Voigt, 1867.

[Truinet, Charles Louis Etienne, and A. E. Roquet (Thoinan).] Les Origines de l'opéra français. Paris, Plon-Nourrit, 1886.

Tufts, George. "Ballad Opera; a List and Some Notes," MA IV (1912–13) 61–86.

Turrini, G. "De Vlaamsche Componist Giovanni Nasco te Verona (1547–1551)," *Tijdschrift der Vereeniging voor Nederl. Muziekgeschiedenis* XIV, No. 3 (1935) 132–59; XV, No. 2 (1937) 84–93. Also in Italian, *Note d'archivio* XIV (1937) 180–225.

Tutenberg, Fritz. "Moderne schwedische Musik und Musiker im Umriss, II: die schwedische Oper," *Zeitschrift für Musik* CVI (1939) 930–34.

—— "Die *opera-buffa* Sinfonie und ihre Beziehungen zur klassischen Sinfonie," AfMw VIII (1926–27) 452–72.

Tuthill, Burnet C. "Howard Hanson," MQ XXII (1936) 140–53.

Tutti i trionfi, carri, mascherate, o Cante carnascialeschi andati per Firenze dal tempo del magnifico Lorenzo de' Medici fino all' anno 1559. Cosmopoli [i.e. Lucca], 1750. 2d ed.

"Ueber das Rezitativ," *Bibliothek der schönen Wissenschaften* XI, No. 2 (1764) 209; XII, No. 1 (1765) 1; XII, No. 2 (1765) 217.

Uffenbach, Johann Friedrich von. Pharasmen; ein Singspiel. Berlin, O. Elsner, 1930.

Uhlenbruch, Fritz. Herforder Musikleben bis zur Mitte des 18. Jahrhunderts. Münster Dissertation, 1926.

Ulibishev, Aleksandr Dmitrievich. Mozart's Opern; kritische Erläuterungen. Leipzig, B&H, 1848. Originally in French.

Unger, Max. "Beethoven und das Wiener Hoftheater im Jahre 1807," *Neues Beethoven Jahrbuch* II (1925) 76–83.

Unterholzner, Ludwig. Giuseppe Verdis Opern-typus. Hannover, A. Madsack, [1933].

Untersteiner, Alfredo. "Agostino Steffani," RMI XIV (1907) 509–34.

Upton, William Treat. The Musical Works of William Henry Fry in the Collections of the Library Company of Philadelphia. Philadelphia, The Free Library of Philadelphia, 1946.

—— "Secular Music in the United States 150 Years Ago," in *Papers of the American Musicological Society, Annual Meeting, 1941 . . . Edited by Gustave Reese* (Printed by the Society [cop. 1946]), pp. 105–11. Contains a list of "certain operas whose librettos were published in the United States before 1800 and which received at least fifteen performances in Philadelphia and New York during that period."

Ursprung, Otto. "*Celos* usw., Text von Calderón, Musik von Hidalgo,— die älteste erhaltene spanische Oper," in *Festschrift Arnold Schering* (Berlin, A. Glas, 1937) pp. 223–40.

—— "Das Sponsus-Spiel," AfMf III (1938) 80–95, 180–92.

—— "Ueber die Aufführung von Monteverdis *Combattimento* und von Peris *Euridice* durch das musikwissenschaftliche Seminar der Universität München," ZfMw XVI (1934) 188–90.

Valdrighi, Luigi Francesco, conte. I Bononcini da Modena. Modena, G. T. Vincenzi, 1882.

Valentin, Caroline. " 'Ach wie ist's möglich dann' von H. von Chézy und seine erste Melodie," in *Festschrift Liliencron* (Leipzig, B&H, 1910) pp. 358–86.

Valentin, Erich. Georg Philipp Telemann. Burg b.M., A. Hopfer, [1931].

—— Hans Pfitzner. Regensburg, G. Bosse, 1939.

Vallas, Léon. Claude Debussy et son temps. Paris, F. Alcan, 1932. Translated as: Claude Debussy, His Life and Works. London, Oxford University Press, 1933.

—— "The Discovery of Musical Germany by Vincent d'Indy in 1873," MQ XXV (1939) 176–94.

—— "Jacques-Simon Maugot," RdM V (1924) 123–26.

—— Un Siècle de musique et de théâtre à Lyon (1688–1789). Lyon, P. Masson, 1932.

Van Vechten, Carl. "Back to Delibes," MQ VIII (1922) 605–10,

Van Vechten, Carl (*Cont.*). "Notes on Gluck's *Armide*," MQ III (1917) 539–47.

—— "Shall We Realize Wagner's Ideals?" MQ II (1916) 387–401.

Vatielli, Francesco. "Le opere comiche di G. B. Martini," RMI XL (1936) 450–76.

—— "Operisti-librettisti dei secoli XVII e XVIII," RMI XLIII (1939) 1–16, 315–32, 605–21.

—— "Riflessi della lotta Gluckista in Italia," RMI XXI (1914) 639–72.

Vautier, Gabriel. "Le Jury de lecture et l'opéra sous la restauration," RHCM X (1910) 13–25, 44–49, 75–78.

Vené, Ruggero. "The Origin of *Opera Buffa*," MQ XXI (1935) 33–38.

Verdi, Giuseppe. I copialettere. [Milano, Stucchi Ceretti, 1913.] Ed. by G. Cesari and A. Luzio, preface by M. Scherillo.

Vetter, Walther. Die Arie bei Gluck. Leipzig Dissertation, 1921.

—— "Georg Christoph Wagenseil als Vorläufer . . . Glucks," ZfMw VIII (1925–26) 385–402.

—— "Gluck's Entwicklung zum Opernreformation," AfMw VI (1924) 165–212.

—— "Glucks Stellung zur tragédie lyrique und opéra comique," ZfMw VII (1924–25) 321–55.

—— "Gluck und seine italienischen Zeitgenossen," ZfMw VII (1924–25) 609–46.

—— "Stilkritische Bemerkungen zur Arienmelodik in Glucks *Orfeo*," ZfMw IV (1921–22) 27–49.

—— "Zur Entwicklungsgeschichte der opera seria um 1750 in Wien," ZfMw XIV (1931–32) 2–28.

Viardot-Garcia, Pauline. "Pauline Viardot-Garcia to Julius Rietz (Letters of Friendship)," MQ I (1915) 350–80, 526–59; II (1916) 32–60.

Vicentino, Nicola. L'antica musica ridotta alla moderna prattica. Roma, A. Barre, 1555.

Vieira, Ernesto. Diccionario biographico de musicos portuguezes; historia e bibliographia da musica em Portugal. Lisboa, M. Moreira & Pinheiro, 1900. 2 vols.

Vienna. Internationale Ausstellung für Musik- und Theaterwesen, 1892. Fach-Katalog der Abtheilung des Königreiches Italien. Wien, [J. N. Vernoy], 1892.

Viereck, Peter. Metapolitics from the Romantics to Hitler. New York, Knopf, 1941.

Villalba, L. "La cuestión de la ópera española; carta abierta," *La Ciudad de Dios* XXXIII, No. 2 (1913) 204–11.

Villarosa, Carlo Antonio de Rosa, Marchese de. Memorie dei compositori di musica del regno di Napoli. Napoli, Stamperia reale, 1840.

[Villeneuve, Josse de.] Lettre sur le méchanisme de l'opéra italien. Ni Guelfe, ni Gibelin; ni Wigh, ni Thoris. Paris, Duchesne; Florence and Paris, Lambert, 1756. German translation by R. Haas, ZfMw VII (1924–25) 129–63. *See also* Bédarida, Henri. "L'Opéra italien jugé par un amateur français en 1756," in *Mélanges de musicologie* (Paris, Droz, 1933) pp. 185–200.

Viollier, Renée. "Les Divertissements de J.-J. Mouret pour la 'Comédie italienne' à Paris," RdM XXIII (1939) 65–71.

—— "Un Opéra-ballet au XVIIIe siècle: *Les Festes ou le triomphe de Thalie*," RdM XVI (1935) 78–86.

Viotta, H. A. "Richard Wagner's verhouding tot die muziekgeschiedenis," in *Gedenkboek . . . Scheurleer* ('s Gravenhage, Nijhoff, 1925) pp. 359–65.

Virella Cassañes, Francisco. La ópera en Barcelona. Barcelona, Redondo y Zumetra, 1888.

Virgilio, Rudolph. Development of Italian Opera in New York. New York, Italian Library of Information, 1938.

Visetti, Albert. "Tendencies on the Operatic Stage in the Nineteenth Century," PMA XXII (1896) 141–51.

Vitale, Roberto. Domenico Cimarosa. Aversa, Noviello, 1929.

Vittadini, Stefano. Il primo libretto del Mefistofele di Arrigo Boito. Milano, Gli amici del museo teatrale alla scala, 1938.

Vivaldi, Antonio; note e documenti sulla vita e sulle opere. Roma, Sansaini, 1939.

Vogel, Emil. Bibliothek der gedruckten weltlichen Vokalmusik Italiens aus den Jahren 1500–1700. Berlin, A. Haack, 1892. New ed. serially in *Music Library Association Notes, Second Series* II, No. 3 (June, 1945) and later numbers.

—— "Claudio Monteverdi; Leben, Werken im Lichte der zeitgenössischen Kritik," VfMw III (1887) 315–450.

—— "Marco da Gagliano," VfMw V (1889) 396–442, 509–68.

Voigt, F. A. "Reinhard Keiser," VfMw VI (1890) 151–203.

Volbach, Fritz. Die Praxis der Händel-Aufführung, 2. Theil: das Händel-Orchester . . . I. Das Streichorchester. Charlottenburg, "Gutenberg," 1899.

Volkmann, Hans. "Domenico Terradellas," ZIMG XIII (1911–12) 306–309.

Wachten, Edmund. "Der einheitliche Grundzug der Strausssschen Formgestaltung," ZfMw XVI (1934) 257–74.

Wagner, Richard. Briefe in Originalausgaben. Leipzig, B&H, [1911–1913]. 17 vols.

—— Gesammelte Schriften und Dichtungen. Leipzig, B&H, n.d. 12 vols. 5th ed.

—— Mein Leben; Volks-Ausgabe. München, Bruckmann, 1914.

—— Opera and Drama. New York, C. Scribner; London, W. Reeves, [1913]. Translated by Edwin Evans.

Wagner, Rudolf. "Beiträge zur Lebensgeschichte Johann Philipp Kriegers und seines Schülers Nikolaus Deinl," ZfMw VIII (1925–26) 146–60.

Wagner, Siegfried. Erinnerungen. Stuttgart, J. Engelhorn, 1923.

Wahl, Eduard. Nicolo Isouard. München, C. Wolf, 1906.

Wahle, Werner. Richard Wagners szenische Visionen und ihre Ausführung im Bühnenbild. Munich Dissertation, 1937.

Waldersee, Paul. "Robert Schumann's *Manfred,*" in Waldersee, *Sammlung musikalischer Vorträge* (Leipzig, B&H, 1879–98) II, 1–20.

Walker, Ernest. A History of Music in England. London, Oxford University Press, [1924]. 2d ed.

Wallaschek, Richard. Das K. k. Hofoperntheater. Wien, Gesellschaft für vervielfältigende Kunst, 1909. ("Die Theater Wiens. 4. Band.")

Walter, Friedrich. Geschichte des Theaters und der Musik am kurpfälzischen Hofe. Leipzig, B&H, 1898.

Waltershausen, Hermann Wolfgang Karl Sartorius, Freiherr (von). Der Freischütz; ein Versuch über die musikalische Romantik. München, Bruckmann, 1920.

—— *Orpheus und Eurydike;* eine operndramaturgische Studie. München, Drei Masken, 1923.

—— Das Siegfried-Idyll, oder, Die Rückkehr zur Natur. München, H. Bruckmann, 1920.

—— *Die Zauberflöte;* eine operndramaturgische Studie. München, H. Bruckmann, 1920.

—— "Zur Dramaturgie des *Fidelio,*" *Neues Beethoven Jahrbuch* I (1924) 142–58.

Wang, Kwang-chi. Ueber die chinesische klassische Oper. Genf, 1934.

Wassermann, Rudolf. Ludwig Spohr als Opernkomponist. München, Huber, 1909.

Weber, Carl Maria, Freiherr von. Sämtliche Schriften. Berlin and Leipzig, Schuster & Loeffler, 1908.

Weber, Max Maria von. Carl Maria von Weber. Leipzig, E. Keil, 1864–66. 3 vols.

Weckerlin, Jean Baptiste. L'Ancienne Chanson populaire en France. Paris, Garnier, 1887.

Wegelin, Oscar. Early American Plays 1714–1830. New York, The Dunlap Society, 1900.

—— Micah Hawkins and the Saw-Mill; a Sketch of the First Successful American Opera and Its Author. New York, privately printed, 1917.

Weigl, Bruno. Die Geschichte des Walzers nebst einem Anhang über die moderne Operette. Langensalza, Beyer, 1910.

Weil, Rudolf. Das Berliner Theaterpublikum unter A. W. Ifflands Direktion (1746–1814). Berlin, Gesellschaft für Theatergeschichte, 1932.

Weilen, Alexander von. Geschichte des Wiener Theaterwesens von den ältesten Zeiten bis zu den Anfängen der Hoftheater. Wien, Gesellschaft für vervielfältigende Kunst, 1899. ("Die Theater Wiens, Bd. I.")

—— Zur Wiener Theatergeschichte; die vom Jahre 1629 bis zum Jahre 1740 am Wiener Hofe zur Aufführung gelangten Werke theatralischen Charakters und Oratorien. Wien, A. Hölder, 1901.

An important supplement to Köchel's *Kaiserliche Hofmusikkapelle;* see corrections in Nettl, "Exzerpte aus der Raudnitzer Textbüchersammlung," SzMw VII (1920) 143–44.

Weingartner, Felix. Bayreuth (1876–1896). Leipzig, B&H, 1904.

—— Lebenserinnerungen. Zürich and Leipzig, Orell Füssli, [1928–29]. 2 vols. Translated as: Buffets and Rewards. London, Hutchinson, [1937].

—— Die Lehre von der Wiedergeburt des musikalischen Dramas. Kiel and Leipzig, Lipsius & Fischer, 1895.

Weissmann, Adolph. "Germany's Latest Music Dramas," MMus IV, No. 4 (May–June, 1927) 20–26.

—— "Richard Wagner; Constructive and Destructive," MQ XI (1925) 138–56.

Wellesz, Egon. "Die Aussetzung des Basso Continuo in der italienischen Oper," in International Musical Society, Fourth Congress Report (London, Novello, 1912) pp. 282–85.

—— Der Beginn des musikalischen Barock und die Anfänge der Oper in Wien. Wien and Leipzig, Wiener literarische Anstalt, 1922.

—— "Ein Bühnenfestspiel aus dem 17. Jahrhundert," Die Musik LII (1914) Qt. 4, pp. 191–217.

—— "Cavalli und der Stil der venetianischen Oper von 1640–1660," SzMw I (1913).

—— "Don Giovanni and the 'dramma giocoso'," Music Review IV (1943) 121–26.

—— "Einige handschriftliche Libretti aus der Frühzeit der Wiener Oper," ZfMw I (1918–19) 278–81.

—— "Francesco Algarotti und seine Stellung zur Musik," SIMG XV (1913–14) 427–39.

—— "Giuseppe Bonno," SIMG XI (1909–10) 395–442.

—— "Die Opern und Oratorien in Wien von 1660–1708," SzMw VI (1919) 5–138.

—— "The Return to the Stage," MMus IV, No. 1 (November–December, 1926) 19–24.

—— "Zwei Studien zur Geschichte der Oper im 17. Jahrhundert," SIMG XV (1913) 124–54.

Welti, Heinrich. "Gluck und Calsabigi," VfMw VII (1891) 26–42.

Wendschuh, Ludwig. Ueber Jos. Haydns Opern. [Halle a. S.], 1896.

Werckmeister, Andreas. Der edlen Music-Kunst Würde, Gebrauch und Missbrauch. Franckfurt, Calvisius, 1691.

Werfel, Franz. Verdi; Roman der Oper. Berlin, Zsolnay, [1924]. Translated as: Verdi; a Novel of the Opera. New York, Simon & Schuster, 1926.

—— Verdi; the Man in His Letters. New York, L. B. Fischer, [1942]. Edited by Franz Werfel and Paul Stefan, translated by Edward Downes.

Werneck-Brueggemann, Fritz. Ueber E. T. A. Hoffmanns Oper Aurora: anlässlich der 3. Funk-Aufführung. Rudolstadt, Edda-Verlag, 1936.

Werner, Arno. "Briefe von J. W. Franck, die Hamburger Oper betreffend," SIMG VII (1905–1906) 125–28.

Werner, Arno (*Cont.*). "Sachsen-Thüringen in der Musikgeschichte," AfMw IV (1922) 322–35.

—— Städtische und fürstliche Musikpflege in Weissenfels bis zum Ende des 18. Jahrhunderts. Leipzig, B&H, 1911.

Werner, Theodor Wilhelm. "Agostino Steffanis Operntheater in Hannover," AfMf III (1938) 65–79.

—— "Zum Neudruck von G. Ph. Telemanns *Pimpinone* in den Reichsdenkmalen," AfMf I (1936) 361–65.

Wessely, Carl. Antike Reste griechischer Musik. [Vienna, 1891.]

Westerman, Gerhart von. Giovanni Porta als Opernkomponist. Munich Dissertation, 1921.

Westphal, Kurt. Die moderne Musik. Leipzig and Berlin, B. G. Teubner, 1928.

—— "Das musikdramatische Prinzip bei Richard Strauss," *Die Musik* (September, 1927) pp. 859–64.

Westrup, Jack Allan. "Monteverdi and the Orchestra," M&L XXI (1940) 230–45.

—— "Monteverdi's *Lamento d'Arianna*," *Music Review* I (1940) 144–54.

—— "The Originality of Monteverde," PMA LX (1933–34) 1–25.

—— Purcell. London, J. M. Dent; New York, E. P. Dutton, [1937].

White, Richard Grant. "Opera in New York," *Century Magazine* I (1881) 686–703, 865–82; II (1882) 31–43, 193–210.

White, Terence. "The Last Scene of Götterdämmerung; a New Production," M&L XVII (1936) 62–64.

Wiel, Taddeo. I codici musicali contariniani del secolo XVII nella R. Biblioteca di S. Marco in Venezia. Venezia, F. Ongania, 1888.

—— "Francesco Cavalli," MA IV (1912–13) 1–19.

—— I teatri musicali di Venezia nel settecento. Venezia, Visentini, 1897.

Wieland, Christoph Martin. Sämmtliche Werke, 26. Band: Singspiele und Abhandlungen. Leipzig, G. J. Göschen, 1796. Contains: "Versuch über das Deutsche Singspiel" (pp. 229–67, 323–42); "Ueber einige ältere Deutsche Singspiele, die den Nahmen Alceste führen" (pp. 269–320).

Wiese, Berthold. Geschichte der italienischen Litteratur. Leipzig and Wien, Bibliographisches Institut, [1898–]1899. Fourth to fifteenth centuries by Wiese; sixteenth century to present by E. Pèrcopo.

Wiesengrund-Adorno, Theodor. "Transatlantic," MMus VII, No. 4 (June–July, 1930) 38–41.

Willms, Franz. Führer zur Oper *Cardillac* von Paul Hindemith. Mainz, B. Schott, [1926].

—— "Paul Hindemith; ein Versuch," *Von neuer Musik* I (1925) 78–123.

Wimmersdorf, W. Oper oder Drama? Die Notwendigkeit des Niederganges der Oper. Rostock i. M., C. J. E. Volckmann, 1905.

Winckelmann, Johann Joachim. Sämtliche Werke. Donauöschingen, Im Verlage deutscher Classiker, 1825–29. 12 vols. Contains "Gedanken über die Nachahmung der griechischen Werke in der Malerei und Bildhauerkunst," I, 1–58; "Geschichte der Kunst des Alterthums," III–VI.

Winesanker, Michael. The Record of English Musical Drama, 1750–1800. Cornell Dissertation, 1944.

Winkelmann, Johann. Josef Myslivecek als Opernkomponist. Vienna Dissertation, 1905.

Winter, Marian Hannah. "American Theatrical Dancing from 1750–1800," MQ XXIV (1938) 58–73.

Winterfeld, Carl von. Alceste, 1674, 1726, 1769, 1776, von Lulli, Händel und Gluck. Berlin, Bote & Bock, 1851.

—— Johannes Gabrieli und sein Zeitalter. Berlin, Schlesinger, 1834. 3 vols.

Winternitz, Giorgio F. "I cimeli belliniani della R. Academia Filarmonica di Bologna," RMI XL (1936) 104–18.

Wirth, Helmut. Joseph Haydn als Dramatiker. Kiel Dissertation, 1937.

Witherspoon, Herbert. "Grand Opera and Its Immediate Problems," MTNA XXVII (1932) 148–49.

Wörner, Karl. "Beiträge zur Geschichte des Leitmotivs in der Oper [Teil I]," ZfMw XIV (1931–32) 151–72.

—— Beiträge zur Geschichte des Leitmotivs in der Oper (Teil 2, 3). Bayreuth, Ellwanger, 1932.

—— "Die Pflege Glucks an der Berliner Oper von 1795–1841," ZfMw XIII (1930–31) 206–16.

Wolff, Hellmuth Christian. Agrippina; eine italienische Jugendoper von Georg Friedrich Händel. Wolfenbüttel, Kallmeyer, 1943.

—— Die venezianische Oper in der zweiten Hälfte des 17. Jahrhunderts. Berlin, Elsner, 1937.

[Wolf-Ferrari, Ermanno.] See special number of Zeitschrift für Musik CVIII, No. 1 (January, 1941).

Wolzogen, Alfred von. Ueber die scenische Darstellung von Mozart's Don Giovanni. Breslau, Leuckart, 1860.

—— Ueber Theater und Musik; historisch-kritische Studien. Breslau, Trewendt, 1860.

Wolzogen, Hans von. Lebensbilder. Regensburg, Bosse, [1923].

—— "Wagners Siegfried," in Waldersee, Sammlung musikalischer Vorträge (Leipzig, B&H, 1879–98) I, 59–80.

Wortsmann, Stephan. Die deutsche Gluckliteratur. Nürnberg, Karl Koch, 1914.

Wotquenne, Alfred. Alphabetisches Verzeichnis der Stücke in Versen aus den dramatischen Werken von Zeno, Metastasio und Goldoni. Leipzig, B&H, 1905.

—— "Baldassare Galuppi (1706–1785); étude bibliographique sur ses œuvres dramatiques," RMI VI (1899) 561–79.

—— Catalogue thématique des œuvres de Chr. W. v. Gluck. Leipzig, B&H, 1904. Ergänzung und Nachträge . . . Leipzig, Reinecke, 1911, ed. by Josef Liebeskind. "Ergänzungen und Berichtigungen," Die Musik XIII (1913–14), Qt. 1, pp. 288–89, by Max Arend.

—— Etude bibliographique sur le compositeur napolitain Luigi Rossi. Bruxelles, Coosemans, 1909.

Wright, Edward. Some Observations Made in Travelling through France, Italy &c in the Years 1720, 1721, and 1722. London, T. Ward and E. Wicksteed, 1730. 2 vols.

Würz, Anton. Franz Lachner als dramatischer Komponist. München, Knorr & Hirth, 1928.

Wyndham, Henry Saxe. The Annals of Covent Garden Theatre from 1732–1897. London, Chatto & Windus, 1906. 2 vols.

Wyzewa, Teodor de. W. A. Mozart: sa vie musicale et son œuvre de l'enfance à la pleine maturité. Paris, Desclée, [1937]. G. de Saint-Foix is joint author of Vols. I and II and sole author of Vol. III.

Young, Karl. The Drama of the Medieval Church. Oxford, Clarendon Press, 1933. 2 vols.

Zademack, Franz. Die Meistersinger von Nürnberg; Richard Wagners Dichtung und ihre Quellen. Berlin, Dom-Verlag, 1921.

Zadig (pseud.?). "Ludovic Halévy," Revue politique et littéraire (1899) No. 2, p. 705.

Zambiasi, G. "Le date (a proposito de G. Verdi); bibliografia," RMI VIII (1901) 408–12.

Zarlino, Gioseffo. Le istituzioni harmoniche. Venetia, [Pietro da Fino?], 1558.

Zavadini, Guido. Gaetano Donizetti. Bergamo, Istituto italiano d'arti grafiche, 1941.

Zawilowski, Konrad. Stanislaus Moniuszko. Vienna Dissertation, 1902.

Zelle, Friedrich. Johann Philipp Förtsch. Berlin, R. Gaertner, 1893.

—— Johann Theile und Nikolaus Adam Strungk. Berlin, R. Gaertner, 1891.

—— Johann Wolfgang Franck. Berlin, R. Gaertner, 1889.

Zeller, Bernhard. Das recitativo accompagnato in den Opern Johann Adolf Hasses. Halle a. S., Hohmann, 1911.

Zelter, Carl Friedrich. "Ein Aufsatz . . . über Georg Benda und seine Oper Romeo und Julie," AMZ XIV (1879) 645–49.

Zenger, Max. Geschichte der Münchner Oper. München, Verlag für praktische Kunstwissenschaft, Dr. F. X. Weizinger & Co., 1923.

Zeno, Apostolo. Lettere. Venezia, F. Sansoni, 1785. 6 vols.

—— Poesie drammatiche. Orleans, Couret de Villeneuve, 1785–86. 11 vols.

Zichy, Géza. Aus meinem Leben. Stuttgart, Deutsche Verlags-Anstalt, 1911–13. 2 vols.

[Zille, Moritz Alexander.] Die Zauberflöte; Text-Erläuterung für alle Verehrer Mozarts. Leipzig, T. Lissner, 1866.

Zingel, Hans Joachim. "Studien zur Geschichte des Harfenspiels in klassischer und romantischer Zeit," AfMf II (1937) 455–65.

Zoref, Fritz. Wesen und Entwicklung des musikalischen Erinnerungsgedankens in der deutschen romantischen Oper. Vienna Dissertation, 1919.

Zucker, Paul. Die Theaterdekoration des Barok. Berlin, R. Kaemmerer, 1925.

Zuckerkandel, Viktor. Prinzipien und Methoden der Instrumentation in Mozarts dramatischen Werken. Vienna Dissertation, 1927.

Zur Nedden, Otto. Die Opern und Oratorien Felix Draesekes. Marburg Dissertation, 1926.

Zurita, Marciano. Historia del género chico. Madrid, Prensa popular, 1920.

Sources of Examples

1–5. Coussemaker, *Drames liturgiques du moyen âge.*

6. Coussemaker, ed. *Œuvres complètes du trouvère Adam de la Halle.*

7. *Ballet comique de la reine* (1582) p. 31.

8. Schneider, *Die Anfänge des Basso Continuo*, pp. 147–48.

9. Solerti, *Gli albori del melodramma.*

10. Eitner, *Publikationen* XXVI, 25.

11. *Ibid.*, p. 22.

12. *I classici della musica italiana* IV, Quaderno 10, p. 20. Realization of bass omitted, signature of one flat added.

13. Caccini, *L'Euridice* (1600).

14. Kretzschmar, *Geschichte der Oper*, p. 38. Realization omitted.

15. Torchi, *Arte musicale* VI, 117–18. Realization omitted.

16–17. Caccini, *L'Euridice* (1600).

18. Eitner, *Publikationen* X, 81–82. Realization omitted; chorus condensed from four staves, reduction omitted.

19. Monteverdi, C.E. XI, 31. Note values halved, score compressed.

20. *Ibid.*, p. 49. Note values halved, bar lines twice as frequent.

21. Monteverdi, *Orfeo,* facsimile of first ed. Figures in brackets correspond to Malipiero's realization, C.E. XI, 59.

22. Monteverdi, *Orfeo,* facsimile of first ed. Last two accidentals under bass notes correspond to Malipiero's realization, C.E. XI, 61.

23. Goldschmidt, *Studien* I, 159–60, bass only. Figures and brackets added.

24. *Ibid.*, p. 230.

25. *Ibid.*, p. 230. Time signature changed, brackets above line added.

26. *Ibid.*, p. 202. Condensed from five staves, names of instruments omitted.

27. *Ibid.*, p. 203. Condensed from five staves.

28. *Ibid.*, pp. 291–93. Condensed from five staves.

29. *Ibid.*, p. 305.

30. *Ibid.*, pp. 299–300. Slurring altered; sharp omitted below bass in measure 12 and before bass note C in measure 14.

31. *Ibid.*, p. 312.

32. Monteverdi, C.E. XIII, 80–81. Realization omitted.

33. *Ibid.*, p. 136. Signature changed from one flat; flat omitted under bass C in measures 1, 4, 8.

34. *Ibid.*, pp. 85–86. Realization omitted.

35. Eitner, *Publikationen* XII, 3, 4. Highest part only of five.

36. *Ibid.*, pp. 19–20. Reduced from four staves; flat added in last measure of bass.

37. *Ibid.*, pp. 79–80. Reduced from four staves; realization omitted.

38. Eitner, *Publikationen* XI, 147. Reduced from four staves; realization omitted.
39. DTOe III², 108. Continuo omitted.
40. Eitner, *Publikationen* XII, 154. Reduced from three staves, realization omitted, E-flat added in signature.
41. DTOe III², 9. Condensed, text omitted.
42. H. Hess, *Die Opern Alessandro Stradellas*, pp. 88–89. Introduction omitted (six measures of two parts over continuo).
43. DdT LV, 102. Bass and realization omitted.
44. *Ibid.*, p. 74. Realization and German text (translation) omitted.
45. DTB XXIII, 119–20. Condensed from five staves; realization omitted.
46. *Ibid.*, p. 159. Accompaniment (three-part strings) omitted.
47. *Ibid.*, pp. 163–64. Condensed from five staves; realization omitted.
48. SB 232. Accompaniment omitted.
49. Lully, *Phaëton* (1683) p. 36.
50. Lully, *Amadis*. Prunières ed. *Opéras* III, 95–96. Condensed from five staves; flat added before last bass note of measure 8.
51. Eitner, *Publikationen* XIV, 87–88. Reduced from six staves, E-flat added in signature.
52. Lully, *Phaëton* (1683).
53. Rameau, C. E. X, *Appendice*, p. 26.
54. *Old English Edition* XXV, 110. Slurs omitted.
55. *Ibid.*, p. 21. Reduced from three staves; realization omitted.
56. *Ibid., pp.* 130–31. Realization omitted.
57. Purcell, C.E. XXVI, 41.
58. Purcell, C.E. IX, 17–18. Reduced from four staves, realization omitted.
59. Purcell, C.E. XIX, 49. Reduced from two staves; realization omitted.
60. MfMg XIII (1881).
61. DTB XXXVIII, 104. Realization omitted; all but one of inserted bar-lines omitted.
62. *Ibid.*, p. 147. Realization omitted.
63. *Das Erbe deutscher Musik, Landschaftsdenkmale Schleswig-Holstein* III, 18. Realization omitted.
64. Händel, C.E. Supplement VI, 104. Reduced from four staves; names of instruments changed from "violino e flauto dolce"; "(Bassi)" changed to "[Continuo]."
65. *Ibid.*, p. 26.
66. DdT XXVII/XXVIII, 38. Reduced from five staves; realization omitted; stage direction translated.
67. *Ibid.*, p. 202. Reduced from five staves.
68. Händel, C.E. LVII, 72. Accompaniment omitted.
69. Händel, C.E. LXVIII, 82–83. Recitative reduced from five staves, aria from six staves.
70. Händel, C.E. XCII. Three string parts omitted; ornamented version of melody by Dr. Putnam Aldrich.

71. Haas, *Aufführungspraxis*, p. 186. Signature changed from two flats.
72. Rolland, *Histoire de l'opéra en Europe*, Supplément musical, p. 9. Reduced from four staves.
73. Eitner, *Publikationen* XIV, 163–64. Reduced from three staves; realization omitted.
74. *Ibid.*, p. 166. Time signature altered from $C\frac{3}{4}$.
75. *Ibid.*, pp. 166–67. Realization omitted in first $2\frac{1}{4}$ measures; string parts condensed from three staves.
76. Dent, *Alessandro Scarlatti*, p. 110. Realization omitted; figure and accidentals in brackets correspond to Dent's realization.
77. Gerber, *Der Operntypus Hasses*, pp. 77–78. Slurs added, other slight changes in notation.
78. DdT XV, 166. Accompaniment reduced from four staves.
79. DTB XXV, 146–47. Accompaniment (first and second violins, viola, continuo) omitted; realization and reduction omitted.
80. DTB XXVI, 144. Accompaniment (four string parts) omitted.
81. DTOe LX, 46–47. Reduced from nine staves.
82. *I classici della musica italiana* XXIII, Quaderno 89–90, p. 11.
83. *I classici della musica italiana* XX, Quaderno 80, pp. 6–7. Reduced from three staves.
84. *Le Théâtre de la foire*, Vol. I.
85. Monsigny, *Le Déserteur*, piano-vocal score, Paris, Alphonse Leduc, no. A.L. 5204, pp. 10–11.
86. Grétry, C. E. I, 43–44. Orchestra parts condensed from seven staves.
87. *The Beggar's Opera*, 2d ed. (1728), p. [45.]. Repeat marks after first double bar omitted to conform with text.
88. Hiller, *Die Jagd* (Leipzig, 1772).
89. Dittersdorf, *Das rote Käppchen*. Ms. Vienna Nationalbibliothek.
90. Subirá, *La tonadilla escénica* III, [16–17].
91. Cherubini. *Les Deux Journées*, piano-vocal score, Universal Ed. 3157, p. 14; text underlaid from another ed., Braunschweig, Meyer, [before 1862].
92. Spontini, *Fernand Cortez*. Leipzig, Hofmeister, plate no. 1135, p. 282. Condensed from three staves.
93. Auber, *La Muette de Portici*. Novello piano-vocal score, p. 137.
94. Meyerbeer, *L'Africaine*. Edition Peters No. 2773, piano-vocal score, p. 127. Reduced from three staves; indication of instruments omitted.
95. Berlioz, *Les Troyens*. Piano-vocal score, Choudens, p. 420. Names of instruments translated; flat added before bass D in measure 11; first eighth rest added in measure 15.
99. Herold, *Le Pré aux clercs*. Piano score, Paris, Léon Grus, plate no. 1746, pp. 72–73.
100. Rossini, *Tancredi*. Piano-vocal score, Paris, Launer, plate no. 3237, pp. 50–51.
101. Bellini, *La sonnambula*. Novello octavo piano-vocal score.

102. Verdi, *Ernani*. Novello piano-vocal score, plate no. 8063, pp. 174–75. Condensed from six staves.
103. Verdi, *La traviata*. G. Schirmer piano-vocal score, p. 108.
104. Verdi, *Otello*. Ricordi piano-vocal score, plate no. 52105, p. 361.
105. Wagner, *Das Liebesverbot*. B&H piano-vocal score, plate no. E.B. 4520, p. 396.
106. Wagner, *Tannhäuser*. Eulenburg small score, plate no. E.E. 4850, pp. 648–49. Reduced from six staves.
107. Wagner, *Lohengrin*. B&H score, plate no. 25700, p. 140.
110. D'Indy, *L'Etranger*. Durand piano-vocal score (1902), pp. 149–50. Some notes enharmonically altered.
111. Debussy, *Pelléas et Mélisande*. Durand piano-vocal score (1907), p. 236.
112. Dukas, *Ariane et Barbe-Bleue*. Durand piano-vocal score (1906), pp. 72–74. Reduced from three or five staves to show only essential harmonic outline; recitatives (two soloists) omitted.
113. Puccini, *Madama Butterfly*. Ricordi piano score, plate no. 110001, p. 123.
114. Giordano, *Andrea Chénier*. Sonzogno piano-vocal score (1896), plate no. 929, pp. 88–89.
115. Montemezzi, *L'amore dei tre re*. Ricordi piano-vocal score, plate no. 114651, pp. 126–27. Reduced from four staves; first two measures notated with signature of three flats instead of three sharps.
116. Kienzl, *Der Evangelimann*. Bote & Bock piano-vocal score (1894), plate no. 14035, pp. 66–67. Upper staff of accompaniment omitted.
117. Pfitzner, *Palestrina*. Piano-vocal score cop. 1916 by Adolph Fürstner (A. 7403, 7415, 7418F), p. 5.
118. Glinka, *A Life for the Czar*. Piano-vocal score, Moscow, n.d., p. 212. Alto voice and accompaniment omitted.
119. Dargomyzhsky, *The Stone Guest*. Bessel & Cie. piano-vocal score, plate no. 5623, p. 132.
120. Mussorgsky, C. E. II, piano-vocal score, Universal Ed. 9313, pp. 324–25. Reduced from seven staves; original Russian transliterated and translated by Dr. Edward Micek.
122. Pedrell, *Los Pirineos*. J. B. Pujol piano-vocal score, plate no. P.25C., pp. 239–40. Time signature, tempo mark, and first "pp" inserted from previous directions.
123. Alfano, *Madonna imperia*. Universal Ed. 8796, p. 93. Reduced in some places from four staves, one stage direction omitted.
124. Ibert, *Angélique*. Heugel piano-vocal score, plate no. H29458, pp. 14–15. Reduced from three or four staves.
125. Honegger, *Antigone*. Senart piano-vocal score, plate no. EMS7297, pp. 51–52.
126. Milhaud, *Médée*. Heugel piano-vocal score, plate no. H31062, p. 84.
127. Berg, *Lulu*. Piano-vocal score, Universal Ed. 10745, p. 231. Accompaniment omitted.

Index

Index

Numbers in boldface type under titles or names
of person represent entries of special importance

Cardillac (Hindemith), 528, 533

Cardoso, Domingo Cyriaco de, 492

Carissimi, Giacomo, 77, 96

Carl Rosa Opera Company, 495

Carmélite, La (Hahn), 433

Carmen (Bizet), 6, 368, **412 f.**, 422

Carnicer, Ramón, 487*n*

Carosse du Saint-Sacrament (Berners), 496

Carr, Benjamin, 500

Carter, Ernest, 503

Caryll, Ivan, 496

Casanova (Rózycki), 480

Casella, Alfredo, 521, 530, 531

Casella, Enrique, 494

Caserio, El (Guridí), 491

Castiglione, Baldassare, Count, quoted, 40

Castor et Pollux (Rameau), 128, 130, 222, 225, 234, 242

Castrati, 85, 103, 195-97; first appearance in opera, 72; prevalence of, 72; famous singers, 74, 193, 196; training: rewards of career; no place in comic opera, 247*n*; disappearance of: replacement by natural voice, 297; last important composers to write castrato roles, 339

Castro, Ricardo, 493

Catalani, Alfredo, 435, 436*n*, 439

Catalonia, regional school of, 491

Catel, Charles-Simon, 302, 325

Catena d'Adone, La (Mazzocchi), 69 f.

Catherine II (The Great), 464

Catone in Utica (Metastasio), 184*n*

Caudella, Eduard, 483

Cauldron of Anwen, The (Holbrooke), 496

Cavalieri, Emilio de, 31, 32, 36, 43, 45, 46, 69

"Cavalier of the Rose, The," *see Rosenkavalier, Der*

Cavalleria rusticana (Mascagni), 436, 437

Cavalli (real name Pier Francesco Caletti-Bruni), 3*n*, 81, 86*n*, **90-95**, 98, 102, 106, 113, 115, 120, 171; a leading figure in Venetian opera, 90; analysis of his music, 91 ff.; first great popular composer of opera, 95; music compared with Cesti's, 96; two operas showing evidence of adaptation to French tastes, 117

Cavatina, defined: use in opera, 213; predecessors of two-part form, 214

Caverne, Le (Lesueur), 303

Cavos, Catterino, 464

Celestina, La (Pedrell), 488

Cellier, Alfred, 496

Celos aun del aire matan (Hidalgo), 271

Celtic legends in opera, 496

Cena delle beffe, La (Giordano), 442

Cendrillon (Isouard), 326

Cendrillon (Massenet), 421

Ceremonial of Spring, The (Stravinsky), 434, 479

Cervantes, 368

Cesti, Marc Antonio, 77, 91*n*, 92*n*, 95-100, 102, 106, 110, 113, 115, 154; music compared with Cavelli's, 96; new trends in music of, 96 ff.

Chabrier, Alexis Emanuel, 415 f., 426

Chadwick, George Whitefield, 506

"Chain of Adonis, The" (Mazzocchi), 69 f.

Chaliapin, Feodor, 470

Chamber operas, 86, 522; English, 140, 497 f.; American, 505, 506

Chambonnières, Jacques Champion, 131

Chant de la cloche, Le (D'Indy), 417

Chapí y Lorente, Ruperto, 487, 488

Characterization, Mozart's vividness of, 285

Characters, in a play, 6; in opera, 7

Charles I (England), 134

Charles II (England), 135, 136

Charles VI, Emperor, 115

Charles IX (France), 27

Charleston, S.C., ballad opera, 500

Charlotte Corday (Georges), 433

"Charon the peaceful shade invites" (Purcell), 140 f.

Charpentier, Gustave, 412, 422, **423-25**, 426, 433

Charpentier, Marc-Antoine, 127*n*

Chartreuse de Parme, La (Sauget), 511

Chausson, Ernest, 415, 419 f.

Chemineau, Le (Leroux), 433

Cherokee, The (Storace), 263

Cherubini, Luigi, 243, **302-4**, 310*n*, 325, 350

"Child King, The" (Bruneau), 423

Chile, opera, 494

Chilpéric (Hervé), 331

"Chinese Ladies, The" (Gluck), 229

Chi soffre, speri (Rospigliosi), 79, 80

"Chocolate Soldier, The" (Straus), 451

Chopin, Frédéric François, and Bellini compared, 342

Chords, side-slipping of, 439; Russian mannerism of alternating, 472

Chorus, in Greek drama, 14 f., 16; stately, of the pastorales, 36, 56, 86; virtual disappearance: its substitute, 86; choral movements of Handel foreshadowed by Purcell, 143; dramatic use by Handel,

Opera *(Continued)*

verdi's attempt to apply full resources of the art of music to opera, 61; steps made by Romans toward establishing main outlines of the structure, 83 *(see* Rome, opera); transformation from court entertainment to modern organization with broad popular support, 84-86; early chamber operas, 86; new features of style developed by Venetian opera, 86, 101 *(see* Venice, opera); Italian, in south German courts, 106-15; French, the only national school able to maintain itself unbroken through eighteenth century, 116 ff.; as conceived by Lully: contrasts between French and Italian, 118 ff. *passim*; weakness and strength of opera as an institution of the state, 125 f.; the style of Rameau, 128-32; Italian and French influences in England: development of its own opera into distinct national type, 133-46 *(see entries under* England); abstract definition of purely national, 147; national, in Germany, 147-64, 227-46, 275-97, 357-73, 374-408, 446-62 *(see entries under* Germany); Singspiel the German equivalent for the term, 149*n (see also* Singspiel); school dramas, 150 ff., 506; operas of Handel, 167-77; origin and development reviewed, 179 ff., 216 ff.; the aristocratic or polyphonic, and the democratic or homophonic, types, 180 f.; the Neapolitan *(q.v.)* school, 181-226; classical compromise operatic form, 184; alteration and patchwork, 188, 191, 228; behavior of singers and audiences, 188-98 *passim*; circumstances under which performed and which caused enthusiasm in their day, 198; constructed of three elements: its history a history of reformations and counter-reformations, 217; influence of changes in literary thought and expression, 218; France the only school of, outside of Italy: its spreading influence, 222; Gluck's and Calzabigi's new ideals for, 237 f.; three revolutionary figures in history of, 244; Gluck's significance, 245 f.; comic elements in early: separation from tragic style, 247; opera seria supplanted: Scarlatti as representative of, 248; comparisons between Italian comic and French serious, 256; Paris the European capital, 301; Revolutionary period and the grand style, 302; climax

under First Empire, 304 *(see also* Grand opera); two with over one thousand performances, 326, 334; forces bringing about changes in: effect upon Italy, 336; Verdi and Italian opera after him, 336-56, 435-44 *(see entries under* Italy); rise and development of national schools, 336, 357, 463-506, 518 *(see under countries, e.g.,* Russia); Bellini the aristocrat of, 342; romantic, in Germany, 357-73; features of romanticism *(q.v.),* 358; virtual dictatorship by Wagner's music dramas, 357; principal difference between features of eighteenth and nineteenth centuries, 358 ff.; factors that have made for popular success in, 393 f.; French, between Franco-Prussian and First World War, 410-34 *(see entries under* France); disappearance of distinction between opéra comique and, 412; postwar progress of orthodox, 503, 508-13; between World War I and II, 503-36; forces encouraging experimental work and those tending to make opera conservative, 507; three main currents in modern, 514 ff.; popularized opera, 514-21; neoclassical school, 522-31; subdivision of neoclassical, committed to atonal technique, 531-36; *see also kinds of opera, e.g.,* Comic; Lyric; *etc.*

"Opera Ball, The" (Heuberger), 333

Opéra ballet, 127; *see also* Ballet

Opera buffa, 5, 247, 248-54; decline of opera seria in favor of: its dominance: outstanding composers, 226; derivation: characteristic form, 248; musical styles: composers and operas, 249 ff.; style advanced by Piccinni, 251; last echoes in Donizetti, 340; Verdi's *Falstaff* the transfiguration of, 355; *see also* Comic opera

Opéra comique, 5; much of it not comic, 6; work called the first, 25; earliest performances in Vienna: influence on Gluck, 230; foundation and development, 247, 254-59, 324-29; compared with earlier and Italian forms, 257; advanced ideas: criticism of social order, 257; leading eighteenth-century composer, 258; distinguished from other forms, 311, 325, 330; two distinct tendencies: romantic comedy, lighter pieces, 324-25; phase of greater sophistication, 327; broadness of term, 331; influence in other countries, 332; disappearance